Castles in the Sand

THE FLORIDA HISTORY AND CULTURE SERIES

UNIVERSITY PRESS OF FLORIDA

Florida A&M University, Tallahassee
Florida Atlantic University, Boca Raton
Florida Gulf Coast University, Ft. Myers
Florida International University, Miami
Florida State University, Tallahassee
New College of Florida, Sarasota
University of Central Florida, Orlando
University of Florida, Gainesville
University of North Florida, Jacksonville
University of South Florida, Tampa
University of West Florida, Pensacola

University Press of Florida
Gainesville · Tallahassee · Tampa · Boca Raton
Pensacola · Orlando · Miami · Jacksonville · Ft. Myers · Sarasota

Castles in the Sand

The Life and Times of Carl Graham Fisher

Mark S. Foster

Foreword by Raymond Arsenault and Gary R. Mormino

First cloth printing, 2000
First paperback printing, 2023

27 26 25 24 23   6 5 4 3 2 1

LIBRARY OF CONGRESS CATALOGING-IN-PUBLICATION DATA
Foster, Mark S.
Castles in the sand : the life and times of Carl Graham Fisher / Mark S. Foster;
foreword by Raymond Arsenault and Gary R. Mormino.
p. cm. — (The Florida history and culture series)
Includes bibliographical references and index.
ISBN 978-0-8130-1809-6 (cloth); ISBN 978-0-8130-8020-8 (pbk.)
1. Fisher, Carl G. (Carl Graham), 1874–1939. 2. Real estate development—
Florida—History. 3. Real estate developers—Florida—Miami Beach—Biography.
4. Miami Beach (Fla.)—Biography. I. Title. II. Series.
CT275.F559 C37 2000
333.73'15'092—dc21
[B]   00-034414

The University Press of Florida is the scholarly publishing agency for the State
University System of Florida, comprising Florida A&M University, Florida
Atlantic University, Florida Gulf Coast University, Florida International
University, Florida State University, New College of Florida, University of Central
Florida, University of Florida, University of North Florida, University of South
Florida, and University of West Florida.

University Press of Florida
2046 NE Waldo Road
Suite 2100
Gainesville, FL 32609
http://upress.ufl.edu

For my loving wife, Laurie

Contents

Figures

Foreword

Castles in the Sand: The Life and Times of Carl Graham Fisher is the fifteenth volume in a new series devoted to the study of Florida history and culture. During the past half-century, the burgeoning population and increasing national and international visibility of Florida have sparked a great deal of popular interest in the state's past, present, and future. As the favorite destination of countless tourists and as the new home for millions of retirees and other migrants, modern Florida has become a demographic, political, and cultural bellwether. Unfortunately, the quantity and quality of the literature on Florida's distinctive heritage and character have not kept pace with the Sunshine State's enhanced status. In an effort to remedy this situation—to provide an accessible and attractive format for the publication of Florida-related books—the University Press of Florida has established the Florida History and Culture Series.

As coeditors of the series, we are committed to the creation of an eclectic but carefully crafted set of books that will provide the field of Florida studies with a new focus and that will encourage Florida researchers and writers to consider the broader implications and context of their work. The series will continue to include standard academic monographs, works of synthesis, memoirs, and anthologies. And, while the series will feature books of historical interest, we encourage authors researching Florida's environment, politics, literature, and popular and material culture to submit their manuscripts for inclusion in the series. We want each book to retain a distinct personality and voice, but at the same time we hope to foster a sense of community and collaboration among Florida scholars.

Castles in the Sand: The Life and Times of Carl Graham Fisher represents a significant addition to our growing literature on modern Florida. The author, Mark S. Foster, a professor of history at the University of Colorado, Denver, provides readers with a refreshing new portrait of the man who made Miami Beach. Deftly blending primary and secondary sources into a graceful, fast-paced narrative, Foster masters the biographer's craft, understanding Carl Fisher as a creative genius, as well as a product of the extraordinary times of the early twentieth century.

Carl G. Fisher was a monumental bundle of energy, a force not seen in South Florida since Henry Flagler. Indeed, Fisher's arrival neatly overlaps Flagler's passing. Customarily, historians compare Fisher's accomplishments with those of his contemporary developers, George Merrick and Addison Mizner. To appreciate Fisher's extraordinary range of talents, however, a comparison with Flagler provides a fuller portrait. Both Flagler and Fisher were regarded as modern Horatio Algers, having succeeded beyond their wildest dreams *before* they set foot in Florida: the former as Rockefeller's partner in the Standard Oil Company, the latter as a promoter and financier. Had Fisher never discovered the barrier island off Miami, he would still be remembered for three stunning accomplishments: the founding of the Indianapolis Motor Speedway, the success of the Prest-O-Lite Company, and his association with the Lincoln and Dixie Highways. Humorist Will Rogers once quipped, with only slight exaggeration, that, were it not for Fisher, "Florida would be known as the Turpentine State."

Foster's retelling of Fisher's arrival in Florida, his early association with Quaker pioneer John Collins, and his dream of hotels and tourists on an isolated barrier island adds a fresh dimension to Miami Beach history. Fisher's inability to sustain the momentum that dazzled Americans in Miami Beach is seen not as an individual failure but as overarching ambition in a stalled boom. Carl Fisher, more than anyone else, would appreciate South Beach today. Readers old and young will appreciate Foster's accounting of long-ago personalities and tales.

Raymond Arsenault and Gary R. Mormino, series editors

Acknowledgments

Perhaps every scholar writing a book belongs in some sort of symbolic debtor's prison on account of past favors that are never repaid. A second offense is failing to mention at least one important contributor. I can repay few of the favors rendered by so many able people; if I have forgotten anyone, please consider the source.

I am grateful to the University of Colorado at Denver for having provided me a Faculty Grant Award, which financed a research trip to the Historical Museum of South Florida. Fernie Baca, assistant vice chancellor for research, provided crucial last-minute help by covering the costs of photographs and permissions. Bill Gates is *not* included in these credits. There were times when I was so frustrated by my computer that I fantasized about extracting my manuscript by cesarean section using baseball bat and crowbar. At such times, several infinitely patient members of our computer information network services group gently took this hopeless Luddite in hand. They include Dallas Jensen, Bitsy Cerny, Jeffrey Beel, Leonid Balaban, Sam Tovbis, Rob Stepnoski, Maureen Christensen, and Linda Mabry.

While examining the Carl G. Fisher Family Papers in South Florida, I received wonderful assistance from Dawn Hugh and several staff members. Sam Boldrick, collection manager at the Miami-Dade Public Library, provided guidance in local secondary sources. I enjoyed a useful visit with Gregory Bush, a member of the History Department at the University of Miami, who provided key insights into Fisher's role in regional development.

In Indiana, Deborah Markisohn provided valuable and timely research assistance, tracking down elusive newspaper columns and rare photographs. Heather R. Munro helped prepare me to use my time productively at the Special Collections Department at the Lilly Library, Indiana University. I am grateful to Eric Mundell of the Indiana Historical Society for directing me to the Walter Dennis Myers Collection, which contains useful information on Fisher's legal troubles with women. Randall Ayers of Social Sciences, Indianapolis-Marion County Public Library, helped me pick my way through voluminous newspaper files relating to Fisher's activities, and Barney Thompson of the Indiana Division of the Indiana State Library helped me with local sources. Joan Cunningham of the Indiana State Archives guided me to several useful state and local encyclopedias. I am also grateful for the assistance of James Hoggatt Jr. and his staff at the Indianapolis Motor Speedway Museum. Annette Miller and Deb Taylor of the Speedway Museum helped me identify and secure useful photographs. Karen A. Rade, director of the Montauk Library, secured and reproduced the photo of Montauk Manor. Jackie Mendenhall, librarian at the Greensburg, Indiana, Public Library also provided useful information on Fisher's early years. At the Bentley Historical Library at the University of Michigan, Anne Frantilla helped me locate insightful letters in the Henry B. Joy and Roy D. Chapin collections, and Kathy Marquis helped me straighten out a lost order for key photographs. By the time I completed my first draft, Mark Davis, of MDTV Productions in Newburyport, Massachusetts, was just completing production of "Mr. Miami Beach," an hour-long American Experience video. Davis generously shared his insights with me before the video first publicly aired, on February 2, 1998.

At my home base, the University of Colorado at Denver, my colleagues have not only been very supportive but have patiently tolerated my endless stories about Carl Fisher and his career. They include Frederick S. Allen, Daniel Caldwell, Mary S. Conroy, Michael Ducey, James

E. Fell Jr., Gabriel Finkelstein, Marie Gingras, Lionel M. Jensen, Pamela W. Laird, Marjorie Levine-Clark, Thomas J. Noel, Carl Pletsch, Myra L. Rich, Chris Sundberg, James Walsh, James Whiteside, and James B. Wolf. Departmental Administrative Assistant Sue Sethney typed countless letters and helped me maintain a sense of proportion and humor when things went wrong. Rudy Witthus, formerly with the Auraria Library, provided crucial early guidance in searching for archival material. As for assistance from reference librarians, nobody surpasses the contribution of Linda Tietjen of the Auraria Library here at the University of Colorado at Denver. She guided me through the bewildering array of databases on the Internet; without her help, I would still be lost out there in cyberspace.

Pamela W. Laird, my colleague at the University of Colorado at Denver, shared her vast knowledge of advertising and promotional endeavors, and Mark H. Rose, an accomplished historian of America's roadways at Florida Atlantic University, deserve special thanks. They both read early, crude drafts of the entire manuscript, offered trenchant insights, and gently guided me away from egregious errors. My stepchildren, Scott and Sarah Maxwell, listened to many Fisher stories. My deepest debt, however, is to my wife, Laurie, who understood my repeated trips and extended absences. She, as much as anyone, bears witness to the loneliness of the writer, and for these and many more reasons, I dedicate this book to her.

Mark S. Foster

Introduction

Carl Graham Fisher was one of the most imaginative, energetic, and versatile entrepreneurs of the early twentieth century. Always fascinated by new technology, he helped pioneer development of products ranging from the first truly satisfactory automobile headlights to diesel engines. He was most captivated by things that moved fast, including bicycles, racing cars, power boats, and airplanes. Fisher was a major figure in promoting the bicycle and its recreational use, racing them himself and selling and servicing them. As a youth, Carl enthusiastically supported the Good Roads Movement.

Early in the new century Fisher turned his attention to automobiles. In his mid-thirties, he and several partners built the Indianapolis Motor Speedway, and in the years before large-scale public funding he spearheaded the drive to build privately funded highways across the United States. Although he was an avid balloonist, Fisher remained on the fringes of aviation; nevertheless, he anticipated transatlantic flights almost a decade before Charles Lindbergh's feat and hoped to participate in the first effort to fly the Atlantic. Although his primary attention was focused elsewhere, Fisher envisioned air passenger service between the United States and Central and South America. As historian David

McCullough pithily observed, "Carl Fisher made a career of betting on the future."[1]

His interest in automobile testing and development, automobile headlights, aviation, diesel engines, and myriad other projects led to Carl Fisher's involvement in an impressive array of technological innovations in the late nineteenth and early twentieth centuries. He loved to tinker and provide encouragement and occasional advice to engineers, but he was not an inspired scientist or inventor like Thomas A. Edison or Charles F. Kettering. Even during his heyday in the mid-1920s, Fisher had only vague ideas about his net worth. He was almost completely out of his element in the world of high finance; stock offerings and bonds never caught his interest. Fisher barely tolerated lawyers and accountants; their concerns were beyond, or at least outside of, his ken, and he paid attention to them only under duress. While he may have admired William C. Durant and Alfred Sloan, whose genius was demonstrated at least in part in their development of new business systems, Fisher did not operate in their orbit. Rather, Fisher relied on gut instinct; even when he was at the peak of his influence, some of his business practices appeared ludicrously old-fashioned, on occasion almost willfully self-destructive.

Fisher was best known to the American public as a promoter of vacation retreats. He loved his work, and it was invariably difficult to distinguish between his work and his play. He and a few associates literally created Miami Beach, dredging it out of coral reef and sand. Fisher was one of the key figures in the spectacular Florida land boom of the early 1920s. Always the speculator, constantly anticipating that the next project would be his biggest yet, Fisher created a gaudy but inherently shaky financial empire that collapsed in the late 1920s because of losses caused by the Florida hurricane of 1926 and reckless overextension at a prospective new development at Montauk, Long Island. Although not fully aware of it at the time, Fisher was finished as a force in American enterprise even before the stock market crash in October 1929. Although Fisher lost his fortune, he lived for another decade, promoting one project after another until the very end.

How can we gauge Carl Fisher's ultimate impact on America? It isn't certain that any answer would interest Fisher himself. He was a *doer*, not a thinker or philosopher: one of the nation's greatest promoters, a latter-day Phineas T. Barnum. His extensive correspondence and business records contain little or no personal reflection, let alone a summing up of his business career. Had he done so, he might have observed that, essentially, he tried to make sport, recreation, and relaxation *accessible* to the quickly emerging, increasingly affluent members of the nation's middle and upper-middle classes. This theme dominated his entrepreneurial career from his days as a "butcher boy" selling magazines and newspapers on passenger trains in Indiana in the 1880s to his final years promoting small-scale tourist attractions in Florida half a century later. As a teenager, Fisher sold and serviced bicycles, which offered a new form of exercise and direct access to relaxation in bucolic settings. Fisher briefly entered the automobile manufacturing derby; significantly, his more popular model was a two-seater, which was sporty rather than utilitarian. Fisher made his first sizable fortune in manufacturing carbide gas headlights. Night driving would enable families to make longer trips and plan more ambitious automobile touring vacations. The Indianapolis Motor Speedway served a practical purpose in facilitating testing automobile design, yet it was far better known by the general public for providing compelling entertainment. Fisher presented a vision of privately financed trans-American highways to Detroit's automobile aristocracy, parts manufacturers, and road contractors. Although both the Lincoln and Dixie Highways ultimately proved functional in permitting long-distance hauling, Fisher essentially "sold" them as national treasures, which would vastly expand vacation opportunities for America's increasing numbers of motoring families. Fisher's ambitious real estate ventures in Miami Beach and Montauk were vacation meccas pure and simple. Throughout his career, Fisher constantly brought the art of promotion to new levels, even if he sometimes offended self-appointed arbiters of good taste.

Throughout his life, Fisher seldom looked backward. Once he completed a project, he wasn't much interested in it. He was far too ambitious, energetic, and curious to spend much time contemplating past achievements. Some of his critics dwelled on his love of a glass of good Scotch, but until very near the end of his life, Fisher's preferred elixir was his next big project, the challenge which "wiser" heads insisted could not be overcome. In his waning years, with his fortune gone, he claimed that he had few regrets; certainly he refused to agonize over past mistakes. For his first six decades, this attitude had served him well. He exuded confidence and optimism; he swept up those surrounding him with his boundless enthusiasm. Fisher possessed a radiant, magnetic personality. He detested being alone, at least until late at night, when he often retreated to his bedroom to enjoy a good book. His friends and associates recalled his ability to mesmerize his listeners as he formulated his dreams of the future. Fisher was constantly surrounded by friends and cronies. During the peak of his career, as he helped mastermind the fabulous Florida land boom of the 1920s, he entertained dozens of guests at his sumptuous home in Miami Beach on an almost nightly basis. Fisher exuded bonhomie. Not surprisingly, when he was out in public the media often surrounded him, and he was usually affable with reporters. He could be both eloquent and expansive when discussing the present or the future. His vision was breathtaking, his enthusiasm infectious.

When asked about the past, however, Fisher frequently displayed impatience, often responding abruptly. When reporters inquired about his family, he provided curt replies that were often evasive and inconsistent. Sensitive observers might have noted a tightening of his jaw, a furtive glance away, a flicker of sadness in his eyes. Although he occasionally mouthed conventional bromides about home and hearth, Fisher appeared evasive, even nervous on the rare occasions when he talked about his roots.

Fisher was a notoriously sloppy record keeper; he left behind fragmented information about even his most successful enterprises and very little about his family tree. One should not assume he had an unhappy introduction to the world based on the paucity of documentation of his past. But there are numerous hints suggesting an emotionally barren upbringing. His father left the family when Fisher was a child; if young Carl experienced any carefree period in his formative years, it must have been exceedingly fleeting. When he was in his early twenties he learned of the death of a brother weeks after the event, through an infrequent letter from his mother. Limited evidence suggests strongly that after his first significant financial success, perhaps even earlier, Carl detached himself both physically and emotionally from his nuclear family. Once he became rich and famous, after he had masterminded much of the early development of Miami Beach, reporters suggested that Carl Fisher had taught Americans how to play. Fisher made the world of adult play his career. Perhaps this was partial compensation for a lost childhood.

A Shaky Foundation

There is virtually nothing in Carl Fisher's background and very early years to suggest the direction his life and career eventually followed. His ancestors included no inspiring role models, and no responsible adult provided significant guidance, let alone inspiration and mentoring. As a youth, Carl was essentially in charge of his own upbringing. As an adult, many of his enterprises revolved around making people forget reality, dismiss workaday concerns, for a few weeks or even a few hours. He genuinely enjoyed making other people happy, and he constantly surrounded himself with active, boisterous people. During most of his working hours, his world throbbed with noise, hoopla, excitement. Could it be that, subconsciously, he was trying to repress memories of his precarious start in life?

Like tens of thousands of other midwesterners born in the last third of the nineteenth century, Carl Graham Fisher's roots were quite ordinary. Fisher's forebears on both sides emigrated from Europe to the East Coast and gradually migrated westward via different paths, eventually converging in Indiana. Apparently, his mother, Ida, came from more distinguished stock than his father, Albert. A year before Fisher's death a distant relative provided an informal sketch of his mother's family roots. William

G. Alexander, a Chicago physician, claimed to have traced Ida Graham Fisher's family origins back as far as eighth-century Scotland. According to Alexander, there were two Graham clans, one from Monkeith, the other from Montclaire. Unfortunately, his claims are suspect—there is about a thousand-year gap in his amateur genealogical effort, and his report contains no dates. He next picked up the family trail in Virginia, where Ida Fisher's grandfather John Gray was allegedly a planter in the late eighteenth century. One of his daughters, Elizabeth Gray, married John Graham. It is uncertain exactly when the union occurred, whether it was before or after they decided to join the growing throng of pioneers following Daniel Boone through the Cumberland Gap and emigrating west to Kentucky. The couple made their home in Harrodsburg and later moved to Martinsburg, Indiana. There, Elizabeth Gray Graham gave birth to Ida Graham, Carl Fisher's mother. To support the notion that there was a touch of "royalty" on the mother's side of the family, the amateur genealogist claimed that Nancy Hanks Lincoln, the martyred president's mother, was a first cousin of one of the Graham women. Such grandiose claims of royal or distinguished lineage cast further doubts on the accuracy of Alexander's findings.[1]

There is a deeper paper trail on his father's side of the family, although it does not go back as far. Carl's great-great-grandfather Phillip Fisher emigrated from Berlin, Germany, to Pennsylvania in 1770. Although there is no record of his having taken part, Phillip may have been uprooted by the fighting during the American Revolution; by 1777 he resided in Pendleton County, which is now in the mountainous region of extreme eastern West Virginia. There is no trace of who Phillip Fisher married, but he had an only son, Jacob. In 1799 Jacob Fisher married Barbara Kyle in Virginia, and the young couple sought a less populated region with more open pastures. Barbara Fisher was soon with child; Jacob's response was to travel to Ohio alone on horseback, where he acquired some land east of Chillicothe, built a cabin, and grew a crop of corn. Jacob returned to Virginia in the fall of 1799 to collect his wife and infant son John and bring them to Ohio. Evidently the young Fisher clan liked the Chillicothe site, since Jacob soon gained title to 200 acres and built a cabin. According to one source, the family moved into the cabin in March 1800.[2]

At the beginning of the nineteenth century, Ohio was still frontier territory. The Northwest Ordinance, a blueprint for settling territory wrested from Great Britain during the American Revolution and Native Americans afterward, had been enacted just thirteen years earlier. Although a few towns along the Ohio River had been founded in the 1770s and 1780s, the interior of Ohio was still remote from "civilization" in 1800.[3] The Fisher cabin had a dirt floor, and living conditions were primitive. Indians were scattered about the region, but they apparently caused little trouble. Crops were generally abundant, and fresh game was plentiful in nearby fields and forests. Jacob Fisher and his clan personified the Jeffersonian prototype of the independent yeoman farmer family, meeting almost all their material needs through their own manual labor. Before Jacob Fisher left the homestead to fight in the War of 1812, he sired a cabin full of farmhands. Barbara gave birth to six children before the war and three more afterward. Carl Fisher's grandfather Jacob Jr. was the last to arrive in 1819. All nine of the Fisher children enjoyed robust health; none died in infancy or childhood, rare good fortune for pioneer families in those days.[4]

Certainly the Fisher clan in Ohio experienced challenges while Jacob was away from home. During the war, while many of the local men were away, some Indians caused trouble; there were frequent thefts and occasional attacks. In one period of "Indian trouble," Barbara Kyle Fisher and other women in the neighborhood herded their broods into a nearby fort for protection every night for two months. Perhaps Barbara had particular reason for worry. A few years earlier two of her nephews had been captured by Indians and held captive for two years before they managed to escape and find their way back to white settlements.

Jacob Fisher and most of his offspring enjoyed good fortune, or at least longevity. Born in 1774, just before the start of the American Revolution, Jacob survived long enough to learn of the Confederate surrender at Appomattox. He died in 1866 at age ninety-two, and his wife, Barbara, lived to the age of seventy-eight, remarkable for a woman who had given birth to and raised nine children.[5]

The pioneering heritage of the Fisher family ended by the middle of the nineteenth century. The next two generations experienced far less tumultuous life journeys. Carl Fisher's grandfather Jacob Fisher Jr. and his father, Albert H. Fisher, located their families in previously settled regions in Ohio and, later, Indiana. As the youngest male and with several brothers ahead of him, Jacob Fisher Jr. had no chance of inheriting any land from his father. He therefore had little choice but to seek his fortune beyond the family farm. There is no record of how Carl Fisher's grandfather supported himself and otherwise spent his early years. The 1830s, however, were years of frantic speculation in canals and land adjacent to these waterways in both Ohio and Indiana, and tens of thousands of newcomers were moving into the region. He may helped build canals, or perhaps he worked as a field hand for neighbors while saving money to buy his own land. Jacob Fisher Jr. married Elenor Wilson of Kentucky in June 1841. He matched his father's record for producing offspring, siring nine children between 1842 and 1862. The fourth child, Albert H. Fisher, was born in 1847.[6]

At this point, Fisher's ancestral trail widens. Albert Fisher, Carl's father, was apparently a footloose young man at the end of the Civil War. He had just turned eighteen and wanted to seek his fortune. During the late 1860s he found himself in Martinsville, Indiana, about forty miles southwest of Indianapolis; here he made the acquaintance of Ida Graham. The young woman had been born and raised in Martinsville, where her family was prominent. Ida's father, John Graham, had gained possession of a sizable land grant in Martinsville and had served as recorder for the county. One can only guess at the reception Albert H. Fisher received from the Grahams when he began courting their daughter. Undoubtedly his social calls were carefully scrutinized. Martinsville was a small town, where everybody knew everybody else's business. The tall, mysterious young man from "somewhere back in Ohio" and the short young woman whom everybody had known for years made a striking couple as they walked past houses and shops, discussing their future plans. Albert finally won Ida's hand, and they were married in about 1870. Not long after their wedding, they moved from Martinsville to Greensburg, another small town located midway between Indianapolis and Madison, Indiana, a large town located on the Ohio River.

In 1870 Indiana was less densely settled than Ohio, but it was nevertheless a generation or two removed from its frontier status. Indiana was originally organized under the Northwest Ordinance of 1787, became a territory in 1800, and entered the Union as the nineteenth state in 1816. By the time Albert and Ida were married, threats to white settlement had long since vanished. General "Mad Anthony" Wayne defeated the Indians at the Battle of Fallen Timbers in 1794. Future president Wil--liam Henry Harrison ultimately broke their resistance at the Battle of Tippecanoe in 1811. The last potentially hostile Indians had been "removed" in 1846. In 1810 the white population of Indiana Territory was just under 25,000 persons. By 1870 it had mushroomed to approximately 1,500,000.[7]

One of the reasons for the state's rapid population growth was the tremendous boom in transportation. The national financial Panic of 1837 had wiped out many speculators in canals. Despite the panic, important canals were built, many of which connected Indiana's numerous rivers and permitted easier flow of goods into the Ohio and Mississippi Rivers on their way to national markets. Improved roads were another boon to the state's economy, as were the railroads that crisscrossed the state by the middle of the nineteenth century.[8] By the mid-1850s, rail lines through Indiana connected upstart cities like Chicago to the East Coast, and local trunk lines linked Indiana businessmen and farmers to larger markets.

Albert and Ida Fisher moved to Greensburg, where town promoters undoubtedly had expansive visions of its potential to become a large city. The location had attracted considerable attention in the past two decades. Town promotion was big business in the Midwest at mid-century, and Greensburg, located midway between the two largest towns in Indiana, appeared ideally situated to enjoy unlimited prosperity. The state's best road, the so-called Michigan Road, connected Madison and Indianapolis and passed through Greensburg. With its accessible location, Greensburg may have hosted runaway slaves passing through Indiana on their way to Canada via the Underground Railroad. Southern Indiana, however, had contained a fairly large number of secessionists in the antebellum era and more than a few Confederate sympathizers during the Civil War. In fact, during the Civil War, some 3,000 Confederate raiders under John Hunt Morgan crossed the Ohio River and ransacked towns and farms as far north as Vernon, which was only twenty-five miles south of Greensburg.[9] As a youngster, Carl Fisher undoubtedly heard many

A young, confident-appearing Carl, age about four. Courtesy of the Historical Museum of Southern Florida.

tales, both truthful and imaginary, about the heroic exploits of Union and Confederate horsemen just a few years before he was born.

Family records contain no clues regarding what attracted Albert and Ida Fisher to Greensburg, nor is there any indication of how Albert planned to support a family. Next to godliness, trustworthiness, and his virtues as a citizen and neighbor, a man in the 1870s was judged by his ability to provide for his family. Albert Fisher knew farm work, but it is uncertain if he possessed other skills. Public records reveal that at age twenty-six, Albert was admitted to the state bar as a lawyer and was sworn in by the clerk of the Decatur County circuit court on November 17, 1873.[10] This, however, was no great achievement. The Indiana state constitution of 1851 stated, "Every person of good moral character, being a voter, shall be entitled to admission to practice in all courts of justice."[11] Carl almost never talked about his father; he evidently knew very little about what Albert did or what jobs he held in and around Greensburg.

Several sources mention that Albert was a heavy drinker. He and Ida separated some time in the late 1870s or early 1880s, although they never formally filed for divorce.

Albert remained with Ida long enough to father three sons: Earle, Carl, and Rollo. Earle was the eldest, and Carl was the middle child, born in Greensburg on January 12, 1874.[12] Then, as now, single-parent families experienced a precarious existence. Soon after her separation from Albert, Ida packed up her brood and moved the family to Indianapolis. Taking boarders into their modest house allowed the family to pay the rent.[13] Ida and her sons probably maintained fruit trees and a vegetable garden, as did most working-class Hoosiers. She also kept chickens, selling the eggs and occasionally butchering one for a family supper. Such practices were common, even in larger towns in the late nineteenth century.

Despite strained economic conditions, Ida Fisher, at least, was ambitious for her sons. Sources described her as a "hard, strong, stubborn, determined" woman, and she saw to it that the boys attended school and toed the line. Although young Carl remained there only through the sixth grade, this placed him at no significant competitive disadvantage, as attending school through the eighth grade did not become compulsory in Indiana until 1897, and only a small percentage of youngsters completed high school.[14] For the Fisher boys, any thoughts of higher education, even had they been so inclined, were clearly out of the question.

Nobody realized it at the time, but young Carl was born with a significant handicap. Years later, he discovered that he had a severe astigmatism. Never having experienced full sight, he may have been unaware of his handicap. In the Midwest in the 1880s, youngsters, particularly boys, were trained to bear their burdens without complaint. Carl could not see the blackboard very well; during his years as a schoolboy, he compensated by selecting a seat near the front of the room. In all likelihood his mother was too distracted by the more pressing needs of putting food on the table to concern herself about her son's poor eyesight. Perhaps Fisher was aware of his disability and deliberately hid it. Despite his poor eyesight, Fisher loved to read, and he was probably as well informed as many of his peers who continued their education into high school.

In later years, Fisher never talked about his childhood or youthful longings. Introspection was not his nature, and we simply do not know if he ever lamented his inability to play baseball like Frank Merriwell or perform the heroic deeds of other celebrated characters in Horatio Alger novels and the *McGuffey Readers*. Nevertheless, the youngster possessed boundless energy and a passion for other physical contests, if not for organized sports. His former wife claimed that Carl earned a reputation as the fastest ice skater in Indianapolis. He loved to run, and he developed a remarkable ability to run backward. One source claimed he could run backward faster than many of his chums could run forward. Carl often stumbled and fell down, which induced his friends to nickname him "Crip." Nevertheless, Carl prided himself on being a daredevil, specializing in balancing acts. He would stand on his head atop tall fences, and he practiced tightrope walking on tightly strung ropes in his backyard. Once he built a pair of stilts so long that he could only mount them from a second story window![15] According to Jerry Fisher, the youngster was also adept at both roller-skating and canoeing and once won a challenging race sponsored by the Indianapolis Canoe Club.[16]

Perhaps young Carl secretly longed to lead the life of Tom Sawyer or Huck Finn, but more immediate realities intruded. By the time he reached the sixth grade, Carl was becoming increasingly frustrated with school. In addition, his family's precarious economic position bothered him deeply. According to one source, Carl simply "stalked out of his sixth-grade study hall, never to return to the classroom." His action was not all that unusual; more than likely, some of his peers had already dropped out of school. Carl allegedly walked into the house and informed his mother that he would be the family's chief provider from that moment forward.[17]

The story may be apocryphal, ingrained in family lore by wishful thinking and years of repetition. Nowhere is there any mention of his older brother Earle and how he might have reacted to such a brash pronouncement from a younger sibling. Published accounts simply dismiss Earle and the younger brother Rollo essentially as ne'er-do-wells, lacking Carl's drive and determination.[18] It was clear from his earliest years, however, that Carl possessed a remarkable ability to combine work and play.

He was mesmerized by speed in any form, and one winter day he staged a risky sled race down a steep hill in which he carried banners advertising a grocery store where he worked.[19]

Although Fisher entered the workforce on at least a part-time basis before he reached his teens, he had prodigious physical energy and a penchant for the most vigorous social activities. In the mid-1880s the bicycle craze was a national phenomenon; in its early years, young men in Indianapolis and across the nation were addicted to high-wheelers, called "ordinaries," which they pedaled about the city streets. The typical "ordinary" had a front wheel with a diameter of approximately five feet, over which the rider was precariously perched. The rear wheel usually measured little more than eighteen or twenty inches; it served as a rudder and provided a minimal degree of balance. Needless to say, "ordinaries" were difficult to ride. The bicycle craze was greatly enhanced by the emergence of the two-wheeled "safeties," which were far easier to master than high-wheelers. By mid-decade the low-slung "safeties" were mass-produced and had been significantly reduced in price. Bicycle enthusiasts were divided in their preference. Some who had fully mastered the tricky and dangerous high-wheelers dismissed those preferring safeties as "sissies." Carl was not attracted by anything that was not a challenge. With his poor eyesight, the youngster possessed little depth perception; as he was riding far above the ground, he could not detect curbs or potholes. Consequently, Carl experienced more than his share of frightening accidents and falls. His companions had no reason to abandon the affectionate nickname of "Crip." Despite being accident-prone, for several years Carl remained staunchly committed to his beloved high-wheeler. Even when at play, Carl enjoyed competing with his peers and attracting attention. A conventional five-foot wheel "ordinary" wasn't enough for him. An avid tinkerer, Fisher once built a high-wheeler with a nine-foot front wheel. Anyone attempting to mount it had to lean it up against a tree or a wall and carefully climb up three "steps" built into the frame, then lower himself down onto the seat. Maintaining balance on the Fisher "ordinary" required far more than average coordination. The unwieldy contraption undoubtedly created a spectacle on the streets of Indianapolis.[20]

When not doing chores for his mother or working for wages, Carl's major recreational pursuit was bicycling. In the summer of 1890 Carl was sixteen, and he and a dozen or so like-minded young cycling enthusiasts formed their own social organization, the Zig-Zag Cycle Club. The founders initially limited membership to those riding "ordinaries." Safety bicycles were just then coming into their stride, and Fisher and his cohorts believed in the more physically challenging, traditional high-wheelers. They eagerly anticipated weekends and long summer evenings when they could gather at their clubhouse and embark on long rides far out into the countryside. Weekend excursions often became marathon riding events, sometimes including jaunts to towns located forty or fifty miles from Indianapolis. Long rides such as these are major athletic challenges a century later, when riding equipment and bicycles are far lighter and more efficient and road surfaces are far better. Back then, the best roads were loose gravel, and the typical road was dirt, often deeply rutted by cart tracks. Maintaining forward movement and balance under such conditions was extremely challenging, and the bicycles had only one gear. Young men enjoying such recreation had to be highly active and physically fit. Young Carl had no inkling at the time, but his experiences on the muddy roads in and around Indianapolis in the early 1890s probably planted the seed of his celebrated initiative to promote transcontinental highways two decades later.[21]

The Zig-Zag Cycle Club attracted young locals from all backgrounds. Carl peddled alongside some youths from elite families, others from working-class families like his own. Perhaps he enjoyed occasional conversations of an elevated nature, in which serious, educated young men attending high school or even bound for college talked about authors, books, and ideas. In his later years, when he had become famous, Fisher became friendly with Indiana's poet laureate, James Whitcomb Riley, whom he frequently entertained in his home. As a youth, he also enjoyed the company of future novelist Booth Tarkington, an Indianapolis contemporary from upper-middle-class origins.[22] Some of his peers had traveled; a few had even been abroad, and he probably learned of distant, mysterious places from them. Others may have discussed music and art.

Some of Carl's experiences in the Zig-Zag Club were probably far less wholesome, at least in the eyes of a typical Victorian era mother. Although the focus of members' activities was tinkering with bicycles, trying out new models, and taking long rides out into the countryside, the young men also enjoyed other diversions. The club attracted mostly single males in their late teens and early twenties, who were exploring their manhood, learning about smoking, liquor, and young women. Sometimes their nocturnal activities became boisterous, overly noisy for neighbors in the quieter sections of Indianapolis. As its membership mushroomed to nearly 200 in the early 1890s, the organization rented several increasingly large clubhouses in or near downtown Indianapolis. A major reason for the frequent moves was that they were forced out by neighbors disturbed by late-night "whoopee." After several moves, the club finally rented a large brick house adjoining the Empire Theater on Delaware Street. This was a burlesque house, and evidently some of the more polished members of the Zig-Zag Club enjoyed reputations as stage-door "Johnny's" to the ladies working next door.[23]

The club lasted only six years, folding its doors in 1896. But this was a critically formative period in Fisher's life, and in certain respects he grew up with the club. Lacking positive male role models at home, Carl searched for them at the club. Although he could and often did charm women, he was clearly more comfortable among men, and he enjoyed locker room camaraderie. He never revealed his introduction to sex; what information or misinformation he picked up from fellow club members remains a mystery. Considering his good looks and remarkable personal charm, however, he may well have enjoyed the company of showgirls. What is clear is that Carl's activities with fellow club members whetted his appetite for speed, racing, and experimenting with machinery. By providing a legitimate outlet for his penchant for racing, the club and the friendships he enjoyed profoundly shaped his future career.

Fisher and a few die-hards held out for the "ordinaries" for several years, even after they let down the barriers and admitted members who preferred the "safeties." The die-hards seemed to delight in outdoing each other in taking the most harebrained risks. A favorite was coasting down long, steep hills, legs off the pedals and slung over the tiny handlebars. Needless to say, striking an unexpected rut or even a small stone could send the contraption spinning out of control and give the daredevil rider a nasty collection of painful bumps, bruises, even broken bones. The young men also found particular enjoyment in playing practical jokes on one another. After reaching an overnight camping spot, one member made an elaborate show of arranging mosquito netting over his bunk. Another rider waited until he was asleep, then took a match to the netting. The perpetrator's identity remained a closely held secret to spare him mayhem from the victim.[24]

Carl Fisher was often in the middle of such shenanigans; decades later, he fondly recalled the camaraderie of his years as a member of the Zig-Zag Cycling Club. For all intents and purposes, the club was his home away from home. Although Carl's brothers were interested in bicycles, no former members of the Zig-Zag Club remembered either Earle or Rollo as having joined the organization. By the time he was a teenager, Carl was clearly the most outgoing and curious member of the family. It seems highly unlikely that he could have felt contentment spending evenings at the family home with his mother and brothers, where entertainment prospects were paltry at best. As Carl reached his late teens, he still performed occasional chores around the house for his mother, helping out as best he could. Most nights he slept there, and he probably spent occasional evenings reading and improving his mind, particularly during inclement weather.

By his late teens, most of Carl's life revolved around wheels, bicycles, and machines. Bicycles constituted his chief diversion, but they also provided his basic source of income. Young Fisher spent most of his waking hours not at play but hard at work. Those who knew Carl well frequently found it hard to distinguish when he was working and when he was playing; his ability to combine the two characterized most of his activities. Throughout his life, he became friends with numerous individuals who would be connected to his later business enterprises. As one of the leaders of the Zig-Zag Cycling Club in the early 1890s, Fisher rubbed elbows and traded barbs with young men who soon became leaders in the fledgling automobile industry and automobile racing. They included the Marmon brothers, Arthur C. Newby, Bob Tyndall, and James A. Allison.[25] The young man was on his own, ready to launch his career.

2

Cracking the Door of Opportunity

In the mid-1920s, after Fisher had achieved fame, reporters and publicists frequently asked him how he got his start in business. Fisher provided several accounts, which varied only slightly. In all likelihood, close friends and numerous publicists wished to embellish his reputation, and they exaggerated the hardships he endured as a youngster. Consciously or otherwise, they tried to fit him into the Horatio Alger mold. Fisher's initial forays into the world of work were entirely conventional, however, his experiences and challenges differing only in detail from those of millions of other young American males in late Victorian America. What is striking about his early years in the workforce was that his experiences were instrumental in establishing the ultimate path his career followed. By the age of twenty, when some of his more "fortunate" contemporaries were still in school, Carl Fisher was already a self-supporting and well-respected businessman. Fisher had already taken big risks, a defining characteristic for his entire business career. He had honed his interpersonal skills and had achieved a solid toehold on the ladder of success.

Some of the published accounts of Carl Fisher's entry into the workforce are pure hyperbole. There is little doubt that Ida Fisher struggled to make ends meet. The charming image of sixth-grade "dropout" Fisher walking into his mother's house with a bag of groceries and announcing that from that point forward he planned to be the chief breadwinner for the family conveys a flattering image of a determined, virtuous, self-sacrificing lad, but other evidence intrudes.[1] Years later, Fisher recalled that he held his first full-time job when he was fifteen.[2] His first paid job was clerking in a grocery store, but it was almost certainly part-time. From his earliest working days, he revealed a penchant for generating publicity by racing down an icy hill in Indianapolis, trailing a banner advertising the store where he worked. In all likelihood, Carl worked at various odd jobs around the store: stocking shelves, arranging produce, sweeping the floor, and making deliveries. The bag of groceries he plopped onto his mother's kitchen table may well have been two-day-old fruits and vegetables his employer gave him for free.

There is considerably more authoritative information on Fisher's next job, which was much more interesting and exciting than working in a grocery store. In the late 1880s railroads not only dominated overland transportation but were a major factor in the nation's burgeoning economy. Visions of careers as engineers, commanding the fast, powerful locomotives that roared over endless, smooth ribbons of steel stirred the imaginations of countless youths. At fifteen, Carl was far too young to drive a train, but he figured out how to ride on one, see the sights, and earn a living at the same time.[3] He obtained a job as a "news butcher" on a narrow-gauge railroad. Essentially, he was a walking newsstand. He passed through day coaches hawking newspapers, magazines, inexpensive books, candy, and tobacco. By all accounts, Carl was an attractive, exceedingly gregarious youth who thoroughly enjoyed interacting with potential customers. He was a natural salesman, and he thrived in this environment.

He employed some rather unorthodox methods to dispose of his stock. He recalled that he devised what looked like an ordinary news butcher's apron, with pockets in front to hold change. When he sensed that his sales pitch was going flat, that the "drummer"[4] he was trying to convince to buy a magazine or cigar was uninterested, he might flip up the front of his apron to reveal a lurid picture of a nude woman. Most of the commercial men riding the rails and plying their trade in the 1880s in central Indiana were not too sophisticated or discriminating. Having piqued a prospect's interest, young Carl often intimated that the cheap books he sold were sexy or downright salacious. Often, Fisher's brash gesture earned a lewd chuckle from a prospective customer, plus a prompt sale of a book and perhaps a cigar to go with it.[5] Naturally, Carl had to select his targets carefully. If he flashed an image of a naked lady to the wrong customer, he could quickly lose his job. This realization forced Fisher to scrutinize potential customers very carefully. Instinctively, he provided himself with superb training, acquiring and honing "people skills" that would significantly enhance his career.

Inevitably, the young entrepreneur made mistakes. On more than one occasion, Carl evidently misread a facial expression and flashed his nude female picture to the wrong patron. Either that, or railroad personnel administrators discovered how young he was. Whatever the reasons, the youngster was fired from his news butcher job, not once but several times. Most beginners would have accepted their fate or even have retreated in humiliation. But Carl demonstrated uncommon pluck. Rather than being discouraged by temporary reversals, the enterprising young man figured several new angles. Sensing that hiring procedures were haphazard and informal and that personnel record-keeping was probably exceedingly inefficient, Carl simply reapplied at other railroad offices, either by rearranging his name or taking assumed names. He was always a step ahead of his bosses. Years later, Fisher recalled,

> I was fired first by the Union News Company office in [the] Louisville division, under my own name. I was the best salesman out of the Union News Company office at that time and the manager was compelled to turn in so much money every day or he would lose his job, so I went out two hours after I was fired from the Louisville, in the Vincennes division under my name backwards using my middle name Graham. They caught me after a time on the Pittsburgh Division and I was fired again from the Pittsburgh end but hired again under the name Carl Graham for the Chicago Division. They fired me from the Chicago Division the first week, so I went to Cincinnati and worked for the Southern News Company on the L & N and the B & O. I won the grand prize offered by our News Company for the sale of more Bob Ingersoll books than any other butcher in the United States.[6]

In important ways, the young man was probably better off earning money and working as a news butcher than he would have been whiling away time and becoming increasingly frustrated in school. Attention Deficit Disorder (ADD) was unknown in the late nineteenth century, but an energetic youngster, unable to see the board clearly, would be bored to death by the repetitious drill and rote memorization teaching techniques practiced at the time. Working as a news butcher, Carl was certainly learning some of the realities of life, and if his store of knowledge grew haphazardly, it developed rapidly. Fisher apparently found plenty of time to read the books he sold, and not all of them were trashy, escapist dime novels. He recalled that he read every book that the Reverend Robert J. "Bob" Ingersoll wrote. One of Ingersoll's advertising flyers claimed that the orator's writings "enable you to live ruggedly, comfortably, sanely. Look at the world from his viewpoint, adopt his attitude and you will find yourself equipped to deal with all life's emergencies, major and minor. So infectious in his gay, humorous viewpoint that you will adopt it before you have read a hundred pages of his winging, buoyant, fighting prose! His attitude is so sensible, so rewarding—so certain of VICTORY!"[7]

Fisher often mentioned Ingersoll's profound effect on his thinking, particularly his emphasis on seeking happiness "here and now." He would build much of his success around helping others to do so as well. Decades later, when Carl was a multimillionaire living in Miami Beach, he had twelve richly bound volumes of Ingersoll's books in his library.

By reading the magazines and newspapers he sold and listening to passengers' talk, young Fisher may have gained some awareness of national and regional politics, the great currency and tariff issues of the day, the development of railroads, and the labor wars of the late nineteenth century. Indiana was in the center of some of the famous railroad disputes. The colorful, deeply committed socialist Eugene V. Debs was busily organizing the American Railroad Union. Debs hailed from Terre Haute, located about a hundred miles almost due west of Indianapolis. More than likely, Fisher saw Debs when he was en route from one labor meeting to another.

Fisher worked as a news butcher for three or four years. Whether he left the enterprise voluntarily or otherwise is largely irrelevant; clearly he had gained all the experience there he needed, and he had outgrown the job. By the time he sold his last newspaper and cigar, he had a good sense of where his future lay. He was fascinated by wheels, but not the kind that rolled across fixed rails.

Fisher's boast of being one of the leading news butchers in the country evidently contained a good deal of truth. Either that or he was unusually thrifty, because he demonstrated a remarkable capacity for accumulating money. By age seventeen he had saved $600, which in 1891 roughly matched an adult male factory worker's average annual salary. Fisher quit hawking newspapers and sundries to railroad passengers and used his stake to open a bicycle repair shop in downtown Indianapolis with his two brothers. Carl was the energy and brains behind the bicycle repair business; neither Earle nor Rollo was ever mentioned in any capacity other than as an employee. Perhaps because Carl put up all or most of the money, he made the key business decisions. In any event, after the repair shop developed into a bicycle sales operation, when they needed to borrow money or extend credit lines, it was Carl who negotiated with prospective lenders and made binding commitments.

Very early in his business career, Fisher acquired a reputation for always being in the vanguard in harnessing and adapting to new technological advances. Ironically, as a bicycle enthusiast with the Zig-Zag Club, Fisher had been one of the very last holdouts against the "safety" bicycle. Once he opened a bicycle repair shop, however, much of his business consisted of repairing punctures of safety bicycle tires. He and his brothers repaired leaks and blowouts for twenty-five cents. In addition, Carl became an immediate supporter of the "tandem," or bicycle-built-for-two when it was introduced in the mid-1890s. He even did it one better; he and a couple of friends tinkered with, then introduced a "triplet" onto the streets of Indianapolis.[8] As the League of American Wheelmen organized more and more local bicycle clubs and increasing numbers of citizens participated in this new form of exercise, the Fisher brothers' business thrived.

After Fisher became a national figure, publicists downplayed his years dealing in bicycles; one has to read their releases and breezy biographical sketches carefully to grasp the fact that he spent almost two decades in the business in Indianapolis. Although Carl pulled off some spectacular publicity stunts, his early rise in business was actually quite gradual. In the two decades book-ending the turn of the century, he slowly expanded his bicycle repair enterprise into retail sales of new and used bicycles, then into motorcycles, and finally into automobiles. Although Fisher occasionally made promotional journeys far beyond the borders of the state, most of those years were spent in and around Indianapolis. He would establish a winter home in Miami shortly before World War I, but his Indiana roots were deep.

As the Fisher brothers started their business, Carl's active association with the Zig-Zag Club clearly provided excellent contacts in the region; by the time the club disbanded, the Fisher shop was a thriving concern. But these years were not a period of uniform prosperity. The financial panic of 1893 evolved into a full-blown national depression, exceeded in intensity only by the Great Depression forty years later. In Indianapolis thousands of men were unemployed: railroad workers, mill workers, small businessmen, construction workers, white-collar clerks, and others. Many families were unable to spend money for recreation; broken bicycles with flats no doubt collected dust in many garages, or youths scraped together the pennies to buy repair kits and learned to fix flats themselves. The Fisher shop occasionally experienced hard times. Apparently, Earle was convinced that opportunities had passed them by, or else he was tired of taking orders from a younger brother. Perhaps he was stirred by the patriotic rhetoric of Colonel Theodore Roosevelt and other "jingoes" urging Americans to take up arms and fight the "evil" Spaniards in Cuba and the Philippines. By the spring of 1898 Earle had left the business and was stationed at Alcatraz Island in San Francisco Bay, courtesy of the United States Army. Ida Fisher occasionally wrote Earle letters filled with local news, including conditions back home at the bicycle shop in Indianapolis. In May, Ida told Earle that Rollo and Carl had only one other worker in the shop, a "cheap boy." Later in the letter, she contradicted herself, stating that there were two men working in the shop and that Carl and Rollo were the "sailsmen [sic]." She failed to mention that ten or twelve men were employed in the rear of the shop repairing bicycles. She concluded, "Rolly gets very blue about business but Carl takes it very well hoping for better times." One month later, in another letter to Earle, Ida had better news to report: "Carl will go to Columbus tonight. Their trade has picked up some, but their profits are small."[9]

Mother Fisher's letters were unintentionally revealing in several other ways. Ida mentioned in passing that Carl was still living at home. In 1898 her middle son was twenty-four, and many of his contemporaries had long since left their parents and had started families of their own. There is no evidence that he thought much about his domestic arrangement, as he showed little inclination to leave the family homestead. At least, that is where he usually slept and took some of his meals. Perhaps it was largely a matter of indifference to domestic matters or sheer convenience. In return for generous contributions to household expenses, the young man was content to permit his mother to take care of his basic domestic needs.

That may be largely because at the end of the century, Carl's attention appeared almost wholly concentrated on business. The bicycle shop may have been temporarily languishing in the spring of 1898, but the young entrepreneur had already tasted considerable success, and he would soon enjoy a good deal more.[10] Carl wanted to do more than simply repair bicycles. A primary challenge was becoming a distributor. To gain the confidence of bicycle producers, one had to become known. Once again, young Fisher demonstrated a keen instinct for combining vocation with avocation. He exhibited unrestrained joyfulness in demonstrating and showing off his products. Carl would retain the capacity to combine business with pleasure for the rest of his career.

With rapid improvements in bicycle technology and with the automobile industry in its infancy at the turn of the century, the general public grew fascinated by machines and speed and thronged to watch speedy, dangerous stunts performed on wheels. In the 1890s, before automobiles could go very fast, bicycle racing became a highly popular form of recreation and entertainment. Carl joined several of his peers from the Zig-Zag Cycling Club as bicycle racers, showing up regularly in regional competitions all around the Midwest. It took both courage and hard work to become a bicycle racer, as the team manager required that his riders learn to fall from a bicycle moving thirty miles per hour without getting hurt. Carl had to practice long hours to develop that aptitude.[11]

One of his closest friends and rivals, Barney Oldfield, later became one of the nation's most famous race car drivers. For a year and a half, Carl competed against Oldfield and many other adventure-seeking midwestern youths on the dusty ovals of county fairgrounds. Fisher's eyesight was a significant, if not immediately noticeable, handicap, and he was a championship level racer only briefly, but he was usually near the front of the pack. Equally important, Fisher was well liked and respected by his peers; bicycle racing provided him the opportunity to cultivate social and business contacts.[12]

Fisher loved the ambience of the bicycle racing circuit and the camaraderie among the riders, but most of all he wanted to succeed in business. In the early 1890s, as safety bicycles were becoming increasingly popular, more manufacturers were entering the business, and increasing numbers of models were being offered. Fisher sensed an opportunity to become a distributor for an up-and-coming brand of bicycle. He was very impressed with the products manufactured by the Pope-Toledo Bicycle Company, so he planned an ambitious campaign to become that company's distributor in Indianapolis. In 1893 the nation was in the throes of a serious depression. Carl was only nineteen years old; his initial challenge was to gain the confidence of both bankers and mature businessmen.

Fisher planned his campaign for the Pope franchise very carefully. He lined up endorsements from several prominent businessmen in Indianapolis. He then boarded a train to Toledo to call on Colonel Albert A. Pope. The following week must have seemed an eternity. Pope put off seeing him for five days. When finally admitted to Pope's office, Carl immediately startled the older man with the audacity of his proposition. Fisher opened with flattery, informing Pope that he was an experienced bicycle racer and that he considered the Pope "Columbia" bicycle the finest available.[13] He then observed that Pope had not yet cracked the Indianapolis market and that central Indiana could be a profitable place to do business. Fisher next made his bid. Pope probably expected Fisher to ask for a dozen units to be introduced on a trial basis. Instead, Fisher asked for a whole carload, several hundred bicycles. He urged Pope to take his proposition seriously and to telephone or telegraph his references back in Indianapolis. Fisher was confident they would back up his claim that he could, and would, sell Pope's bicycles. He told Pope that if he was provided units at factory cost and sold them at full retail price, both men would reap a solid profit; equally important, Pope would have his entree into Indianapolis. Pope told Fisher that he "had more nerve than a government mule," but he was intrigued. He directed the young man to come back to his office in two days. Evidently his inquiries concerning Fisher's reputation and integrity satisfied him, for he accepted the terms.[14]

At this juncture, Fisher launched the first great publicity stunt of his illustrious career. He eventually became one of the most flamboyant promoters of the first half of the twentieth century and would be closely identified with the fabled "ballyhoo" of the 1920s. In the early 1890s he was still an unknown in central Indiana. That would soon change.

Even before age twenty, Fisher demonstrated that he was willing to risk everything on a single roll of the dice. Upon his return to Indianapolis, he went immediately to one of the bankers who had recommended him to Pope. He informed the executive that his stake was down to $400, and he needed an additional $500 for publicity purposes. Carl got the money. Anticipating prompt delivery of Pope's bicycles, Fisher wanted to sell them quickly. A key item in his strategy was having negotiated to purchase the bicycles at factory cost. Fisher figured that his per unit markup would be sufficient to more than offset the cost of giving away fifty units as prizes. As he promised his banking associate, he used the $500 loan for publicity. With part of the money, he arranged for his friend George Bumbaugh to make a thousand durable toy balloons capable of remaining aloft for hours, even days, when filled with illuminating gas. Fisher planned to outfit each with a tag and a number. He then purchased several full-page ads in a local newspaper announcing that the balloons would be released into the air over Indianapolis on a given date and that individuals finding balloons with one of the fifty "lucky" numbers would win a free bicycle.

The announcement caused a sensation. Newspapers all across the state picked up the story, and Fisher received enormous amounts of publicity in return for the money spent on the newspaper ads. According to one account, "Every hill-billy who could steal the time off on the appointed day was out waiting for his release of the balloons." According to Jerry Fisher, "Some Hoosiers were so eager to get a free bike that they loaded rounds into their shotguns and shot at the balloons as though they were hunting geese."[15] Some of the balloons drifted for several days before being shot down or falling to earth without assistance. As the enterprising young man anticipated, the publicity continued for several days, and Fisher's name remained in the news. Fisher arranged for the bicycles to be given away by the mayor of Indianapolis, and several prominent merchants participated in the elaborate ceremony. As a result of Fisher's stunt, not only did the sale of Pope bicycles jump from a few hundred to thousands across the state, but both Fisher and Pope made a nice profit. Fisher became a distributor for Pope bicycles. The publicity stunt truly launched Fisher as a businessman before he was twenty; he was a young man to keep an eye on.[16]

Fisher was expanding his horizons and becoming more ambitious. If one of the most critical elements of entrepreneurial success is the instinct for perceiving opportunities, perhaps an even more vital quality is the ability to *create* them. Forging opportunities almost invariably entails risks; one needs a rock-solid core of inner confidence and the steely nerves of a gambler to confront the very real possibility of failure caused by one false step. From this point forward, Fisher thrived in the excitement of uncertainty. Many of his friends were content to survive in the bicycle business, earning just enough to pay their daily expenses. Repairing bicycles might produce a living wage for the foreseeable future, and the young man with limited ambition could no doubt enjoy life in the shop handling machines he knew and jawing with his cronies. But in moving aggressively into bicycle sales, Fisher had already shown that he clearly wanted more. The young entrepreneur sensed that if he could earn good money selling one brand of bicycles, he should do even better if he offered a range of brands.

The nineteen-year-old next traveled to Columbus, Ohio, to call on George C. Erland, another of the nation's leading bicycle manufacturers. He informed Erland that he wanted to set up the biggest bicycle showroom in Indianapolis, a location where he could retail every major brand. This step would require significant capital. Erland was impressed with Fisher's confidence and his appearance as a seasoned salesman. He was also impressed with the young man's background in bicycle racing and the fact that his bicycle shop was already providing a livelihood for several people. Erland provided him critical underwriting to expand his operation, eventually extending $50,000 worth of credit. This was an astonishing act of faith in a young man from humble origins owning virtually no tangible assets. Fisher was still legally a minor; had he failed, Erland could have been left in the lurch. In this case, Erland's instincts served him well. With his new source of funding, Carl was not only able to rent a premier showroom in Indianapolis, but he could fill it with glittering new bicycles of every major brand. Fisher's bike shop thrived, and Erland enjoyed larger profits through increased sales of his bikes. Fisher never forgot Erland's act of faith; long after he gained fame, he remained grateful to the older man and offered him lucrative inside deals on many of his later investments.[17]

By the late 1890s, it appeared that all of Indianapolis had gone batty over bicycling. To some, it seemed as if the two-wheeled sport rivaled baseball as the national game (basketball had not yet captivated Hoosier hearts). Fisher's well-to-do chum and erstwhile racing rival Arthur C. Newby capitalized on the craze by building an impressive quarter-mile wooden racing oval north of Fall Creek and just off Central Avenue. The oval, completed and opened to the public in July 1898, offered seating in covered grandstands for up to 2,000 racing fans who paid admissions ranging upward from twenty-five cents. The more expensive viewing areas were box seats, located up front, just ten feet above the wooden track. The advantage over road races for spectators was that the action was always visible. The track's steeply banked curved ends allowed racers to achieve high speeds; sixty years later, many old-timers in Indianapolis shared fond memories of working hard to earn a quarter, then spending a glorious, exciting afternoon at the Newby oval, watching cyclists whiz round and round.[18]

Fisher remained an enigma to the end of his life. He gained a reputation around Indianapolis as a show-off, for good reason. Critics who did not know him well may have passed his showmanship off as sheer hubris, but in face-to-face interaction, the young man was quiet and unassuming when attention was focused directly on him. The key to understanding Carl Fisher was recognizing that he would do virtually anything to draw the spotlight to his business. While he could appeal to older men such as Pope and Erland as a sober, sensible young entrepreneur, some of his wilder promotional stunts suggested a sophomoric lack of good sense. To further publicize the bicycle showroom, he and his brothers built what they billed as "the largest bicycle in the world" and announced that Carl himself would ride it around the streets of Indianapolis. On the announced day, they unveiled a huge contraption more than twenty feet high which Carl mounted from a second-story window. Police had to divert their attention from more mundane concerns to hold back curious onlookers who undoubtedly expected the foolhardy young man to break his neck.[19]

The early twentieth century witnessed daredevils like Harry Houdini managing seemingly impossible escapes, and a handful of reckless individuals had themselves launched over Niagara Falls in barrels and other devices. These spectacular events invariably attracted large crowds. As historian Gregory W. Bush has suggested, by the turn of the century, American entrepreneurs, armed with the new insights of behavioral psychologists regarding the collective behavior of large crowds, had learned how to appeal to the masses in carefully orchestrated settings.[20] Directly or indirectly, such knowledge fattened their pocketbooks. It is highly unlikely that Carl Fisher had ever dipped into the writings of psychologists and social scientists such as Gustav Le Bon and Robert E. Park, but he intuitively sensed how to manipulate large gatherings of interested, excited witnesses. Thus, with appropriate fanfare, Carl announced that he would ride a bicycle across a tightrope stretched between the roofs of two twelve-story downtown buildings. He had practiced tightrope walking in his family's backyard since he was a boy, but balancing on a clothesline a few feet off the ground was a much different proposition than remaining upright on a bicycle and pedaling across a rope twelve stories up. Young Fisher exuded confidence; to add to the drama, he wrapped himself up in a padded suit, which would have done no good had he fallen. Two men held ropes attached to the handlebar of the bicycle, but they would have provided little, if any, protection had Carl lost his balance. Fortunately, the intrepid trickster safely negotiated the length of the rope, to the relief and cheers of the curious throng below.[21]

The local police maintained a love-hate relationship with Fisher. On a personal, one-to-one basis, Fisher included many beat cops as friends. But his stunts created real hazards to public safety, and they occasionally interrupted traffic flow in downtown Indianapolis. Apparently, Fisher never considered the possibility that an impressionable child or adolescent might try to imitate his most daring acts, with tragic results. The police department often tried to prevent Fisher's stunts, which were invariably advertised days in advance through local newspapers in order to generate maximum publicity and ensure large audiences.

In another typically flamboyant promotion, Fisher announced that he would throw a bicycle off the top of a building; the lucky individual who retrieved the frame and turned it into his shop would receive a brand new bicycle. The police were determined to nip this scheme in the bud, and they confidently placed patrolmen in front of the building the night before the scheduled event to deny Fisher access to its roof. Evidently the young promoter had a mole in the department to inform him of the plan, or he had a superb sense of anticipation. Carl hid himself and the bicycle inside the building before the police set up their watch. At the appointed hour, to the consternation of the police, Fisher's head popped over the roof, and, as promised, he dropped the bicycle onto the street below. The next few minutes resembled a *Keystone Kops* comedy. Onlookers scrambled to recover the mangled frame. Out-of-shape police, sputtering with indignation, lumbered up the stairs to arrest the arrogant perpetrator of the deed. Fisher, meanwhile, slipped down a back staircase and vanished. This time the police were determined not to let him get away with breaking the law, and they waited at his shop with a court summons. Once again, the young promoter was a step ahead of them. Fisher, in the meantime, had calmly walked to the local police precinct to surrender; from there, he phoned his shop and advised the picketing officers where he could be found. The young entrepreneur clearly enjoyed the last laugh; the ensuing publicity was easily worth the price of his arraignment and fine.[22]

Fisher's aggressive publicity and promotional activities allowed him to develop the largest and most active bicycle shop in Indianapolis. Indianapolis was a good place for a young entrepreneur. In 1890 the city's population was just over 75,000; ten years later it had grown to just over 105,000, and by 1910 it would be almost 170,000. In 1892 the business was located at 76 Pennsylvania Avenue; three years later, he moved next door to 64 Pennsylvania Avenue. Dimensions for the ground-level store and basement were 18 feet across and 150 feet from front to back. The enormous rear of the store contained a large repair shop which employed a dozen men in 1896. Fisher and one of his brothers were assisted in sales by at least two "traveling men." Besides Pope's and Erland's models, Fisher and his associates offered a wide variety of brand names, including Clipper, Grande, Maroon, Stearns, and Smalleys. By 1896, the severe national depression that had begun in 1893 was easing. The business sold over one hundred units each week, and the Stearns unit had become the most popular brand. Fisher's shop was also headquarters for the local chapter of the League of American Wheelmen and its female counterpart, the Wheelwomen.[23]

Although Carl appeared most in his element when he was out among the public, promoting one of his enterprises, he was equally happy tinkering endlessly with machinery and experimenting with new ideas. One winter when bicycle repair work and sales were slow, Carl invented a sled with a very light frame, which he raced through the snowbound streets and countryside near Indianapolis. While other mechanically minded men were experimenting with engines to power wheeled carriages, Carl was instinctively drawn into their fold. He had been an avid bicycle racer, and he owned a bicycle shop. Fisher began devoting some of his spare time to motorcycles, and he and his brothers sold a few dozen of them from the shop. Motorcycles, however, never became a major Fisher interest.

Fisher was becoming far more interested in the emerging automobile industry. Historian Al Bloemaker claimed that Fisher actually owned the first automobile in Indianapolis.[24] If so, it was more of a toy: an imported two-and-a-half-horsepower French De Dion Bouton motor tricycle that cost him $650 in 1898.[25] Full-size turn-of-the-century automobiles were expensive playthings for the wealthy, costing several thousand dollars. By then, Carl Fisher had a promising future, but he was not yet rich. But the young man had always been interested in cars. A newspaper account recalled an amusing incident in the 1890s involving Carl and a local man who did own one. The man had allegedly managed to draw the chugging contraption up to his home and park it near the curb, with its engine running. At the time, automobiles were curiosities, and the scene attracted onlookers. The man opened his barn door, intending to park the vehicle inside. Young Fisher was inspecting the automobile when the owner returned. Perhaps the man had experienced sufficient stress negotiating the streets in an unfamiliar, balky contraption, or perhaps Fisher looked cool and confident. The owner allegedly asked him if he knew how to drive an automobile. Fisher may never have driven one, but he was eager to try it out, so he replied in the affirmative. The man said that if Fisher could park it in the garage, he would give him a quarter. According to the account, Fisher jumped into the seat and pulled the most likely looking lever toward him. The car lurched forward and Fisher directed it toward the barn. Seeing he was about to hit the back wall, he reversed the direction of the lever, and the car backed out of the door. He repeated the movements three times. The exasperated owner bawled out to Fisher, "I thought you knew how to run an automobile." Fisher allegedly retorted, "Well, I had it in the barn three times. Why didn't you shut the door."[26] There was no mention of whether the young man received his quarter. This story may be spurious, but it is vintage Fisher.

Even if he didn't actually own the first car on the city's streets, Fisher and automobiles became inextricably intertwined in the history of Indianapolis. His involvement began when Fisher and several of his friends and rivals on the bicycle racing circuit made a natural transition into automobile racing. At the turn of the century, hundreds of young men with a sense of romance, adventure, modest mechanical skills, and a little ambition had dreams of glory on the automobile racing circuit. It seemed that every other tank town in the Midwest had a dirt racing oval, where growing crowds ventured to watch young daredevils test their increasingly fast and powerful racing machines against both the clock and each other. Many of the tracks were dangerously rutted and unsafe. The machines themselves were experimental and often unreliable, and they were being tested at unprecedented speeds, all too often by young drivers with far too much courage and too little skill. As racing became faster, it became extremely dangerous; predictably, speed and danger attracted ever larger crowds.

A more cautious, conservative young entrepreneur might have confined his activities to selling motor vehicles from the floor of a show room. But prudence and an inactive lifestyle held no charm for Carl. The young habitually consider themselves immortal, and for a man who had ridden a bicycle on a tightrope twelve stories above the street, the dangers of automobile racing probably appeared inconsequential. Very likely, too, his choice of friends influenced his entry into the automobile field. In 1900 Carl and Barney Oldfield, his old pal from bicycle racing days, journeyed to New York to attend a major automobile show. They were equally mesmerized, and both young men acquired vehicles, which they drove back home to Indianapolis over tortuous roads. They, too, dreamed more about speed than profits.

Over the next decade, automobile racing became an integral part of Fisher's life. He never matched the fame enjoyed by Oldfield, who stood at the pinnacle in racing circles and whose name became synonymous with speed and daring in the early twentieth century, but Carl enjoyed considerable success of his own. Beginning in the spring of 1901, Fisher, Oldfield, Arthur C. Newby, and several other chums from the defunct Zig-Zag Club barnstormed across the Midwest, appearing at dozens of local, regional, and state automobile races. They labeled themselves "the world's most daring automobile racers."[27] In an era when recklessness seemingly ran rampant, this was quite a boast. Apparently, gullible racing fans in small towns believed them, for the tour returned huge profits. The partners charged a flat $500 appearance fee, refundable only if the promoter failed to clear that amount. According to one source, in a single season, Carl cleared $20,000![28]

The claim that they were the region's greatest racers may have appeared justified by mid-decade. Carl and his friends were constantly tinkering with old racers and trying to build bigger, better, and faster ones. In at least one race, Carl achieved a spectacular success. According to his publicists, in 1904 the thirty-year-old racer set a world's record for two miles from a running start in a modified Mohawk racer at the Harlem dirt track near Chicago. His time was two minutes and two seconds.[29] Although the record did not last long, the young man could take pride in having been, for one shining moment, a world record holder.[30]

Memorable as this moment was, there was an earlier incident which Fisher and his associates must have tried hard to forget. Carl and brother Earle had built a pair of racers, and in 1903 they participated in a county fair demonstration in Zanesville, Ohio. During the contest, Carl was driving, and his brother was seated beside him, serving as mechanic. Suddenly their engine burst into a ball of flames. Carl skidded in his own oil, and he was unable to control the racer as it careened toward a fence at the end of the track. The vehicle slammed through the fence, flipped over end to end, and plunged into a crowd of spectators. Miraculously, Carl and Earle dragged themselves out of the wreckage, suffering only cuts and bruises. Unfortunately, numerous spectators were not so fortunate. Two were killed outright, and another dozen sustained varying degrees of injuries. One account held that the Fisher brothers barely escaped with their lives, claiming that they went into hiding for the rest of the day while a lynch mob searched house to house for them. Allegedly a town constable helped them escape after dark. Even if later accounts embellished the incident, it would be strange indeed if the brothers weren't seared by memories of the crash and feelings of guilt. When questioned years later about how many had died, Fisher sadly replied, "I don't know. They were dying for the next two years."[31] He seldom referred to the episode later in life.

The accident in Zanesville and his role in it bothered Fisher, as did serious injuries to some of his racing peers. Although he purportedly set the world speed record for two miles from a running start the next year, his personal participation in racing generally tapered off. One of Carl's last major personal flings in racing was his effort to win the prestigious Vanderbilt Cup. Annoyed because foreign racers were taking most of the laurels, Fisher commissioned the Premier Motor Company to build him a big, fast racer with plenty of "guts." For one of the few times in his life, Carl outsmarted himself. Premier engineers built and delivered the vehicle before the race rules were mailed out. Fisher's behemoth weighed 2,500 pounds, and the weight limit was announced as 2,200 pounds. Try as they might, Fisher and his mechanics could not strip 300 pounds from the machine, and he was forced to watch from the sidelines.[32]

By the middle of the decade, racing cars were becoming much faster and more durable, and new speed and distance records were being set, seemingly on a weekly basis. Fisher was never frightened by a challenge, but it was becoming harder and harder to stay on top. Fisher turned thirty in 1904, a comparatively youthful age for race car drivers. But his poor eyesight was a notable handicap, particularly at higher speeds, and he was beginning to sense that it was time for him to devote more attention to promoting and marketing vehicles rather than driving them for thrills.

A young entrepreneur with a bright future: Carl Fisher in his early twenties. Courtesy of the Historical Museum of Southern Florida.

Perhaps his decision to retire from racing ovals was most influenced by his increasing realization that American racing cars simply could not compete with the best the Europeans had to offer, that his talents might be put to better use promoting top-notch racing on this side of the Atlantic. In 1905 Carl joined an American team that ventured to France to compete in the James Gordon Bennett Cup races. They were completely outclassed by most of the Europeans, not because they were better racers but because they had better cars. Fisher later contended, only half in jest, that French, British, and German cars could "go uphill faster than the American cars can come down."[33] He did not enjoy his journey to France, but there was one positive outcome. While on the Continent, he had so much trouble with his vision that he finally consulted several oculists. Eventually he was outfitted with his first pair of glasses, and for the first time in his life he could see well. Why he waited until age thirty-one to address his need for spectacles remains a mystery. In later years he was something of a hypochondriac, paying close attention to some bodily afflictions while blithely ignoring others. As a young man, he may have considered eyeglasses the mark of a sedentary individual; perhaps he considered them unflattering to his appearance.

A few years later, Fisher would return to automobile racing in a big way as builder and promoter of one of the most famous racetracks in the world, the Indianapolis Motor Speedway. If the United States was not on the cutting edge of race car development, other events were unfolding that quickly established its position as the world's leading manufacturer of passenger vehicles. At the beginning of the twentieth century, most automobile producers were small-time operators, turning out just a few dozen units per month from overgrown blacksmith shops. A decade later, dozens of the fledgling producers had been driven out of the industry by larger-scale, increasingly efficient producers. Henry Ford, of course, led the transformation of the industry, when his huge Highland Park facility turned out 19,000 Model T's in 1910, its first full year of production; just two years later, output quadrupled.[34] Across town, William C. "Billy" Durant was busy organizing General Motors, which would eventually wrest leadership of the automobile industry away from Ford.[35]

Ford's greatest contribution, of course, was to create a simple, functional automobile that was within the price range of the average American. Before the mass-produced Model T appeared, motor vehicles had essentially been toys for the rich. By mass-producing Model T's, Ford managed to drop prices dramatically. Rock-bottom prices would not be reached until the mid-1920s, but the effects were beginning to be felt by late in the first decade of the twentieth century. Rival manufacturers were also beginning to think of producing vehicles for farmers and the rapidly expanding middle class. Men interested in acquiring dealerships began thinking of mass markets rather than small numbers of sales to a few wealthy customers.

It was a situation ripe for an individual of Fisher's temperament. Fisher was and always had been a born salesman. He was extremely effective courting rich potential investors for his manifold projects on a one-to-one basis. And later in life he was surrounded by a circle of wealthy friends and admirers. But he was equally in his element appealing to the multitudes. After returning to Indianapolis from the races in Europe, he enthusiastically plunged back into selling virtually anything on wheels. As Fisher shifted his attention to more adult-oriented, expensive products, one might logically expect that he would tone down the "excess" in his promotional activities. Fisher never fit a conventional mold, however; his promotional techniques became increasingly audacious and ambitious.

His primary attention had long since shifted from bicycles to automobiles. By then, the police and the public in Indianapolis were used to Fisher's extravaganzas; if the former were tired of them, the latter evidently could not get their fill. By now, his most widely known nickname had changed from "Crip" to "Crazy Carl." But his notoriety gained him admirers among men who counted, particularly certain automobile manufacturers, and by 1907 he was selling several makes from his showroom in downtown Indianapolis. One fairly popular brand was the Stoddard-Dayton. As he had when selling bicycles, Fisher would do almost anything to keep both the brand name and his name before the public. Fisher announced that on a given day he would push a Stoddard-Dayton off the top of a downtown building, a drop of seven or eight stories. He apparently recruited both newspapermen and some of his friends in the police department to help with his scheme. Several news stories circulated to the effect that the stunt was highly dangerous, and they debated whether it should be allowed. Other writers scoffed at the "nervous Nellies" and argued that the stunt should go forward. The free publicity naturally heightened interest, and on the appointed day, the streets were packed with curious spectators.

Fisher then unveiled the second part of his plan. As the crowd waited in anticipation, several policemen dramatically "rushed" the building and began ascending the stairs in a staged effort to stop the proceedings. Fisher had had the vehicle raised to the roof of the building the previous evening. As the police were ascending the staircases, Fisher dramatically appeared at the edge of the roof, next to the vehicle, which was seemingly teetering on the edge. He had nailed the door from the staircase to the roof, apparently to prevent the police from interfering with his stunt unless they chose to batter down the door. One can imagine Fisher's friendly accomplices inside the building loudly shouting imprecations and banging on the roof opening, adding to the drama. With the crowd excited to a fever pitch, Fisher finally pushed the vehicle off the roof, and it plummeted to the street below.

This scene, too, had been carefully prearranged. Unknown to witnesses, Fisher had worked with company engineers to produce a "one-of-a-kind" model, structurally reinforced at key places to withstand the shock of the landing.[36] The vehicle had also been outfitted with special tires, which were only slightly inflated so as to soften the impact and prevent the car from bouncing back too far into the air and perhaps flipping over. How they prevented the vehicle from flipping over as it fell several stories remains a mystery, but Fisher's luck held. The vehicle landed with a crash but remained upright. Carl had enlisted his brothers Earle and Rollo into the caper, and they waited at street level, ready to spring into action. Before the crowd regained its wits, one brother leaped forward and hopped into the driver's seat, while the other turned the crank. Amazingly, the motor sputtered to life, and the driver would have driven the car away had he not been surrounded by the enthusiastic spectators. To gathering reporters, Fisher soberly claimed that his chief goal was to prove that the Stoddard-Dayton was the sturdiest vehicle available.[37]

One senses that by then the young entrepreneur was addicted to the limelight, for this was but one of many of his stunts promoting the Stoddard-Dayton. On October 30, 1908, he pulled off another startling

A typical, headline-grabbing promotional stunt. Carl Fisher and George Bumbaugh fly a car over Indianapolis on Halloween 1908. Courtesy of *Indianapolis News*, November 2, 1908.

promotional coup. By then, Fisher's friend George Bumbaugh, who had designed and produced a thousand smaller balloons for his bicycle giveaway a few years earlier, had become expert in building and flying much larger ones. Carl asked Bumbaugh to design a sphere capable of lifting an automobile from the ground and remaining aloft for several hours. The young designer, no doubt intrigued by the publicity he would receive, agreed to take on the challenge.

In his usual manner, Carl worked up imaginative publicity for the impending display. Not only would the balloon lift the vehicle off the ground, but he would be riding in the driver's seat. He vowed he would ride the balloon wherever it took him, and when it landed he would drive the vehicle back to Indianapolis. Fisher's caper went off smoothly, without any apparent hitches. The day following Fisher's stunt the *Indianapolis News* described the scene: "Indianapolis had never before had more craning necks than yesterday afternoon when thousands watched as Carl G. Fisher sailed through the sky in an automobile attached to a balloon.

The novel spectacle was one never before seen in any part of the world, and the people forgot their business affairs and worries while they stood in open-mouthed astonishment as the giant balloon and its unusual load drifted lazily across the city."[38]

The spectators weren't actually witnessing what they thought they were seeing, however; once again, the crafty promoter engaged in some sleight of hand. Those who gathered for the liftoff naturally assumed that he was using a standardly equipped vehicle. But Fisher knew that the balloon would have been unable to lift a fully loaded car, particularly with him sitting in it. So he stripped the "flight model" of virtually all heavy parts, including the engine. None of the modifications were visible, and the spectators and public were apparently fooled. Not knowing which way the wind would blow, Fisher had arranged for several teams of confederates to drive fully equipped Stoddard-Daytons in different directions from town. When the balloon landed, the nearest car was to rush to the site, where Fisher would take the wheel and drive back into town while his helpers hid the evidence before any curious onlookers gathered at the site. Amazingly, Carl pulled off the stunt, and he triumphantly drove back into Indianapolis, once again a local hero. Fisher later admitted that had any enterprising reporter exercised a bit more initiative and followed the balloon while in flight to its final landing site, his gimmick would have been exposed. Once again, however, Fisher's luck held.[39] Even better, big city newspapers across the country picked up the story.[40] For a fleeting moment in the fall of 1908, Fisher became a national figure, and he clearly reveled in the attention.

Carl and his chum George Bumbaugh made many ascents in balloons, entering numerous regional and national races. Ballooning became an important avocation for Carl; clearly he enjoyed its sporting aspects, and perhaps its dangers. It also served a larger purpose in keeping his name constantly before the public. Fisher's imagination always worked overtime; not long after his Stoddard-Dayton stunt, he announced that he and Bumbaugh were planning to fly a balloon eastward across the Atlantic Ocean. They envisioned a 40,000-cubic-foot sphere, attached to which would be twenty "supply" balloons containing about 2,000 cubic feet, which would refuel the main balloon when needed. They were quoted as claiming that it "would be an easy matter to bleed the smaller balloons into the large bag while in the clouds." The arrangement sounded like something dreamed up by Rube Goldberg. As of December 1908, Fisher and Bumbaugh were allegedly waiting only for scientific advice as to the ideal launching point. They were considering locations from Florida to Boston.[41]

The two friends never made that trip, but the next summer they participated in a balloon race over land that turned out to be almost as risky. Fisher was at the center of organizing and promoting a national championship for balloonists. The meet, held at the newly completed Indianapolis Motor Speedway in early June, was labeled "America's Cup" for balloonists. The object was to remain aloft for the longest period and cover the greatest distance from Indianapolis. Hence judicious fuel consumption and skill in catching the best wind currents would, presumably, determine the winner. Fisher and Bumbaugh didn't win the competition, but they experienced one of the wildest rides. They remained aloft for almost two days, finally landing near Nashville, Tennessee. Soon after they landed, Fisher phoned back to reporters in Indianapolis: "We are safe and sound, thanks to the poor marksmanship of a number of farmers. They began firing on us when we were in Brown County, Indiana, and have kept up target practice ever since. . . . It has been a regular fusillade down here in Tennessee." Fisher recalled catching a wind current over a river valley; "it was certainly a hair raising experience. We shot up 14,000 feet and over with such rapidity that I expected the gas to explode any minute." At another point, the balloon allegedly spun out of control while they plummeted downward. Once safely on the ground, Fisher exclaimed, "As for the trophy for the longest time in the air, I gave it and would not care to win it."[42] Carl probably exaggerated the risks; that made better copy.

By late 1908 Fisher seemed addicted to anything related to automobiles. He and several associates decided to join the throngs of entrepreneurs producing automobiles. Arthur C. Newby, James A. Allison, and Robert H. Hassler joined forces with Fisher. In the summer of 1909 they announced formation of the Empire Motor Car Company; the founders would take over the struggling Mohawk Cycle Works at 29th and Elmyra Streets on the outskirts of Indianapolis. They claimed they could turn out between one and two thousand six-cylinder runabouts in the next year, priced in the $800–850 range. The Empire Motor Car Company would produce two models, the A and the slightly more expensive B. The former would be a two-seater up front with a rumble seat in the rear. The latter, named the "Little Aristocrat," was designed as a "performance" vehicle with a longer hood and bucket seats.

Fisher and his associates crowed that the Aristocrat would be inexpensive but that it would "perform as well as the most costly car you can buy."[43] They probably committed a tactical blunder because the renowned racers inevitably conjured up images of a powerful, highly competitive racing car. In fact, equipped with a twenty-horsepower engine, even the sportily equipped Aristocrat had a top speed of about thirty-five miles per hour. According to one historian of the company, the founders would have been wiser to promote their "saucy little car" as a vehicle that "could get one wherever he wanted to go—and look cute as a bug doing it."[44] Test drives even under optimal conditions at local racetracks demonstrated that even a souped-up Empire was at best a decent passenger car.

Fisher and his partners had, in a sense, painted themselves into a corner. The design of the vehicle implied performance; the A model could seat only two passengers comfortably. Hence the Empire models would fit the needs of only a very small number of potential buyers: childless couples or those sufficiently affluent to afford more than one automobile. Very few American families considered ownership of more than one car early in the twentieth century. Forty or fifty years later, Fisher and his allies might have found a niche, but they were too far ahead of the consumer market in 1909 and 1910. Realizing that their fledgling enterprise was already in trouble early in 1910, the partners resorted to a marketing gimmick that has long been associated with the industry: announcing next year's models very early. In late June 1910, the Empire Company was the first in the industry to announce its 1911 cars. The company offered only one model, although advertising copy attempted to hide this fact.[45] Even though the partners hired promising designer Harry C. Stutz, whose renowned Bearcat would become one of the most sought after symbols of the Roaring Twenties a decade later, his suggestions could not reverse the Empire Company's sagging prospects.

The Empire Motor Car Company made almost no impact on the automobile industry even in Indiana, let alone in the United States. By 1909 there were at least sixty-seven automobile companies in the Hoosier State employing almost 6,800 workers. The total value of their output that year was almost $24 million.[46] Unfortunately, only Studebaker, located in South Bend, showed much staying power, keeping its doors open until 1963.[47] Howard H. Peckham offered a partially convincing explanation for why the Hoosier State never became a force in automobile manufacturing. Unlike Detroit, which was home to Henry Ford, William Durant, the Dodge brothers, Walter Chrysler, Alvan Macauley, and a host of other luminaries, no Indiana city boasted a critical mass of entrepreneurs focused on a single industry. In addition, most Detroit auto men concentrated on family cars. In Indiana, the objectives of automobile entrepreneurs were more scattered.[48] For example, the Studebaker brothers were also turning out wagons and carriages; Fisher was at least as interested in racing cars as family vehicles. What Peckham failed to mention was that, unlike Detroit, no Indiana city contained an infrastructure of highly knowledgeable employees at every stage of manufacturing design.[49]

Although the Empire Motor Car Company remained in business for several more years, Fisher and his partners dropped out of the business in 1911 and sold the company's assets to investors in Pennsylvania. In later years, Fisher seldom discussed his brief foray into automobile manufacturing, and few traces of the company's existence remain today. Unlike his commitments to most projects, Fisher's entry into the manufacturing end of the automobile industry appeared tentative, almost halfhearted. The partners did not make huge personal investments in the company, so their losses were sustainable. When the company was sold, the partners received only $80,000. Beverly Kimes, who traced the company's brief history, suggested that although Fisher and his partners were extremely competent automobile men, their interests were too divided; they were all pursuing other important projects, and nobody really took responsibility for the Empire Company. She concluded: "The Empire was in the midst of an identity crisis and, alas, it would never find itself. . . . The Empire's problem had been that . . . it simply could not compete against a gifted, dynamic man [Henry Ford] whose sole obsession was the Model T. The Empire never really had a chance. Hardly any cars like it did."[50]

By the beginning of the second decade of the twentieth century, Fisher's interests had expanded far beyond marketing or even producing automobiles. He was well on the way to earning his initial fortune through his substantial share of the Prest-O-Lite Company, a manufacturer of the first practical headlights for automobiles. In addition, Fisher had recently spearheaded construction of the Indianapolis Motor Speedway. He had retired from driving fast cars but became passionately involved in organizing and promoting auto races. He sold his interest in the Empire Company in 1911. He would remain in automobile sales through World War I but gradually lost interest in the business. Although Fisher maintained his showrooms in Indianapolis and represented numerous automobile manufacturers, subordinates essentially ran these offices. When the national sales manager of the Reo Motor Car Company complained that the Fisher agency in Indianapolis was not doing enough to promote his company's automobiles in the spring of 1919, Fisher replied that Reo was not delivering sufficient numbers of units, that the volume of business did not warrant special treatment, and that many other manufacturers wanted Fisher to represent them. When the manager continued his remonstrations, Fisher criticized the Reo touring car as outmoded and too expensive.[51] From the tone of his letters, Fisher clearly considered himself an expert on what would appeal to American buyers, at least in the Midwest. By the end of 1920, he was becoming increasingly irritated at the time and effort needed to run his sales office in Indianapolis; he was distressed at the inability of his hired managers to make sound decisions without consulting him at every turn and bothering him with relatively trivial questions. Even more bothersome to him was the high salaries he was paying to salesmen, only a few of whom were proving their worth.[52] Clearly his sense of romance with certain facets of the automobile industry was starting to wane. By then, however, other facets of the burgeoning industry had made him rich.

3

The Initial Fortune

In hindsight, it almost appears that Fisher's first fortune was dumped into his lap, that he was nearly a passive beneficiary of a serendipitous windfall. Unlike his experience in bicycles and automobile merchandising, where it took him years to become influential, Carl became a force in the automobile headlight business almost overnight. He did not have to develop a carefully thought-out strategy to gain access and penetrate the field; instead, Fisher received an unexpected offer from an inventor who was frustrated by his own failure to enter the field.

The early twentieth century was a mostly optimistic period in which Americans collectively possessed a tremendous faith in science and the possibilities of technological "fixes" for even the stiffest and most intransigent problems.[1] As technology historian Cecilia Tichi noted, mainstream magazines were regaling readers with real and anticipated technological triumphs: "The middle-class male reader heard his magazines tell him that 'in this country we have gone further in engineering than any other people,' that 'in the progress of engineering we are contributing more than our share,' and that 'civil engineers have supplied the grand arches and ribs of steel which made it possible thus to excel in vastness every building enterprise which earth in its unnumbered centuries has borne upon its bosom.'"[2]

A nearly universal trait of successful entrepreneurs is that, somehow, they have a sixth sense for positioning themselves to *attract* opportunities. Individuals who are excited by new ideas, who thrive on tinkering with new gadgets, often attract like-minded cohorts. Fisher had always been intrigued by machines, what they could be made to do, how their performance could be improved. Many of his friends shared this fascination, and they spent countless hours around automobiles, tweaking engines, testing new fuels, trying to make cars run longer and faster.

Just as the new industry attracted hundreds of men intent on producing the next huge success on wheels, so did it draw thousands of entrepreneurs who envisioned earning fortunes supplying indispensable new parts and accessories. At the turn of the century, travel by automobile was exciting and adventurous, but it could also be frustrating, unpleasant, even dangerous.[3] There was unlimited potential for improving automotive performance, safety, ease of operation, and comfort for passengers. Improvements in automobile headlights were critically needed. Although roads were primitive and almost all travel was during daylight hours, breakdowns frequently upset the best-laid plans, and adventurers sometimes found themselves forced to drive after dark. Some early cars used kerosene lanterns suspended over radiators. Another device was the carbide gas lamp, in which calcium carbide was dissolved by slow addition of water and produced light. Not only did these devices provide minimal illumination, but incessant jostling and even moderate winds often extinguished the flames. It did not take a genius to understand that as road surfaces gradually improved and automobiles gained speed, dependable headlights providing significant illumination would be necessary for night travel; the market was untapped and virtually unlimited.

The dazzling opportunities in the automotive field attracted thousands of potential contributors. Good businessmen were a rarer breed than inventors, or, to be precise, would-be inventors. Men with reputations as sound businessmen soon found themselves besieged by inventors, each convinced that he had created the inspired gadget that would revolutionize the industry. Many of them possessed good ideas, but they lacked either the capital or the entrepreneurial skills needed to publicize and market them.

Thus Carl must not have been too surprised when, in 1904, an inventor named P. C. "Fred" Avery approached him with an idea for improving automobile headlights. Avery was a tinkerer who loved to experiment, and he had obtained rights to a French patent for a method of converting compressed carbide gas into a bright light. Unfortunately, Avery was no salesman, and he didn't possess sufficient capital to develop methods for bringing the concept to the marketplace. According to one account, Carl was leaving his automobile shop for his daily lunch at Pop Haynes's restaurant in Indianapolis when he noticed a man grumpily loading a tank into a battered car. Fisher walked over to find out what was going on. The man was Fred Avery. "I've left this tank in your shop for weeks and you haven't even taken the trouble to look at it," Avery fumed. Fisher tried to mollify him, replying, "Why, the boys were afraid to touch it—they said it would blow up."[4] Fisher asked what the device was for, and Avery testily retorted that it was a compressed gas headlight that would allow people to drive at night.

Fisher was entranced. With his marginal vision, he had always had trouble with night driving, and he immediately perceived the possibilities of the device. He forgot all about lunch. A bit later, he caught up to his friend and partner James Allison and excitedly spelled out the possibilities. Allison, whose caution and attention to detail were in marked contrast to Fisher's infectious enthusiasm and flair, probed for details, but he agreed to take a look. The two men asked Avery for the opportunity to investigate the device; Avery granted their request, but not too willingly. The truth was that he had exhausted his resources and his patience, and he had been peddling the invention from city to city, hoping someone would take a chance on it. In fact, the concept had gained some earlier acceptance, as it was used to illuminate buoys and lighthouses. By 1904 Avery was tired of trying to market it; he just wanted to sell out his right to the patent and make a little money.

Why Fisher pursued this particular opportunity while ignoring others remains a mystery, but timing probably played an important role. Many circumstances in his life would seemingly have dictated that he exercise caution in making additional commitments. Most of his money was already tied up in his bicycle and automobile shops. He didn't have extra capital lying around; he didn't even have a home of his own but was still living with his mother. But he was thirty years old in 1904, and perhaps he decided that it was time to take another gamble, just as he had as a nineteen-year-old in borrowing money to promote Colonel Pope's bicycles.

Whatever their motives, Fisher and Allison decided to form a public company and sell stock. Sources vary in stating the precise amount of personal funds invested and the number of shares issued, but evidently the amounts were small. Fisher and Allison each invested somewhere between $2,000 and $10,000 of their own funds.[5] Within two years, Avery had dropped out of the partnership, realizing a very modest return for his years of effort. The two remaining partners attracted a handful of other friends and speculators to risk small sums, in most cases no more than a few hundred dollars.

In the fall of 1904, caution in committing to the enterprise appeared wise, as fame and profits seemed exceedingly remote. Clearly there was a huge potential market for bright, reliable automobile headlights, but the obstacles were formidable. The partners may have underestimated the challenges at the beginning, but they faced years of dirty, dangerous work. Had they accurately forecast future problems, they might never have taken the plunge. Their first task was to figure how to compress the gas into containers small enough to fit onto the running board of the average sized vehicle. Second, the container had to be leak-proof and reasonably safe to operate. Next, they had to figure out what types of tubing and control valves would most efficiently feed a steady supply of the gas to the headlamps. Finally, in addition to developing a marketing plan, they had to service and refill empty containers. In other words, how could customers dependent on compressed gas quickly replenish their supply? Would they need to purchase multiple containers? If compressed gas headlights achieved widespread acceptance, would the partners have to establish factories in other parts of the country?

The corporation was founded on September 6, 1904, "for the purpose of manufacturing, assembling, handling and selling lamps, reflectors, receptacles and gas for automobiles, carriages, mines, buoys, and all other machines and things in which artificial gas is necessary or required to be used."[6] The first item of business was to set up shop and try to figure out how to harness their promising source of energy. According to Carl's future wife, Jane, they located a "dilapidated shed in a poor section of Indianapolis" and began work. They donned goggles to protect their eyes and thick bandages for their hands and started experimenting. Their first hire was Jack Noble, whom they put to work filling tanks with an old-fashioned hand pump. Noble also became their first salesman, venturing around Indianapolis trying to persuade automobile owners to give the headlights a try. One of the easier challenges the partners faced was naming their company. One day, Allison asked Fisher for ideas, and after thinking for a few moments, he commented, "Presto means quick and light is what we're making—why not call it Prest-O-Lite?" Allison liked it, and the name stuck.[7]

Perhaps their most serious dilemma was balancing volume production and profitability with product safety. To provide a salable commodity, they had to compress a considerable quantity of gas into containers small enough to mount on running boards of cars but large enough that they wouldn't have to be refilled too often. If all these demands were met, customers might decide that they were useful and convenient and would keep using them. As Fisher and his associates forced more gas into a fixed amount of space, however, the danger of explosions multiplied exponentially. Higher pressure required more durable, heavier tanks. In addition, valves and tubing had to be extremely reliable, carefully engineered, and of the highest possible quality. Increased pressure obviously compounded engineering challenges. The trick was to devise durable, leak-proof, reasonably light, and inexpensive tanks that were capable of withstanding high pressures even after multiple refillings.

This formidable task challenged their perseverance, bravery, and ingenuity for years. Gas explosions were a constant, terrifying threat and an expensive headache. In fact, Fisher and his partners operated plants at numerous locations in Indianapolis, several of which were severely damaged by explosions. One of the early plants was at 28th and Pennsylvania Streets; another was located at 229 South East Street.[8] A third facility was on South Street, just west of East Street. None of them lasted very long.

The first serious explosion occurred on August 17, 1907, and many employees had narrow escapes. A second occurred just four months later, on December 20. In the second blowup, Elmer Jessup, an employee, was killed and three other workers were seriously injured. Flying steel was scattered about the neighborhood, but, miraculously, no nearby residents were killed or injured.

Only six months later, the most serious explosion yet in Indianapolis rocked Prest-O-Lite. This one dominated regional headlines for days. On June 6, 1908, the *Indianapolis News* contained a front-page story, "Prest-O-Lite Lets Go Again." The force of the blast shattered windows in buildings half a mile distant. Pieces of iron weighing several hundred pounds were hurled into the air and landed hundreds of feet from the plant. Incredibly, nobody was killed, even though the explosion occurred during working hours when about thirty employees were in the building. One workman suffered a broken leg when he jumped from a second-story window. Several others were burned, although papers reported that none of the injuries were serious. Most of the damage occurred outside of the Prest-O-Lite plant. St. James Infirmary, located nearby, was badly damaged, and numerous patients were in shock. Witnesses recounted that glass windows in the infirmary shattered with such force that glass slivers penetrated interior walls inside the infirmary. The blast also did such serious damage to firehouse No. 2 that the building eventually had to be torn down.[9]

It did not take long for public outrage to surface. Local citizens had grown jittery enough over the previous mishaps, but this major jolt was too much. Prominent citizens demanded action. One Dr. Pfaff, who was attending victims of the explosion, declared, "The construction of the Prestolite [*sic*] works so near the hospital was nothing short of criminal . . . it seemed plain to me that, sooner or later, just such an explosion would occur. The erection of that plant so near a hospital was something that a wise and self-respecting community should not have allowed."[10]

Fisher and Allison must have finally realized that they needed to make conciliatory gestures toward the citizens of Indianapolis. According to one published account, after one of the earlier explosions, they had arrogantly challenged local citizens to try to throw them out. "At that time the Prest-O-Lite people were declaring they would resist any action by the city to make them move, if they had to take it through every court in the country. That was their principal argument—that they would fight the case so long that the property owners would gain little by their efforts."[11]

The account of the partners' attitudes may have been spurious; naked confrontation was not Carl Fisher's style. After a third explosion in a year, however, the Prest-O-Lite partners sensed that their luck was nearing an end. Although they believed they had solved their safety problems and that they could make the plant much safer, they also realized that a future explosion in a congested area might cost many lives. In addition, they understood that public sentiment was turning against them. It was time to settle claims against them and the company. They faced numerous lawsuits. Although courtroom proceedings were serious business, there were lighter moments. One local citizen of German descent claimed that the explosion had blown the lids off three barrels of sauerkraut he'd had in his yard and that "exposure to the air injured his kraut." One paper reported that the story appealed to Fisher's sense of humor and he asked the man what the damages were. When told that $2 would cover it, Fisher handed over the money with a grin.[12]

Fortunately for Fisher, Allison, and Prest-O-Lite, public attention was soon diverted away from them and toward squabbling and blame throwing by city officials. Accusations flew about whether earlier ordinances affecting chemical processing were stringent enough and why certain regulations already on the books had not been enforced. The mayor and the city council engaged in heated arguments without coming to a resolution. The council finally passed an ordinance prohibiting Prest-O-Lite from conducting certain operations within city limits.[13] The respite allowed Fisher and Allison to plan their retreat from downtown Indianapolis in an orderly manner, and the partners eventually were allowed back into a less densely settled area of the city, under more carefully regulated conditions.

As Prest-O-Lite prospered and business expanded, the company set up plants in numerous cities across the United States, from Bayonne, New Jersey, to Los Angeles. Vastly expanded production under varying conditions caused dangers to multiply. Explosions and industrial accidents were a constant concern. Fisher and Allison even set up a system of telegraph codes through which they and local plant managers kept each other informed about disasters. As Prest-O-Lite expanded production to plants scattered across the nation, Carl found himself constantly in court, defending the corporation against lawsuits, most of them involving personal injuries and violations of local public safety ordinances. Allison spent most of his time running the plants and taking care of the books.[14]

But the worst disaster to occur in a Prest-O-Lite plant was not caused by chemicals. In December 1911 the partners were constructing a new plant in an industrial section of Indianapolis when interior concrete walls collapsed, burying more than two dozen men in tons of rubble. Ten workers eventually died, and many more were injured. Newspapers featured the story on the front pages for days, with lengthy accounts of frantic rescue attempts; gruesome stories of men horribly maimed; tales of victims in such pain that they had to be administered morphine shots while pinned in the wreckage; sad stories of pitiful, forlorn, and desperate widows and mothers who lost their sole means of support.

Predictably, the search for culprits began even before the last body was recovered. Once again, the partners were fortunate in that local politicians immediately pointed fingers at each other. In fact, the accident was not their fault, and they escaped subsequent investigations with their reputations largely intact. The plant had originally been designed as a two-story facility. Later, the partners asked for a third story to be added. They had hired a reputable architectural firm, and draftsmen drew up plans for a third floor. Senior architects presumably examined and approved the plans. In their haste to get the project finished, the architects overlooked city ordinances requiring approval by the building inspector's office. Technically, the contractors were at fault. Various public officials, however, hoped to capitalize on the tragedy. The mayor blamed the city's building inspector, claiming that inspection laws were far too lax. The inspector countered that his budget was ridiculously small and that he lacked the personnel necessary to enforce more than a fraction of the laws already in place, let alone come up with more exacting codes.[15]

The Prest-O-Lite disaster in Indianapolis attracted national attention. Safety engineers and specialists in building materials combed the wreckage. Extensive investigations failed to pinpoint precise causes for the disaster, but most experts consulted eventually focused on the fact that the concrete walls had been poured in unusually warm November weather and that a cold spell had arrived before the concrete had completely set.

Prest-O-Lite's frequent explosions posed a great danger to urban residents. Carl and his partners were fortunate that most citizen anger was directed against public officials rather than themselves, as this December 9, 1911, *Indianapolis Star* political cartoon suggests. Courtesy of Indiana State Archives.

The resulting contraction of the concrete weakened the walls, which had not been sufficiently buttressed with supports. The company's role in the tragedy was tenuous, difficult to prove. Several workmen claimed that they had informed bosses that some of the walls were bulging, and a few even testified that they were so worried they decided to quit their jobs.[16] But foremen were not experienced civil engineers; fixing blame on them for not *anticipating* a collapse was not a serious option for prosecutors.

A grand jury was active in the investigation almost from the beginning, and at the end of December it issued a report essentially clearing all parties of blame. It found that there were no violations of criminal laws in construction of the building, and that nobody was liable. Consequently, no indictments were returned.[17] Cartoonists lambasted public officials' unwillingness to assign blame.

When the building collapse occurred, Fisher was far from the scene in sunny South Florida. He didn't learn of the tragedy until days later when a telegram from Allison finally reached him. In Fisher's absence, his partner handled key matters for the company. Allison set up a $1,000 charity fund, to be administered by public agencies, to take care of the immediate needs of family members of victims. Allison and Fisher must have been relieved to escape responsibility for the disaster, at least in the public's eyes.

The disaster at the Indianapolis plant may have profoundly affected the direction of Fisher's career. In the fall of 1911 Prest-O-Lite had been gearing up to manufacture a new invention, the electric self-starter for automobiles. Earlier that year, Charles F. Kettering, an engineer working for Delco, had designed a successful self-starter for automobiles.[18] Before that time, starting an automobile required considerable manual dexterity, brute strength, and, on occasion, infinite patience. The task could be dangerous as well. Hand cranks that failed to disengage from the crankshaft at the proper moment occasionally struck operators, causing serious injuries. Thus Kettering's device was a dazzling breakthrough. Through their mutual interest in virtually all things related to automobiles, Fisher and Allison knew the inventor from Dayton, Ohio, well. They sensed that he had produced a winner; they, too, were thrilled by the prospect of future markets and were determined to get a share of them. The new Prest-O-Lite building in Indianapolis had been designed to include space for manufacturing self-starters. Had the building not been so heavily damaged, delaying production, Fisher's and Allison's careers might have taken very different paths. They might have achieved a significant toehold in the self-starter business and focused most of their energy on automobile parts and services.

As it turned out, 1911 was a pivotal year for the partners, one in which they went off in different directions. Despite repeated explosions and a barrage of lawsuits, Prest-O-Lite earned large profits. Indianapolis remained headquarters for the company. But the manufacturing facilities were inadequate; they had only 90,000 square feet of space in scattered locations in the city, and they needed space for a new, modern plant. Fisher and Allison evidently spread rumors that they were considering moving their corporate headquarters away from the region. If they were bluffing, it worked. Once the furor over the building collapse died down, local politicians, fearful of losing a major employer, enacted ordinances more friendly to manufacturers. Civic leaders let the partners know that new plant facilities would be welcome in Indianapolis, preferably some distance away from congested neighborhoods.[19]

By the end of 1911, Fisher was also heavily involved in developing an automobile racing oval several miles west of downtown Indianapolis, and it made sense to look for property for the Prest-O-Lite Company in the same general area. Ninety years ago, the area that became known worldwide as Speedway was a bucolic retreat with small farms and scattered individual dwellings. There was a waiting station for the Ben Hur interurban electric line, which operated between Indianapolis and Crawfordsville. The Baltimore and Ohio Railroad also ran tracks through the area, but there were few other signs of settlement. For Fisher and Allison, the location seemed ideal. The land was cheap. The railroad could deliver industrial supplies to the plant and ship filled tanks back to customers, and the interurban lines would carry workers to and from Indianapolis.

During 1911 and 1912 Prest-O-Lite prospered. As demands for the product grew and the company added more workers, the partners decided to build a company town, where employees could live close to their work. By 1913, in association with a rising local real-estate agent, Lem H. Trotter, the partners set up the Speedway Realty Company and were offering small lots suitable for modest wooden bungalows within walking distance of the main plant.[20] The original terms for lots were $10 down and $10 per month, without interest. More companies moved into the area just before World War I, and the partners realized additional profits through selling land to other workers.[21] The new plant was more than three times the size of its predecessor downtown: it contained more than 280,000 square feet of floor space and cost about $500,000 to build.[22]

Prest-O-Lite Company became a gold mine for several reasons. Despite a spate of accidents, Fisher and Allison eventually discovered methods for making more durable tanks that were safer to fill and handle. One critical advance was to use a thin asbestos lining to protect the inside of the tanks. This lining did not eliminate all danger, but the horrendous explosions that marred the early years were far less frequent. In addition, the partners developed techniques for compressing the gas into increasingly compact tanks, which drivers found far more handy than cumbersome, undependable carbide gas lamps.[23]

Equally significant, the partners realized that fast, dependable service to customers was the linchpin for the survival and growth of their enterprise, and they honed it to a fine edge. Essentially, they became pioneers in overnight delivery. In later years, Fisher claimed that customers located up to 200 miles away from the nearest Prest-O-Lite facility could take empty tanks to the local train station as late as 4:00 p.m. and have them serviced and back in their hands the next day. Company agents collected empty containers and made sure that they reached the Prest-O-Lite facility no later than midnight. Once at the plant, they could be filled by workers on the graveyard shift and shipped out in early morning trains to waiting customers. Until they grew accustomed to such convenience, some customers were startled to find refilled tanks back in their hands so quickly.[24]

As their empire expanded and profits accumulated, Fisher and Allison attracted more and more attention. Inventors of new and improved automotive products deluged them with propositions. The partners were well aware of the axiom that fools and their money are soon parted. For the most part, they were savvy businessmen, but even they could get sucked in occasionally. One of their most memorable, almost comical, lapses in judgment was their investment in a "miracle" fuel called Zolene. For centuries, humans have been mesmerized by the vision of propelling devices effortlessly through perpetual motion techniques and means of operating machinery with cheap and virtually inexhaustible fuel. An enterprising promoter from Dayton, Ohio, claimed to have invented a gasoline substitute consisting of water and a secret ingredient. Fisher traveled to Dayton and was sufficiently impressed to invite the inventor to Indianapolis for a demonstration. At the racetrack, the man performed his magic in front of Fisher and his suspicious engineers. First, he boiled water in a tea kettle, then dropped a handful of white cubes, which looked like camphor, into the kettle. Finally, he took a small vial from his vest pocket. Fisher asked what it was. "That's the secret," replied the inventor. He wouldn't let Fisher examine the bottle but added it, along with the solution, into the empty tank of one of Fisher's vehicles. Fisher got into the driver's seat and an assistant cranked up the car. To their amazement, it started, and Fisher drove it around the track.

Fisher was beside himself with excitement. Allison, typically the more cautious and skeptical of the two, was equally enthralled. No wonder. Before some of the big domestic petroleum reserve discoveries of the 1920s, gasoline was not cheap, and early automobiles consumed it in large quantities. The partners' imaginations ran wild. If they could acquire the rights to Zolene, they might be able to dominate the production and distribution of at least one form of cheap fuel for years, if not decades. They might even overthrow Standard Oil and other petroleum giants! Only one of Fisher's associates was dubious, stating that "making gasoline out of water is contrary to every law in chemistry." But Fisher and Allison were mesmerized by the "magic" vial. Fisher exclaimed, "I'd give $10,000 to find out what's in that bottle. He won't even let me smell it." Eventually, Fisher and Allison snapped up the bait, paid the inventor $30,000 for the formula rights, and set up a Zolene experimental operation at Speedway. According to Jane Fisher, local newspaper headlines "hailed him as the Messiah of a people that had become automobile conscious."[25] Within weeks of being the subject of such encomiums, the partners must have wanted to hide in embarrassment. Once they finally had their hands on the "magic" vial, Fisher's more scientifically trained engineers soon learned that the bosses had been bilked. Zolene was a craftily concocted hoax. Perhaps the partners were embarrassed at being so easily hoodwinked for they never revealed what the vial contained.

At first glance, Fisher and Allison appear to have been foolish to have fallen for Zolene. In hindsight, it was clear that there were no magic shortcuts to cheap energy, but in the minds of many Americans in the first decade of the twentieth century, no major technological challenge appeared insurmountable. The year before the founding of Prest-O-Lite, the Wright brothers had successfully launched the first airplane. The automobile business had been transformed since Fisher and Allison bought the rights to Fred Avery's patent just a few years earlier. The most obvious change was Henry Ford's revolutionary production techniques and innovations in mass marketing. In the first years of the new century, enterprising auto men thought in terms of producing a few thousand vehicles annually. Ford had raised the stakes a hundredfold.

As the 1910s began, tensions were rising in Europe, and World War I would soon interrupt automobile production, at least temporarily. Nevertheless, farsighted automobile men envisioned future markets of a million or more units per year. To bring these dreams to fruition, cars would have to be made and marketed more cheaply, and they had to be easy to operate. Ford was achieving these goals. Such startling advances in volume production generated exciting prospects of huge new markets, but they also introduced potential perils. Fisher and Allison realized that with the perfection and widespread use of the electric self-starter, it was but a matter of time until electricity would be used for headlights. They were conducting their own experiments with electric headlights, and they were convinced that this was the technology of the future. Even if it took years to develop reliable and economical electric headlights, the stakes in the headlight market would grow higher; competition would inevitably become much stiffer. Those years were dominated by huge corporate consolidations and mergers, and Fisher and Allison realized that the playing field would be dominated by those with deep pockets and large research and development staffs.

Fisher and Allison began to consider selling out. Timing was of the essence, and by 1913 the partners realized that the right moment had arrived to reap their profits and quit the game. Fortunately for Fisher and Allison, Union Carbide Corporation had been making overtures to purchase Prest-O-Lite Company for the past few years. Union Carbide understood the automotive future just as well as Fisher and Allison did, but the company had other uses in mind for the facilities. Union Carbide realized that the containers produced by Fisher and Allison had a dozen or so other marketable uses. The market for conveniently sized containers for acetylene welding was very inviting. Union Carbide had access to far more capital than the Indianapolis entrepreneurs, and it wanted Prest-O-Lite's facilities so as to launch large-scale production of these and other containers. In addition, the company had discovered other applications for the gasses, from welding to medical purposes. Eventually, Union Carbide offered the partners roughly $9 million for their business, and the sale was consummated. The partners divided the proceeds, each receiving a combination of cash and stock in Union Carbide.[26]

The two partners' reactions to becoming instant multimillionaires were completely different. Allison proclaimed, "From now on, I'm going to be the goddamnedest laziest man in the whole goddamned universe."[27] He essentially retired, "setting up an experimental engineering firm at Speedway, where he spent the rest of his working life tinkering with the machinery he loved."[28] By contrast, Fisher immediately plunged his new capital into ever more ambitious enterprises. Nevertheless, during the exhilarating years when he and Allison were masterminding Prest-O-Lite, he may have sensed that other aspects of life were passing him by and that he deserved to engage in occasional leisure activities.

In his thirties, Fisher was still trim and athletic, possessing phenomenal physical stamina. As a youth he expended a good deal of energy racing bicycles, and later he experienced adrenaline surges as he raced fast cars. At some point after he gained a measure of wealth, Fisher took up tennis, perhaps in part because it provided lots of exercise in a brief time period. Fisher did not possess the flowing, smooth moves of a natural athlete, but he made up for any such lack with an energetic, slashing style. Whatever sport he engaged in, whether driving cars, racing boats, riding polo ponies, or playing tennis, he enjoyed immensely. One of the few sports that failed to intrigue him was golf.

Fisher was still a bachelor in his mid-thirties, and he evidently devoted considerable time to chasing women; perhaps he succeeded too well in this endeavor. Carl was of medium height, compact, and handsome, and many women were attracted to him. His magnetic appeal undoubtedly intensified as his fortune grew. At one point early in the twentieth century he was briefly engaged to a woman named Emma Messing. Emma's sister once commented rather bluntly on his sex appeal: "Carl Fisher has the most kissable mouth I have *ever* seen in my life" (emphasis in original).[29] Neither Carl nor Emma revealed reasons for their breakup, but it was friendly, and they stayed in touch for the rest of their lives.[30]

If Fisher managed to remain on good terms with his former fiancée, he did not always fare as well with other women. In fact, several women took him to court for alleged breaches of promise. One of his attorneys, Walter Dennis Myers, defended him in numerous cases. Years later, Myers reminisced, "Somehow [Fisher's] genius did not extend to women, wise as he was in the ways of this world. Ten different females in the hands of jackleg lawyers tried to blackmail him." According to Myers, Fisher didn't fare too well in court: "Breach of promise cases . . . are hard to defend when the promises are alleged to have been made orally; it is hell and high water when they are put on paper, however deficient the writer may have been in describing romance." Myers recalled that of ten "blackmail" cases he handled, six plaintiffs won damages, although he claimed that typical settlements were "[on] terms that may have brought the jackleg attorney a new suit of clothes."[31]

At least one plaintiff won considerably more than that. In October 1912, Gertrude W. Hassler, formerly a professional opera soprano, sued Fisher for breach of promise. She claimed a relationship with the defendant dating from 1903, when she was in her mid-twenties. According to her courtroom testimony, Fisher "paid her constant attention and promised repeatedly to marry her." In addition, when Fisher became ill, he allegedly "insisted that she be his nurse and at one time induced her to take up her residence with his mother, with whom he lived." When she filed suit, Hassler alleged that for six years Fisher was her only escort and that he forbade her to see other men. Finally, he allegedly forbade her to study music or sing in public, saying that she sang "well enough to suit him."[32]

The lawsuit was considerably more complicated, involving business matters as well. Hassler claimed that she was Fisher's most valued assistant, "his eyes and ears," for many years. "She allege[d] that when Prest-O-Lite gas was invented she advised the defendant, wrote his advertising matter and became 'his memory' by reminding him of what he asked her not to let him forget. The assistance given the defendant by the plaintiff, she [said], caused his fortune to grow to $1,000,000." She asked for $500,000 "balm." Just how "devastated" Hassler was by Fisher's alleged betrayal is suspect. She waited for three years after Fisher's marriage to file suit, by which time his fortune had grown substantially. Fisher was irritated at her claims, but Hassler had kept some of his correspondence, which in some cases was rather steamy. When the case went to trial, her lawyers were able to produce several witnesses who had seen the two lovers together and had heard Fisher talk of a future with Hassler after they were married. Hassler made a far better witness than Fisher; on the stand, she gave an emotional account of their relationship that moved several courtroom witnesses to tears. In contrast, when he testified, Fisher appeared cavalier in his treatment of the affair. After a sensational trial that lasted several days, attracted overflow crowds to the courtroom, and made front-page headlines, the case went to a jury, which awarded Hassler $50,000.[33] Given his penchant for "misunderstandings" with women, it was undoubtedly fortunate that he remained a bachelor until his mid-thirties. Anyone who became involved with him romantically was in for a wild and bumpy ride.

It was probably fitting that his future bride, Jane Watts, first set eyes on Fisher as he was drifting over Indianapolis in his Stoddard-Dayton automobile, suspended from a balloon on that glorious fall day in 1908. At the time, she was a fourteen-year-old schoolgirl. Jane recalled that he was already the talk of the town and that "Carl had been our idol at Shortridge High School. To our parents, Carl was the automobile tycoon who was helping to put Indiana on the map, but to the children, Carl was a daring hero and a champion. . . . I belonged to a girl's club—fan club it would be called now—that was in love with Carl Fisher *en masse*" (emphasis in original).[34]

Jane Watts perhaps went a bit further in her admiration for Fisher than her peers; she claimed that she filled a scrapbook with newspaper clippings, pictures, and stories of his exploits. A few months after Fisher's balloon caper above the streets of Indianapolis, she attended a large party at a local country club with her parents and brother, and she was dressed in clothing that was sophisticated for a fifteen-year-old. Suddenly, she found herself standing face to face with her idol. For a moment she stood stock-still, staring at Fisher, mesmerized by his "dark magnetism." Finally, her brother jolted her out of her reverie by poking her in the ribs and urging her to move along. The young girl claimed to have caught Fisher's eye and that he allegedly murmured just loud enough for her to hear, "There goes the girl I'm going to marry."

The teenager and her idol were not formally introduced that evening. Jane claimed that a few days later she came down with the "grippe," and her parents left her with a neighbor to recover while they went visiting. While they were gone, the Watts house allegedly caught fire; all the teenager could think about was her precious Fisher scrapbook going up in flames. Young Jane recounted that in a panic she called Fisher's business number, introduced herself as the young lady he had seen at the country club, and told him that her house was on fire. Allegedly, the business mogul quietly reassured her, "I'll be right over, little honey."[35]

Such accounts of their first meeting are probably overblown. Unfortunately, historians possess few materials concerning the courtship of Fisher and Jane Watts other than the breathless first-person recollections of a star-struck fifteen-year-old. Fisher was virtually silent about the events leading up to his first marriage; friends and associates basically reiterated accounts penned by Jane. It is safe to say that Jane took the courtship far more seriously than Carl. First and foremost was their age difference; she was fifteen and he was thirty-four when they began their relationship. There were, too, the inevitable gender differences in attitudes toward matrimony. In the early twentieth century, ideal husbands were expected to be silent, strong, competent "providers"; middle-class girls were trained to be housewives, to take care of and even pamper their men. For many women, love and marriage defined their existence.[36] This description certainly characterized Jane Watts.

Evidence suggests that Fisher approached courtship and marriage far more casually. Conduct perceived as chauvinistic today was not so defined ninety years ago; it was routine and normal behavior for many husbands and even for lovers consciously practicing good behavior during courtship. Yet Fisher's attitude toward women appears crass even for those days. In his lodgings he displayed a leather pillow embroidered with the declaration: "A Woman is Just a Woman, But a Cigar Is a Smoke."[37] If Jane Watts ever saw the pillow in their months of courtship, she would have been wise to have taken it as a portent.

They began their courtship in June 1909. Fisher was an extremely busy man of affairs, with several projects moving forward simultaneously. He fit time with Jane Watts in between business appointments, but he courted her at a fast and furious pace. Jane reminisced at length about her overpowering suitor: "Altogether, I found Carl so dazzling that at first I couldn't look at him." She had never ridden in an automobile, and Carl took her out on numerous rides. He drove her to his job sites, and he took her on long, fast sojourns on dusty roads out into the countryside far beyond Indianapolis. Jane recalled that "In My Merry Oldsmobile" was their "courting song," and they would share the lyrics with the birds as they buzzed along, enjoying warm summer breezes.

Perhaps the couple journeyed outside of the city to escape tensions on the home front. Jane's family was divided over the affair. Her stepfather, James Buchanan Watts, was a farm implements salesman and a great admirer of Fisher, but he was highly skeptical of the affair: "What does a big man like Carl Fisher see in a kid like you?" he asked her. Perhaps he was masking his fear that Fisher might be taking advantage of her when they were far from prying eyes. Jane, however, recounted that her mother was quietly supportive of the romance: "Mama, bless her, had kept silent through these hectic weeks."[38]

Indeed, this time was hectic! In the summer of 1909 Fisher and Allison still owned Prest-O-Lite, a full-time operation by itself. In addition, Fisher was not only involved in laying down the original surface of what eventually became perhaps the most famous racetrack in the world, the Indianapolis Motor Speedway, but was continuing to manufacture automobiles through the Empire Motor Car Company. In addition, his showrooms and shops in and around Indianapolis sold and serviced various brands of cars. If all of these activities weren't enough, he was personally promoting and competing in regional and national balloon races. Early in their courtship, Carl moved quickly. One of their first dates, he allegedly said softly to Jane, "You know, Jane, I'm going to marry you." Jane claimed that she could only reply, "Yes, I know."[39]

By the fall of 1909 Carl abruptly decided that the hearts and flowers aspect of their relationship had gone on long enough. Returning from a hazardous balloon ride that ended when he and his longtime friend and sidekick George Bumbaugh had crash-landed their balloon in the mountains of West Virginia, Carl announced to Jane that they should be married right away. His "proposal" did not exactly reek with romance: "I've a Prest-O-Lite suit out in Los Angeles. . . . If we marry now, you can come on the trip. I'm tired of traveling alone. . . . I've got to cut out this

Thirty-five-year-old Carl and fifteen-year-old Jane Watts posed cozily shortly before their marriage in October 1909. Courtesy of the Historical Museum of Southern Florida.

courting business and get back to work." Years later, in her biography of her former husband, Jane understated, "From the beginning, he took a rare amount of understanding on my part."[40]

Obviously Jane acquiesced in Carl's determination to end the suspense and form a permanent union. They agreed, or perhaps Carl decreed, that they would be married on October 23, 1909. Virtually every aspect of the wedding arrangements, ceremony, and honeymoon was bizarre. In the nineteenth century, and even into the early twentieth century, marriages of older men and young women were not unusual. Nevertheless, Carl was clearly embarrassed that Jane was only fifteen, and he asked that she claim to be twenty-four when he introduced her to friends.[41] Jane was a statuesque, full-figured woman, and she could successfully hide her true age when among casual acquaintances.

In the hours before they were married, Carl's behavior became strange, cavalier, even cruel. They had agreed on a small, private ceremony at the Watts home. The night before the wedding, while Jane's mother was bustling about the house making sure everything was in place, Fisher's black servant, William Galloway, appeared at the doorstep. According to Jane, "He seemed a little apologetic. 'Mister Fisher ain't much for fuss and feathers, ma'am,' he told my mother. Mother had no way of knowing the message contained a warning." A bit later, the warning became more specific. Fisher phoned his bride-to-be and informed her, "If you want to get married, you'll have to get the preacher. I don't know any preachers." According to Jane, he abruptly hung up.

The preacher story is probably apocryphal because it is almost inconceivable that neither party had thought about a presiding official until then. Fisher was, admittedly, up to his neck in business and other lawsuits, but he must have been aware of the technicalities of forming a legal union. Jane might have been dazzled by the whirlwind nature of her romance, but surely her parents would have demanded an explanation from Fisher for his bizarre actions. Perhaps a more sophisticated, less smitten young woman would have called the wedding off right then and there. But Jane and her family were evidently determined to go through with the event.

Three years later, at his breach-of-faith trial, Jane would discover another reason for Fisher's wild behavior in the days surrounding their nuptials. It seems that virtually up to the moment Carl and Jane exchanged vows, Gertrude Hassler was exerting enormous pressure on him to resolve their differences. At that time, Hassler still had visions of a permanent union with Fisher, and she telephoned him frequently and pleaded with him to see her. In fact, the night before his wedding to Jane, Hassler swore she had talked to Fisher at length and that she had repeatedly asked him to take her to Omaha. She had ended the conversation only after extracting a promise from Fisher that she would see him "tomorrow," the very day he was to be married![42]

Thankfully, Jane was oblivious to her fiancé's last-minute dealings with an erstwhile jealous lover. As if she hadn't experienced sufficient stress the previous evening, the prospective bride was awakened the next morning at 6 a.m. by a pouring rain and the blaring sounds of a German street band under her window. Fisher had thoughtfully arranged for the "entertainment," and Jane's anguished entreaties failed to interrupt their full repertoire of songs. Barely half an hour later, florists began arriving at the Watts home in droves. The family had already decorated the house for the nuptials, but Fisher, in his heavy-handed attempt at providing his own vision of a romantic atmosphere, had ordered numerous floral arrangements. Despite the chaos and confusion, the ceremony eventually took place, more or less on schedule. Fisher's family consisted only of his mother and brother Earle. His other brother, Rollo, had died, and his father had long since been banished from his mother's household.

Years later, Jane recalled how flustered Carl appeared during the ceremony. "All the time the minister was talking, Carl kept running his fingers under his collar. In a wild-eyed sort of way he seemed to be glaring at me as if I were a total stranger." She attributed his nervousness to the fact that she was, for the first time in his presence, formally dressed. She concluded her description of the frenetic nuptials with a startling description of Fisher's nervousness: "The minister was still talking when Carl, red-faced and perspiring, seized my hand and shoved the ring at me wildly. 'Here take it! . . . Good God, we must be married by this time.'"[43]

That was just the beginning of unpleasant, stressful surprises for the young bride. Fisher had reserved a drawing room on a train headed for the West Coast. According to Jane's account, as soon as they got to the train and were in their quarters, Carl abruptly took out a knife and started cutting away at the gold braid on her dress. Jane started crying, but he kept at it, explaining, "I just naturally can't stand gold braid." When all the braid was gone, he grinned and concluded, "That's the way I like my woman, little wench, unadorned, the way God made her." Jane must have thought he had sex on his mind, but such was not the case. He handed her a magazine and said he had to finish up some business. "Honey, I've got to see a man about a boat—I'll be back." He was gone for hours. Jane was summarily abandoned on her wedding night, and she may have wished she was home with her family. She cried herself to sleep. Later, she woke up to see her new husband smiling down at her. "I'm sorry, honey, but this boat man was on board.-" Jane concluded, "There would always be men, business, big money and big deals. They came first."[44]

Fisher's behavior in the days before and after his wedding was clearly boorish and crude. Jane, of course, was just fifteen when they were married; she would feel totally dominated during their seventeen years together. Yet it took Jane many years to conclude that their marriage had to end. She evidently believed that Fisher's heart was in the right place and that some of his most inexplicable behavior was rooted in his awkward efforts to do something spectacular for her. In some warped way, she was right. The wedding night fiasco was essentially the result of Fisher's spontaneous, unilateral decision that when his business affairs permitted, he and Jane should have a spectacular honeymoon; for this, they needed a yacht. Unbeknownst to Jane, Carl had arranged for Clement C. Avery, a boatbuilder, to book a ticket on their train. The two men had sat up for hours, poring over plans for the boat. Carl was fond of grand gestures, but it took Jane some time to get used to them. On their wedding trip, they visited a jewelry store, and Jane was mooning over a toilet set of solid gold. As Carl urged her to take it if she wanted it, she hesitantly asked the jeweler the price. When told it was $1,500, she insisted they leave the shop. "I didn't believe there was that much money in the world." Later, she would become accustomed to their wealth and would spend ten or fifty times that amount without batting an eyelash.

Back home in Indianapolis after the honeymoon to the West Coast, Jane promptly discovered she would be living in a man's world, *his* world. A few years before their marriage, Carl had finally moved from his mother's house into a home of his own. Carl's bedroom in his former bachelor's quarters was decorated in early cowboy: basically in wood and leather, with lots of hooks for hanging things. A stand on one side of his bed always held a jar of salted peanuts. Above the bed were paintings of Lincoln and Napoleon, plus a patch of sandpaper which Carl used to light matches. There was a spittoon next to the bed; in fact, they were scattered about the house. This is evidently when Jane learned that her husband ate peanuts and smoked cigars in bed. One can only imagine the odors in the room, let alone the aroma of Fisher's breath when he turned out the lights. Jane recalled that there wasn't an ounce of femininity in the room; then and there, she must have understood what an uphill battle she faced. Quickly shedding her girlish naiveté, she wisely decided to concentrate her energies on one item at a time. "My bridal struggles against that spittoon resembled the crusades of Carrie Nation." However valiant her fight, Jane lost. The spittoon stayed.[45] If Jane ever shared her husband's bedroom for sleeping, she did not do so for long. In about 1911 Carl purchased a large country home in Indianapolis which they named Blossom Heath. There, Jane had her own daintily appointed bedroom.[46]

Within weeks of their marriage, Carl apparently had second thoughts about using the yacht he had ordered on his wedding night for any honeymoon trip. It took about a month to finish the boat, and by that time he at least was settled into married life. He thought that instead of a honeymoon trip, he would prefer to take a trip down the Mississippi River to New Orleans and perhaps travel as far as Florida with some of his buddies. He and his friends had, after all, been working at a frenetic pace, and Fisher wanted to escape for a while. When it slowly dawned on Jane that she wasn't going to be invited, she finally put her foot down, insisting that she go along. Carl tried to talk her out of it, claiming she'd be uncomfortable and that she'd feel out of place. But she was determined to go and finally won the battle.

Once on board, she might have had second thoughts. The men—Fisher and his business associates Harry Buschmann and John Levi—put her through a sophomoric hazing ritual, challenging her to take a chew of tobacco and bite the head off a captured fish. Jane claimed that she called their bluff, and slowly she was accepted into their company. In some ways, they did "rough it," Jane recalled. The bathtub she had looked forward to using had been converted into a coal bin, so Jane had to douse herself with river water when she wanted a bath. Despite the complete male dominance, Jane managed gradually to participate in and enjoy the rough bonhomie, at least until they got to New Orleans. They docked there on Christmas Eve, whereupon the three men abruptly left her on board with Fisher's servant, Galloway, and headed for the tenderloin district.

Jane had already put up with a lot, but she wasn't mentally prepared for this new insult. She had decorated a tree and had envisioned a romantic, sentimental celebration. Instead, she grew increasingly fearful as Christmas Day dawned. Then she heard them—three rollicking drunks descending down the dock, voices loud and harsh in the morning mist. It appeared that they had been waylaid by police officers during their peregrinations the previous evening. It all seemed perfectly normal to Fisher, as he cheerfully regaled his shattered young wife with the details. Fisher reported buying an expensive bracelet, his Christmas gift to Jane, in a jewelry store. Even though he paid cash, the store owner was evidently suspicious at the appearance of three free-spending, shabbily dressed men reeking of river smells. He called the police, who allegedly detained the three men for a time. After they were released, John Levi purchased a roasted pig, evidently intended as a hostess present for Jane. On the way back to the boat, they converted the pig into a football, merrily passing it back and forth. As Jane recalled, "The game was interrupted by a second appearance of the New Orleans police, who unreasonably declared grown men could not play football with a roast pig—at least not after midnight in New Orleans."[47] One wonders if even a teenage bride would accept such an imaginative tale at face value.

Thus in the tumultuous first two months of her marriage, Jane Fisher was rudely introduced to the less attractive side of her husband's character. He was, in many ways, immature, selfish, and thoughtless. Both in business and in his marriage, he blithely assumed that others shared his interests. Carl's penchant for self-indulgence once he acquired riches may have been unconscious compensation for the privations he had experienced earlier in life. Perhaps Jane instinctively sensed this and learned to forgive his excesses. But Fisher's behavior was maddeningly complex and inconsistent. On rare occasions he could be contemplative, enormously sensitive, even romantic. He showered Jane with expensive and occasionally thoughtful gifts. When in the right mood, momentarily unencumbered by the enormous pressures of his mounting business commitments, his attention to Jane totally captivated her. She lived for those infrequent, precious moments when she had Carl completely to herself, and she treasured them long afterward. Jane sensed that she was married to a great and highly unusual man; for years, being a part of his exciting universe, even on the fringes, would be enough for her. After she finally left Fisher, Jane married again several times. But no other husband could match Carl in sheer energy, fascination, and excitement. "I couldn't do it. I divorced; I married again and again. I couldn't stay married to them because life was just too drab. . . . Living with Carl Fisher was like living in a circus: there was something going on—something exciting going on—every minute of the day . . . it was living. It was excitement, aliveness that I never found again."[48]

4

Building a Brickyard

From his earliest years, Carl Fisher was absolutely fascinated by anything that moved fast. He also enjoyed attracting attention. He learned to balance himself on the top of picket fences and trained himself to run backward about as fast as his chums ran forward. He sledded recklessly down icy hills with an advertising banner streaming along behind him. As a member of the Zig-Zag Club he had always been in the midst of the fastest, most strenuous, most dangerous bicycle races. The invention of motor-powered bicycles and racing cars came at the perfect moment for Fisher. He was fascinated by how engines worked and driven to learn how to make machines move faster and longer. Carl was perfectly positioned in place, time, attitude, and aptitude to become one of the most important early promoters of automobile racing in the United States.

In all of his automobile-related endeavors, beginning shortly after the turn of the century, a larger purpose influenced his actions. Like other farsighted automobile men, Fisher instinctively grasped the machine's potential for transforming Americans' lives, if not the national culture. He was a sportsman and simply loved fast automobiles, and this was a major reason why he led development of a racing oval in Indianapolis. In the early years of the century, Fisher clearly saw what the automobile was doing for Detroit. He dreamed of making Indianapolis a worthy rival.

If the city did not manufacture as many automobiles as Detroit, perhaps it could attract many of the ancillary supplies and parts businesses. Carl and his partner, James Allison, were doing their part with Prest-O-Lite. These automotive enterprises promised to invigorate the economies of cities that attracted them. Across the upper Midwest, in cities such as Cadillac, Toledo, Dayton, Akron, and Youngstown, civic boosters harbored similar dreams. The competition would be stiff, and Fisher wanted Indianapolis to win its share. At the very least, an impressive motor speedway could provide a superb testing ground for men and machines, new metals, parts, and experimental automotive equipment. In a sense, Fisher assumed personal responsibility for advancing this nation's automotive technology on several fronts simultaneously.

After attending the 1900 automobile show in New York and driving numerous makes and models, Fisher added automobiles to his bicycle showroom in downtown Indianapolis. Most entrepreneurs might be satisfied with doing one thing well, such as selling an up-and-coming, fashionable product, but not Carl Fisher. He had to know what was going on under the hood, and he intuitively understood that automobile racing was a critical ingredient in designing and building better cars. Poor eyesight had forced Carl to abandon driving racing cars himself, but "retirement" from the racing circuit would not relegate him to obscurity. In fact, it was perhaps a blessing in disguise, as it encouraged him to apply his superb promotional skills to one of the sports he loved. Although Henry Ford was simultaneously engaged in the manufacturing experiments that ultimately made the United States the world's undisputed leader in automobile production for half a century, the motor vehicle had been invented in Europe. In the early 1900s, Europeans were still the leaders in experimentation and design. Most American racing men were profoundly impressed by the sleek, durable, and speedy European makes that occasionally appeared in formal races in the East.[1]

In the first decade of the twentieth century, Americans were growing accustomed to the idea of racing automobiles. But most racing occurred in locations poorly suited to the task, such as flat dirt tracks at county fairgrounds. Not only did they become muddy in poor weather and very dusty under dry conditions, but they quickly developed deep ruts and were extremely dangerous for both competitors and spectators. A fast-moving vehicle could easily flip over when caught in a deep rut while the driver was trying to maneuver. Looking back on his accident at Zanesville, Fisher might have been tempted to blame the racing facilities at least as much as his own handling of his vehicle. Nevertheless, there was enormous interest in racing, and the Indianapolis Automobile Racing Association actively sponsored races at the Indiana Fairgrounds at least as early as 1905. On November 4 of that year, W. F. Clemens won a 100-mile race in just under two hours.[2]

By mid-decade Fisher had plenty of reasons to be dissatisfied with America's prospects in automobile racing. His first overseas trip, a visit to the James Gordon Bennett Cup Races in France as a member of the United States team in 1905, was in some respects an upsetting, depressing experience. Not only was the racecourse across twisting mountain roads extremely dangerous, but it was quickly apparent that the French and Italians had more experience driving under such conditions and that they had far better cars. "The possibility of an American victory was so remote that I completely lost interest," Fisher later recalled.[3] He was out of sorts for most of the trip. Part of the reason may have been that he couldn't convince French chefs to feed him American steak, potatoes, and apple pie, his staples. Writing four decades later, Carl's former wife, Jane, unwittingly revealed his provincialism, noting that he "hated European food, and the foreign languages maddened him. When in Italy he found a cook in a restaurant who had worked in America and could fry potatoes and make apple pie, he took the man along for the rest of the tour."[4] Jane claimed that the visit soured Fisher on Europe for years and that when they acquired wealth, he was little interested in returning except to attend two major races. Jane maneuvered her husband into making a brief visit in 1914, which he abruptly terminated when World War I broke out.

However stressful his first European trip may have been, the experience intensified Fisher's determination to do something to improve his country's automobile racing prospects. Carl ruminated at length about the possibility of developing facilities exclusively for automobile racing. He reasoned that such testing sites could serve three purposes. First, by allowing automobile manufacturers a place to test their machines to the limit under controlled conditions, a racetrack would stimulate far more rapid technological advances and more sophisticated safety features. Second, a dedicated racetrack might draw large numbers of paying fans and become a profitable venture. Third, a renowned racing venue might stimulate the development of automotive industries in Indiana.

Despite his sour memory of his initial voyage to Europe, Fisher returned briefly in 1907. In England he visited an enormous estate owned by Hugh Fortesque Locke-King, where he saw the mammoth Brooklands racetrack under construction.[5] The experience was an epiphany for Fisher. Upon his return stateside, he began thinking in earnest about building the greatest racetrack in the world.

Fisher's concept was amazingly farsighted, in that he instinctively understood that short tracks of a mile or less in circumference would be ill-suited for the speeds racing machines might reach in future years. Indeed, he originally imagined a huge oval racetrack somewhere between three and five miles in circumference. Carl perceived little attraction in short track or point-to-point races, explaining his logic in an open letter to the editor of *Motor Age*. "There is no question in my mind that track racing on mile tracks is doomed. . . . To the spectators there is very little enjoyment in seeing a 25 or 50 mile road race where immense crowds throng the course and where only fleeting glimpses can be had of the cars as they come and go down the road. There is no accommodation for the public in a race of this kind."[6] Fisher urged American manufacturers to cut advertising expenses and support automobile racing. What they needed was a place where they could test their vehicles at high speeds over long distances, and Fisher grew increasingly determined to provide just such a facility.

French Lick, Indiana, was Fisher's first choice of location. The exquisitely named resort in the rolling hills of southern Indiana was already known for its high-stakes gambling. Two large hotels already existed there, so Fisher undoubtedly dreamed of high rollers becoming involved in the newest sport. In addition, railroad lines offered easy access for crowds from reasonably close big towns in Indiana, Kentucky, and Illinois, which might be induced to take day trips and pay entry fees to watch racing. Fisher hesitated, influenced perhaps by the financial panic of 1907; he may have reasoned that the setback would lessen the numbers of vacationers with deep pockets. This pause probably doomed French Lick as a potential racing site. Deeper deliberation convinced Fisher that the plot at French Lick was not large enough to accommodate a five-mile track. In the long run, Fisher's decision probably saved him from many headaches because the land he had selected tended to flood in late May.[7]

Over the next year or so, Fisher was preoccupied with other business interests. He was expanding his automobile lines in his showroom in Indianapolis, and he and several partners were in the process of putting together the Empire Motor Car Company. Plans for a racing speedway seemed to be on hold, if not permanently scotched. But Fisher developed an amazing ability to keep several balls in the air simultaneously, and evidently the project was never far from his mind. Late in 1908 Carl and one of his real estate associates, Lem Trotter, drove from Indianapolis to Dayton, Ohio. The anticipated short drive became an odyssey. On the return trip, the car overheated twice, and just inside the Indiana border the vehicle blew out the third tire of the day. A projected one-day journey had turned into a fiasco. Fisher kept grumbling to Trotter about how unreliable American cars were and that the nation really needed a huge test track. Trotter challenged Fisher to stop griping and start acting. "You've been talking about a racetrack ever since you got back from Europe," Trotter said bluntly. "If you think it would make money, why don't you build it yourself." Decades later, Trotter claimed, "I just kept nagging [Fisher and three partners]. There never was all four of them together until the last few conversations."[8]

Perhaps Trotter's words ignited Fisher and the three other men he drew into the group. From then on during the business trip, Fisher talked of little else. He grilled Trotter to think of a spot where he might build. Trotter had the "perfect" spot in mind. It was a 320-acre plot known as the old Pressley farm, located about five miles west of downtown Indianapolis. By the time they got home, Fisher had commissioned his associate to inquire about purchasing the site. Trotter sounded out the owners, who confided that they might be persuaded to part with it for $80,000. Fisher consulted with his erstwhile racing associate and Prest-O-Lite partner, Jim Allison. The latter was as excited by the notion as Fisher, and he readily agreed to the plan. The two speculators approached three other mutual friends: longtime racing chum Arthur C. Newby, carburetor manufacturer Frank H. Wheeler, and Indianapolis banker Stoughton Fletcher.

All but Fletcher joined the combine. It didn't take Fisher long to figure out that a half-section of land would not be large enough for the track he envisioned. Eventually, the partners purchased additional adjacent land and controlled 539 acres. On February 8, 1909, they filed incorporation papers under the name of Indianapolis Motor Speedway Company, capitalized at $250,000. Of the total invested, Fisher and Allison each subscribed $75,000; Newby and Wheeler $50,000 each.[9]

If they planned to host any races in 1909, they would have to get a track built quickly. The partners agreed to hire Park T. Andrews, an engineer from New York, to design the track. Fisher was determined that the track should be three miles in circumference. Andrews, however, urged them to construct a two-and-a-half-mile rectangle with banked and rounded corners. Fisher wanted to hold out for a three-mile track, but Andrews astutely pointed out that if they did so, there would be no room on the grounds for a comfortable grandstand, capable of seating tens of thousands of potential racing fans.[10] Fisher clearly possessed a large ego, but he yielded to the expert.

As if he didn't already have enough on his mind, in the summer of 1909 Fisher was feverishly courting his future bride, Jane Watts. She recalled that her seasoned swain was consumed by the building project and that he drove her out to see the construction almost every time they went for a ride. The partners wanted to host events during the 1909 racing season, so haste was imperative, and two or more shifts of dozens of men worked twenty hours a day to hasten construction. Intimates recalled that Carl was seemingly in the midst of it all, driving himself to exhaustion. His enthusiasm reinforced his energy, and when local reporters came out to see the work in progress, Fisher gaily took them on a speedy lap of the unfinished track. The scribes were unnerved by their wild, bumpy ride.

The first official function at the motor speedway was not an automobile competition but a balloon race. Fisher, an avid balloonist, hoped a spectacular liftoff and various other attractions would publicize the new track and lure paying fans. The event was staged on June 5, 1909. It did indeed attract paying customers, but they only numbered about 3,400. An estimated 40,000 other locals figured they could see plenty of action from the outskirts without paying to sit in the stands. Once aloft in his balloon, Carl theatrically unfurled six American flags and showered both paying customers and freeloaders with dozens of red roses.

If the initial balloon extravaganza raised little revenue, it gained Fisher and his partners excellent publicity, a precious commodity. Unfortunately, for the racing season itself, publicity would not be so favorable. In their haste to promote exciting racing, the partners planned the initial construction phase poorly. They decided on a macadam surface of crushed rock, gravel, limestone, and tar oil. This surface was fine for ordinary automobile travel at speeds common in the early twentieth century, but it would quickly prove to be far too fragile for constant pounding by heavy, fast-moving experimental vehicles. In hindsight, it is obvious that in their effort to attract star racers and stage big races, the partners downplayed concerns over the track itself. A motorcycle race in July should have provided clear warning signals, had they been inclined to heed them. Several motorbikes overturned, and the cyclists warned of uncommonly dangerous surface conditions. If the track couldn't accommodate relatively light motorcycles, how would it stand up to the constant pounding of racing vehicles several times heavier? Fisher and his partners insisted that the kinks could be worked out before the next major event, scheduled for Labor Day weekend.

In retrospect, it is clear that they should have listened more carefully to the warnings from the motorcycle riders. Racing car drivers were also using the track for practice runs, and the surface was causing them near spills and other types of trouble. Three days of racing were scheduled. On the first day, the 250-mile Prest-O-Lite Trophy race had to be flagged off when the surface started to break up into huge slabs, which created deep potholes. American Automobile Association officials monitoring the races wanted to call off the next two days of racing. But Fisher insisted on providing the large crowds what he had promised to give them. He informed officials that the next day's races were no longer than 100 miles and that he could get the track in shape in time. That night his crews worked frantically to repair the damage; the second day, races went off without a hitch before 25,000 fans.

On the third day, 35,000 fans showed up, expecting thrills and excitement. They got far more than they bargained for. They witnessed carnage on the track and in the stands. The feature event was the 300-mile Wheeler-Schebler Trophy Race. All went well for the first 100 miles, but then the track began to break up again. Huge ruts appeared, particularly at the southwest corner of the track. Herb Lytle hooked a rut and swerved into the infield. He was not hurt, and he immediately rejoined the chase. A few laps later, Charley Merz was less fortunate. He lost control of his huge National racing machine and hurtled off of the track and into a crowd of spectators. Merz's riding mechanic, Claude Kellem, was killed instantly, as were two spectators. In separate mishaps two other persons were killed, including one driver and another spectator. Nevertheless, the race went on. A few laps later, Bruce Keen's Marmon crashed into a pedestrian bridge near the southeast corner, seriously weakening the structure. That was too much for starter Fred Wagner, who finally called off the remainder of the race.

For Fisher, the most visible of the racetrack partners, the Labor Day festivities were a public relations disaster. The tragedy did not show him in his best light. Publicly, Carl tried to put the best face on the proceedings by implying that he made the decision to stop the races in consideration of public safety. Perhaps trying to deflect further criticism, he made more promises: "To insure the safety of the public and the participants alike," Fisher intoned, "we are ready to spend $100,000 or more to make this a reality." In fact, Fisher had been bitterly disappointed by interruption of the final race.[11]

Fisher was deeply shaken by the multiple tragedies in the inaugural series of races at Indianapolis. His mind undoubtedly flashed back to that awful day in Zanesville, Ohio, a few years earlier where he and his brother Earle had crashed into a crowd, causing several fatalities. In the eyes of citizens of Indianapolis and many other cities, his Prest-O-Lite factories were ticking time bombs waiting to go off. The energetic entrepreneur must have felt very uncomfortable once again having his name actively associated with death and mayhem. Perhaps he should not have blamed himself too much. As Rich Taylor, a historian of the Indianapolis 500, suggested, "The basic problem was the unbelievably rapid advance in technology, which moved too quickly for race organizers to handle."[12]

Whatever his private feelings, Fisher learned a very valuable lesson from the disasters at the racetrack. In the interests of speeding up construction and having the track ready for the announced opening day, the partners had cut corners and had compromised on quality of the building materials. Although few blamed Carl directly for the deaths, he felt that his reputation had been tarnished. From this point forward, when Fisher was associated with building projects, he insisted that they be constructed of the strongest and most durable materials available and that workmanship should be superior. A certain amount of public hand-wringing might have been offered by any owner or manager of a facility that had hosted such a tragedy, but evidently Fisher's promises were genuine. He did his best to make amends for the disaster. When he announced plans to upgrade the safety of the track, he was far more deeply committed to constructing a high-quality product than many realized. Fisher was determined not only to make the track as safe as humanly possible but to make it the finest in the world, a state-of-the-art facility that would attract the greatest international racers to future events.

Fisher and his partners consulted track designer Park Andrews, who suggested that they rebuild with either concrete or bricks. Although bricks were twice as expensive as concrete, the partners opted for bricks. One reason was probably that Fisher coaxed one of his associates, Arthur Newby, to cover their cost, perhaps in part because Newby had very deep pockets at the time.[13] Resurfacing began within a month of the disastrous races at the track. First, construction crews leveled the existing track and spread an additional two inches of sand over the original material. Next they laid a total of 3.2 million bricks on the surface. In addition, they constructed a 9-inch-thick, 33-inch-high concrete retaining wall to prevent out-of-control vehicles from hurtling into crowds of spectators. The entire rebuilding phase took just sixty-three days. When construction ended a week before Christmas 1909, the partners ceremoniously proclaimed that the final brick was gold; in fact, it was a mixture of bronze and brass from melted-down carburetors.[14] Although the weather was bitterly cold, the partners immediately staged a series of exhibition races.

Lewis Strang drove a 200-horsepower Fiat to a new American record for two laps, or five miles, at 91.81 miles per hour, and he also set a new record for a quarter of a mile on a straightaway of 111.86 miles per hour. For the recent bridegroom, the day marked at least partial vindication for the disasters of the previous summer.[15]

With the track finally finished, the promoters had to determine how best to use it. They had built a masterpiece of a racing facility, but they clearly needed new ideas for promoting races. The 1910 racing season was unremarkable. A series of short automobile races drew disappointing crowds.[16] Fisher and his associates also experimented with air races and aviation shows at the facility. Carl even brought in Orville and Wilbur Wright in an effort to stir up enthusiasm. Carl and Jane hosted the famous aviators at their new home, called Blossom Heath; she found the pair socially inept and taciturn, "the strangest men I had ever met."[17] Even the presence of the Wright brothers failed to create the hoped-for sensation.[18] As with the balloon ascension the previous year, penny-pinching viewers realized they could see almost as much action from across the street as they could from the grandstand. Why pay for what you could see for free?

The partners realized that to make the track a success, they had to revamp their thinking. Before the 1911 racing season, they made some striking and farsighted decisions. Fisher had attended several prestigious races in Europe that attracted tens of thousands of spectators. He had been impressed with both the quality of the races and the competition, as well as with the caliber of fans attracted to the big European races. In the eyes of a homespun Hoosier, these events exuded "class." In the years leading up to construction of the track at Indianapolis, Carl had been an active participant in the first generation of track races on American soil. While he had fond memories of some of his races and many warm friendships from those years, he thought the United States could do better than the undistinguished hodgepodge of short races around dirt tracks at county fairgrounds. Fisher wanted to challenge the Europeans. He imagined an extravaganza, a spectacular one-of-a-kind event that would attract the world's best racers to Indianapolis. His partners evidently shared his ambition. They seriously considered staging a twenty-four-hour event because many drivers and manufacturers liked the idea of putting both men and machines to such an ultimate test of stamina. In addition, marketers of many automotive products drooled over the advertising value of such a unique event. Fisher's partner Arthur Newby initially favored the twenty-four-hour event but eventually saw the value of shortening the time and distance. "Personally, I like 24 hours," he declared. "But even a thousand miles is too long for the spectators. We need a distance that can be run in a single day. Six or seven hours is about enough. Five hundred miles is just about right." If Newby was responsible for setting the length of the race, Carl Fisher was very likely the inspiration for establishing the date. The 1911 race would be run on Memorial Day; the tradition has been maintained ever since.[19]

When Jane Fisher wrote her account of life with her husband, she referred to the crowd at the initial Indianapolis 500 race as "that first thin cavalcade of horse-drawn vehicles, with here a car and there a car, that set out for the races on Memorial Day, 1911."[20] Although generally prone to exaggeration when providing numbers, in this case Jane's description of the level of interest the race attracted was overly modest. Fisher and his partners had assiduously promoted the race, appealing to racers across the nation, even around the world, to make an appearance at the inaugural Indianapolis 500. In future years, of course, landing a spot in the starting field for the race would become a career highlight for many racers. But in 1911, convincing racers to make the trek to Indianapolis took a lot of salesmanship, and Fisher worked hard at this task for many months before the event. Some were ultimately won over by the prospect of cash prizes: the total purse for the inaugural Indianapolis 500 race eventually reached a then unheard-of $27,550, which dazzled many young men tinkering with machines in their garages. The promoters also had to attract tens of thousands of paying customers because they would not only lose money but would be embarrassed if they put on a stirring race in front of scattered fans. Fortunately, their hard work paid off. On race day, a crowd of between 75,000 and 80,000 people paid a dollar apiece to sit in the stands and watch the spectacle.

By modern-day standards, arrangement of starting positions and rules concerning the vehicles themselves were startlingly casual. Today, only highly trained teams of racers, backed by countless technicians and engineers and financed by corporate millions can hope to compete in In-

Lineup at the inaugural Indianapolis 500 race on May 30, 1911. Carl Fisher's pace car is on the far right in the front row. Courtesy of Indianapolis Motor Speedway Corporation.

dianapolis. Ninety years ago, however, a young man with a dream and a knack for experimenting with machinery could drive in the Indianapolis 500. The only entry requirements for the inaugural race were that the vehicle's engine displacement had to be 500 cubic inches or less and that it be able to run a quarter of a mile at better than seventy-five miles per hour. Beyond that, the racers were lined up according to the dates on which they posted their entries. Evidently, Fisher and his associates wanted to reward those racers who made early commitments. Particularly in the early years, there were many experimental racing machines, and their speeds varied considerably. Because faster machines were scattered among slower-moving vehicles, the informal starting arrangement almost guaranteed accidents. With memories of some of the previous racing days at the speedway relatively fresh, some ghoulish witnesses may have been attracted by the prospect of seeing more carnage on the bricks.

What they saw instead was a memorable road race. Promptly at 10:00 a.m. Carl Fisher, dressed in a white suit and driving a Stoddard-Dayton roadster, led the pace lap, then ducked into the infield as starter Fred Wagner dropped the flag. Forty souped-up vehicles of wildly varying size, design and engine displacement roared down the track. From the very start it was an exciting event, the lead changing repeatedly in the early laps. There were several serious crashes, most of them in the early going. Twenty-eight of the machines that started were forced out of the race, and only a dozen racers completed the 200-lap journey. On his twelfth lap, Arthur Greiner collided with the wall leading into the backstretch. His mechanic was thrown onto the track and was instantly killed. Fortunately, there were no other serious injuries. In the last stages of the race, a local Indianapolis boy, Ray Harroun, began to pull away in his yellow Marmon with black trim, and he took the checkered flag as the first Indianapolis 500 winner. His average speed was 74.59 miles per hour. Harroun's vehicle completed the journey in a bit over six and a half hours. The finish was by no means the nip-and-tuck conclusion modern-day fans expect. His closest challenger, Ralph Mulford, who drove a white Lozier, was about a minute and a half behind Harroun, with third-place finisher David Bruce-Brown crossing the line more than ten minutes behind Mulford.[21]

Fisher was exultant, and so were his associates. There had been one fatality, but fair-minded critics had to admit that the cause was a driver's error, not a defect of the track. In fact, the brickyard had stood up to the pounding of heavy vehicles remarkably well, and drivers and mechanics proclaimed the facility as one of the best, if not the finest racetrack in the world. The evening after the race, dozens of friends and well-wishers crowded into Blossom Heath. They celebrated far into the night and began drawing up plans for an even more ambitious race the next year.

There were some important changes before the 1912 race. Total prize money doubled to $55,875, making the Indianapolis 500 "the highest paying sporting event in the world."[22] The winner would pocket $20,000; second was worth $10,000, and third, $5,000. The tenth-place finisher would take home $1,400. Ticket prices increased as well. Fans willing to stand in the infield or take less desirable seats could still get in for $1, but prices ranged all the way up to box seats at the start and finish line costing $10. Surprisingly, considering the number of accidents the previous year, the race organizers did not arrange starting positions according to lap speed demonstrated on the track. Drivers did, however, have to complete a whole lap at seventy-five miles per hour or faster to qualify. The partners realized that they had been lucky with the relative safety of the previous year's event, and they limited entries to thirty-three machines. An American had won the inaugural race, and Fisher personally hoped that Americans might continue to compete effectively; however, he and his partners also desired the prestige of attracting a strong international field.

European drivers and their machines began to make their presence felt. In the 1912 contest Italian Ralph De Palma did everything but win the race. After Teddy Tetzlaff led the first two laps, De Palma, driving a shiny, powerful Mercedes, took over and led for the next 196 laps. On the 199th lap, however, a broken connecting rod forced his car off of the track. Jane Fisher recalled being dazzled by the Italian's gallantry. With his car out of the race, De Palma and his mechanic pushed his car past the grandstand. Masking his bitter disappointment, he turned and smiled and waved to the crowd; local racing fans gave De Palma a rousing ovation

At the end of the 1912 Indianapolis 500 race, Ralph De Palma's racer broke down with just over a lap to go. The intrepid driver and his mechanic gallantly pushed the car across the finish line, receiving an ovation from spectators. Courtesy of Indianapolis Motor Speedway Corporation.

for his sportsmanship.[23] American Joe Dawson passed by and went on to win the race with an average speed of 78.72 miles per hour. Back then, a driver had to complete the entire 500 miles to be eligible for any portion of the total purse, so De Palma received nothing. Ralph Mulford, who had finished second in the 1911 race, was not so fortunate the next year, but he was determined to win some money, and he nursed his faltering machine across the finish line two and a half hours behind Dawson. His average speed was 56.29 miles per hour, the slowest speed of any finisher in the track's long history. The intrepid Mulford earned $1,200 for his trouble.[24]

By its third year Fisher's plans for making the event a serious international competition began to bear fruit. More European drivers showed up, and several European automobile firms entered machines. The qualifying standard of finishing one lap of the track at seventy-five miles per hour or better remained in force, but starting positions were not determined until the night before the race, when drivers drew lots. At the time starting positions were not critical in a 500-mile race. Prudent drivers managed their vehicles conservatively in the first laps, intent largely on avoiding collisions and not falling too far behind leaders. As the field spread out, they could concentrate on creating a balance of maximum speed and minimal wear and tear on their vehicles. The 1913 race resulted in the first of many victories by a foreign driver and the largest margin of victory in the history of the track. Jules Goux, driving a French Peugeot, completed the 200 laps more then thirteen minutes ahead of runner-up Spencer Wishart. The race historian Jack C. Fox claims that his margin of victory might have been even larger had not the Frenchman consumed champagne at several of six pit stops, ostensibly meant for engine maintenance.[25]

Jane Fisher may understandably have exaggerated her husband's impact on the Indianapolis 500; after all, dozens of men played important roles in converting the race into an American institution. But she recalled that her husband was totally enthralled with every aspect of racing and that he personally managed some of the minutest details. Fisher converted Blossom Heath into an informal hotel for out-of-town guests. For days preceding the race, the growing staff had to remain flexible and expect any number of house guests. Lots of friends and acquantances needed somewhere to stay, and Jane recalled that one room in their house was filled to the ceiling with extra bedding and cots. Thirty or forty guests might show up for any meal. Fisher was naturally gregarious and loved people. When he was home, he presided over the festivities, but he left the work of managing the household to his young wife. When he was tending to other duties, Jane was left to entertain guests. On race day, she accompanied their guests to choice seats in her private box. But there were many tasks to keep track of. As she recalled, "I would always be up at four o'clock on race day." After arranging breakfast for several dozen guests, she would prepare to head to the track. "Hampers of sandwiches and fried chicken and gallons of hot coffee and lemonade had to be packed by Galloway to serve at noon in the grandstand. All the spectators brought lunch to Speedway Day. It was the biggest picnic in the world."[26]

Carl seemed to be everywhere at the racetrack. The night before the race, he might join the drivers at the drawing of starting positions. Jane recalled that he invariably soiled his racing day suit when he got down into the pit area and that he even helped racers figure out mechanical problems. Fisher thoroughly relished his self-appointed role of driving the pace car in the early years, and Jane always drew a big sigh of relief when she was assured that he had managed to get out of harm's way once the starter's green flag dropped. During the race itself, Fisher was often one of the first on the scene of any crash, doing what he could to aid stricken drivers and machines. After the race was finished, Fisher remained on the scene until the last prize was awarded, the last congratulatory statement issued, the last champagne toast presented. Later that night, he might bring another score or so of friends, casual acquaintances, and hangers-on to their annual postrace party at Blossom Heath.[27] For Jane Fisher, race day must have been an exhausting ordeal. For Carl, it was sheer electricity; it seemed as if he could run for days on sheer adrenalin.

As World War I loomed, European teams and drivers demonstrated their superiority over American entries at Indianapolis. In 1914, a few months before the assassination of the Archduke Franz Ferdinand and commencement of hostilities in the Great War, the fourth edition of the Indianapolis 500 unfolded. In that race, Europeans, led by René Thomas, swept the first four places. Thomas's Delage set a new speed record of

82.47 miles per hour. The first American across the line was Fisher's life-long chum Barney Oldfield, who finished fifth, more then twenty minutes behind the winner.

The next year saw several changes, both in the physical facilities at the track and management of the race itself. A new grandstand was erected, and additional garages were built to house racers' vehicles. Piston displacement for engines was lowered again to 300 cubic inches. Drivers had to achieve at least eighty miles per hour for their one-lap timed run, and for the first time, starting positions were determined by qualifying times. The fastest qualifier garnered the pole position, along with the number 1 painted on his machine. The second fastest qualifier lined up alongside him in the front row and sported number 2, and so on. The 1915 race also brought the first "rainout" and postponement. Heavy rains and flood conditions forced race day back to May 31. Ralph De Palma, tough-luck driver in 1912, gained victorious redemption, driving his Mercedes to a new record average pace of 89.84 miles per hour.[28]

Carl and his associates had achieved their dream. By 1916, five years after the inaugural race, the Memorial Day event at Indianapolis had become an elite race. In the words of a reporter for *Leslie's Weekly*, "This two-and-a-half mile course has become historical. It is the cradle of the automobile track race, the melting pot of design, and the training ground for many a world-famed driver."[29]

By the late spring of 1916 the war in Europe had degenerated into an agonizing stalemate. Millions of soldiers of both the Allies and Central Powers were entrenched in nearly impregnable defensive positions. Imperious demands by muddle-headed politicians on both sides for glorious victory had forced generals to order huge, senseless offensives engaging hundreds of thousands of soldiers, which invariably led to wholesale slaughter. American citizens read accounts of the savage fighting and thanked Providence for the presence of the Atlantic Ocean. So far, at least, President Woodrow Wilson had managed to keep the United States out of the war, although national policies clearly favored the Allies. In fact, the United States's continued neutrality was partly the result of the Central Powers' determination, up to that point, to avoid a direct confrontation.

Although the United States was not yet directly involved in the fighting, World War I already affected many Americans in significant ways, including automobile racing. There was a Memorial Day race at the Indianapolis Speedway in 1916, but a lack of new entries from Europe induced race officials to shorten the contest to 300 miles. Nevertheless, Italian Dario Resta drew away from the field in his Peugeot, becoming the fourth European in succession to win at Indianapolis. Later that season, there was a one-day series of races at the track in September, including 20-mile, 50-mile, and 100-mile events, but they atracted a disappointingly small crowd of about 10,000. When the United States formally entered the war on the Allied side in April 1917, the promoters decided not to conduct races as long as the war lasted. The 1917 and 1918 Indianapolis 500 races were canceled.

Even before the nation declared war, Carl Fisher sensed that such a decision was inevitable, and he actively promoted putting the track to patriotic use for as long as the federal government might be able to use it. As an active balloonist for almost a decade and friend of the Wright brothers, Carl had long been fascinated by aviation. In 1915 he had written an article envisioning a time when airplanes could defend the nation from attack, and he advocated building a huge fleet of 10,000 planes for that purpose. A few months after the United States declared war, Carl demonstrated that his thinking about potential uses of aircraft was far ahead of that of many military men. Although one role of the fleet of planes would be to protect American coastlines from enemy attack, he also envisioned aircraft as offensive weapons, capable of bombing enemy production plants.[30] Federal aviation officials respected his expertise in ballooning, and he was appointed to the National Advisory Committee on Aeronautics.[31] The "technological enthusiast" merged patriotism with his ambition to be positioned on the thrilling frontier of development of machines that would travel farther, faster, and higher than ever before.

The Hoosier entrepreneur had absolutely no tolerance for delays and red tape, and he was not content to serve as a passive member of any government committee. Even before the nation's formal entry into the war, Fisher offered the racetrack as an ideal location for a military aviation school. In the early twentieth century, automobile men and flyers were basically cut from the same mold. Many of them knew each other, and some moved in both arenas. For example, Fisher's erstwhile friend Eddie Rickenbacker had been a race car driver, and he went on to become a celebrated World War I flying ace. Later, Rickenbacker would take over management and eventually ownership of the Indianapolis Motor Speedway from Fisher and his associates.

Thus Fisher's interest in establishing an aviation school for the government merged naturally with his other interests. In a letter to John Oliver LaGorce, another close friend and Washington insider, Fisher boasted: "We have everything in Indianapolis that the Government needs. . . . If there is any way to cut the red tape from a bundle of five Curtiss machines, six extra engines and 15% of miscellaneous parts for these engines, and authority from anybody who can give it to go ahead, I will guarantee that we can have a better aviation school in Indianapolis, running full tilt, in sixty days, and can turn out better aviators for the Government than any other place in the country."[32] Although he did his share of grumbling about government corruption and incompetence, Fisher felt deeply patriotic. A week after the United States formally entered the war, Fisher made it clear to one subordinate that profits from any such venture were unimportant. "I haven't any companies to promote, nothing to sell—and I want you to keep your mouth absolutely closed regarding any plans that I may mention to you. My personal effort will be to lend such services as I can to the Government, without charge . . . don't get mixed up on the idea that this is a promoting scheme."[33]

By midsummer 1917, Fisher was hip-deep in organizing the flight school at Indianapolis. In addition to building hangars and clearing runways for novice airmen, he actively sought cooperation from communities across Indiana and adjacent states in establishing flight routes airmen could follow. Eighty years ago, flyers relied heavily on landmarks for directions. Directional signals on tall buildings, coded numbers on the tops of barns, even signs in the middle of fields all aided flyers who might otherwise get lost. Since not all training occurred during daylight hours, Fisher also encouraged public officials in towns along proposed routes to place directional signals and lights in prominent locations. Fisher personally solicited several dozen city and small town officials. One such letter

informed them that the first training route in America was between Mc-
Cook Field in Dayton, Ohio, and Chanute Field in Rantoul, Illinois, with
Indianapolis in the middle. Flight trainers wanted bright beacon lights
strung together at approximately ten-mile intervals, pointed skyward at
an angle of twenty degrees. The unique angle would presumably make
them instantly recognizable. Fisher's task was to persuade town officials
not only to put up the lights but to pay for the installation, maintenance,
and electricity. He offered to have an Indianapolis company install the
lights at a "fixed price" but noted that maintaining them would give work
to local electricians. Fisher's pitches avoided mawkish appeals to patriotism, instead subtly suggesting that up-to-date communities would unquestionably assist the war effort in this and any number of other modest
ways.[34]

Fisher had undertaken a large job, and he relished the challenge.
In mid-July he informed Howard E. Coffin of the Aircraft Production
Board that he had already secured access for aviation cadets at forty-eight
landing fields between Indianapolis and Richmond, Indiana. Assuming
that flyers were being trained at facilities across the nation, a coherent,
uniform system of directional signals needed to be created and put in
place, and he offered his own set of signals for consideration. As Fisher
noted, "It will certainly be confusing if a man in New Jersey who wants
to mark a few buildings gets up a code of signals of his own and if a man
in Illinois has a different idea of signals." In a second letter to Coffin the
same day, he outlined an ambitious proposal for creating inspirational
movies showing former automobile workers proudly and happily building airplanes.[35]

Fisher was usually extremely generous in acknowledging the contributions of others who worked with him on projects, so it is surprising that
in his correspondence with government officials, he seldom, if ever, mentioned his associates. Obviously, he did not convert the racetrack to an
aviation training facility by himself. In late September, Fisher informed
Coffin that he and unnamed associates had built two hangars at the track,
an aviation tower, and floodlights for night landings. In addition, they had
acquired access and provided appropriate markings at 135 airfields between Eaton, Ohio, and Rantoul, Illinois. Flying distance was 220 miles,

and the greatest distance between any emergency landing areas was between 3 and 4 miles. He promised that lighting along the entire route would be completed within the next month. Finally, Fisher suggested that if military decision makers found this type of training facility useful, "we can extend it in any direction thought necessary, and it would be quite feasible to have lights put up clear across the continent."[36]

The government failed to take Fisher up on his offer to mastermind development of a national aviation training network, but he continued to make improvements in the regional system. In September 1918 the *Philadelphia Sunday Magazine* published a highly flattering account of the work that Fisher had done for the military's flying program. In addition to praising Fisher's energy and patriotism, the article described the project in detail and noted several improvements instituted in the previous year. Neophyte flyers engaged in night training, particularly in marginal or even slightly cloudy weather, might lose track of the beams from searchlights. Thus a system of backup directional signals was set up for pilots who strayed seriously off course. If they wandered twenty miles too far south, they would see red arrows pointing due north; if they flew too far north, green arrows pointed south.[37]

Despite Fisher's imaginative and energetic work for the government, there were critics. Some cynics both inside and outside the government evidently questioned his motives or assumed graft was somehow involved. A report surfaced that $40,000 had been spent on the facilities at the racetrack, and suspicious bureaucrats demanded an accounting. Fisher indignantly denied the allegations. In addition, he pointed out that most of the costs of lighting had been paid for not by the federal government but by towns along the flyers' paths. To buttress his own reputation, he observed that he had put in hundreds of hours of work and had invested thousands of his own dollars without asking for any compensation. To one official, Fisher complained, "I never sent the Government a bill for the route and only at their request made twice in writing, so I really don't see where you should be criticising [*sic*] this matter."[38] Evidently finding a sympathetic ear, Fisher vented at length to the same official: "I do not give an eternal d— for the investigating committee regarding any of the work I have been connected with, and I think that the criticisms that are now being freely passed about tend to disorganize the Signal Corps and it takes the heart and spirit out of the engineers."[39] A few months later, Fisher complained to a private correspondent, "You don't recognize the differences bet(ween) war times and ordinary times. I've had more trouble in the past twelve months in financing my obligations to the government and other interests than I've had in fifteen years, and as long as this war lasts I can see this situation continuing."[40] No charges were ever filed against Fisher or anyone else promoting aviation training in Indianapolis. Ultimately, the endeavor cost Fisher several thousand dollars; he clearly made no profit from it. Nevertheless, as one analyst observed, he "got no thanks in return."[41]

Following the end of World War I and armistice in November 1918, Fisher and his partners at Indianapolis could finally think of resuming automobile racing. They staged a race in the spring of 1919, but they chose May 31 rather than May 30 to avoid interfering with the pomp and solemnity of the first Memorial Day following the Great War. According to Jane Fisher, a local newspaper had protested that running the race on Memorial Day would be "rank desecration of a national holiday." The year following the armistice saw a disturbing national hysteria labeled the Red Scare; no prudent businessman or promoter wanted to do anything that might appear unpatriotic.[42] In a fitting display of such "patriotism," Fisher had hired national guardsmen to line the track before the opening ceremony the following day. Local guard unit officials, however, thought the festivities were inappropriate for use of the soldiers' uniforms. This time, Fisher did not cave in. In thirty-six hours before the event, he made frantic arrangements with willing outfitters to get every man in uniform. Participants received their uniforms twenty minutes before they took their place along the side of the track. Once again, the fabled Fisher luck held, with a very vigorous assist from the determined promoter himself.[43]

Fisher may have secretly hoped that drivers from Allied countries would be too distracted by the recent hostilities to pose a challenge to American drivers, let alone continue their victory streak. As usual, he rooted for an American victory but was sportsmanlike about the result. An American driver won with a foreign vehicle. Highlights of the 1919 race were René Thomas's one-lap track record of 104.7 miles per hour and Howard "Howdy" Wilcox's winning 88.05 mile-per-hour average for the 200 laps in his Peugeot. Most observers at Indianapolis rejoiced. Like Ray Harroun eight years earlier, Wilcox was not just an American but a local man from Indianapolis. The race was particularly meaningful for Fisher. As his wife, Jane, wrote, "Carl had his private victory. Tested in the 'bricklined crucible of the cornfields,' America had at last proved to be worthy of first place in world competition. Speedway was all he had asked of it—a testing ground for machines and for men."[44]

Although all of Fisher's promotions were designed to publicize his name and enhance his enterprises, they increasingly became larger civic gestures. Using a balloon to suspend himself and his Stoddard-Dayton above Indianapolis in 1908 may have simply looked like a cheap, if daring, publicity stunt, but photos of the event appeared all over the country and generated publicity for the city. Fisher worked hard to build an automobile sales organization that would be the largest in the state only in part for the potential profits; he clearly wanted Indianapolis to be a hub for automobile sales and servicing, if not for the entire Midwest, then at least for Indiana. Prest-O-Lite provided Fisher his initial fortune, but he also imagined it as but one of many potential automobile product companies in the region. Promotion of Speedway City reflected not only his interest in providing housing for Prest-O-Lite workers but for encouraging development of another manufacturing district in the city.

Although he was closely connected to many of the most powerful automobile manufacturers in Detroit and avidly boosted the commercial prospects of his city, Fisher never succeeded in persuading any of them to shift their operations south to Indianapolis. After World War I, however, Fisher continued to devote considerable energy to promoting Indianapolis. In October 1919, he proudly imformed Harold Wills of Ford Motor Company that he had helped engineer a big contract for a carburetor manufacturer to produce those items in Indianapolis and suggested that Ford would be wise to look to Indianapolis for these and other car parts.[45] In the months before the 1920 Indianapolis 500, Fisher was busy reconverting the racetrack and surrounding area from military to peacetime use. He thought that if he and his associates could transform the racetrack into a multipurpose facility, it would further enhance the prestige of the race and simultaneously boost Indianapolis. He hoped to add swimming pools, golf courses, and even polo grounds in hopes of inducing European aristocrats interested in automobile racing to extend their visits to Indianapolis.[46] Fisher was, even then, creating a winter tourist mecca in South Florida at Miami Beach. Could he help turn Indianapolis into an attractive destination for vacationers during other parts of the year?[47]

The 1920 race brought several innovations. Maximum engine displacement dropped to 183 cubic inches, which matched International Formula standards. In addition, for the first time, four-lap qualification runs determined the order of the start, a system still in use today. During the race, lap prizes were awarded for the first time from a $20,000 fund. As an added incentive to be at the head of the pack, the leader of each of the 200 laps won $100. Prize money increased as well; a total of $93,550 was distributed. The winner was Gaston Chevrolet, who was driving a Monroe. After four years out of the winner's circle, American automobiles had won for two years in a row.[48]

By the early 1920s, however, Fisher's primary business and sporting interests had shifted south to Florida. He and Jane were spending less and less time in Indianapolis. To be sure, Miami Beach was hot, sticky, and almost uninhabited during the off-season, but Indianapolis was not a great deal cooler. Equally important, Fisher had discovered that the Indiana climate played havoc with his allergies; he and Jane customarily sought relief from heat, humidity, and various air pollutants near major bodies of water. In 1921 Fisher arranged for one of his most astute publicity men, Steve Hannagan, to take over promoting the Indianapolis 500. Two years later, Fisher explored the possibility of selling his shares in the track to his erstwhile friend and partner in many ventures James Allison, and the two men dickered for a time over reasonable valuation of outstanding shares.[49] For the time being, Fisher retained his interest in the track, although Allison assumed the presidency of the organization in 1924. Before long, Allison also became interested in selling out, and their other major partner, Arthur Newby, was agreeable. They offered the facility first to Thomas W. Milton, a recent champion in the event. But Milton had neither the capital nor the business experience to consider the proposition seriously. On August 15, 1927, they finally sold the track to a group headed by Eddie Rickenbacker for $650,000 plus interest, to be paid in three installments. A year later, Fisher was still trying to sell his remaining real estate interests in the town of Speedway.[50]

After he sold his shares in the Indianapolis Motor Speedway to Rickenbacker, Fisher exchanged reminiscences about automobile racing with the World War I flying ace and frequently provided detailed advice on pricing of seats and concessions and many other facets of promoting the Indianapolis 500.[51] Both during and after Fisher's years of intense commitment to the Indianapolis racing scene, he was active in promoting the development of tracks elsewhere. In 1915 he and Arthur Newby were appointed to the board of directors for the proposed Sheepshead Bay Speedway in Brooklyn. Fisher assisted directly in design and construction of a two-mile board track there, and he held stock in the venture for a time. According to one scholar, "Fisher saw the track well on its way, then relinquished his position to Harry Harkness."[52] He was also an automotive visionary. As early as 1919, he imagined a place where automobile experimentation could be stretched to the limit. "The most ideal place for an automobile race is not the Indianapolis Motor Speedway or any other speedway that was ever built, but it is on the Great Salt Desert in Nevada, which is 25 miles wide and 100 miles long, with not a pimple on it as large as a mosquito egg." He did not think such a location would be used for that purpose, "for the reason that there is nobody there to see it."[53] Decades later, however, Fisher's technological foresight was demonstrated when the Bonneville Salt Flats in western Utah became the site of many important automotive land speed records.

Fisher's interest in automobile racing after World War I was generally limited to smaller projects. In 1920 he actively promoted a speedway in Cuba.[54] Although he invested heavily in Miami Beach real estate in the mid-1920s, he found time to mastermind construction of a wooden track in Miami, which held races in 1926. His Fulford-by-the-Sea track hosted spectacular time trials, where cars reached speeds of 140 miles per hour in the Carl G. Fisher Cup race on January 30, 1926; some 20,000 spectators witnessed these spectacular runs. Unfortunately, a devastating hurricane in 1926 reduced the wooden track to kindling and splinters, and the facility was never rebuilt.[55]

In good times or bad, promoting fast driving machines was never far from Fisher's mind. Even after his fortune vanished and he was reduced to living on a modest pension provided by old friends and business associates, Fisher was still full of ideas for promoting automobile racing, even building new tracks. In the summer of 1935 he gave useful ideas for enhancing the safety of spectators to one of his former employees who was still involved in the Indianapolis 500.[56] Eddie Rickenbacker still kept in touch; in the spring of 1936 Fisher tried to interest him in staging a major race in southern Florida. "In January and February there is [*sic*] easily 100,000 people in this community to draw from, and a race, if properly staged, would draw a very large crowd from all parts of the State, and you can hardly make a mistake with the weather."[57] Evidently Rickenbacker demonstrated at least mild interest; two weeks later, Fisher wrote him again, discussing possible locations and estimating costs of acquiring property for a track.[58] Nothing ever came of these tentative initiatives, but they helped keep Fisher connected to the sporting world and many of his old friends and associates. Racing had been a vital part of his life for four decades. Except for the haunting memory of the deaths he and his brother caused at Zanesville, Fisher was justifiably proud of his achievements as a racer and a promoter.

Roads Worthy of a Nation

In the late eighteenth and early nineteenth centuries, the founders of the new American nation repeatedly evoked highly idealized images of a society steeped in Roman republican virtue. Roman influence was particularly evident in architecture and painting.[1] Consciously or unconsciously, many politicians imitated the public conduct of notable Roman senators and emperors. Perhaps they chose the wrong role models. Unfortunately, the new republic's leaders did not follow the example of Roman engineers, who constructed more than 50,000 miles of road. In the United States, little progress was made in road building during the republic's first century. Most decent roads were financed privately. The only major road project underwritten by the federal government was the National Road from Cumberland, Maryland, to Wheeling, West Virginia, which was completed in 1817. Henry Clay's "American System" eventually generated millions of dollars of federal government support for important internal improvements, including canals, port improvements, and eventually railroads, but his initiative might actually have delayed improvement of roads. The handful of brave inventors who envisioned applying steam power to freewheeled overland transportation had little, if any, government support. As late as 1903 there were 2.3 million miles of so-called roads in the United States, but more than 90 percent were almost impassable, "horse-belly deep in mud in spring and thick with dust in summer, frozen in iron-hard ruts in winter."[2]

If the United States was ever to boast decent public roads, identifiable political constituencies would have to step forward. The initial boost for improved public roads came from various sources. Carl Fisher was in the midst of most of them. The bicycle craze had arrived in full force in the 1890s, as millions of Americans took up riding the new safety models. Active riders found city streets confining because they were often filled with commercial wagons, carriages, and pedestrians. In response, in the 1890s the League of American Wheelmen formed a powerful interest group. Representatives of this somewhat elitist organization pressured local governments to improve country roads, at least those within a day's outing from cities and towns.[3] Publications such as the *Carriage Monthly* and the *Horseless Age* also lobbied hard for better roads. As a youthful racer and bicycle entrepreneur, Carl Fisher enthusiastically applauded their initiatives.

"Unimproved" roads typified the nation's highways until after World War I. To promote automobile use and travel, the Lincoln Highway Association aimed to build a wholly "improved" road between New York and San Francisco. Courtesy of Lincoln Highway Association.

But would any entity assume responsibility for building roads? At the turn of the century, roads were almost exclusively the responsibility of local governments. By 1912 there was still no federal funding for highways, and no less than twenty states also provided no public support.[4] This lack largely explains why there was little or no coordination in road building across long distances.

Fisher made a significant contribution to the nation's effort to pull its wagons and vehicles out of the muck and send them on their journeys along direct routes across smooth, dependable surfaces. When he first became actively involved in promoting highways, many "good roads" supporters held strong opinions about what *should* be done, but nobody presented practical plans for achieving results. Although dozens of other individuals made significant contributions, Fisher essentially provided a missing link, a jump-start toward the beginning of a national highway system.[5] Between 1912 and the end of World War I, he provided a clear vision of what needed to be done, and he was a vital force in coordinating the initial steps toward achieving it. By the time Fisher effectively ended his participation in private sponsorship of long-distance highways shortly after the armistice in 1918, the federal government was taking responsibility for them.

The initial push for long-distance highways came not from practical businessmen but from intrepid, energetic adventurers. Fisher was not part of this group. At the turn of the century, several ambitious individuals set out on coast-to-coast automobile trips. Not all claims for "first crossings" are believable. According to a history of the Lincoln Highway, in 1898 J. M. Murdoch and his family journeyed from Los Angeles to New York in thirty-two days.[6] Given the miserable state of the nation's roads and the alleged time elapsed, such a claim is difficult to accept. Other sources state that Horatio N. Jackson and Sewell K. Crocker were the first to complete the trip in 1903, covering forty-five hundred miles of primitive roads from San Francisco to New York in sixty-one days.[7]

Businessmen soon entered the campaign for better roads. In 1904, Boston millionaire Charles J. Glidden sponsored the first of his famous "Glidden tours," in which convoys of automobiles traversed hundreds of miles over several weeks, competing for various prizes. Although the chief focus was the automobiles themselves and which might be the most comfortable and reliable, these tours eventually reached every part of the country and highlighted the desirability of improved roads.

By the second decade of the twentieth century, the automobile mania was in full swing. At Indianapolis and elsewhere, manufacturers had tested and demonstrated machines capable of sustaining breathtaking speed over long distances. Such automotive triumphs fired the imaginations of tens of thousands of witnesses concerning the potential use of less powerful but more easily manageable automobiles over the American landscape. Equally important, automobile ownership was no longer a mark of distinction. Henry Ford had introduced the Model T in 1908, and his highly efficient assembly-line production system rapidly reduced the price of reliable transportation. From a few thousand vehicles owned by wealthy adventurers in 1900, registrations approached the half-million mark a decade later.

This was when Fisher entered the highway arena. In later years, after he had gained fame as a promoter of highways, Fisher never claimed that he had experienced an epiphany, a defining moment when he felt a calling to become a leader in the movement for better roads. But he frequently recounted an experience one evening early in the century when he was driving in an open touring car with two companions. Night fell, along with a downpour. "We guessed our way along . . . until we came to a place where the road forked three ways. None of us could remember which of the three roads we had followed in driving out. There was a pole nearby with a sign on the top of it, but it was as black as the inside of your pocket and the sign was too high to read. . . . I climbed up to the sign, scratched a match and read it. It said 'Chew Battle Ax Plug.'"[8]

At about the same time, another car man, Packard Motors president Henry B. Joy, was experiencing similar frustration with overland travel. Perhaps inspired by the cross-country feats of Jackson and Crocker, Joy was trying to drive his Packard west from Omaha. He asked his dealer in the city to direct him to the road west from Omaha. The dealer informed him there were no roads, but he accompanied Joy to the edge of the city. They reached a barbed wire fence. "Take down this fence and drive on and when you come to the next fence, take that down and go on again." "A little farther," Joy reported, "and there were no fences, no fields, nothing but two ruts across the prairie."[9]

Roads were a lot like the weather; everybody grumbled about them, but nobody had yet mounted a successful effort to improve them, at least not on a national level. It is highly unlikely that Carl Fisher had ever heard of Theodore Dehone Judah, who had imagined the first transcontinental railroad, but Fisher's experience in highways paralleled Judah's in railroads. Not only did Judah dream about a transcontinental railroad, but he worked out a possible route. Initially, Judah thought construction of such a line would be a privately funded project. Judah was an executive of the Central Pacific Railroad when it was organized in 1861. He managed to inspire Leland Stanford with the same vision. The two men quickly dropped the notion of depending wholly on private capital, enlisting the support of both the city of San Francisco and the California legislature. Even in the midst of the Civil War, the project excited the imagination of Washington's influential decision makers, and President Abraham Lincoln signed the Pacific Railroad Act on July 1, 1862. Seven years later, the last rails were joined at Promontory, Utah. Judah's vision had become reality in less than a decade.[10]

Half a century later, Fisher and several associates were about to follow Judah's example. According to Jane Fisher, Jim Allison, Fisher's longtime friend and partner, was the first to learn of his dream of a coast-to-coast highway and his thoughts about who should finance it. "The automobile industry should be willing to finance a road across the country. Think of what it would do for the American automobile."[11] Fisher also wrote to a longtime friend, Elbert Hubbard, a prominent automotive writer who was in a strategic position to influence public opinion through his magazine articles: "The highways of America are built chiefly of politics whereas the proper material is crushed rock or concrete."[12]

As a former automobile racer, a partner in Prest-O-Lite, and builder of the Indianapolis Motor Speedway, Fisher had intimate ties with Detroit's first generation of automobile men. Many of them came to the Indianapolis 500; Fisher hosted a lot of them in his home, and he undoubtedly shared with them his dream of converting Indianapolis into a major player in the automobile industry. While few of the Detroit men shared Fisher's enthusiasm for decentralizing the automobile business, they respected and liked him. When he issued an invitation to some of the most influential auto men to join him for dinner at the Duetches Haus Hotel in Indianapolis on September 1, 1912, he had a far bigger agenda than simply feeding them a big meal and promoting the next year's Memorial Day race. After they had finished their strudel, loosened their belts, and lit their cigars, Fisher got to the main point of the gathering. It was up to them to address the shameful state of the nation's highways. "'A road across the United States,' Fisher shouted to the crowd at the Duetches Haus dinner, 'Let's build it before we're too old to enjoy it!'" His words clearly excited his listeners. Fisher suggested that $10 million, if wisely managed and carefully spent, could create a direct and passable highway from New York to San Francisco. The funds would supply the materials; local labor would provide the muscle. The road could be finished by May 1, 1915, in time to accommodate a caravan of 25,000 automobiles trekking across the nation to the Pan-Pacific Exposition in San Francisco. Once again, Fisher had placed himself at the forefront in promoting the latest and most up-to-date technology. Swept up in Fisher's enthusiasm, the Detroit men pledged $300,000 that night. Frank A. Seiberling, president of Goodyear Tire Company, quickly matched that sum without even consulting his board of directors.[13]

The project was off to a rousing start, and people were excited. The initial stage of euphoria must not be allowed to wither. Fisher developed a deliberate two-pronged strategy. He realized that for the project to succeed, it had to have enthusiastic backing from the automobile industry in Detroit. In addition, he needed the support of the general public. The route would traverse the nation and pass through hundreds of small towns and several big cities. Local chambers of commerce, booster organizations, and service clubs must become involved. Ordinary Americans needed to feel a stake in the project, a sense of participation, including a belief that completion of a transcontinental highway would enhance their sense of national pride.

Ironically, during the fall of 1912, Fisher was also heavily involved in improving roads at the local level. He entered politics for the first and only time in his life. He sought and was given the Progressive Party nomination for county commissioner for Marion County, Indiana, the county in which Indianapolis was located. Fisher's chief reason for running for commissioner was to improve roads in the region, and he talked of little else in the campaign. If elected, Fisher offered to return his entire commissioner's salary of $2,500 to the county treasury and to match that figure with a contribution of his own, as long as the money would be used to improve roads. His basic argument was that poor roads cost far more money than good ones. He noted that neither businessmen nor ordinary citizens usually thought of the hidden costs of inconvenient and difficult physical movement. Yet these same individuals were extremely leery of highly visible and costly public works such as good roads.

Fisher claimed that such thinking was shortsighted. The aspiring politician did not do a great deal of public speaking, but when he did, he urged listeners to think about the long term and stop allowing local officials simply to patch up inadequate streets and unpaved roads but to spend a little more money to do the job right: "I can not understand the folly of men who will throw thousands and hundreds of thousands of dollars annually into the gulf of oblivion which the poor road really is. Just a little money wisely expended goes farther and brings richer results than all the thousands that are thrown into the mudholes in the shape of loose gravel."

His opponents attacked Fisher indirectly, claiming that his transcontinental highway was an elitist scheme to divert public funds into a project that would accommodate only a few expensive toys of wealthy men and families who could afford to take long vacations and travel coast to coast. One opponent evidently charged that farmers wouldn't be allowed to use the highway and that trucks might be denied access. Fisher categorically denied these allegations. "Nothing could be farther from the truth. No one ever heard of building or trying to build a public highway for motor vehicles exclusively."[14] Although Fisher ran an energetic race and gained endorsements from some of the leading men in Indianapolis, he lost to his Democratic opponent by about the same ratio of votes Theodore Roosevelt lost to Woodrow Wilson in Marion County. Like Roosevelt, Fisher at least had the satisfaction of drawing more votes than his Republican rival. He received 17,478 out of a total vote of about 57,000.[15]

Why Fisher ran for a local office at the same time he was masterminding a national campaign to construct a coast-to-coast highway is a mystery. He never discussed his aborted political career in later years; few of those who described his career even mentioned it. In the fall of 1912, however, he devoted much of his energy to the transcontinental highway plan. During the first months, enthusiasm was high. Money from pledges and contributions rolled in. Some automobile men responded generously. In addition to Frank Seiberling's $300,000, Henry Joy of Packard Motors pledged $150,000, and Willys-Overland offered the same amount. Within a few months $4 million had been raised. Fisher and a group of shrewd publicists ran a national campaign to attract as many small contributions as possible, pledges of as little as $5 so that people all over the nation would feel they were part of something patriotic and grand.

The single most influential automobile magnate in the United States, however, Henry Ford, failed to provide a dime's worth of support. By the time Fisher spearheaded the venture, Ford's factory at Highland Park was disgorging hundreds of thousands of automobiles a year onto primitive streets and roads. Who would benefit more from good roads than the industry's biggest producer? Ford's own company magazine, *Ford Times*, had repeatedly preached the same message Fisher did. Carl had entertained Ford personally at the Indianapolis 500, and he had good contacts in the Ford Motor Company. Thus he confidently expected that Ford would provide generous support. When his first approach to the enigmatic and cantankerous magnate failed to yield results, Fisher went to Detroit and found Ford at the Detroit Fair, appraising pigs in a pigpen. Fisher launched into his most convincing spiel. Ford took it all in and replied, "Come to my office tomorrow and bring your papers. I'll sign up." Fisher was overjoyed and invited several friends to celebrate with him at a victory dinner in a Detroit hotel. The next day, when Fisher arrived at Ford's office, he was shocked to learn through an intermediary that Ford had changed his mind and would not contribute after all.[16] In a letter to Fisher, a prominent Ford executive, James Couzens, explained his own reasoning, which apparently won over his mentor: "Frankly, the writer is not very favorably disposed to the plan, because as long as private interests are willing to build good roads for the general public, the general public will not be very interested in building good roads for itself. I believe in spending money to educate the public to the necessity of building good roads, and let everybody contribute their share in proper taxes."[17] Ironically, Henry Ford, who feared immigration and urbanization and was so reactionary in much of his thinking about labor unions and many social issues, was far ahead of his peers when it came to envisioning the federal government's central role in the future of the nation's highways.[18]

One critical issue was what to call the venture. In his initial address to the automobile men in September 1912, Fisher referred to the project as the "Coast-to-Coast Rock Highway." The title was neither descriptive nor particularly inspiring, so Fisher and his friends deliberated long and hard about the best name for the road. They wanted something patriotic and of national significance. Henry Joy suggested calling it the Jefferson Highway, partly in an effort to attract southern support in Congress in the event federal funding ever became a possibility. According to one source, Fisher had wanted to use the name "Lincoln Highway" from the start. He had idolized Lincoln from his early years and proudly displayed pictures of the martyred president in his home. Although some promoters worried that the name choice would alienate some southerners, they ultimately determined that it would more than compensate by generating strong support in other parts of the nation. They labeled their organization the Lincoln Highway Association.[19]

By early 1913, Fisher was experiencing significant concerns about his own role in the organization. Many news stories had been published, and he had been interviewed by numerous writers; some of them were calling it the "Fisher Highway." He realized that if he was too closely identified with the project, if too many citizens felt that the project was "his," public support could quickly vanish. In his initial rush of enthusiasm for the project, one supporter had written to Fisher, predicting that a magnificent statue would someday be built, honoring him as the father of the first transcontinental highway. Fisher had written back, "I am not much into statuary—and right now I think it is a good time to pull out personally and take away from our possible subscribers the idea that this road plan is mine. If any particular noise is made for any particular person or small clique of persons, this plan is going to suffer."[20] Then, too, he sensed how soft the support for the project was within the automobile industry. Through long association with the industry's leaders, he knew that many of them had enormous egos and a need to feel important, in charge. Perhaps the fact that he hadn't started it was the real reason why Henry Ford had refused to join the effort. Fisher was keenly aware that, at least within the fledgling automobile aristocracy, he was an outsider if for no reason other than that he was from Indianapolis.[21] It might be a good idea for someone other than himself to head up the Lincoln Highway Association.

Henry B. Joy of Packard Motors appeared to be a perfect fit. Joy was a highly respected insider in Detroit, president of one of the most prestigious automobile companies in the country. He also symbolized what would later be called the Eastern Establishment. He was a graduate of both Andover and Yale. In addition to his role at Packard, he was a director for several blue-chip corporations. Joy's wife, Helen Newberry Joy, had been prominent in Detroit society even before cars became important. As one writer noted, "Because her family was pre-automobile she always outranked the rest of Gasoline Society." Joy had natural connections which it would take Fisher years to forge. Even better, Joy was just as enthusiastic about the venture as Fisher and equally committed. Late in life, Joy claimed that leading the Lincoln Highway Association was his most significant achievement.[22] Joy recruited some of America's leading automobile men to play significant roles in the organization. They included Roy B. Chapin, president of Hudson Motors; Frank Seiberling, president of Goodyear Tire and Rubber; William C. "Billy" Durant, who first revived Buick and later masterminded General Motors; and John N. Willys, later chairman of the board of Willys-Overland.[23] Other prominent men representing industries with direct interest in road building joined the group. One of the first tasks they faced was securing the right to call themselves the Lincoln Highway Association. Another group of highway promoters had earlier seized the name Lincoln Highway for a proposed Lincoln Memorial Road from Washington to Gettysburg. Congress, however, had chosen to fund the Lincoln Memorial instead, so the naming issue was resolved in the Fisher group's favor.[24]

With Joy at the helm, leaders of the Lincoln Highway Association met in Detroit on July 1, 1913, and created a formal organization. Carl was installed as vice president even though he was not present at the meeting. Instead, Fisher, the Hoosier Motor Club of Indianapolis, and the Indiana Auto Manufacturers Association jointly organized a convoy of vehicles manufactured in Indiana to embark on a publicity trip from Indianapolis to California. When news of the proposed journey spread, many observers mistakenly assumed that it was sponsored by the Lincoln Highway Association. Civic leaders and chambers of commerce officials in hundreds of communities west of Indianapolis contacted Fisher and his associates, pleading to be included on the route. Promoters in Price, Utah, were even more persistent than most. A group of boosters from Price visited Indianapolis to lobby for a visit from the cavalcade. When reminded that there was no road for automobiles, they promised to build one. The Price men fulfilled their pledge, but their larger hopes were dashed when the Lincoln Highway eventually passed about one hundred miles north of the town. Politicians in Nevada were more successful. The legislature rushed through a $25,000 appropriation for road improvements, and the Lincoln Highway eventually traversed the entire width of the state, passing through Ely and Reno.[25]

The ostensible purpose of the Hoosier cavalcade from Indianapolis was to promote Indiana automobiles. In that sense, the journey was a failure because most of the brand names of cars making the journey soon passed into history. They included the American, Apperson, Empire (built by Fisher), Haynes, Henderson, Marmon, McFarland, Pathfinder "40," Pilot "60," and Premier.[26]

By 1913 cross-continent automobile trips were still arduous, but they were no longer a novelty. After all, pioneering drivers had crossed the nation at least a decade earlier, and the famous Glidden Tours had passed through many sections over the past few years. But because Fisher accompanied the group and because he was so closely identified with the Lincoln Highway, the "Hoosier Trailblazers" attracted enormous publicity. Most commentators paid far more attention to the path selected by the Hoosiers, as an indication of the future Lincoln Highway route, than they did toward the Indiana-produced cars. Governors from several states through which the vehicles passed accompanied the dusty drivers for at least part of the drive and paid them glowing tributes at every stop along the way. Nevada governor Tasker Oddie met the caravan at the Utah-Nevada state line with his own eight-car posse and accompanied the flatlanders all the way to the California line, nearly a five-hundred-mile journey.[27] Even as Fisher and his associates headed west, governors in several states were pushing for good roads legislation. California governor Hiram Johnson assured Fisher that the Golden State would pay the entire bill for construction of the Lincoln Highway through the tortuous terrain of the Sierra Nevada Mountains and all the way into Oakland. Fisher was thrilled at the news; this meant that the Lincoln Highway Association could concentrate more effort on attracting support in states possessing more wide open spaces, where road construction would be far less expensive.

There was serious business to transact along the way, but basically Carl treated the 1913 trip as a lark with his automobile-driving cronies. Jane Fisher had wanted to go along, but Carl refused her plea. She described the convoy which she waved off from downtown Indianapolis: "They were weighted down with equipment worthy of an expedition into darkest Africa. Each carried ropes and an extra oil-burning lantern, block and tackle, mud hooks and chains, shovels and picks, water bags, tents and food—in all, equipment and provision to suffice for days if lost in the mountains or deserts."[28]

The entire journey took thirty-four days. They could have made better time, but towns through which they passed greeted them like conquering heroes and detained the caravan as long as possible. After a few weeks, Fisher must have felt that he could not tolerate another long-winded political speech or digest yet another rubbery chicken dinner. When the party had hotel accommodations in towns, they were not always first class. In Grand Junction, Colorado, the tourists were assaulted by bedbugs, and Fisher allegedly retreated to the roof of a nearby chicken coop to try to get some sleep.[29] Carl was happiest on the road, mastering mechanical breakdowns, rescuing fellow drivers buried to their axles in mud, and mending flats. The convoy endured blazing heat on the deserts; fierce winds in the mountain passes of Wyoming; and nights lying on the bare ground in sleeping bags, occasionally fending off scorpions and rattlesnakes.[30]

Fisher was having a grand time. Two-thirds of the way into his trip he apparently felt guilty for having excluded his young wife. He finally telephoned Jane and urged her to catch the midnight train out of Indianapolis headed west. They hooked up in Lake Tahoe, and Jane accompanied the triumphant caravan as it snaked down the mountains into Sacramento and finally to the shores of the Pacific Ocean in San Francisco. Over the final miles, the caravan was followed by hundreds of automobiles, and they passed through streets festooned with flags and thousands of cheering spectators.[31] The sunburned drivers may well have felt like victorious generals being greeted by admiring throngs in Rome.

They didn't bask in their glory for long. If the Hoosier Trailblazers were not officially the pathfinders for the Lincoln Highway, knowledgeable observers realized that their observations and recommendations would be vital in determining the final route. Politicians in virtually every town with even the slightest possibility of being on the route of the Lincoln Highway raised the hopes of their constituents and presented glowing visions of prosperity once the road passed through their regions. Evidently, Fisher had tolerated the politicking along the way, but Henry Joy, who joined the tour after it got under way, found it nettling. According to Lincoln Highway historian Drake Hokanson, the two men had fundamental disagreements regarding publicity strategies. "Fisher saw gain for the highway by pitting states against states and possible routes against one another to see who would produce the best promises about future highway improvements should the highway pass their doors. . . . Directness was all that mattered to Joy . . . he sought a route that would take advantage of easy terrain and natural paths . . . avoiding congestion and narrow roadways."[32] Colonel Sidney D. Waldon, a member of the National Association of Highway Manufacturers, had made several journeys to the West. Roy D. Chapin solicited his recommendation for a route. Waldon concurred with Joy.[33] Directness and the least possible variation in climate and elevation were the keys to success. Their ideas generally prevailed.

Joy, Fisher, and their associates knew that they could not afford to make too many promises, even of a veiled nature, to too many politicians and regional boosters. They knew full well that most politicians were going to be disappointed. To be a practical, useful route, the Lincoln Highway had to cut a relatively straight path across the nation, allowing for significant topographical constraints. If they caved in to insistent boosters for one out-of-the-way destination, they would be under increasing pressure to accommodate others, and the highway would serve little practical use. As Fisher noted in an address to the Conference of Governors at Colorado Springs in late August 1913, "A transcontinental highway that wound from large city to large city, from one wonder of nature to another would indeed be a devious and winding journey in this great America of ours."[34]

Nevertheless, the decision makers associated with the Lincoln Highway project realized that enormous personal and political tact had to be employed in the process of unveiling the final route. On rare occasions, Fisher stumbled. He may have been somewhat indiscreet in virtually promising that the Lincoln Highway would traverse Kansas and at least part of Colorado. At least, that is what the governors of Kansas and Colorado believed; they had offered enormous political support for the road, as long as it took the route they thought they had nailed down.[35] When Joy and Fisher addressed the Conference of Governors in Colorado Springs in the late summer of 1913, they unfurled a map revealing the route. With the exception of the link between Reno, Nevada, and Salt Lake City, Utah, the western section of the route basically followed what is today Interstate 80 from Sacramento to Chicago, often within eyesight of the first transcontinental railroad line, completed almost fifty years earlier. From Chicago to New York, it followed the line of what eventually became the Indiana, Ohio, Pennsylvania, and New Jersey turnpike system. Newly elected governor Elias M. Ammons of Colorado was particularly incensed that his state was left out. He besieged the Lincoln Highway directors with appeals and petitions, and they tentatively agreed to add a "dogleg" from Big Springs, Nebraska, down to Denver, then back up to the main highway at Cheyenne, Wyoming. Dozens of other groups flooded them with similar demands. If an exception had been made for Denver, why not for them as well? The directors finally bit the bullet, canceled plans to include Colorado, and opted for the functional, direct route.[36]

By the early fall of 1913, however, all the association had done was generate publicity and raise money. The associates were more than a bit concerned with the latter task. Not surprisingly, after an initial rush of enthusiasm donations had tapered off. Nevertheless, a year after Fisher's initial appeal they had about $4 million in contributions and pledges, much of it in the form of building materials. For example, A. Y. Gowan of the Lehigh Portland Cement Company promised 1.5 million barrels of his product, with the possibility of doubling that amount. Obviously, his industry would reap priceless publicity if the project moved forward quickly.[37] But there was little cash on hand, in part because fund-raisers had originally informed many of those who made pledges that they did not need to come up with the funds until the association had $10 million fully committed. The founders had determined that it would be best to include the "masses" in the project, encouraging small donations, even pennies from schoolchildren. One unanticipated problem with this strategy was that many unsophisticated donors expected almost immediate results. Administrative costs alone sapped much of the scant cash on hand. In September 1913, for example, after the route was announced, the organization sent out 75,000 fliers and other types of mail answering inquiries. The association's secretary Arthur Pardington had solicited major contributions from 3,000 millionaires but received little response.[38]

Fisher, Joy, and their associates huddled to devise a new financing strategy. Sober planning soon made it clear that $10 million, if not a drop in the bucket, was far less than the total eventual needs for construction of the highway. By 1914 they decided to put most of their efforts into raising in-kind contributions: building materials and equipment. They had no foundation of qualified construction engineers, material supplies, and experienced workers. They had to leave it to states, counties, and cities to underwrite most other costs, including labor.[39]

A gigantic, complicated physical task challenged the association. A semblance of a road already existed along virtually the entire route. Most of it was unpaved. Road surfaces varied considerably but included a few miles of concrete and a few hundred miles of gravel road. Most of the rest was "unimproved," which usually meant ruts in the dirt. Under perfect weather conditions the unimproved surface was passable, but it was insufferably dusty in dry weather, impassable muck when it rained.

Not until the fall of 1914 was the first actual improvement of the Lincoln Highway finished, a modest "seedling" one-mile length of concrete road near DeKalb, Illinois. It took a good deal of cooperation from many directions. The state of Illinois provided road equipment and engineers who supervised preliminary grading. Local businessmen raised $2,000 from public donations and another $3,000 from the county supervisors. In addition, local officials appealed to the Lincoln Highway Association, which arranged for provision of 2,000 barrels of cement by the Marquette Company. The finished strip was only ten feet wide, but

A section of the Lincoln Highway before improvement work began.

The same section of road after improvements were made. Photos courtesy of Lincoln Highway Association.

it generated much enthusiasm.[40] The Lincoln Highway proved to be an excellent laboratory for experimenting with building materials, widths, and construction techniques.

One mile of improved highway was down, with more than 3,000 miles to go. Virtually every small project had to be completed within a unique, often complex local economic, social, and political environment. Different interest groups had to be consulted, courted, and appeased. The next year, 1915, saw modest progress. Four more seedling miles were finished: two miles in Nebraska, one each in Illinois and Indiana. These sections were wider than the DeKalb effort, fifteen to sixteen feet across.[41]

Fisher and his cohorts planted their seedlings wisely, choosing rural locations, far away from roughly comparable urban street paving. Hence the contrast between muddy, rutted roads and smooth, level concrete was dramatic. In the context of the more market-driven consumer economy that was emerging in the United States virtually simultaneously, their strategy was clearly to create widespread desire for the best roads money could buy. In addition, they spaced their experiments widely, hoping that local and regional interest groups would exert sufficient political pressure to persuade appropriate governing bodies to fill in the gaps. Lincoln Highway officials repeatedly emphasized that *local* decision makers would control the building projects.

In some respects, the association's overall promotional strategy appeared shrewd, but it was fundamentally flawed. Through dramatic showmanship and heavy publicity, the Lincoln Highway Association had initially created enormous interest in better highways. By dangling the vision of possible inclusion along the Lincoln Highway route, the leaders of the association had raised the hopes of hundreds of regional and small town interest groups across the country. By delaying announcement of the final routes, they strung these businessmen and politicians along for many months. Most of them experienced severe disappointment when they learned their interests would not be served. In retaliation, some of them became opponents of the Lincoln Highway Association. Political and civic leaders in Colorado voiced a typical response once they learned that the state would be left out. As one analyst observed, after the association shelved plans to construct the dogleg from western Nebraska into

Denver in 1915, "within that state little good was ever said about the Lincoln Highway."[42]

An even more fundamental reason for lack of sustained support for the program was the basic dichotomy between the interests of the decidedly elitist Lincoln Highway Association and the great masses of Americans. Sponsors of the highway might attract small contributions from tens of thousands of subscribers, but for most Americans, a coast-to-coast highway was little more than a romantic vision, irrelevant to their daily transportation needs. True, prices of motor vehicles had dropped dramatically since the turn of the century, and in 1910 about one-half million Americans owned automobiles; thus motor vehicles were no longer toys for the rich.[43] But most owners used them for short trips in local areas.[44] Farm-to-market roads facilitating rural free delivery and easier communication over short distances were of more concern to most driving Americans than were coast-to-coast highways. Some farmers disdainfully rejected major highways as "peacock alleys," designed primarily for the rich in their fancy cars.[45] Thus utilitarian roads serving local needs naturally attracted most of the attention of rural and small town politicians.

During the years the highway was under construction, several drivers established speed records for cross-country trips. In 1916, Bobby Hammond drove an Empire roadster from San Francisco to New York in just six days, ten hours, and fifty-nine minutes. Fisher's automobile company had manufactured Empires a few years earlier, and Carl himself may have been behind Hammond's effort. Later that year, two other drivers completed the journey even faster. According to the Lincoln Highway Association, the purpose of the trips was to show that the highway was a real road that would permit expeditious travel.[46] Farmers and some local interests may well have viewed the speed attempts as further evidence that the highway was built for rich sportsmen with too much time on their hands.

Carl Fisher obviously understood that many urban and rural automobile owners were beginning to consider automobiles necessities; unfortunately, he never shared his thoughts on the subject. During the years he promoted the Lincoln Highway, Fisher was also building a resort paradise in South Florida, and he appeared more in tune with entrepreneurs who envisioned the automobile as a recreational and leisure device.[47] Fisher was no populist, and neither were his associates in the Lincoln Highway Association.

In addition to dealing with competing visions regarding primary purposes for roads, Fisher and his colleagues were realizing that outside events were quickly supplanting the role of the Lincoln Highway Association. By the mid-1910s, the federal government had begun taking the leading role in developing modern highways. If one discounts its role in constructing the National Road, its initial commitment to road building actually went back to the early 1890s. In response to mounting pressure from the League of American Wheelmen, agricultural and rural constituencies vowing to "get the farmer out of the mud," and other groups, the Department of Agriculture sponsored an agency called the Office of Public Roads (OPR). Highly sensitive to the issue of states' rights, in the first decade of the twentieth century the OPR essentially limited its role to providing engineering advice on road building to state and local bodies requesting it. By the early 1910s, however, OPR representatives were presenting thousands of lectures annually to interested local commercial and civic groups. In addition, the federal government established various agencies for the development and dissemination of advanced engineering concepts, as well as sampling and testing various road-building materials. Increasingly, locales interested in improving their roads shifted attention from the private to the public sector.[48]

Carl Fisher was well aware of these developments. As an unsuccessful candidate for Marion County commissioner on the Progressive Party ticket in the fall of 1912, he had centered his campaign on the need for improved roads, and his speeches stressed the growing responsibility of public agencies to provide them. One of the central beliefs of early twentieth-century progressives was the ability to solve virtually any problem through the combination of good intentions, honesty, scientific reason, and professionalism.[49] The small-scale "demonstration projects" sponsored by the Lincoln Highway Association were hardly new initiatives. The Department of Agriculture, through the OPR, had completed hundreds of such projects before the outbreak of World War I.

By the time the war started, Fisher had large projects on his plate in addition to the Lincoln Highway. He and Jane had visited Miami in 1912.

They were so captivated by South Florida that Carl had become deeply involved in real estate development there, and by 1914 they were spending more time in Miami than in Indianapolis. He and James Allison had sold most of their interest in Prest-O-Lite, which gave Fisher even less reason to remain in Indianapolis. In the mid-1910s Fisher was simultaneously involved in promoting yet another transcontinental route, the Dixie Highway. This road, when finished, would funnel tens of thousands of northern vacationers to the Deep South during winter.

World War I brought major changes in the relationship of the federal government to business, labor unions, even the general population. As historian David M. Kennedy has ably demonstrated, federal agencies became far more of a presence in the daily lives of most Americans.[50] This heightened involvement noticeably affected road and highway development. Government officials in Washington formed various agencies committed to developing a "national defense" highway system, capable of assisting railroads and ships in transporting massive amounts of manufactured goods, natural resources, food, and human beings to where they were most needed to aid the Allied cause. Ironically, a coast-to-coast journey by a large convoy of military trucks in the summer of 1919, several months after the armistice, demonstrated the potential for highways to carry large amounts of commercial freight—a purpose Fisher had only dimly perceived.

Many patriotic Americans were deeply involved in the war effort. Carl had converted the Indianapolis Motor Speedway into an aviation school. This was a good time to cut back on his involvement in a private organization that might conceivably find itself working at cross purposes with the government. At least that was the advice he received from Roy D. Chapin, president of Hudson Motors, in December 1917: "The Government is going to dominate the building of practically every mile of really improved highways in this country from now forward, as long as the war may last." Chapin urged Lincoln Highway officials to lobby aggressively to get huge sections of the Lincoln Highway designated as critical for national defense. Chapin advised moving the Lincoln Highway Association's offices to Washington to be nearer the action, but Fisher resisted. So far, federal politicians had delivered far more windy rhetoric than tangible support about the need for good roads. Fisher urged holding off on significant lobbying efforts and the necessary expenses accompanying them until they knew better which way the wind was blowing.[51]

Fisher's active work on behalf of the association dropped off precipitously during 1918 as he concentrated most of his attention on facilitating training of pilots in Indianapolis and promoting development in Miami Beach. He had other smaller projects in the works as well. Nevertheless, several other founders continued to press for completion of the Lincoln Highway, and their efforts appeared to be paying off. An annual report at the end of 1918 claimed that the highway was "the best known road on this continent, if not the whole world," being completely marked along the entire route. The association claimed that it was possible "in dry weather" to load up a five-ton truck in New York and drive it to San Francisco "on a definite schedule." The report claimed that 65 percent of the route was covered with "all-weather" material. All this had been achieved without any direct support from the federal government. In its first five years, the association spent a little over $200,000 promoting the highway. The balance of its income was spent on materials. As a result, in addition to millions of dollars and in-kind contributions from private sources, city, county, and state agencies had spent just over $15 million on the highway. The founders were justifiably proud of their achievement to date, but there was still work to be done. "Western states with long distances to cover and small populations to draw upon need outside help for the completion of their sections." The report hinted at the possibility of lining up for federal support because contributions from private sources were drying up.[52]

Drake Hokanson neatly summed up the long-term impact of the Lincoln Highway Association: "The country simply could not go long with millions of cars on dirt roads; the change was inevitable. What the Lincoln Highway did was speed up the process; it made the public accept the idea of long roads built not for local convenience but for the benefit of everyone—roads for the nation, not just the county. This was the Fisher idea."[53] The association continued to function for several more years, but when it became clear that public agencies would dominate future road building, it quickly lost momentum and relevance. Following World War I, Fisher essentially lost interest in the organization. When invited by the association's new president, A. F. Bement, to attend a meeting in New York in the spring of 1920, Fisher replied, "I don't know of a single thing that I can advise regarding the continuation of the Lincoln Highway other than this: That the American people generally don't seem to be very enthusiastic for the assistance of such an organization as the Lincoln Highway—and I have, a long time since, lost a lot of my interest and pep in these highway associations for the reasons above stated."[54]

Fisher significantly cut back his own financial support to the Lincoln Highway Association. In his initial rush of enthusiasm for the effort, he actually pledged one-third of his estate in the event of his death. By 1920 his position had shifted significantly. His fortune had grown by millions of dollars, but he felt far less reason to contribute. He cut the association wholly out of his will, substituting a token $2,500 annual contribution for ten years. Part of the reason was that he thought he had carried a disproportionate share of the load. If private groups were to play any significant part in the nation's future road building, it was time for others with more direct stake in improved roads to step forward. As Fisher explained, "The lack of interest taken by some of the automobile manufacturers, for instance, in this work where they are vitally concerned and even the lack of interest of communities where their very life almost is at stake—has greatly changed my mind and plans." Fisher's old Lincoln Highway associate Henry B. Joy tried to interpret Fisher's decision positively: "Your proposed gift of $2,500 per year for ten years is splendid and generous. It may even accomplish more good than the larger bequest of one-third of your wealth contingent upon your demise." In other words, a little cash now might be worth far more at some undetermined future date.[55]

At this point, Fisher's positions on private versus public responsibility for road building were not always clear or consistent. Even after Congress passed two major highway bills, he argued that Detroit automobile manufacturers were taking very short-term views of even their own best interests, let alone those of the American public. As he noted in a passionate letter to Detroit Automobile Club manager W. S. Gilbreath in the fall of 1921, "I might incidentally tell you that I am darn good and sore at the various automobile companies, sundries companies, etc., who are making millions out of the automobile business and who will not help support road building programs. There is absolutely no incentive, nowadays, for people to purchase touring automobiles. . . . Why should I, entirely out of the automobile business, waste a lot of time and a lot of money in promoting touring roads for the automobile companies who are too selfish to do their share. I am just about to the point where I would like to tell them all to go to Hell."[56] His general irritation with Detroit auto men may have been influenced by the fact that he was simultaneously engaged in somewhat testy exchanges with several manufacturers whose makes were offered in his automobile showroom in Indianapolis. By the early 1920s, Fisher was, consciously or otherwise, cutting some of his ties to the automobile industry. What he never did explain was why automobile men should increase private support for road building when the federal government was clearly assuming primary responsibility for through routes. Perhaps his venting against automobile companies was related to their limited underwriting of lobbying efforts for increased federal funding for roads.

In his final years, Fisher became more philosophical about energy spent promoting the Lincoln Highway. In early 1938, he waxed nostalgic to a close associate and two-time Indianapolis 500 race winner Thomas W. Milton, "I got the movement pretty well started when Mr. Joy and Mr. Seiberling and Mr. Chapin came in, and they really deserve more credit for the success of the undertaking than myself." Fisher shared the story about why Henry Ford slipped off of his baited hook: "I sold Henry Ford the idea of coming in with us, and he himself suggested that he would tie a tag on every Ford automobile made, calling for a $5.00 extra subscription to help build the road, but Couzens talked him out of it."[57]

Fisher intentionally discounted his role in promoting highways in the years immediately preceding World War I. His romance with privately organized national highways was short, but for a few years, his commitment was intense. During the years he was associated with the Lincoln Highway he spearheaded yet another major road-building project, the Dixie Highway. In the latter project, his motive was decidedly less altruistic than the former. By then, he was a major developer in Miami Beach, and the southern terminus for the Dixie Highway would deposit thousands of tourists into his spanking new vacation paradise, Miami Beach.

6

Touring Through Dixieland

In most important respects, Fisher's initiative in promoting a major north-south national highway paralleled his work on the Lincoln Highway. Clearly he hoped that by facilitating interstate journeys, major highways would enhance the overall appeal of the automobile. Thus, as with the Lincoln Highway, Fisher hoped to attract major support from the Detroit automotive interests for the north-south project. The two projects unfolded in the same general time period. Fisher initiated the Lincoln Highway in the fall of 1912, the north-south project two years later. Finally, Fisher lost interest in and curtailed his participation in both efforts at about the same time and for essentially the same reason. By the end of World War I it was evident that the federal government would provide most if not all of the funding for major interstate highways.[1]

Yet there were major differences in Fisher's work on the Lincoln Highway and what would be labeled the Dixie Highway. His personal stake in the latter project was fairly transparent. By the autumn of 1914, when he first publicized the idea of a north-south highway, Fisher was developing real estate in Miami Beach, Florida. Hence he had a significant financial stake in the success of the Dixie Highway. If successful, it could deliver tens of thousands of motoring vacationers to his community each winter.

This would obviously enhance the value of property in the region and directly serve his financial interests. Second, by 1914 Fisher had developed considerable political sophistication. It had been two years since he had run a spirited, if losing, campaign for Marion County road commissioner on the Progressive Party ticket in Indianapolis. In the interim, he had widened contact with politicians from the local to the national level. His work on the Lincoln Highway project had provided him with national visibility. Fisher understood that most major road-building projects were going to be publicly financed. Correspondence reveals that he aggressively used both his increased knowledge of road-building techniques and growing political contacts to push the Dixie Highway.

The Great War was breaking out in the fall of 1914, when Fisher's enthusiasm for big highway projects was at its peak. Publicity for the Lincoln Highway was overwhelmingly favorable, and both private and public pledges for support of the road were being honored. Although very little actual construction had been completed, it seemed as if the pieces were falling into place. William Herschell, a reporter for the *Indianapolis News*, was working at his desk when he received a phone call from Fisher. The two men were friendly, and Fisher had given Herschell scoops before. He said, "Want a good story? Come over and let's talk." The reporter hustled over to Fisher's office on Capitol Avenue. The entrepreneur greeted Herschell with the question, "How do you think the country would take a proposal to build a great highway from Indianapolis to Miami, Florida?"[2]

Herschell, an astute reporter, immediately realized the significance of the interview. Reflecting on the conversation a decade later, he noted, "It was a tremendous thing, a partnership of the north and south in an intersectional enterprise." He got to the crux of the matter when he concluded, "Fisher said it could be done and when he said it—well, it could be done."[3]

Was Fisher the true originator of the idea of the Dixie Highway, or did he, like many individuals credited with important new theories or inspired insights, simply articulate and publicize dreams that had been present in the minds of many for years? The truth does not matter much. In the minds of some opinion-makers, perhaps the most positive effect of the recently concluded Spanish-American War was that it had reunited

North and South behind a "patriotic" venture. In 1914 the fiftieth an-
niversary of the end of the Civil War was approaching, and many pub-
lic-spirited individuals consciously sought affirmation of the healing of
the long-festering wounds caused by the nation's bloodiest war. Wouldn't
a magnificent new highway provide a symbolic new bond? When approached for a public endorsement of the Lincoln Highway project,
President Wilson, a southerner, "expressed the hope that in the not too
distant future a highway, modeled after the Lincoln Highway, might
link the North and South together and make 'the imaginary Mason and
Dixon line . . . once and for all a thing of the past.'"[4] Historian Howard
L. Preston has traced important southern initiatives in promoting good
roads dating from the 1890s.[5]

The Dixie Highway project differed from the Lincoln Highway effort in another key respect. In lining up support for the east-west transcontinental road, Fisher first approached private interests, namely key
automobile men in Detroit and other cities with important automotive-
related industries. In the Dixie Highway endeavor, he concentrated the
initial campaign on key politicians. His first target was Indiana governor
Samuel M. Ralston. Although he initially imagined a road originating
in Indianapolis, further deliberation convinced Carl of the wisdom of
extending any north-south interstate farther north. In a letter to Ralston
in early December 1914, he urged the governor to "take the initiative in
the creation of an interstate highway from Chicago, Illinois to Miami,
Florida." Fisher argued that "there were many Midwestern automobile
owners who would like to travel to the South" but found it impossible
because "there is no chance for them to drive thru. The roads in Tennessee and some parts of Georgia are simply Hell." The Dixie Highway, he
stated, would "do more good for the South than if they should get ten
cents for their cotton," and it would "mean hundreds of millions of dollars
to Indiana in the next twenty-five years."[6]

Fisher's initiative galvanized the governor. A week after receiving
Carl's communication, he was firing off letters to fellow governors in other states, talking up the idea. Ralston invited governors of several states
to meet in Chattanooga in the spring of 1915 to develop plans for a co-
operative and, presumably, publicly funded road-building venture. In the
early weeks of 1915, as news of the project circulated widely, chambers of

commerce and booster organizations in countless towns and cities across the South and Midwest sprang into action. Each civic group dreamed of convincing conference delegates that its community deserved inclusion in the proposed route.

As Governor Ralston courted fellow state governors, Fisher developed other valuable political contacts. One of his most valuable recruits was Tom Taggart, a wheelhorse in the Democratic Party at numerous levels. Irish-born Taggart had been mayor of Indianapolis at the turn of the century and later chaired the state Democratic committee before moving on to the national Democratic committee. In 1916 he would be appointed to the United States Senate before losing a special election to Republican James E. Watson the same year. In addition to his political contacts, Taggart possessed an affable personality and significant business connections. He owned and managed the French Lick Hotel and was chairman of the Fletcher National Bank. In all likelihood, the two men had become friendly a few years earlier when Fisher was considering building an automobile racetrack in the resort area of French Lick. Taggart had also served on the state road commission, and he, like Fisher, was a passionate supporter of the good roads movement.[7]

Fisher, Taggart, and Ralston realized that to achieve success they had to garner broad-based support from many states and various interest groups. It would be politically astute for the initial planning meeting to be sponsored by a private group rather than a public agency. Consequently, the Chattanooga Automobile Club officially hosted such a gathering in the spring of 1915. Excitement mounted to a fever pitch. When the conference opened on April 3, there were 5,000 representatives from 200 communities and ten states. President Wilson graced the proceedings with a congratulatory telegram praising the delegates "upon the inauguration . . . of the Dixie Highway project."[8] Ralston gave one of the major addresses, making a calculated, emotional appeal to southern delegates: "I like to think of the proposed Dixie Highway, or if you please, the Robert E. Lee Highway, as an advance agent of social intercourse, mutual understanding and national unity and good will, through the heart of our beloved common country." He continued, "The Dixie Highway will allow people of North and South to get to know each other better. . . . Heretofore, most communication has been east to west. The automobile will help mold people together in a homogeneous mass." Although much of his speech was forgettable political rhetoric, Ralston made one prescient observation. Wholly new funding strategies must be developed: those advocating "Dixie Highways and similar highways should not fail to recognize the fact that one of the first problems to the solution of which they must address themselves is a radical overhauling of state highway laws; and in connection therewith, to the securing of federal aid for road construction and maintenance."[9]

Ralston's focus on the ultimate need for federal subsidies for interstate roads was one of the few substantial comments to come from the conference. Most other speakers indulged in windy and self-serving pleas for special consideration for their constituents, real or imagined. Many fine- sounding resolutions were read into the record of the conference proceedings and dutifully reported by newspapers. The one tangible achievement of the conference was official organization of the Dixie Highway Association, essentially a carbon copy of the Lincoln Highway Association model. The Dixie Highway Association initially included two appointed representatives from each of ten states. Fisher and Taggart were the obvious choices to represent Indiana. Apparently, most delegates left the conference convinced that political action would generate critically needed public funding.

The leaders of the Dixie Highway movement faced enormous challenges. Most of the nation's traffic moved along an east-west axis, and many decision makers hoped those routes could be improved first. Hence Dixie Highway enthusiasts often found themselves toward the back of the line when seeking public funding. Other than securing significant funding for actual work on the road, the most obvious hurdle was determining a final route. Inevitably, there would be far more disappointed advocates of good roads than winners. Would those whose towns and districts lost out in the sweepstakes take out their frustrations against the winners by opposing state and local efforts to secure funding? In addition, it seemed that advocates of sophisticated or even serviceable interstate roads represented a fairly narrow constituency. In all of the states along the proposed route, thousands of farmers had little or no interest in through roads.

Many of them seldom ventured more than a few miles from their farms. Hence they understandably preferred that scarce public funding be devoted to adequate farm-to-market roads.

Conflict between farmers and "elitist" advocates of highways serving bicycling, touring, and vacation purposes had become an increasingly contentious political issue during the preceding thirty years.[10] As a prominent advocate of good roads, Governor Ralston was well aware of the debate and controversy before helping launch the Dixie Highway organization. A year earlier, farmers complained that state road bills primarily benefited "city automobile owners." One farmer wrote to the *Indianapolis Star*, "If the farmers had to pay their road tax in money you could not get more than half of the gravel on the roads as we do with the present system." One of his basic complaints was that farmers' property was highly visible, impossible to hide from tax collectors, whereas urban property holders often camouflaged their assets in corporate trusts and less easily identifiable paper assets. Another angry farmer wrote directly to Ralston: "I wish to enter my most vigorous protest against the bill that compels the farmer to pay his road tax in cash. . . . We work out our road tax at a season of the year when our labor can best be spared from the care of our crops and it is that money saved to the farmer that we can lily [*sic*] spare to pay out at some stranger's discretion."[11]

The fundamental disagreement between rural and urban constituents over road-building priorities was not resolved during the Progressive era, and vestiges of the conflict still surface four score years later.[12] But Dixie Highway officials were most immediately concerned with the delicate political challenge of placating a sufficient number of interest groups to assure both initial and sustaining work on the highway while ultimately building a reasonably direct road. Short-term political realities had to be balanced against long-term objectives. In the months following the Chattanooga gathering, this may well have appeared a near impossible challenge. There was constant bickering between rival interests. Even Fisher, one of the two Indiana representatives, found himself under fire. The *South Bend Tribune*, a Republican paper, criticized Ralston's appointment of not one but two Indianapolis men to the association, complaining that there should have been better geographical representation.

Carl Fisher taking a break, perhaps somewhere along the Dixie Highway. Courtesy of the Historical Museum of Southern Florida.

Ralston defended his choices by stressing the road-building expertise of both nominees.[13]

Determining the final route was an even stickier challenge. In the weeks following the Chattanooga conference, boosters from dozens of cities applied constant pressure against the association. Individual members endured unrelenting lobbying efforts, both subtle and crudely self-serving. Had the association accommodated even half of the towns and cities vying for inclusion, the route would have meandered so aimlessly that it would have added several hundred miles to the journey. Fisher had originally conceived of a route taking a fairly straight line from Indianapolis to Miami. In addition to Indiana and Florida, the route would have passed through Kentucky, Tennessee, and Georgia. Lobbying efforts by interested parties eventually convinced association planners to expand the scope of the project. One analyst claimed: "The Dixie Highway was to have a long and arduous struggle over more than a decade before it was a fully-completed route between Miami and the Midwest. Acrimonious arguments over the route the highway would take ate up much of the pure enthusiasm for the project."[14]

The end product essentially resembled a two-pronged fork, originating far north of Indianapolis in Sault Ste. Marie, on Michigan's Upper Peninsula. The route divided into two branches at Mackinaw, reconverging at the final destination, Miami. The western division passed along the eastern shore of Lake Michigan, through central Indiana, Kentucky, and Tennessee, through western Georgia into Tallahassee, Florida, and finally down through central Florida into Miami. The eastern division hugged the shoreline of Lake Huron and passed through Detroit, then traversed western Ohio, eastern Kentucky, and Tennessee before dipping into western North Carolina and western South Carolina. The eastern segment reached the East Coast at Savannah, then followed the coastline all the way to Miami. Illinois was included by providing a road straight south from Chicago to Danville, then east to Indianapolis. The two main branches were connected by several east-west links at various points along the route. Considering the enormous number of conflicting interests and dissonant voices, Dixie Highway officials did a remarkable job of laying out two routes that made logistical as well as political sense. The eastern division made a fairly straight line from northern Michigan to Miami. The western branch was more indirect and circuitous, largely because political pressure induced planners to route it through more large, important cities.

Devising a final route and drawing lines on maps were necessary tasks, but the roads remained to be built. The association was intent on providing quick, tangible results. Suellen Hoy claimed that "road construction was rapid; within a year, one of the last barriers—the Nashville-Chattanooga link—was nearly completed. Then in September 1916, Ralston and Fisher attended a lively celebration in Martinsville, Indiana, which signaled the opening of the Dixie Highway from Indianapolis to Miami."[15]

To be sure, announcement of a successful road was made and duly celebrated, but in 1916, the work was only beginning. Funding remained problematical; it was a rickety combination of state taxes, bonds originated by counties through which the road passed, and scattered contributions from car dealers and manufacturers, auto clubs, and private citizens. As a result, progress was very uneven. By the end of 1916, a few stretches were either in place or largely completed. In late October a group of Dixie Highway officials inspected a section of the highway between Cincinnati and Chattanooga. They drove a Model 86 Overland touring car, and they visited with local officials in addition to surveying the quality of the main roads inspected. Over that particular route, they reported that all sections of the planned highway had been "provided for." They noted that in Kenton County, Kentucky, just across the river from Cincinnati, county officials had already begun replacing serviceable macadam roads with concrete. "Three miles of permanent paving has been constructed with preparations made for four miles additional. In a few years the entire mileage of the highway through this county will be of concrete."[16]

As the inspection party proceeded south, they discovered that in and near large cities and towns and important county seats, road construction was a priority, and they often traversed smooth highways. In sparsely settled rural and mountain areas, however, they often faced primitive driving conditions. Residents in many counties were desperately poor, and they had maintained antipathy and suspicion toward public officials at least since Reconstruction. Even the most enthusiastic boosters of the Dixie Highway must have realized that providing good roads through the forests, swamps, and mountain ranges in various parts of the Deep South might take decades.

In the early fall of 1916, a second "official" inspection party departed from Chicago, determined to take the road all the way to Miami. Fisher joined the foray south. He was unfamiliar with southern terrain, mountains, and roads, so he happily yielded leadership to the association's field secretary, W. S. Gilbreath. They left on October 5, and the first few days were largely uneventful, even routine. Challenges soon confronted them, however. As the pioneering touring committee approached Chattanooga, they may well have wished Daniel Boone was accompanying them. They became hopelessly lost in hilly terrain somewhere in southern Tennessee. A reception committee in Chattanooga eagerly awaited the tourists. As the evening lengthened and the tourists failed to arrive, committee members first grew restive, then anxious. Finally, they "sent a trapper familiar with the mountains to hunt up the lost party." It didn't take him long to find the beleaguered group, and he reportedly called out cheerfully, "Come on, fellers, I'll guide you to Chattanooga." Evidently, he set too fast a pace down the mountain. "In and out he darted like a firefly, and the caravan was lost again. However, the tourists finally wound their way around Lookout Mountain and into Chattanooga just as day was dawning. The reception committee had gone to bed. It did not take the tourists long to follow suit."[17]

The official Chicago-to-Miami tour provided other equally memorable incidents. Sometimes, they were the ones providing help. Evidently, they enjoyed challenges and taking risks because at one point, perhaps trying to make up time and avoid overly zealous reception committees, they drove a narrow road through the Florida Everglades after dark. About midnight, they encountered an elderly gentleman and his wife mired axle-deep in mud. "The Dixie Highway tourists, after carrying logs and fence rails long distances, finally extricated the car and then with much difficulty themselves. The old man and his wife had prayed for help—and it came."[18]

Dixie Highway organizers and officials declared the Chicago-to-Miami run a huge success. Despite encountering detours, getting lost, and delays caused when civic groups in virtually every town through which they passed threw some sort of function, they completed the journey in fifteen days. When the tired, intrepid tourists finally pulled up to Biscayne Bay, opposite the sparkling new resort town which Carl Fisher was dredging out of the mangrove swamps on the other side of the water, they undoubtedly welcomed the final and most extravagant civic celebration of the trip. Fisher had helped plan the reception, and both he and his fellow trekkers were ready to be feted. There was no more driving to face the next day, so they could party the night away.

The Chicago-to-Miami journey by these drivers in October 1916 marked the first successful passage of "tourists" over the Dixie Highway, but major improvements were needed before the road would be a national asset or before it would significantly increase the flow of vacationers from north to south. After all, it had taken a group of skilled drivers fully fifteen days to make the trip.[19] Even allowing for time lost to civic welcomes, the journey was very strenuous. In 1916 railroads could safely transport families from northern cities to Miami in reasonable comfort in a day or two, a fraction of the time required for an automobile trip.

Fisher's enthusiasm for and commitment to the Dixie Highway project peaked with the Chicago-to-Miami trip. The journey ended in Miami in late October, which was the beginning of the tourist season there, and development of Miami Beach had become his primary entrepreneurial interest. In all likelihood, he remained in town after his fellow Dixie Highway associates headed back north. The eastern division of the highway featured a road from Detroit through to Miami, and Fisher was actively recruiting prominent automobile men as investors and residents in Miami Beach. Thus Fisher possessed a personal and financial stake in continuing his association with the project. Yet one senses that, as with the Lincoln Highway, his hitherto exuberant, infectious enthusiasm for the project began to wane. By the next year, the United States had entered World War I, and Fisher had taken on the responsibility of organizing the army air corps training routes in Indiana, Illinois, and Ohio. In addition, he was organizing flight training in South Florida.

Fisher did, however, have one more financial reason for maintaining some interest in both highway projects. During World War I he became a major supporter of the Kentucky Rock Asphalt Company; by 1919 he had invested a bit over $200,000 and held about 20 percent of its market shares.[20] This enterprise produced an experimental form of road surfacing that competed with gravel, macadam, pure asphalt, and cement. The company was located in the heart of Dixie Highway country, and it marketed local materials. If its surfacing won approval from civil engineers and road-building experts, the company might well garner lucrative contracts with the Dixie Highway Association and other road-building projects.

Fisher was little concerned with conflict-of-interest issues. Eighty years ago a considerably different business ethic prevailed, and few businessmen were sensitive to situations that would raise red flags today. To opinion-makers well positioned to affect the success or failure of the Dixie Highway, Carl aggressively hawked Kentucky Rock Asphalt products. Fisher enthusiastically promoted the benefits of the company's road surfacing materials to his friend William T. Anderson, editor of the *Macon* (Georgia) *Daily Telegraph*, whose endorsement of any product might well influence regional engineers considering highway contracts. Anderson was a powerful journalist; it may have been no coincidence that two branches of the Dixie Highway converged in Macon. In one pitch to Anderson, Fisher claimed that he had previously been a "very strong concrete man," but he had discovered that too many road contractors skimmed on jobs because of the cost of building materials. "Every time a contractor can keep a barrel of cement out of the concrete paving job, he is about four dollars ahead—and a great many see to it that they keep out a good many thousand barrels on a big job." He argued that concrete was not only more expensive than competing materials, but it was difficult to repair. In contrast, "Kentucky Rock Asphalt will wear just as well as the concrete and costs less money. It can be laid with ordinary labor . . . [and] it is much easier to patch."[21]

In contrast to his direct, personal interest in promoting road-building materials to Dixie Highway officials and other potential investors, Fisher was somewhat more circumspect in lobbying directly for consideration of particular routes for the road itself. As one of Indiana's two members of the association, Fisher received many petitions promoting individual communities and specific routes. In most cases he politely replied that final decisions depended heavily on technical recommendations by engineers and compromises arranged by local and regional authorities. But he occasionally intervened, particularly when alternative routes into his hometown of Indianapolis were under review. The link to the western branch of the highway from Chicago ran due south to Danville, Illinois, then almost due east through Indianapolis before turning south again. Drivers would have saved hours had the highway from Danville veered southeast to join the Dixie Highway in Paoli, Indiana. In lobbying for selection of "practically a bee line for 143 miles" route between South Bend and Indianapolis, Fisher advised the Indiana State Highway Commission, "In my estimation it would be a grave mistake to select any other road with a narrow right-of-way, numerous crooks and curves in and out through villages in a more or less roundabout way."[22] Fisher's recommendations obviously carried weight; the eventual layout of the Dixie Highway included a straight section from South Bend to Indianapolis.

During World War I Fisher's perspectives broadened considerably, and he was directly involved with the preparedness campaign. Transportation of goods and services was a vital wartime need, and as the nation prepared for war, the infrastructure was being tested to the limit. Railroad trains and ships carried the bulk of the load, but for the first time, federal legislators aggressively promoted expanding the role of highways. The Federal-Aid Road Act of 1916 had directly committed $75 million in federal funds, and grants were doled out during the war. Many private groups and public agencies actively pursued a far more ambitious program of federal aid to highways. These efforts eventually produced the Federal Highway Act of 1921, which effectively inaugurated the initial network of national highways.[23]

Although deeply committed to promoting the Dixie Highway to serve his own financial interests in Miami Beach, Fisher perceived its potentially larger role. In a letter to his friend Roy D. Chapin, an experienced Detroit automobile executive serving the government as a dollar-a-year transportation adviser, Fisher hinted at the possibility that roads might relieve railroads of some of their enormous burden, particularly in less densely populated, remote areas. In the spring of 1918 he noted, "Just now the railroads are particularly congested in the South—and if there ever was a time when it seemed necessary to complete the connection between Chattanooga and the Ohio River, both by way of Knoxville and by way of Nashville, then certainly we have arrived at the proper time to do this work." Ever the patriot, Fisher was not so subtly reminding Chapin that he and his Dixie Highway associates were ready to serve the nation, but, in addition, they were patiently waiting in line for building materials that might be used on what Fisher considered other less viable projects. Furthermore, completion of this section of road would enhance, not retard, the development of the national transportation system. "If the completion of these roads called for a large quantity of road material to be handled by the railroads, I would not advocate the work being done now—but I happen to know that the road material to complete these roads or at least to complete the basic foundation for these roads, is right on the mountains by the millions of tons."[24] In other words, with minimal cooperation from federal-level decision makers and perhaps millions of dollars in contracts for Kentucky Rock Asphalt products, Fisher and his associates could do their part for the war effort.[25]

In the years following World War I, Fisher did little on behalf of the Dixie Highway Association other than keeping track of seemingly countless local and regional initiatives related to financing small sections of the road. Would a certain county road commission recommend that a specific road-building bond issue be put to a vote? Had a goodhearted but politically inexperienced new mayor consulted all of the key engineers before asking a city council for authorization for funding for a small section of the proposed road?

In most cases, Fisher took a passive role, but he occasionally participated in micromanagement of local politics. On rare occasions, Fisher dealt with state-level issues, and his correspondence revealed how he and other Dixie Highway men conducted their business. In March 1919, association president Mike M. Allison expressed optimism that the Tennessee legislature would pass a $50 million bond issue for a state system of permanent roads. Allison strongly implied that the organization had been active in improving the prospects for passage of the bill. "We were fortunate in getting a good committee in the main, which entered heartily into the proposition and made a tour of the state holding twenty-one or more meetings." He observed that V. D. L. Robinson, the assistant secretary of the organization, had accompanied them on the tour. Allison confidently continued, "We have checked up on the members of both houses and it seems as though we will have a good majority in favor of the bill." He assured Fisher that he would closely monitor its progress: "The bill will come up for final action in about ten days and I am leaving for Nashville Wednesday and expect to stay on the job until the legislature has acted."[26]

In the same informative letter, Allison provided a broad-brush outline of the Dixie Highway Association's efforts in other parts of the South. He noted that "we have been taking somewhat of an active part in the Georgia and North Carolina campaigns and the prospects are exceedingly bright that both of these states will materially increase their state road funds which will enable them to build permanent roads along the routing of the Dixie Highway." Allison also expressed confidence that the Kentucky legislature would provide financial support for roads not covered by newly received federal funds. Like most southern road officials, he welcomed the free and widespread use of convict labor to lower road-building costs sufficiently to enhance the likelihood of political support.[27]

In the next few weeks and months, Allison's euphoria would turn to despair, as one rickety regional political alliance after another fell apart. Five weeks later, he sadly informed Fisher that the Tennessee bill had failed, at least the portion that would have directly aided the Dixie Highway. Farming interests had evidently persuaded legislatures to shift emphasis at the last moment. According to Allison, "The bill passed by the legislature fail[ed] to provide for any permanent or through highways. The road tax is apportioned out to all the counties of the state and will result in building a few miles of road in each county which can not be connected up."[28] Less than two weeks later, another booster and friend of the association, A. F. Sanford, president of the *Knoxville Journal and Tribune*, informed Fisher that things looked little better in Kentucky than in his state, Tennessee: "Permanent roads legislation in Kentucky is so far away and the difficulties ahead for completing the Western branch of the Dixie Highway between Nashville and Chattanooga are so great and uncertain as to result, that our best bet now is to knock out [one] small section."[29] In other words, provincial interests usually prevailed. Dixie Highway planners had to maintain sufficient stamina to facilitate building scores, if not hundreds, of short segments if the entire project was to succeed.

Although Fisher's stamina was fine, he was losing patience with the Dixie Highway project. After receiving another discouraging report on Tennessee prospects from Mike Allison, Fisher replied acerbically: "You know what I think of all the rock and material they have in Tennessee for the roads and the fact that the people there won't even pick up the rock along the road and throw it into the holes—and when I think of all the mudholes we went thru before we got to Jellico—well—it wouldn't do for me to put it on paper." He continued, "Really, some of the people of Tennessee ought to be ashamed of themselves for the roads they have. Fisher mentioned another short segment of road in the state which was just $5,000 short in its budget and remarked that he could easily contribute the money himself, "BUT I'M DAMNED IF I AM GOING TO GIVE UP FIVE THOUSAND DOLLARS TO A BUNCH OF PEOPLE WHO WON'T HELP THEMSELVES."[30] Five years later, according to Fisher, roads in Dixie were still deplorable. In a 1924 letter to Allison, he stated, "I wouldn't go over the Dixie Highway, or any other highway from here to Chicago in an automobile for the whole state of Indiana, or Tennessee either for that matter. The road from here to Jacksonville is much worse than it was five years ago; and it is almost as bad as it was when we came over it."[31]

At the end of 1919 the association's secretary prepared a comprehensive report on work completed that year. He noted that in numerous states, the work of paving at least one through road along the Dixie Highway route was completed or at least "provided for." Northern states such as Ohio, Illinois, and Michigan had met most if not all of their commitments and promises. Although residents in the northern part of the state might not support through routes, the Florida legislature had responded well, perhaps because of Fisher's close ties to local politicians in Miami, who were able to exert significant pressure on state officials. In addition, Florida politicians were expected to react enthusiastically to any project manifestly dedicated to promoting one of its most vital new industries, tourism.

Although Dixie Highway spokesmen emphasized the positives and pointed to significant additions to the Dixie Highway south of the Ohio River, most of the problems lay in the former Confederacy. Like Fisher, the secretary could find little good to say about the efforts of the Tennessee legislature. His report praised Georgia for raising bond issues sufficient to pave 25 percent of the Dixie Highway route in 1919, but huge sections remained unimproved, particularly in the southern part of the state. For example, he described the road between Macon and Jacksonville as "almost impassable sand," which was "known by every tourist who has attempted to go to Florida."[32] The message was clear: there was no end of work in sight.

Fisher was not a particularly introspective individual, especially when he was extremely busy. As the 1920s dawned, he was involved in many important projects. If he ever assessed his role in highway promotion, he never put his thoughts on paper. But it is likely that his reactions to the Lincoln and Dixie Highways were virtually identical at that time. He had given a good deal to both efforts, serving essentially as the inspiration and one of the big idea men behind both projects. The federal government was moving inexorably, if ponderously, into the highway building business. New bureaucratic structures were emerging, such as the American Association of State Highway Officials (AASHO). Fisher had served as a transitional figure, a bridge between amateur, privately funded, and professional, publicly funded road building. A new generation of professionally trained road construction engineers was primed to assume command of this segment of the nation's infrastructure. Fisher clearly sensed that private road-building consortiums had outlived their usefulness. In the future, roads would primarily serve traffic needs rather than private interests.[33]

It was time to move on. By the summer of 1921 Fisher disengaged himself from the Dixie Highway Association's affairs, or at least its day-to-day business. Mike Allison wrote a newsy letter, bringing Fisher up-to-date on association affairs and expressing regret that he hadn't been able to attend the annual meeting of the board of directors. By then, Miami Beach was booming, and Fisher was deeply committed to its development. As with the Lincoln Highway Association, Carl commenced sending regular contributions to the Dixie Highway Association in lieu of a significant commitment of time and energy. Allison thanked Fisher profusely for the financial support but hinted strongly that the group really needed his expertise, since he was reelected to the board in absentia.[34]

Fisher resisted Allison's entreaties. He felt that he had pulled far more than his share of the weight for years; it was time for others to step forward.[35] Fisher continued sending donations, but from then on, his only additional involvement was occasional advice. Late in 1921 he congratulated President Allison on the progress made by the association. He noted that with passage of the Federal Highway Act the federal government would carry much of the expense of building national highways. Perhaps it was time for the organization to develop new strategies. He suggested capitalizing on the surge of negative attitudes toward armaments: "It seems to me that it would be a good time right now to jump into some publicity regarding the amount of roads that could be built in America if only one fifth of the money appropriated for the Navy could be applied to roads. Nowadays a first class battleship costs about $50 million. With the grades already established, the Dixie Highway from Mackinac to Miami could be a boulevard for the cost of one battleship."[36] From that point forward, the future of the Dixie Highway was in the hands of others. By then, his compelling commitment was building a sparkling resort city from the marshes and mangrove swamps just off Biscayne Bay in Miami, Florida.

7

The Accidental Tourist

In 1970, Polly Redford, a Miami Beach historian, wrote, "If ever a man made a city, Carl Fisher made Miami Beach—from the ground right up to its bathing beauties. Even today it still bears the stamp of his personality. So Miami Beach begins with Carl Fisher."[1] Although local memories of Fisher have faded, his impact on the entire region of South Florida was immense. Fisher helped transform the tone and pace of development of the east coast of Florida, beginning in the 1920s. Before examining Carl Fisher's role in creating a vacation paradise, however, we should look at the backdrop of what South Florida was like before he arrived.

When Fisher first laid eyes on the region in 1910, Miami was a relatively sleepy southern town, featuring a warm, sunny climate in the winter, oppressive heat and humidity, and swarms of mosquitoes in the summer. But there were already signs that Miami had promise as a tourist mecca. A half-dozen or so entrepreneurs were working assiduously to develop the region.

There was nothing preordained about Fisher's arrival in South Florida; it was almost wholly accidental. It was actually the result of a belated "honeymoon" trip gone awry. When he married Jane Watts in October 1909, Fisher had browbeaten his young bride into forgoing a formal honeymoon. Instead, Carl reluctantly allowed Jane to join him and his chums on a riotous trip down the Mississippi River to New Orleans, which ended in the 1909 Christmas morning fiasco.[2]

If the "honeymoon" yacht trip aboard the *Eph* had been unpredictable through Christmas, it became even wilder afterward. Departing New Orleans, Fisher and his doughty crew headed out into the Gulf of Mexico, where they almost immediately encountered stormy weather. Jane later claimed it had been a hurricane; however, Howard Kleinberg, a historian of Miami Beach, checked weather records for the date and discovered no hurricane warnings.[3] Fisher grounded the vessel in the sand in an emergency maneuver. They were in a remote location in Mobile Bay; evidently they had lost their bearings and did not know where help could be found. They had no sense that friends and family members were extremely worried about their fate. According to Jane, they had been given up as lost at sea. Apparently, other boats had gone down, and there were some deaths. At the time, the intrepid voyagers thoroughly enjoyed the adventure, acting like Robinson Crusoe and his shipmates. Jane claimed that they lived like beachcombers. "We ate canned goods and beautiful big fish we caught with our hands in the shallows of low tide, and immense oysters we pried from the rocks."[4]

According to Jane, ten days after their disappearance, a passing oyster fisherman found them and helped them locate a winch to get the yacht back into the water. They docked at Mobile; only then did they discover the turmoil their disappearance had caused. Jane insisted that it would be a good idea for them to return to Indianapolis as quickly as possible to reassure their temporarily bereaved families. For once, her spouse acceded to her wishes. Carl made arrangements to have the yacht shipped back to Indianapolis on a flatcar.

Here, fate intervened. Railroad officials informed Carl at the last minute that a bridge along the route was too low to accommodate the vessel. The boat would have to be moved in some other manner. Had the bridge been a few feet higher, Fisher might never have discovered South Florida, and the fate of Miami Beach could have been considerably different.[5]

Fisher recruited a shipmate, John H. Levi, to take care of the boat. Levi agreed to captain the boat around the Florida Keys and up the East

Coast to Jacksonville. Carl and Jane returned to Indianapolis in the dead of winter, then waited for word about the yacht. Almost two weeks later, a cryptic message came by telegram: ARRIVED SAFELY. MIAMI PRETTY LITTLE TOWN. WHY NOT MEET ME HERE INSTEAD OF JACKSONVILLE? JOHN. The couple was more than willing to escape the cold and dreariness of winter in Indiana so they caught a train to Miami. Jane recalled that they pulled into a "dirty, drab Florida East Coast railroad station" on a beautiful February morning in 1910. They fell in love with the soft, warm air and "jasmine-scented Miami moonlight."[6] Always decisive and occasionally impulsive, Carl immediately bought two lots on Biscayne Bay, where he and Jane would build a winter home. As John Levi had promised, the *Eph* was safely docked in the harbor, and the couple jumped aboard to familiarize themselves with the waterways in and around Miami.

Miami was a relatively new and inconsequential town then, having been incorporated only fourteen years earlier, and its population in 1910 was just under 10,000. The east coast of Florida, however, had a lengthy and interesting history of Spanish discovery and rapid conquest, long-term neglect, rediscovery in the late nineteenth century, and tentative development from that time forward. As many schoolchildren know, Spanish explorer Ponce de Leon sailed the east coast of Florida in search of gold, spices, and other riches, including the fabled Fountain of Youth. The year was 1513, almost 400 years before the Fishers' visit.[7] At the time, the area where Miami would later be settled looked unpromising to the Spaniards, who settled in St. Augustine, 300 miles farther north. The Miami area was occupied occasionally by a semino-madic tribe named the Tequesta by the Spanish. The Tequesta did not survive for long, wiped out by imported Spanish diseases.[8] The Spanish made numerous unsuccessful, and usually bloody, attempts to settle along both the Atlantic and Gulf Coasts of South Florida in the sixteenth century. According to Charles E. Nash, historian of early Miami Beach, the French had somewhat more success settling Florida because they made friends with Indians rather than attempt to subjugate them. The French monarchy never felt sufficient interest in the region to make any significant commitment there.[9]

Although the region experienced several transfers of ownership, involving the Spanish, English, and the United States over the next 350 years, Florida experienced little additional white settlement until the mid-nineteenth century. Henry M. Flagler became a major force in developing Florida. One of his biographers argued that "Florida had been and remained until well after the Civil War the last frontier area east of the great [Mississippi] river."[10] Flagler, a powerful lawyer and one of the architects of John D. Rockefeller's innovative corporate structure, had "retired" from the petroleum business in the mid-1880s and moved to St. Augustine.[11] A wealthy man in his own right, Flagler immediately perceived Florida's potential for tourism, and he constructed several large hotels along the state's east coast. He intended to convert St. Augustine into the "Newport of the South." The fabulous Ponce de Leon Hotel, at the time the largest concrete structure in the world, opened in St. Augustine in 1888.[12] The resort attracted thousands of chilled northern aristocrats and socially ambitious parvenus.

By the late 1890s, the trip south was far easier than it had been a decade earlier. In the early 1880s, visitors had to travel largely over water. A decade later, Flagler had connected most of the east coast of Florida to the North by railroad lines. St. Augustine, however, had its drawbacks as a tourist mecca, most often weather. It was far enough north that winter often brought nippy temperatures, and citrus orchards located just a few miles inland experienced frequent, devastating freezes. Flagler, ever the shrewd entrepreneur, encouraged farmers to grow crops which his railroads could transport north; however, frosts regularly cut severely into freight tonnage in the 1880s. Thus Flagler began promoting tourism and agricultural development farther south along the coast. In the early 1890s he touted Palm Beach as the "Queen of Winter Resorts." His anchor in Palm Beach, the Royal Poinciana, opened in 1894 and was both the largest hotel and the largest wooden structure in the world. Six stories high, with several wings, the luxurious facility contained over a thousand rooms and was electrified throughout.[13]

Flagler was also the most influential businessman during Miami's initial burst of development. By the early 1890s, he had determined to extend his East Coast Lines railroad all the way to Key West. Flagler sensed

Miami's tourist potential; farther south than Palm Beach, it might be slightly warmer in the winter. Even better, it was almost totally undeveloped. When Flagler's railroad line into Miami opened on April 21, 1896, it had a population of 300; the city officially incorporated three months later. Flagler opened the first of two hotels in Miami, the Royal Palm, on Christmas Day 1896. In addition to railroads and hotels, Flagler invested in many city services, including its first hospital, the waterworks, and Miami Electric Light and Power.[14]

The town Carl and Jane Fisher visited in 1910 was evolving quickly as a center of tourism. During the winter of 1910, local hotels hosted over 100,000 patrons.[15] Miami Beach, however, was nonexistent. Looking east across Biscayne Bay in 1910, residents of Miami viewed an uninviting sight: a long, low tangle of mangrove swamp. Beach areas north and south of Miami were attractive but difficult to reach. There had been little commercial beach development. For most of the nineteenth century, the handful of settlers along beachfront areas of South Florida had made their livings salvaging wreckage from ships that went aground offshore. Beginning in the 1870s the federal government established several refuge houses along the coast to aid shipwreck victims. The first actual structure in what became Miami Beach was a refuge house, opened in 1883. Most of the earliest dwellings were built with salvaged ships' timbers, which could later be covered with shingles and various sidings that were shipped in.[16] One of the most notable events in the area's early history was the wreck of a vessel containing a huge wine shipment in November 1886. Perhaps anticipating the entrepreneurial spirit of the bootleggers who would swarm the same beaches forty years later, refuge house manager John Peacock rescued thousands of bottles of the precious fluid. Finders were allowed to keep the spoils.[17]

Thirty years before the Fishers' arrival, other pioneers perceived that the sandy soil adjoining the mangrove islands had agricultural potential. Henry Lum was the first farmer known to have planted crops, and his son Charles allegedly built the first house on the land that later became Miami Beach.[18] The elder Lum and his family arrived in the area in 1882 with hopes of raising coconut trees and exporting the product to northern consumers. It was a fine concept except for two critical flaws. First, the soil generally resisted Lum's trees. Second, getting coconuts to market proved far more difficult and expensive than Lum anticipated. Until Flagler's rail line connected Miami to the North, the coconuts had to be shipped by boat. Even after rail lines opened, getting the product across the bay to railroad loading platforms was difficult. The Lum family sensed the land's commercial possibilities, but others had more impact on development of the region.

Even though they never met, Fisher revered Flagler and later erected a statue in his honor. Lum's business activities were also concluded by the time Fisher arrived in South Florida. The energetic Hoosier, however, had extensive dealings with several other regional pioneers.

Few individuals exerted more influence on the early evolution of Miami Beach than John Collins. Born in 1837, Collins was a New Jersey Quaker, a successful farmer, and a founder of the Garden State's horticultural society. He was already wealthy when he arrived in Florida in the mid-1890s, but he sought both a warmer winter climate and interesting challenges. Collins was in his late fifties when he first arrived, and he dabbled in several Florida investments, including pears and coconuts, before deciding to concentrate on avocados. He guessed that affluent Americans were developing a marked appetite for this exotic fruit.

By 1907, at age seventy, Collins owned a narrow, five-mile-long strip of land between Biscayne Bay and the Atlantic Ocean. Younger family members in New Jersey came to Miami to check out the patriarch's investment and returned home shaking their heads. Collins's vision would be extremely difficult to effect. First, the land, for which he had paid about $2 per acre, was overgrown with pine and palmetto trees; it cost $300 per acre just to clear it by hand labor for planting. Collins had experience with large farm implements, and he rigged up more than a dozen heavy tractors outfitted with knife-bladed wheels to hack through the pine roots. This innovation allegedly reduced clearing costs by 90 percent. Planting, nurturing, and harvesting avocados was even more challenging. The delicate trees had to be "shipped, planted, wrapped in burlap to protect them from the ocean spray, watered by a system of wells and pumps and sheltered from wind by hand-planted shelter belts of Australian pine."[19] When his trees began yielding fruit, shipping and storing the crop presented additional challenges. Getting his harvest into Miami, where it could be sent north on Flagler's railroad, was a monumental task because heavily laden farm boats kept getting tangled in the pesky turtlegrass flats of North Bay. By 1911 Collins was fully committed to avocados, but the project was hemorrhaging money. Now he insisted to family members that tens of thousands of dollars be spent on dredging a canal, which could cut the distance from the farm to Miami by half.

Collins and his wife had three sons, Arthur, Irving, and Lester, and a daughter, Katherine. The children and their spouses were deeply involved in the family enterprises. As John Collins diverted increasing amounts of the family's assets into growing avocados, his children insisted on finding out more details of where the family's fortune was going. The old man's will would prevail; it was, after all, his money. But the children hoped to rein him in somewhat. Being devout Quakers, they could not imagine where their father had acquired his gambling spirit. They planned a return visit to Miami in 1911, a year after Carl Fisher had first seen it.

Who had the initial vision of the potential of Miami Beach as a prominent resort area? Was it Carl Fisher or one or more members of the Collins family? Evidence strongly suggests the latter. As longtime residents of New Jersey, the Collinses were familiar with several of the successful late nineteenth-century resort towns along the state's coast. During their visit to Miami in 1911, the children evidently came to the conclusion that though the farm might eventually break even, the beachfront property had far more potential as a seaside resort. Collectively, they confronted John Collins and explained their alternative vision. The old man listened, then supposedly replied, "Yes, it might make another Atlantic City at that."[20] They agreed that John Collins would continue to operate and manage the farm and that the younger generation would establish a real estate company and develop and sell land. Irving, Arthur, and Lester Collins, and Katherine and Thomas Pancoast established the Miami Beach Improvement Company. Their commitment to this enterprise moved the center of family operations from New Jersey to Florida, although it is inconceivable that any of them could have imagined the impact they and other like-minded developers would exert on one of the nation's foremost future playgrounds.

Back across the bay, Miami may have been a sparsely settled small town in terms of permanent residents, but its population swelled with approximately 10,000 tourists in the winter of 1911; most visitors spent only a few days, but some stayed for months. Moreover, enthusiastic boosters of the town had immodest ambitions. Miami residents enjoyed some of the finer things in life: parks and libraries, tearooms and restaurants. They could see movies at the Elite Theater, "air-conditioned" in the summertime by fans blowing air across blocks of ice. But Miamians could not easily find an escape from the heat at the beach because little beach space was easily accessible. For a generation, businessmen had been developing a harbor on the Miami side of Biscayne Bay; commercial development quickly consumed what little natural beachfront the locals had once enjoyed. The big ships inside the bay discharged oil and fuel residue, making recreational use of the harbor less attractive. In addition, dredging equipment used to keep one or more channels open for seagoing vessels further polluted the water, as had efforts to drain nearby Everglades swamps. Muck-filled water from the latter effort flowed past the ship ways and docks. From the spattered, oily docks on the Miami side of the bay, the closest sights were mostly derelict warehouses and seedy commercial establishments.[21] When Carl and Jane Fisher arrived, the harbor was not a pretty sight.

A few small-time local businessmen had made modest efforts to provide access to sea breezes and recreation at nearby waterfront locations. Polly Redford noted that locals could enjoy the ocean if they made a determined effort. They first had to journey to the Miami Beach side of the bay, usually by one of Biscayne Navigation's ferries. "Just north of the ship channel a couple of bathhouses, grandly called casinos, had sprung up on the oceanfront, and a long rickety boardwalk had been nailed across the mangrove roots to a small dock on the bayside." The boardwalk offered access to "fairyland," free to ferry patrons and costing twenty-five cents to those who had provided their own transportation across the bay. For an additional fee, patrons could rent shapeless, itchy wool bathing suits for the day. Redford called the casinos "the beginning of the pleasure industry in Miami Beach."[22]

Considering the work already done by Henry Flagler not far north of Miami and the shortage of leisure-related amenities in a region noted for its balmy winter temperatures, it is hardly surprising that the Collins and Pancoast families sensed the potential to develop resorts in the area.[23]

John Collins masterminded and ramrodded the next link in the development of Miami Beach. By 1910, the automobile was quickly emerging as Americans' preferred mode of ground transportation.[24] Ironically, it was the oldest member of the Collins clan who sensed that if Miami Beach was ever to become a viable resort community, access to the mainland by automobile was of critical importance. An automobile bridge crossing two and a half miles of open water was needed. Collins determined that he would build it.

When rumors of Collins's bridge project surfaced, he encountered immediate opposition. The Biscayne Navigation Company, which provided ferry service across the bay, complained that its business would be ruined. The company initially convinced the county commission to deny Collins the required permits, but Collins gained the support of one of Miami's most influential lawyers. Frank Shutts had paved the way for Flagler's entry into the city, and he owned Miami's morning newspaper. It helped that John Collins had an instinct for showmanship. He drove his car to the ferry pier and demanded transportation for both himself and his vehicle across the bay. Ferry officials protested that their vessels were designed only for pedestrians. Shutts's reporters ridiculed the ferry operators. Collins had made his point; without "automobile service" by the company, he was being denied "full use" of his land across the bay.[25]

Collins finally received permission to build the bridge in May 1912.[26] If he succeeded, it would be the longest wooden bridge in the world. In principle the project appeared easy enough because the bay was relatively shallow. Heavy timber supporting twenty-four-foot planks would provide a two-lane road. But there were daunting obstacles. Foot-thick logs used for supports would only last for two years in saltwater. A bridge constructed with unprotected wooden supports would be under repair so often and in so many different places that it would be virtually useless. The wooden supports had to be protected, and concrete piling had not yet been invented. To meet this challenge, Collins devised a multistep solution. His construction team first riveted iron "jackets" into cylinders, which were lowered into the water. Next, the wooden logs were inserted into the cylinders. Finally, concrete was poured into the cylinders to fill in the open spaces between the wood and iron.

Once construction commenced in the late spring of 1912, the chief problem was financial. Building costs far exceeded the family's original estimates. Costs of the "iron coating" process for protecting the wooden beams greatly exceeded estimates. The completed structure would require more than the 2,000 sets of iron-encased pilings originally planned. Costs per mile soon reached $50,000. As Polly Redford noted, "Straining their credit in Miami and New Jersey to the limit, Collins and his family were able to spend six months and 100,000 1912 dollars on their bridge, only to run out of money less than half a mile short of the Beach. In November 1912 there she lay: the world's longest vehicular bridge leading nowhere."[27]

Carl Fisher entered the picture at this critical juncture, having recently decided to establish wintertime roots in South Florida. He and Jane had first visited Miami Beach more than two and a half years earlier. During their initial visit, they stayed for only a week, but warm days and cool nights, the smell of flowers in the air, and the strong whiff of future prospects convinced Fisher to make a deeper commitment. The entrepreneur from Indiana often made his important decisions, even those with long-range implications, on gut instinct. Snap decisions did not faze him in the least. Fisher had acquired two lots, and not long after they departed for the North, he purchased sight unseen a lovely winter home on Miami's Brickell Avenue which he had seen advertised in a brochure. They bought the house from Alonso Bliss, who had made a fortune in herbal medicines and real estate.[28] Since the structure was shaded by tall trees, they named it Shadows.

Carl was exceedingly busy with affairs in the North for most of the year. During these years, he was negotiating to sell Prest-O-Lite, organizing the Indianapolis 500 automobile race, and founding the Lincoln Highway Association. Nevertheless, in 1911 and 1912, he and Jane made time to spend several weeks in Miami each season. Jane was still a teenager, and everything was new to her. She was thrilled to be married to a wealthy man, and she loved the high life in Miami. Luncheons, teas, parties, and planning for both her husband's and her own social gatherings at the Shadows occupied Jane's days. One guest at a luncheon arranged by the youthful hostess in 1915 described an elegant dining room setting, "darkened, and candles with silver and pink shades . . . everyone had a rose for a favor." She stated that Carl had dropped in and that she liked him "very much."[29] Undoubtedly, he didn't stay long. Although he could easily afford it, a life of repose, with long, leisurely lunches would never suit Carl.

When Fisher and James Allison sold Prest-O-Lite and took their millions, Fisher undoubtedly chuckled over his partner's intention of becoming "the goddamnedest laziest man in the whole goddamned universe."[30] He probably verbalized similar sentiments to Jane, but he was constitutionally incapable of indulging in sheer play, disconnected from any business interest. If he and Jane were going to spend weeks each year in Miami, Fisher knew that he would be unhappy if he lay on the beach and dabbled in recreation. Work was his tonic; he had to find something meaningful to do.

As it turned out, he met John Collins; the Fisher, Collins, and Pancoast families established intimate business connections that profoundly influenced the development of Miami Beach. On the surface, the pairing appeared strange. Fisher was breezy, flamboyant, aggressive, an impulsive gambler, and a casually profane man who seldom entered a church willingly. His associates were devout Quakers; in addition, they were generally soft-spoken, conservative, and deliberate in reaching business decisions. The Collins and Pancoast men immediately sensed Fisher's magnetism, however, and they quickly developed a deep respect for his rock-solid integrity. For decades, the parties routinely conducted business with only a handshake as a bond.[31]

Accounts differ as to how Fisher and John Collins met and who initiated their business connection. Jane offered two significantly different accounts, essentially attributing their association to Fisher's admiration of the older man's grit, plus Carl's innate generosity. According to Jane, she and Carl were casually exploring the backwaters and estuaries serving Biscayne Bay in a power boat, accompanied by his associate John Levi (a future mayor of Miami). They were somewhere in Indian Creek, out of sight of the bay, when they encountered the startling sight of an impeccably dressed, wiry septuagenarian standing on the shore, far out in the "wilderness." In Jane's words, "Fisher asked Collins for directions back to the Bay, and a conversation developed." Earlier, Fisher had seen the unfinished bridge, named "Collins's Folly" by some unsympathetic locals. Collins put a brave face on his predicament, but Fisher learned that he was near the end of his rope. His avocado crop was rotting on the trees, and his chances of finishing the bridge appeared unpromising. The planks in place covering the completed section were already warping under the relentless sun and salt spray.

By Jane's account, when they returned to the Shadows, her husband was bubbling with enthusiasm over their encounter with Collins. "Carl came back after meeting John Collins in one of his eager and excited moods. He walked the floor, talking. 'Why, that little Quaker is the bravest man I ever met, Jane. Imagine starting a gigantic project like that bridge at seventy-five—an age when most men are ready to sit down and die! And the sweetest, cleanest, finest person, Jane.' I listened, recognizing the symptoms. 'What are you going to do about him, dear?' I asked, and Carl said firmly, 'I'm going to help John Collins.'"[32] Fisher's help took the form of a $50,000 loan, which Collins secured by giving Fisher title to approximately 200 acres of land on the ocean side of Biscayne Bay. This was how Carl got started in Miami Beach.

Two decades after Jane's account was published, Polly Redford was researching her history of Miami Beach, and she interviewed Jane Fisher in 1967. Jane's verbal recollection of their meeting with Collins was somewhat different. They were lost somewhere in Indian Creek when they saw Collins: "There stood a little man. He was a very short man. He had a white beard—it was a white goatee—and the whitest shirt and the bluest suit that I have ever seen. He wore a bow tie, a polka-dot blue and white tie. It impressed me to see a man so immaculately dressed standing amidst all this wild territory." Fisher asked Collins for directions back to the bay, and Collins responded, in his distinctive Quaker manner. "My husband thanked him and did not ask his name: neither did the little man. We did as he suggested, and found ourselves back in Biscayne Bay and back home and didn't even talk about our encounter with this gentleman."[33]

Jane's conflicting accounts of their first encounter vary in comparatively minor ways. Fisher's hookup with John Collins was undoubtedly the catalyst for his initial involvement in developing Miami Beach. More than likely, others assisted in forming their partnership. Frank Shutts, the newspaper owner who had helped Collins gain permits to build the bridge, undoubtedly felt more than a little responsibility for seeing the project finished. Shutts had a high profile in Miami; like any power broker, he had influential friends, plus critics who would enjoy seeing him embarrassed. That some cynics were calling the unfinished bridge "Collins' Folly" must have rankled him; he obviously had a personal stake in helping Collins.

Like Fisher, Shutts also had Indiana roots, and he had undoubtedly known of Fisher's exploits long before his fellow Hoosier arrived in Miami. Shutts's professional training as a newspaper man led him to probe any prominent new arrival's daily activities and future plans. In another segment of her extensive oral history interview with Polly Redford, Jane Fisher stated that although Fisher had not mentioned helping Collins at the time of their initial meeting, he visited with Shutts about a week later. Jane identified Shutts as the instigator of Fisher's notion of loaning $50,000 to Collins.[34]

After Miami Beach became one of the most renowned playgrounds in the world, Fisher often received acclaim as its premier developer, even its founding father. Fisher, after all, bailed out Collins when apparently nobody else would put up the money. Without the bridge, Miami Beach might never have been built, or so such reasoning went. Others resented such emphasis on finishing the bridge, most notably the Lummus brothers, who loaned Collins the much larger sum he needed to begin building the bridge. They, too, were pioneers in Miami and, later, Miami Beach. J. N. (John) Lummus was a native of Bronson, Florida, where he had been a railroad telegrapher. He came to Miami in 1895, and once Flagler's line was opened, he worked as a train dispatcher between 1896 and 1902. He immediately sensed the area's potential and entered the banking profession early in the new century. His brother J. E. (James) Lummus arrived in Miami a year later and opened a general merchandise store, which he owned until 1908. When Flagler extended his railroad line toward Key West, J. E. won a commissary contract, yielding sufficient profits for him to organize another bank. The brothers joined forces and entered the title abstract business, then founded yet another bank in 1911. They were up-and-coming businessmen in Miami in the early 1910s who also sensed the region's potential. The Lummus brothers platted land in what became Miami Beach *before either Fisher or the Collins-Pancoast families did so*. They purchased 600 acres at the south end of the beach; they, too, were destined to be major players in the area's development.[35]

Jane's biography breathlessly claimed that Carl provided the inspiration for Miami Beach. She noted that in return for his $50,000 loan, Collins gave Fisher bridge bonds and a strip of land 1,800 feet wide, running from Biscayne Bay to the Atlantic. In addition, Fisher purchased another 260 acres. Shortly after they met Collins, Carl took Jane over to the property. "No one knew why Carl wanted this ribbon of swamp. . . . When later we went by boat to inspect the new property, I protested. We walked, stepping gingerly and slapping at mosquitoes. . . . An old alligator roared its resentment at our invasion of [its] age-old jungle. Mosquitoes blackened our white clothing. Jungle flies as large as horse flies, wanted for our blood. . . . I can recall how disgruntled I was. . . . I refused to find any charm in this deserted strip of ugly land. . . . But Carl was like a man seeing visions." Taking a stick and drawing lines in the sand, Carl bubbled, "Look, honey, I'm going to build a city here! A city like magic, like romantic places you read about and dream about, but never see. It's going to be a place where the old can grow young, and the young never grow old—the sort of place Ponce de Leon dreamed about."[36]

By Jane's published account, her husband laid out his "vision" for Miami Beach in November 1912. Still, the concept of Miami Beach's dazzling future, either as a residential area or a glittering resort, was not original with Fisher. When John Collins announced plans to build his bridge, several businessmen started speculating on property on the east side of the bay. When he received his permit from the county, more speculators entered the bidding, and once work commenced, a trickle of investors became a stream. In May 1912, six months before Carl's alleged "vision," the real estate firm of Bendle and Anderson promoted its lots by claiming in a newspaper advertisement that Miami Beach was "destined to become . . . a year round residence section and winter play ground for the multitudes."[37] On August 18, 1912, the *Miami Herald* crooned, "Five years from now—that is the maximum mind you—there will be an East Miami . . . with paved roads running up and down a perfect beach, then will homeseekers and investors grab at a chance to secure holdings in a place so ideally located."[38]

If Miami Beach's destiny as one of the nation's premier resort communities appears obvious even to casual observers today, there were many doubters ninety years ago. They had excellent reasons for negativism. Most of the area was shifting sand and mangrove swamps. The swamps were infested with unpleasant and sometimes dangerous animals. Worst of all were the mosquitoes. Jane Fisher's experience was shared by the early pioneers in the area. When the Pancoasts built one of the first homes there, they hoped that indoor living would provide relief from the pests, but Russell Pancoast recalled: "The mosquitoes were beyond belief. Also the sand flies were bad, and if anyone went into the house, they were sprayed immediately after they came through the screen door—which always opened out instead of opening in. . . . Then, after you sprayed yourself and the mosquitoes, you were able to go through the rest of the house."[39]

Thus in the late fall of 1912, Miami Beach was still a distant vision. Biographers and historians might debate about who was the most farsighted and made the most critical initial commitments, but all were united by the vision of booming real estate. A few investors, including Fisher, perceived its potential as a resort community. The majority probably hoped to turn a quick profit by selling off lots for modest single-family homes. When Carl Fisher knelt in the sand and drew a rough outline of "his" future city, trying to interest his mosquito-covered wife in the area's potential, he initially envisioned a town dominated by small houses and perhaps a hotel or two. He had little inkling of the size and difficulty of the challenge of turning his vague dreams into reality. Once committed to the concept of building a city out of the sand late in 1912, however, Fisher devoted much of his prodigious energy and risked millions of dollars to realizing that vision over the next two decades.

Morning Sun

Just what Carl Fisher imagined doing with his property on the east side of Biscayne Bay when he acquired it late in 1912 remains unclear. The only certainty is that he greatly underestimated the task before him even to create land that was salable at any price. Some sandy areas were wholly out of the water, but much of the property was muck and mangrove forests at or just below sea level. If he had visions of fancy hotels and sumptuous winter homes, such as those gracing established resorts farther north on the Florida coast, he apparently shared them only with Jane. Back home in Indianapolis, Carl informed a few friends and associates that he would spend about $75,000 developing a winter resort. They could get in on the ground floor if they were interested. Few cautious Hoosiers bought Carl's real estate. They undoubtedly slapped him on the back, wished him luck, and promptly forgot his invitation.

Evidently, Fisher initially imagined building an attractive community containing relatively modest, single-family homes, plus a few small hotels to accommodate guests. Creating and developing land at Miami Beach, however, quickly evolved into a massive, enormously expensive commitment. Miami Beach did not explode onto the nation's consciousness as a fabulous resort area until the early 1920s, fully ten years after Fisher and a few other like-minded promoters began serious work on it. For years, expenses mounted, while revenues lagged far behind. As red ink flowed, Carl gradually raised the stakes, and at the end of World War I his vision of a resort community crystallized. When Fisher became a nationally acclaimed resort impresario in the mid-1920s, the uninitiated assumed that fortune had fallen easily into his lap. Few had any inkling of the sometimes desperate decade-long struggle that preceded the reaping of profits. To understand Miami Beach and the Jazz Age fully, one must have a grasp of the lean years immediately preceding.

When Fisher first announced plans to develop property that was then under water, many residents of Miami thought he was losing his mind. When Collins started building his bridge in the summer of 1912 there was some interest in his family's Miami Beach Improvement Company property and the Lummus brothers' Ocean Beach lots. At least they owned solid land, above sea level. Creating hundreds of acres of new property out of sand seemed preposterous to many. Miamians probably thought his nickname, "Crazy Carl," was well chosen. As one of them put it, "Do you have to be a damned fool to make money? A fellow named Carl Fisher is pumping tons of sand into a swamp when there are already millions of solid acres in Florida nobody is using."[1]

Controversy arose over who deserves credit as the true founder of Miami Beach. Since they began their initiatives before Fisher got started, the Collins and Pancoast families could lay a legitimate claim, as could the Lummus brothers. As Polly Redford observed, "Fisher partisans . . . always said that who got there first is of no importance compared to who *did* the most."[2] To the renowned humorist Will Rogers, it was no contest; Carl Fisher had "done more novel things, even before he ever heard of Florida, than any man I ever met . . . [he] rehearsed the mosquitoes 'till they wouldn't bite you until after you bought.'"[3]

All three claims have merit, but in late 1912 and early 1913, the developers shared a vision of the area's future and had enormous incentive to coordinate efforts rather than bicker. To a remarkable extent, they did just that. Before large-scale dredging of Biscayne Bay could begin, they needed authorization from both the state of Florida and the Army Corps of Engineers. There was no environmental controversy because there was virtually no sense ninety years ago that mangrove swamps and coral reefs would ever be in short supply. The state was happy to have private developers undertake dredging operations that at a later date taxpayers might demand be performed at public expense. In arranging permits, Fisher cooperated with the other developers in sharing lobbying and legal expenses. He was justifiably confident that the Army Corps of Engineers would approve the project; contracts for dredging operations were let a week before J. N. Lummus and Frank Shutts's law partner, Crate Bowen, returned from Washington with permits in hand.

Dredging began in the early summer of 1913, shortly before John Collins finished building his bridge. On June 12, there was a grand opening celebration of the structure. Local politicians and other dignitaries made appropriate remarks, and a cavalcade of cars rattled two and a half miles across the bridge from Miami and then turned around and drove back. Fisher could not attend; he was far away in Indianapolis, organizing the initial Hoosier caravan cross-country automobile tour.

As he contemplated the task before him, Fisher quickly sensed that he would have to increase his investment. Early in 1913 he scuttled his original $75,000 estimate and announced that he would spend two years and $250,000 to create land. Within weeks, he revised that estimate upward. Fisher and his partners planned to generate 6 million cubic yards of fill to create new property. They would eventually dredge a basin 12 feet deep, 1,500 feet wide, and almost two miles long. While he was up north, concentrating on the Lincoln Highway and Indianapolis 500 concerns, Fisher left his trusted associate John Levi in charge of the crews and machinery.

Although no rival to the Panama Canal, which was nearing completion in the summer of 1913 and would open the next year, dredging in Biscayne Bay was an incredibly difficult, frustrating task. The engineering challenge was basic: clearing mangrove trees and other forms of vegetation, moving sand and rock, and shaping the new "fill" into solid land. Much of the work was appallingly difficult manual labor. Levi hired gangs of black laborers to clear the mangrove trees by hand. It seemed that every physical element conspired against them. Mangrove trees look innocuous enough from a distance: lush, low, very green. But each tree contained dozens of thick, iron-tough roots sinking into the water or sand. The men usually worked in knee-deep water, hacking out trees with

Many Floridians thought Fisher was crazy for spending millions of dollars in the 1910s to create land near Miami when so much of what already existed had not been sold. Courtesy of the Historical Museum of Southern Florida.

machetes. Levi's initial schedule of two-hour shifts followed by ten-minute breaks quickly exhausted even the strongest men.

Other factors compounded the challenge. The clearing of mangrove trees began in the summer, when the heat and humidity were oppressive. Pests and potentially dangerous predators made difficult work even harder. Crocodiles were never a problem because noise and heavy machinery quickly drove them to quieter waters, but workers feared them and were always on guard. Poisonous snakes were an infrequent presence, but a few men were bitten. Worst of all were the mosquitoes and sand flies, absent only when strong breezes blew. When the air was still, workers' light-colored shirts were often blackened by the swarms. Job foremen finally introduced smudge pots and built bonfires of dried palmetto leaves, which helped control the mosquitoes, but the smoke irritated eyes, lungs, and nostrils.

What made Levi's (and presumably Fisher's) decision to use hand labor to clear the land mystifying is that, by some accounts, several years earlier John Collins had developed a far easier, faster, and less expensive way of clearing land. He had ordered two sixteen-ton, thirty-five-horsepower tractors fitted with special knife-bladed wheels. According to Charles E. Nash, "The knives chopped up the buried scrub palmetto roots that had been giving so much trouble. Special gang-plows brought them to the surface and permitted their quick removal. The cost of clearing was reduced to about $30 an acre, for the tractor did more work in a day than fifty men."[4]

Finishing the job required changes. Clearing mangrove trees down to the roots by hand was both slow and ruinously expensive. Levi and his foremen decided to cut some corners, limiting mangrove clearing to the branches themselves. They left about a foot or two of roots above the water line. They figured that dredges could cover the roots with heavy sludge, which would subsequently be reshaped into usable land and reinforced after it dried out.

Another critical task was building a permanent shoreline. Florida residents living on beachfront property had learned the hard way that sand often shifted rapidly; what appeared to be firm soil well back of the shoreline might be covered by water a few months later. Fisher and his associates decided, therefore, to concentrate first on developing land on the bay side rather than areas facing the ocean. Levi's men dredged coral and muck from the bottom, creating mounds on the shoreline. Next, pile drivers drove rows of wooden timbers into the ground, forming a bulkhead shoreline that was reinforced with steel cables.

The reshaping of the bay was slow and expensive. Three huge dredges scooped fill from the bay and poured it into desired locations. The largest of the dredges was powered by a 1,000-horsepower engine and could move 20,000 cubic yards of fill in twenty-four hours.[5] The work was slow because the sludge that was dredged, then forced through mile-long pipes by pressure and poured into required locations, was a watery mixture of lime deposits, sand, and water which, according to one source, was about the consistency and color of Cream of Wheat. The workers called it "soup." It took at least a week, often longer, for the substance to congeal to the point that it could support any significant weight. The "soup" was also full of marine life that rotted and then dried. On one occasion, a working mule plunged into the "soup" and died, adding to the stench. Workers and passersby were swathed in ungodly smells. Six more months were required for the sun and rain to complete the "sweetening" process.[6] Only then could the new land be developed.

The newly formed land looked strange. Wholly barren of vegetation after it dried, the hardpan was extremely light in color. In bright sunlight, the surface produced a strong glare, almost like mountain snow. The surface stood about five feet above water level at high tide. The built-up area looked somewhat like a giant flattened angel food cake. When the winds blew, sand clouds hung over it, stinging the faces of nearby boaters, fishermen, and swimmers.[7]

During the first summer of work, Fisher was seldom on hand. Following the Hoosier cavalcade trip west, he managed a quick August visit south to check on progress. Levi remained in charge of day-to-day operations. But Fisher was appalled at the cost of the process and desperately sought money-saving innovations. He had revised cost estimates for preparing land upward several times but was still unprepared for the huge bills pouring into his offices. Jane later claimed that expenses mounted to $50,000 a day![8] Her figure was undoubtedly an exaggeration, but expenses spiraled upward.[9]

Fisher had originally planned to build a sea wall and provide landfill for about 200 acres, but the job was quickly expanding in scope and difficulty. Friends like James Allison assessed the project and begged him to stop. They were afraid the project would literally suck up his entire fortune. At times, Fisher shared their fear. In the words of one Miami Beach historian, "As the operation siphoned $50,000 a day from his fortune, he shouted 'Goddamn!' incessantly. The man who had completed five grades of school was circumscribed in his vocabulary, and 'goddamn!' had to serve a host of disparate enthusiasms."[10] Despite his financial worries, Carl occasionally injected a note of capriciousness and fun into his work. To move men and material along the developing shoreline, Fisher constructed a railroad about a mile in length. He then printed lifetime passes and, as a joke, sent them to presidents of numerous major lines. He was amused and delighted when several recipients reciprocated.[11]

Absentee management of his project wouldn't do over the long term. Carl returned to Miami in the fall of 1913 ready to plunge back into the development work full-time. There were, Jane recalled, some desperate times, and she, too, feared that the doubters were right. "'Crazy Carl Fisher' were words I heard again. It did seem mad to pour a fortune into making more Florida land, when so much was already going to waste. The jungle itself seemed to protest in every possible way against this intrusion by man. Malaria, mosquitoes and lack of water fought invasion. But Carl had started something, and it was not easy for him to give it up."[12]

What probably kept Fisher going was that there were some satisfying triumphs and thrilling moments. During one trip to Indianapolis, he bemoaned his inability to clear mangroves efficiently. Either he had not yet talked to Collins about his problem or he had tried Collins's tractors and found them wanting. One morning an old friend, Al Webb, dropped by Fisher's office. Webb was a mechanic who had raced cars with Fisher a decade earlier. As Carl laid out his problem, Webb replied, "It's a funny coincidence, but I've been working on a plow to clear some land I have on the West Coast." Fisher had an inspiration. "Build one for me, Al. The biggest plow you can build." A few weeks later Webb shipped a huge contraption to Miami. It was so large and heavy that a special barge was needed to move it across the bay to the job site. Webb came down himself to operate the plow. Fisher watched him start it up. "The three-cornered blade slipped down into the land and ripped up the tough little palmettos as if they were ferns. Under the heaving palmettos the upturned land fairly boiled. Carl was on his feet whooping, 'Look at 'em boil, Al, look at 'em boil!'" He ran along beside the tractor like an excited boy. 'Boil, you goddamn roots, boil!'" According to Jane, the tired workers joined in jubilant chorus: "Boil, ol' roots, white man say boil."[13]

The plow was an important innovation; it cleared ten acres per day, saving thousands of man-hours of labor. The mangrove tree problem remained, but Webb helped solve that one too. He wrapped a long steel chain around dozens of mangrove trees, then attached the chain to his plow. "Their trunks snapped with a sound like machine-gun fire as the matted mangroves gave. All at last was cleared."[14] The workers were supposedly just as thrilled as their boss was. According to Jane, he took time to get to know them. He talked to everybody, and he was a good listener. Jane concluded, "Men respected Jim Allison, but they loved Carl. . . . Carl's praise, so softly spoken, would move mountains."[15]

For many tasks, such as landscaping and building hotels, golf courses, tennis courts, and polo fields, he needed skilled architects, designers, and managers. Fisher had a dynamic, engaging personality and was working on big, exciting projects; therefore, ambitious and imaginative men found working in his orbit very stimulating. Although some of his designers and managers had egos exceeding their talents, Fisher attracted some very talented individuals who worked for him for many years.

His greater need was for hundreds of manual laborers, most of whom had limited contact with Fisher himself. His wife somewhat exaggerated Carl's rapport with laborers. In the second decade of the twentieth century, management and labor were in almost constant conflict. In dealing with large numbers of manual workers, Fisher was affected by the same labor problems plaguing employers across the United States. World War I brought severe inflation. Prices doubled between 1914 and 1920, but wages increased only 60 percent. Workers saw big industrialists reaping huge wartime profits even after they pledged not to strike during the duration of the conflict. They were understandably restive and wanted their share. Management, by contrast, sensed it had gained the upper hand over workers and was determined to maintain its dominance. The postwar period ushered in a period of severe labor unrest at the national level, involving vicious suppression of organized labor during the infamous Red Scare of 1919.[16]

Fisher was a notorious "soft touch"; the lucky worker who attracted his personal attention with a particularly effective sob story might reap a windfall. He bailed more than one employee out of a severe financial jam. Obviously, Carl could not personally attend to the needs of hundreds of men; he had to leave day-to-day management of workers to his foremen, many of whom were far more callused than he was. Much as it pained Fisher personally, mutual distrust sometimes marred relationships between his managers and some workers during the building years in Miami Beach. In a letter to Fisher in September 1919, one of his real estate salesmen, Harry S. Bastain, assessed the local labor situation in very negative terms. Craftsmen were demanding higher wages in Miami Beach than in Miami. Plumbers charged $8 per day in Miami, $8.50 plus carfare in Miami Beach. The differential was small, but it was irritating. In addition, Bastain claimed that on one building job, plumbers charged

$10 per day for a "boss plumber" whose contributions to the task were negligible. Bastain informed his boss that many of the influential business leaders in Miami were determined to head an aggressive campaign to convert Miami to an open-shop town. They would commence their efforts in January 1920. The only reason for the delay was that there were many building projects in progress, and they wanted to wait until work was relatively slow.[17]

Fisher shared some typical businessmen's views toward labor, but he understood that at least in South Florida, unions held strong cards. The "slow" period anticipated by some employers didn't come, at least not during the first half of the decade. In September 1920, Fisher lamented to the governor of Louisiana that he had "just gone thru a seven months argument with Unions at Miami, Florida. The Unions, with their coercion and their manipulation of affairs at Miami, have cost me a good many hundreds of thousands."[18] Four years later, labor problems still bothered many employers, including Fisher. In October 1924, John W. Levi, who had been with Fisher for years and was by then secretary-treasurer for one of Fisher's real estate companies, informed his boss that "the labor situation here is still about as rotten as it possibly could be." Levi claimed that the local newspapers, determined to sustain a uniformly positive image of the South Florida region in the midst of an unprecedented land boom, refused to print any negative news, including what he perceived as the truth about the labor situation. Levi urged Fisher to throw out the unions, even if they had to act unilaterally: "We have just got to get our own organization of the different trades, our own supply house and our own little mill, if necessary, and go to it on our own hook regardless of the unions."[19] Levi was largely venting his frustration: Fisher sensed it would be unrealistic to follow his advice and wisely avoided the issue. Labor problems did occasionally frustrate Fisher, though, just as they did other entrepreneurs.

In many ways, Fisher's attitude toward labor mirrored that toward racial minorities. He was tolerant and open-handed as long as neither labor nor minorities appeared threatening. Fisher could be appalled at the rawness of racial prejudice in the era of Jim Crow. Jane recalled an incident when a black worker at the Indianapolis racetrack was horribly maimed on the job. Fisher allegedly took him in his own car to the nearest hospital, only to be informed by an intern that the hospital wouldn't "treat niggers." The worker died before Fisher could get him to another hospital. Jane claimed that Carl was so infuriated that he vowed to put the "white" hospital out of business and did so.[20] Fisher gave liberally to black charities and educational institutions, and he had a warm, open relationship with his valet of thirty years, William Galloway. Away from public view and among his male cronies, however, Fisher exchanged crude racial jokes, and he cooperated with other businessmen in Miami Beach in discouraging blacks from enjoying the beach—it might be bad for business.[21]

Labor union issues and race relations were not at the forefront of Fisher's concerns in 1913. After months of creating a solid foundation for a new community, by one account, Fisher had poured about $2 million into his project.[22] The land still looked more like a moonscape than anything habitable. In Fisher's mind, at least, it would take many more months, if not years, to create significant amounts of marketable property. Carl and his associates opened real estate offices, but lot prices were low and sales were sluggish. A few other real estate agents joined them. The Lummus brothers and the Collinses and Pancoasts had less capital than Fisher. In fact, the Lummus brothers borrowed $150,000 from Fisher at 8 percent interest to develop their acreage.[23] His friendly rivals faced even more pressure than Fisher to shorten the turnaround time between development of property and cash sales.

Lot sales at Miami Beach actually began in February 1913, five months before the Collins bridge opened. Collins ran full-page ads touting Miami Beach as the "Atlantic City of Florida," then hired a flamboyant auctioneer, Edward F. "Doc" Dammers, to hawk property. Dammers "lured people over to the Beach with a wagonload of free gifts—cut glass, bric-a-brac, Oriental rugs, dinner sets, and solid gold watches." Attracted by free boat rides and the chance to win valuable "gifts," 300 people showed up the first day. They crossed the bay on wooden barges, towed by tugs. Dammers would raffle off a few gimcracks to get the crowd excited, then sell a few lots, and then repeat the cycle. Three days of intense effort yielded $66,000 in sales. Terms were 50 percent cash, the remainder in monthly installments.[24]

Fisher watched the proceedings and was amused at the showman's antics. Dammers would go on to bigger and better things, achieving national prominence when he teamed with three-time Democratic presidential nominee William Jennings Bryan in promoting nearby Coral Gables in the mid-1920s. In early 1913, Fisher, for the time in his life and for several reasons, shied away from flashy showmanship to promote his projects. With millions in the bank from his recent sale of Prest-O-Lite, he did not need quick cash. Fisher sensed that buyers would pay much higher prices for land that was fully developed, with lush plantings, streets, and access to water, sanitation, and basic utilities, than for undeveloped lots. Dammers was selling lots for between $250 and $300. If Miami Beach developed as Fisher hoped, property would continue to increase in value. Carl sold a few lots and built a modest hotel, assuming that the big money would come later. In addition, by the spring of 1913, Jane was breaking into local society, and Fisher was also forging alliances with Miami's power elite. Unlike the Collins, Lummus, and Pancoast families, he and Jane were newcomers, and Carl may have sensed that close association with comparatively crude huckstering would damage their chances of acceptance by "polite" society. In future years, society would be of far more interest to Jane than to her husband.

In the meantime, there was a city to build and services to provide. Over the next several years, Fisher divided attention between developing property and providing required utilities. After his newly formed land dried out, Fisher hired Fred Hoerger, his assistant gardener in Indianapolis, to move south and take charge of landscaping. It was a huge challenge and an enormous increase in responsibility, but Fisher liked the young man and had faith he could do the job. Hoerger, in turn, hired hundreds of black workers, many of them women and children, to plant new vegetation. Jane Fisher claimed that "each sprig of grass had to be set out by hand," a task employees called 'spriggin.'"[25] Hoerger scoured catalogs of rare, exotic plants from around the world, searching for species that would thrive in Miami's climate. In 1916 Fisher turned the landscaping work over to two expert Japanese horticulturists, Shigezo Tashiro and Kotaro Suto. By 1917, they had developed lush, groomed landscape covering more than 200 acres. Polly Redford recounted that Tashiro and

Suto remained with Fisher for several years, "prospering along with their gardens."[26]

Dredging the swamps and creating land eliminated the worst of the mosquito problem, but there was much more to be done. Fisher gradually transformed his vision from a community featuring modest hotels and small homes to a splashy resort community with stately homes for well-to-do vacationers. In addition to visually enticing landscaping, there would be golf courses, polo grounds, and tennis courts, bathing casinos and groomed beaches, plus luxurious hotels and exclusive retail shops. Other developers, however, had their own dreams, and growth was uncontrolled. So much construction commenced virtually simultaneously between late 1913 and the end of the decade that it is difficult to make sense of it. In those frantic years, the "Beach's" appearance changed dramatically month by month.

Even as Fisher was dredging and developing land for a vacation paradise, he decided that he and Jane should abandon their comfortable home on Brickell Avenue in Miami and build a new one in Miami Beach. Jane was not too happy about the idea. In Miami she had a lovely home, new friends, and a full social life. As usual, however, Carl's wishes prevailed. The couple built a splendid new home called Beach Shadows. Although opposed to the move at the beginning, Jane determined to view it as an adventure. She eventually grew to love the house itself, which was "enchanting, spacious and cool." In the beginning, however, she felt like a pioneer. For a time the home was isolated in "wilderness," surrounded by cranes, dredges, and lots of hot, sweaty workmen. Jane recalled, "I might have been keeping home on a desert island. Every item of food, every stick of furniture or building material, even the water we drank, was transported by wagon or barge or truck across Biscayne Bay."[27] Carl was constantly surrounded by prospective clients, old cronies, and casual acquaintances. He was an exceedingly gregarious man who loved to entertain. Even in such "primitive" conditions, Jane had to be ready to host large numbers of guests at any time.

One of the emerging resort community's priorities was passable streets. Although developers drew them on maps, most remained sandy trails until World War I. Fully paved roads would not be completed until the 1920s. Basic utilities were equally critical. In the first few years after

Miami Beach development around World War I. There were a few modest hotels, a few moderately priced homes, and lots of cheap land. Courtesy of the Historical Museum of Southern Florida.

the land was dredged, energy customers "had to take their chances with the old Miami Electric Light & Power Company's inadequate current, which arrived at the beach—if it arrived at all—by fits and starts and at scandalous prices."[28] Fisher grew impatient. In May 1919 he finally took the bit in his teeth, organized the Miami Beach Electric Company, and began building a power plant.

In the six years following the opening of John Collins's bridge in the summer of 1913, the population of Miami almost doubled. Miami Beach incorporated in 1915, and its population also mushroomed. Traffic between the two municipalities grew to the point that Collins's bridge quickly became obsolete. The Lummus brothers, who owned the land at the point where a new causeway could enter Miami Beach, pressed public officials to build a new causeway to the developing town. Although bond issues were subsequently approved, World War I prevented any such development for several years. After the war, public officials responded with two projects; a new causeway was opened in 1920, and the Collins bridge was dismantled and replaced by the Venetian Way, which finally opened in 1926.[29]

Public officials in Miami had turned a deaf ear to Fisher's and his real estate partners' entreaties that they provide public transportation directly to Miami Beach. So Fisher, a dedicated "automobile man," joined with the Pancoast, Collins, and Lummus families in organizing a street railway company in 1919. A streetcar line would benefit developers by making it easier for prospective buyers to visit their real estate offices and to view the area. It would make Miami more accessible for residents of Miami Beach and vice versa. Obviously, this development would enhance the value of all of their real estate. The line started in downtown Miami, crossed the causeway, and made a "leisurely loop" of developing Miami Beach, then returned to Miami. For patrons just wanting a sight-seeing excursion, the ride took about an hour and cost a nickel.

In later years, Fisher complained to one local politician that his civic efforts had never been appreciated.[30] One historian noted, however, that streetcars served his interests as much as anybody's. By the time they finished their rides, "passengers had seen nearly every salable piece of property in Miami Beach," which of course was the purpose of this otherwise unprofitable public utility. For Miami real estate men would not bring their customers to the Beach in those days. The trip was too long: it was easier to show lots on the mainland. Anyone who asked about Beach property was told horror stories about snakes and alligators, mosquitoes and sand flies. That was why Carl and his associates put in streetcars: so that people could see Miami Beach for themselves. The ride made a pleasant excursion."[31]

Despite the distraction and initial expense of helping establish utilities, Fisher devoted constant attention to promoting Miami Beach and selling lots, quickly eclipsing the efforts of his friendly rivals. Fisher inaugurated his first serious promotional effort in Miami Beach on December 10, 1913, when the Alton Beach Realty Company opened its doors. Carl had been riding on a train and saw a freight car belonging to the Chicago and Alton Railroad. For some reason, he was attracted to the latter name and called his initial large development Alton Beach. Carl's promotional release, printed in the *Miami Herald*, read: "Transformed from a wilderness into a park, almost in an instant as though by the waving of a magic wand, Alton Beach today seems a fairy land, and the story of its development during the past twelve months reads like a romance, to which, however 'finis' has by no means been written, for each day sees some new beauty added to it."[32] Adjacent to this oleaginous press release, Fisher provided a listing of all improvements made on his property. The ad encompassed two full columns of small print. Not only did he list what he had done; he soberly promised many more improvements in the future.

Such matter-of-fact press listing of improvements was uncharacteristic of Fisher, as were his early advertisements for Alton Beach. A year later, perhaps trying to lure staid Palm Beach investors just a little farther south, one of Fisher's advertising men wrote: "We invite the closest analysis and investigation of this property. There is no uncertainty about Miami's Ocean Front Property. There is only a limited amount and will have a permanent value because of its desirability. Every lot in Alton Beach has a permanent value and those offered in this first sub-division are particularly choice and attractive for a home and investment."[33] As he had done in his *Miami Herald* advertisement a year earlier, he listed details about some of the spectacular additions he had made, supported by lifeless statistics.

In 1913 and 1914 even the conservative Collins and Pancoast families were presenting more enthusiastic, imaginative advertisements for their properties. They emphasized that owning Miami Beach property could be fun. Fisher, on the other hand, had momentarily abandoned the Barnumesque come-ons that had characterized his publicity campaigns promoting bicycles, automobile races, and the like back in Indiana. He refused to hire "Doc" Dammers to auction off his lots, perhaps because the flashy, charismatic showman did not match up well with Fisher's recently adopted conservative style. When Dan Hardie, a local sheriff who moonlighted by running a bathing beach and dance hall for the Lummus brothers at their end of the beach, approached Fisher, asking for a $500 donation to bring a carnival to the area as a tourist attraction, Fisher demurred: "Dan, I'll give you five hundred to keep it away."[34]

In the mid-1920s, when the Florida land boom was the talk of the nation, Miami was its focal point. George Merrick's Coral Gables development, centered about five miles southwest of downtown Miami, rivaled Fisher's work in Miami Beach, and both promoters were wallowing in money. By then, it seemed, one could find hundreds of men on the street, in the bars, sitting in lounge chairs by swimming pools, or walking down the fairways of local golf courses who *claimed* that they had seen the boom coming, that any smart men should have realized it was inevitable. When queried closely, it turned out that virtually all of them had failed to invest in the early days.

In the mid-1910s, Fisher was one of the handful of risk-takers willing to commit heavily in Miami Beach. He sat in his Alton Beach Realty Company offices with hundreds of lots for sale but very few customers. At the south end of the beach, the Lummus brothers weren't doing any better. Farther north, John Collins and the Pancoasts were also staring at vacant lots. Carl and Jane had built their sumptuous $65,000 Miami Beach home, expecting that it would soon be surrounded by others. Although local papers marveled at the expense and publicized its opening, few other well-heeled families joined them. Fisher's staid appeals weren't drawing many buyers; other methods of creating demand were needed.

Fisher and other developers sensed that incorporation might provide a stimulus. In 1915 thirty-three registered voters qualified as permanent residents on the ocean side of Biscayne Bay. By law, a minimum of twenty-five persons had to sign a petition for a vote on incorporation. The interested developers quickly rounded up the required signatures, and Miami Beach was duly incorporated on March 26, 1915. J. N. Lummus was the first mayor.[35] There was some discussion over the appropriate name for the new town. "Ocean Beach" was considered, but the present name prevailed. Promoters obviously believed verbal association with their larger neighbor across the bay would enhance appeal, particularly to potential investors outside of the state.

In the short term, incorporation provided little help with land sales. On rare occasions, even Fisher grew discouraged. At times he could not even give property away. Just before World War I Fisher offered free lots to anyone who would build a home. Only six people accepted his offer. He offered to finance home construction for families brave enough to homestead at Miami Beach; again, only a handful of people responded, "for few people wanted to live in the Miami Beach boondocks if they couldn't be right on the sea."[36] Finally, Fisher offered 600 feet of prime oceanfront property to anyone who would build a $100,000 hotel on it. Jane Fisher recalled that "those who heard his offer hooted it down," confident that nobody would be crazy enough to pour good money down a rat hole. A few years later, N. B. T. Roney built a $2.8 million hotel on the same site.[37] Some of those who had refused Fisher's earlier offer of free, or at least inexpensive, land managed to tell stories on themselves. Fisher's good friend from his Dixie Highway days William T. Anderson, editor and owner of the *Macon* (Ga.) *Telegraph*, recalled that Fisher had offered him property but that he had thought the Miami Beach project was "pretty crazy." Anderson ruefully recalled, "A few years later that lot sold for 18,000; two weeks later the purchaser sold it for 22,000; and thirty days later the second purchaser sold it for 56,000."[38]

Fisher realized all along that he would probably have to build hotels himself; they would anchor commercial development, stimulate residential lot prices, and demonstrate that Miami Beach indeed had a future. Despite having already poured a fortune into creating land, he alone among local developers had sufficiently deep pockets to continue improving property on a large scale. For the present at least, the Collins and Pancoast families and the Lummus brothers needed to retrieve capital, so they generally sold their land as comparatively inexpensive, semideveloped residential property.

In contrast, Fisher built the beach's first hotel. The Lincoln Hotel, a modest thirty-five-room facility, opened just before the United States entered World War I. Carl hoped that millionaires who might otherwise have vacationed in Europe would visit Miami Beach instead.[39] It was on Lincoln Road, the area's primary east-west street on the beach. Lincoln Road was just off the entrance to the new causeway to Miami, which was in the initial stages of construction. Fisher believed it would become the most important commercial boulevard in the area. These and later developments, which focused most attention in Miami Beach on Fisher's property, would lead to considerable future jealousy on the part of the Lummus brothers.

In some respects, Fisher may actually have been agreeably distracted by the advent of World War I. The conflict provided him tangible worries other than his own unfinished projects and deepening financial commitments. As with the Indianapolis Motor Speedway, Carl offered his Miami Beach property, which by then included polo fields, for flight training. The Lummus brothers actually beat him to the punch in offering land for training military pilots.[40]

Fisher was right that military officials were interested in locating certain facilities in the Miami area, and they discussed several possibilities with him. By late 1917 Fisher was already well known because of his work organizing training fields in the Midwest. A few months after the United States entered the war, the navy approached Fisher concerning the possibility of establishing a patrol boat base on his property in Miami Beach.[41] Nothing came of this inquiry, but late in the year the air corps considered establishing an air field there.

Confusion surrounded Fisher's dealings with military officials. For a time, he didn't know what they had in mind for South Florida. Evidently, one or more officers mentioned rather casually the notion of flying a few training aircraft into makeshift airfields on a very occasional basis. Small-scale ideas soon became more elaborate. Fisher reviewed the situation in a late December 1917 letter to one liaison officer: "When I first took the matter up with you and Bragg, it was my idea that you just wanted to send one or two machines down here for a week's work. As the proposition is now put up by Bragg, you want to construct a hangar, the field must be enlarged, a large number of trees must be cut down." Fisher was laying out polo fields, and most of the work had already been performed; therefore, he was somewhat reluctant to modify it: "I have a first class property here, with approximately $2 million invested, and I don't want to see any cheap looking barns built on it." He would, however, sacrifice the improvements if compensation was fair. He listed the expense of converting the property to aircraft landing strips, requesting only that the government pick up the tab.[42]

Fisher was baffled at the lack of advance planning by military officials. The nation had declared war on the Central Powers on April 2, 1917. Although military officials established training facilities fairly quickly, they evidently gave little thought to the changing seasons. In Fisher's mind, at least, winter caught them completely unprepared. Northern training fields were essentially useless four or five months of the year. Fisher had not been approached about using his Miami Beach property until early in the winter of 1917. In early January 1918, he reflected on this lack of foresight: "The government has spent several million dollars on aviation fields and hasn't one now that is any good for work at this time of year in the South." He portrayed himself as the consummate patriot, prepared to rescue government officials from their folly: "I outlined a contract which I think will protect me from having the field entirely ruined, and at the same time give the Government the best flying field there is in the United States, and keep it that way."[43]

During early 1918, Fisher's work on polo fields ceased, and some of his property serviced training planes. Several hangars were erected. There was some controversy over the amount of money spent to convert Fisher's property to military use. Some newsmen raised the possibility that the whole arrangement was a small-sized boondoggle, claiming that $40,000 had been wasted on a flying field in Miami, another $40,000 for training facilities. Fisher angrily defended both projects. Fisher claimed that only $3,000 had been spent for establishing facilities for night training flights in the Midwest, much of it covered by local chambers of commerce. He observed that only $14,000 was used for hangars and alterations of the fields in Miami Beach and that he had asked only for rent of a dollar per year.

Although Fisher repeatedly complained about the frustrations of working with government officials, he clearly found his work in aviation during World War I enormously stimulating. He was totally in his element dealing with machines, which remained a lifelong passion. When working with aviation in the late 1910s, Carl was acutely aware that he was on the cutting edge of new technology. As World War I reached its climax late in the summer of 1918 and stirring accounts of the exploits of fighter pilot aces such as Baron Manfred von Richthofen, Billy Mitchell, and Eddie Rickenbacker made headlines, Fisher was brimming with enthusiasm for the future of aviation. Occasionally, his imagination ran wild. In August 1918, he predicted a transatlantic airplane flight, along with his intense desire to be personally involved in making it happen. "For a long time I have been very anxious to be a passenger on the first plane to go across. . . . I am willing to donate $50,000 towards the expense of building a successful machine . . . and that will afford me an opportunity to work as a mechanic on the first trip."[44]

Armistice Day on November 11, 1918, brought an end to the hideous slaughter of World War I. For Fisher, it meant that he could devote full attention to peacetime issues. Nevertheless, for the next twenty years, he promoted aviation in Miami. Immediately after the war, Fisher explored the idea of installing airship service along a triangular route, connecting Miami, Key West, and Havana, Cuba.[45] He personally visited Havana to consult with government officials, and a flurry of specific proposals and correspondence followed. Fisher was even more interested in promoting cooperation over issues involving tourism in the region and polo matches between Cuban and American teams. His interest in dirigibles hovering over South Florida eventually dwindled.

In addition to promoting highway and aviation access to South Florida, Fisher also promoted expansion of passenger ship service to the port of Miami. Despite the recent *Titanic* disaster, ocean voyages had been popular among the rich before the war and figured to be so again following the armistice. Naturally, improved steamship service would further enhance South Florida's emergence as a tourist mecca, indirectly enhancing the value of Fisher's land. Although Fisher participated with Cuban officials and several other partners in forming a steamship company, it failed when the national economy suffered a short-lived postwar recession in 1921.[46]

Was Fisher's work promoting Miami selfless or self-seeking? After he became rich and famous, his publicists tried to portray him as a quietly influential, behind-the-scenes performer of good deeds for the welfare of South Florida in general, Miami Beach in particular. Fisher performed important public service for Miami Beach, and he was generous to a fault. His business associates, even his competitors, repeatedly remarked that Fisher's ethics were above reproach. Others noted that he usually bent over backward to give the other fellow a fair shake. Yet however ethical his business dealings were, any portrayal of him shying away from publicity is preposterous. He soon abandoned the sober, dignified marketing tactics he had briefly used before World War I. Like Phineas T. Barnum and Harry Houdini, Fisher's life revolved around showmanship, energetic display, and risk-taking. In the summer of 1919 an attorney friend wrote to Fisher, who was in Indianapolis, "They got off a good joke on you at the Theater the other night. The comedian asked what was love, and the answer was that it was the one thing in Miami that Carl G. Fisher didn't control. It caused a real laugh."[47] If Fisher sometimes demurred when credited with doing too much, it was most likely the result of a slowly growing awareness that excessive self-promotion could hurt him in the long run.

The development of Miami Beach would be the crowning achievement of his career. When the 1920s opened, Fisher was convinced of the region's future; he could only shake his head in disbelief that many others failed to see it. By New Year's Eve 1920, most of the "Beach's" infrastructure was completed, and his hardest work was behind him. Nevertheless, in the first year or two of the new decade, Fisher faced continued frustrations. The nation was recovering slowly from the ravages of the international influenza pandemic of 1918–19, the Red Scare of 1919–20, and a brief but serious postwar depression in 1920–21. Idealism appeared to be an old-fashioned, vanishing commodity, replaced by a hard, brittle-shelled cynicism. The advent of Prohibition in 1920 framed the contrast between public morality and private behavior.

Ironically, the Roaring Twenties opened on a sour note. In sunny South Florida, however, Carl refused to be dragged down by cynicism or gloom. Like the Lincoln and Dixie Highways and even the Indianapolis Motor Speedway, the development of Miami Beach was geared toward encouraging his countrymen to cast aside their inhibitions and experience adventure. All of these projects were connected, directly or indirectly, to exciting new technologies associated with speed. Fisher sensed that Miami Beach was the perfect retreat from workaday cares. Months, maybe years, of hard work lay ahead before his tropical playground became reality. But Fisher was convinced it was just a matter of time. After 1920, Fisher's primary challenge in Miami Beach was providing finishing touches.

9

Dressing Up the Beach

By the end of World War I, Fisher had firmly established his vision of what he hoped to create in Miami Beach: a vacation paradise. Resorts were not new additions to the American landscape. Cindy S. Aron systematically tracked their evolution in the United States since the Civil War, finding antecedents dating from the late eighteenth century.[1] But Americans did not easily or naturally adapt themselves to scheduled leisure. For centuries, extended periods of time when adults were not working usually meant hardship for families. Aron observed that most Americans felt ambivalent toward leisure, vacations in particular. Moral authorities understood and slowly came to accept the idea of the restorative benefits of rest and relaxation, yet they wrestled with concerns that vacations went against Puritanical views of virtue and self-denial. As Aron observed, between the Civil War and World War II, "Americans struggled to fashion forms of vacationing that would allow them to reconcile their desire for leisure with persistent cultural dictates about the importance of work and the dangers of play. Vacation places became sites where these tensions were mediated and tested, if never fully resolved."[2] Critics charged that rather than providing physical recuperation, intellectual stimulation, and moral regeneration, many resort communities presented far too many unhealthy "temptations" and encouraged patrons to slip too easily into a softening degeneracy.

Fisher developed what was, in the 1920s, a breathtakingly modern, even futuristic-appearing resort community in Miami Beach. Whereas most nineteenth-century retreats, including Henry M. Flagler's development in Palm Beach, emphasized sedentary recuperation and restoration, Fisher's new resort featured action, including a third "r," *recreation*.[3] From the art deco architectural style gracing several of his hotels and many commercial structures to the dazzling variety of entertainments and games offered to visitors, Fisher consciously and "carefully scripted scenes."[4] Although Hal Rothman was assessing late twentieth-century tourism in the West when he wrote, "Tourist space is specially scripted to keep visitors at the center of the picture while simultaneously cloaking, manipulating, and even deceiving them into believing that their experience is the locals' life, reality and view of the world,"[5] this description essentially mirrors Fisher's achievement at Miami Beach in the 1920s. One of the primary objectives of the impresarios of late twentieth-century leisure was the ability to "purposely create another level of experience that masquerades or prepares for so-called authentic experience, blurring any line that may remain and often making the replica even more seductive than the original."[6] The secret of Fisher's ultimate success in Miami Beach was his ability to draw visitors into a fantasy world. In essence, he taught many serious, sober-minded, and well-heeled Americans how to play.

As the 1920s opened, however, many workaday chores remained. In their effort to enhance interest in Miami Beach real estate, Fisher and his cohorts had founded a streetcar line in 1919. Two years later, he was trying to unload it. He certainly realized that it would not make money from fares; at a nickel per ride, breaking even was obviously a pipe dream. But having performed what they considered a "public service" for Miami, they thought the city should take it over. Fisher informed Frank Shutts, a mover and shaker in Miami, that building the electric light plant and the street railway to Miami Beach were "the biggest thing we have done for the Beach. But we don't need this outfit any more and I don't care to be burdened with either the investment or the troubles that go with it." Fisher offered to sell both utilities back to the city at what he claimed as their "actual cost." To sweeten the deal, he offered to throw in "at cost" eleven acres of land which he had created along the new county causeway desired by Miami for dock space.[7] Unfortunately for Fisher and his associates, the Miami authorities refused to bite. A month later he was still trying to sell the utilities. He wanted other beneficiaries to assume their share of the burden and proposed that they be taken over by "a large number of real estate people."[8] Fisher was willing to take a bookkeeping loss of as much as $200,000 just to get rid of them. This effort to unload a cumbersome burden also failed. Five months later he and his partners were still operating streetcar lines, and they were tired of offering a service that also benefited rival real estate entrepreneurs, particularly in Miami. But Fisher sounded like an experienced streetcar line operator, a bit more resigned to remaining in that field for the foreseeable future. He complained about mounting traffic congestion and "jitney" operators who worked only during prime hours and robbed his line of critical patronage.[9] Coming from a man who had done so much to promote the street railway's chief rival, the automobile, such complaints are a bit disingenuous.

As these negotiations suggest, Fisher's relationships with businessmen and politicians in Miami were often tense. A major factor was resentment and jealousy on the part of those who considered Fisher an interloper, even a threat. Many of these men and their families had lived in Florida for at least a generation before Carl and Jane discovered Miami in 1910. Some of them had been making huge efforts, at least in their own eyes, to develop the area. Yet by World War I it was Fisher, nicknamed "king" of Miami Beach by some newspapers, who was attracting national attention.[10] Perhaps, too, some of them resented Fisher's "style." He was a midwesterner with a lot of money who exuded glamour, at least in their eyes. His young, beautiful wife was clearly socially ambitious, and he surrounded himself with expensive adult toys, mainly cars and boats. In addition, most of his critics had business interests on the Miami side of Biscayne Bay. Almost all of Fisher's investment was in Miami Beach. Miami entrepreneurs generally viewed "the Beach" as a competitor, a new, intrusive development that threatened their own investments.

Fisher, in contrast, expressed amazement that his rivals in Miami could not perceive the larger picture. He considered himself an open-handed and farsighted developer, working long hours, sometimes anonymously, for the benefit of the entire region. With every dollar he invested in Miami Beach, he was contributing to the city's economy. He bought construction materials in Miami. He hired Miami workers, who paid rents to Miami landlords and purchased food and clothing in Miami stores. He deposited money in Miami banks, and he had helped build the city's infrastructure through his investments in public utilities. In addition, he and his top-level managers spent considerable time in Tallahassee, lobbying state legislators for funds for infrastructure improvements in both Miami Beach and Miami. Carl did sometimes act in a maddeningly patronizing manner. On more than one occasion, he essentially lectured his rivals, trying to get them to understand the benefits he was offering them. Fisher insisted to one associate in September 1921, "I am as much interested in the city of Miami as I am in the city of Miami Beach." A few weeks later, after his offer of land "at cost" for dock space was rejected, he proclaimed, "I was in hopes that the people of Miami would realize how much cheaper it would be for them to have the harbor away from the most beautiful part of the city."[11] Some of his critics dismissed his efforts as shameless grandstanding. Not surprisingly, such conflicting perceptions contributed to the uneasy relationship between Fisher and the Miami entrepreneurs. Only after Fisher lost his fortune did some of them soften their attitudes toward him.

In addition, Fisher craved recognition for his efforts to promote the region in general, and on rare occasions he could be petty when anticipated encomiums were not forthcoming. Shortly before the new decade opened, Fisher calculated the funds he had expended for the general benefit of the regional business community. As the 1919 fiscal year ended in June of that year, Carl claimed that he was carrying an excessive share of advertising expense. To be sure, announcements of real estate in national publications benefited him, but Fisher argued that they also worked to the advantage of all real estate agents. Fisher revealed that he alone had spent $35,000 advertising Alton Beach property. Fisher claimed that such advertising not only attracted buyers who would be interested in his property, but "the average person [would] buy where he can get the best location at the best price." He suggested that all interested real estate agents pool their resources and write advertising copy that would aid them all, while cutting expenses: "I don't feel like carrying this whole load myself, and I think that each year we should chip into a fund for advertising purposes and have one man handle the entire proposition for all of us."[12]

Eventually, Fisher's promotional efforts induced others to help out. The most influential contributions came at the national level, when the *Saturday Evening Post* writer and famed historical novelist Kenneth Roberts wrote several articles on the Florida land boom which appeared between 1922 and 1926. These, along with sketches by other writers in magazines and newspapers across the country, helped feed the emerging boom.[13]

Even when good times finally swept Fisher and almost all Miami real estate developers into the frenzied bonanza of the Florida land boom, Fisher was an occasional target for nay-sayers. In the summer of 1925, Fisher once again offered land for the expansion of Miami's harbor facilities, which were becoming increasingly crowded. John W. Watson, a state senator representing Miami, publicly questioned Fisher's motives, claiming in a newspaper editorial that Fisher stood to reap a windfall if local decision makers took him up on his offer.[14] Carl often ignored criticism, assuming that responsible and fair-minded adults would eventually concede the truth. In this case, however, his honesty had been questioned, and his temper snapped. In a three-page, single-spaced reply, he ripped into his adversary, laying out his side of the controversy. Fisher noted that he had come to Miami thirteen years earlier and that "nobody in Miami has worked as hard as I have for deep water or has spent one-tenth—yes, I will say one-fiftieth as much as I have in efforts and real cash to promote deep water."

According to Fisher, selfish and shortsighted opponents had rebuffed his offer to sell additional land for dock facilities at cost. By his reckoning, opponents insisted on crowding as much dock space as possible onto Miami's downtown waterfront on the west side of Biscayne Bay. Too many ships were trying to unload goods onto docks that were crammed together. Spreading out commercial docks was simple common sense. Chamber of Commerce officials and Miami politicians, however, feared that Fisher intended to siphon off millions of dollars of business and tax revenues to Miami Beach. Fisher chided Watson for playing to the crowd: "Your attitude on this subject is just as foolish as Mr. Sewell's, and if you persist in building on Miami's waterfront you will, to a great extent, be responsible for the wasting of millions of dollars by the city of Miami and the people." Fisher insisted that monetary gain was not and never had been his objective: "Neither were my efforts in building Miami Beach *entirely* from the dollar standpoint; in fact, there was no thought in my mind when I entered this development to make money off of it" (emphasis added).[15]

By the summer of 1925, Fisher was finally raking in huge profits—millions of dollars every month—and such a claim undoubtedly appeared disingenuous, especially to his enemies. Five years earlier, visions of fabulous wealth would have appeared far-fetched because so much work remained to be done. Still, by the summer of 1920 Fisher felt better about his Miami Beach prospects than ever before. A fundamental reason was that he had finally clarified in his own mind precisely the types of vacationers he hoped to attract. Before the war, he had vague notions of luring the Palm Beach crowd farther south, of catering to the entrenched Anglo-Saxon power elites centered in Boston, New York, and Philadelphia. His staid advertisements of Alton Beach property had reflected this conservative marketing approach. After the war, Fisher totally altered his selling strategy. He was on intimate, or at least friendly, terms with many of Detroit's "gasoline aristocracy."[16] They were young, energetic, had millions of dollars to spend, and, Fisher believed, they needed to be taught how to play. There were similar groups of upstart entrepreneurs throughout the Midwest and elsewhere. The old money eastern elites might dismiss them as crude, pushy parvenus, but to Fisher they represented a potential gold mine.

Fisher imagined a giant adult playground under the sun. Well-heeled visitors would be able to enjoy virtually any form of expensive outdoor recreation they chose and some indoor diversions as well. When his Shangri-la was finished, vacationers would stay in fabulous luxury hotels. They could either swim in the ocean or loll about in freshwater pools. They might choose between a couple of sets of tennis or a round of golf, a morning of yachting or a day of deep-sea fishing. If young and energetic, they could mount horses and play polo. More sedentary guests could stroll over to cages set up nearby to gaze at exotic birds brought in from the West Indies. Perhaps they might choose to sit back with refreshing drinks in hand and watch yachting and power boat races or scheduled tennis matches between some of the finest amateurs and professionals in America. For those who preferred indoor sports, there were lessons and competitions in bridge, mahjongg, and other games. He imagined that hotel guests would eventually buy his lots and build expensive homes. In the vacation retreat of Fisher's imagination, boredom on the beach would be an oxymoron.

Although Fisher was determined to create a far livelier atmosphere than that of Palm Beach, he believed that certain activities would sully the area's image, and he was sensitive to outsiders' perception of Miami Beach. Although he was an enthusiastic boxing fan, he didn't want Miami Beach to host either boxing or wrestling matches. When the city council received an application from a promoter who wished to build a facility to host such events, Fisher voiced reservations to fellow developer Thomas J. Pancoast: "There is plenty of room for them in the city of Miami and the city seems to like this form of sports, why not let them have it. These things never draw desirable people out to the Beach . . . and if any building is erected at the Beach it certainly is not going to be permanent or anything we could be proud of."[17]

One of Fisher's first and most ambitious efforts to promote exotic sports in Miami Beach was laying out polo fields. He probably witnessed his first polo match when he journeyed to Europe to participate in international automobile races in 1905. The idea may well have occurred to him when he dreamed initially of attracting the more conservative eastern crowd. Jane fully intended to enter society in Miami, Indianapolis, or wherever else they might live; she may have influenced his thinking. A historian of Miami Beach observed, "Some of the richest people in America played the sport and if Fisher could create a polo paradise in Miami Beach, he could lure those people to his tropical paradise and sell them on investing in and promoting his adventure."[18]

Jane adored the glittering social life surrounding polo. By 1919 she had been married to Carl for ten years, and she was no longer the wide-eyed, innocent teenager from a comfortable, if provincial, middle-class Indianapolis home. But she was still childless and only twenty-five, and she focused most of her energy on running the household and planning parties. Jane loved the mystery and romantic airs surrounding Cuban cavalry officers and the exquisite social graces of the long, lean English riders. She recalled one dazzling evening when she and Carl hosted 350 guests at a sit-down dinner: "The dining room open[ed] on the sea, palms and stars, while the native music throbbed on through the night. At intervals, Reinald Werrenrath sang arias that thrilled Metropolitan listeners in New York, and Sybil Cromer, a lovely figure in Spanish costume, crooned Cuban songs from the balcony." Carl, always unpredictable, disappeared midway through the evening and retired to their bedroom. Jane staggered into the room as the sun came up; Carl woke up from a sound sleep and cheerfully observed that it had been a lovely party. He allowed that he had a great time, adding, "Only I knew when to go to bed."[19]

Whatever his original incentive for investing in the sport, Fisher initially laid out polo grounds in both Miami Beach and inside the track of the Indianapolis Motor Speedway. Polo required a vast amount of space, so Fisher's decision to build and maintain fields at Miami Beach was a major commitment, particularly after land values skyrocketed. In 1918 Fisher had plenty of empty land, including a large parcel just east of Alton Road near Lincoln Road. At that point he didn't know much about polo, but he was willing to listen to "experts," who persuaded him to spend $40,000 to bring clay from the Everglades, level it out, and plant the right variety of grass. World War I delayed his plans for showing off the sport because army aircraft used the fields temporarily. After the armistice, he rushed the project to completion. Carl purchased his own team of polo ponies and ceremoniously paraded them across the Collins bridge onto his freshly rebuilt field. On February 20, 1919, the first polo match ever played in Florida took place at Fisher's state-of-the-art facility, named the Flamingo Polo Grounds.[20] An estimated 2,000 people showed up, including many socially prominent visitors to South Florida. Fisher beamed with satisfaction as he worked the crowd; he had stolen a march on the stuffed shirts in Palm Beach.

Polo entailed enormous expense because Fisher always went first class. One associate estimated that by 1923, when the Florida land boom was finally beginning to take off, Fisher had already spent $2 million for stables, barns, clubhouses, and other amenities. This did not include salaries for professionals who played there or daily maintenance. In preparation for a single heavily promoted championship match, Carl imported an entire polo team from England, complete with their horses, at his own expense, which amounted to $50,000. He housed the players at his spanking-new King Cole Hotel and fed them "English-style, sideboard breakfasts of kippers and kidneys."[21]

Fisher and his men were extremely busy building the resort city, selling real estate, and tending to a dozen other projects; the boss seldom truly relaxed. Even when fishing, Carl was usually talking to a guest about buying some of his land. But he really took to polo. In about 1920, at age forty-six, he learned to ride a horse and play the game. Unlike many of the long, lean, youthful players, Fisher had a short, stubby body and limited eyesight. But he had courage and tenacity, along with enormous enthusiasm for the game. When he played, he demonstrated more aggressiveness than finesse. Carl was a consummate sportsman and insisted on fair play.

Fisher may have initially promoted polo in order to help attract the so-called smart set to Miami Beach, but he was soon smitten with the sport. To one associate in the automobile business in Detroit who described the boating "bug," Fisher replied, "I find that when you get the Polo bug it is just the same thing, only worse." He mentioned buying a horse "that I really believe is the ugliest horse in the world until you get on him and see his eyes commence to shine—and then he is about the prettiest thing you ever looked at."[22] Fisher promoted polo aggressively to the "gasoline aristocracy," apparently attempting to "cultivate" them socially. He assiduously courted Edsel Ford, son of the founder of Ford Motor Company. One of Edsel's associates visited Miami Beach in the summer of 1924 and examined Fisher's vastly expanded facilities. By then there were six polo fields and all necessary amenities. The spokesmen evidently disclosed that Edsel loved polo. Fisher wrote to the Ford scion, "I am very glad to hear this, for the reason that I don't know of any better sport and exercise in the world than polo—if you go at the job carefully and don't attempt horses that are beyond you there is practically no danger other than bruises and bumps which naturally come from a game that is quite strenuous." Fisher also successfully recruited Harvey Firestone and other notables involved directly or indirectly with the automobile business.[23]

On one occasion, polo matches brought Fisher distinct embarrassment. He had invited a Cuban team to play a match early in 1920. All was smiles and handshakes before the match, particularly when Fisher presented the Cuban captain with a fine saddle horse. During regulation play, covering six periods, or chukkers, the Cubans shut out the Americans 4–0. They had won fair and square. The match should have been over. But the Americans persuaded the Cubans to extend the match two more chukkers.[24] The Cubans remained on top, after which the Americans demanded yet two more tries. As Fisher recounted in a letter to a polo-playing friend, "The Cubans were worn out, and without anybody to look after their horses, and I don't think they particularly favored the extra two periods.—but the last period was the most disgraceful thing of the whole affair." The American captain had evidently arranged with the time keeper to keep the clock running as long as it took to wear down the Cubans and win. "This was the most frightful abuse of horses I have seen in a long time, and it was also taking a very unsportsmanlike advantage of the confidence the Cubans had placed in us. . . . I told the Cubans I was very sorry and that it was not my idea of clean sport." Evidently the Cuban captain accepted Fisher's apology. In future weeks, Carl corresponded with him and Cuban officials about promoting both the sport of polo and tourism in general in Havana.[25]

There were other setbacks in Fisher's recruiting campaign. He convinced dozens of successful middle-aged men to saddle up. On at least one occasion, this had tragic results. Julius Fleischmann, founder of the formidable yeast fortune, played a vigorous game of polo, dismounted from his horse, and promptly collapsed and died of a heart attack. Although shaken by his friend's death, Fisher did not miss a trick when it came to promoting Miami Beach. He reminded one of his publicity men to insist that reporters use a Miami Beach dateline when reporting the tragedy.[26] Given the age and lack of physical condition of some of Fisher's polo recruits, it is surprising that such incidents did not occur more often.

Tennis and golf were also crucial ingredients for making Miami Beach a winter playground. Fisher was personally far more interested in tennis, which he played with reckless enthusiasm, if limited skill. In fact, since there were usually considerable intervals between polo matches, tennis constituted the only regular vigorous exercise he got. Tennis courts did not take up much space, particularly compared to polo and golf. Fisher included numerous tennis courts in his hotel plans. In addition, he sponsored tennis tournaments in Miami Beach, offering sumptuous free board and lodging, plus prizes generous enough to attract many of the top tennis amateurs and professionals. Bill Tilden, Vincent Richards, Helen Wills, and other tennis stars of the Jazz Age entertained paying guests with dazzling exhibitions of skill. Carl also arranged for certain tennis stars to reside for weeks at his hotels, rubbing shoulders with paying guests and contributing to the overall ambience.[27]

Fisher was personally far less enthusiastic about golf. He played occasionally, but the sport suited neither his skills nor his temperament. He once stated that if he hit a good shot, he couldn't see it, and if he hit a bad shot, he didn't want to see it.[28] He informed his friend James M. Cox, the 1920 Democratic nominee for president, that after building one course in the late 1920s he played just nine holes, losing eleven golf balls in the process.[29] But Carl knew that golf was taking America by storm in the 1920s and was particularly popular among the nouveaux riches. Vacationers to South Florida demanded it, so Fisher happily provided it.[30] He wasn't concerned over where courses were built, as long as they would soon dot the entire region.

Fisher persistently prodded rival developers across the bay to build more courses. To S. Bobo Dean of the *Miami Metropolis*, Fisher noted, "Golf seems to be going over the country like wildfire. The golf clubs over the country and the memberships are increasing twenty to thirty percent each year." Carl informed Dean that Aiken, South Carolina, was a favorite retreat for the wealthy, partly because it was aggressively catering to golfers. What Fisher called a "jerkwater town back in the woods" had two eighteen-hole courses, plus a nine-hole layout, and was planning two more long courses. Fisher needled, "Doesn't it look ridiculous that Miami and Miami Beach cannot have more than two 18-hole courses at this time? About half of us have been asleep on this golf situation in Miami."[31] As Fisher wrote to one golf promoter in Miami, "I am heartily in favor of one, two, three or a half dozen Golf courses on the Miami side of the Bay. . . . I can't think of anything better than for Miami to be known as a

Fisher would do almost anything to generate publicity. Rosie the elephant patiently
assists in this captivating publicity photo promoting golf. Courtesy of the Historical
Museum of Southern Florida.

golf metropolis in the Winter time."[32] Fisher even volunteered to provide
some of the capital to build courses across the bay.

At the same time he advocated cooperation with Miami, Fisher wanted
to guarantee that Miami Beach fully capitalized on the emerging golf
craze. He confidently announced that he would build the finest championship golf courses in South Florida. He proved to be a man of his word.
Most local courses were flat as a pancake, reflecting the topography of the
region. Not Fisher's. He had course designers include artificial mounds
and occasional gullies to give his resort courses individuality and character. By the early 1920s, Fisher was hobnobbing with celebrities from
many fields: politics, entertainment, sports, and occasionally the arts. One
of his best friends was John Oliver LaGorce, associate editor of *National
Geographic Magazine*. To honor his friend, Fisher sponsored the Miami
Beach LaGorce Open Golf Tournament, offering a lush purse: $15,000
in total prizes. This was enough to attract many of the top stars of the

day, including Gene Sarazen, Tommy Armour, Johnny Farrell, and Light-Horse Harry Cooper. Each of the eighteen holes of one of his golf courses in Miami Beach was named in honor of one of his friends or associates in business or professional entertainment. Honorees included heavyweight boxing champion Gene Tunney, sportswriter Grantland Rice, comedian Will Rogers, and Indiana poet laureate James Whitcomb Riley.

Fisher's primary love in Florida was the ocean; boats, even more than polo and tennis, were his passion. Developing land was expensive, but there were thousands of square miles of ocean within easy reach of Miami Beach. It cost money to build docks and maintain beach facilities, but use of the ocean itself was free. Fisher seemed happiest when he was organizing deep-sea fishing trips, a sailing regatta, or a speedboat competition. Midwestern sportsmen sponsored numerous speedboat races in and around Detroit during the summer season, and Carl had frequently hobnobbed with racers and boat mechanics during these competitions. He invited boat designers and developers of powerful engines by the dozen to spend weeks and even entire winter seasons in Miami Beach, and he sometimes covered all their expenses. Speedboat races in Miami Beach during the winter months were a natural fit, and Fisher staged his first races there during the 1913–14 season. Since the waters were too shallow on the Miami Beach side of Biscayne Bay, he ran the races on the Miami side and built temporary grandstands for spectators at Eleventh Street.

Before World War I, the speedboat races basically mirrored the Indianapolis 500 automobile races in promoting new technology, speed, and excitement for business purposes, but they were also social gatherings for Carl and his friends, excuses to get together to eat, drink, and match their machines in friendly competition. Elements of this clubby camaraderie would always surround the events, but over the years, Fisher's power boat races grew increasingly competitive. Bigger purses brought far more public recognition, larger numbers of entries, and faster speeds. Fisher insisted on maintaining control of the promotions, and he wanted to guarantee spectators that they would see racing as and when advertised. In observing competition elsewhere, Fisher had been amazed when Detroit's famous Gold Cup races had been delayed by days because of engine fires, mechanical breakdowns, and false starts. One season they were finally called off altogether because of bad weather. Carl had been appalled at the sloppiness of the Detroit races, and he was determined to do better. In South Florida, Fisher always insisted on running his races on schedule, even if inclement weather threatened. No matter how influential the sponsor of a boat might be, if a driver couldn't get his entry to the starting line on time, race officials were instructed to begin without him. Fisher's guarantee of races was not too much of a gamble because competitions usually began in late December, after the hurricane season.

The 1919 Miami Regatta was a typical Fisher promotion, once he decided to go "big time." He offered a $5,000 trophy to the American Power Boat Association if it would help him stage a series of races to begin at 3 p.m. "regardless of weather, sea, or any other factors, including the owners' or spectators' wishes." The races, including heats and finals in various divisions, covered several days. Fisher's longtime friend and engine designer James Allison helped sponsor the regatta by providing $1,000 prizes to each division winner. Just as with automobile racing at

Carl Fisher's first love in South Florida was the water. He hosted some of the nation's most glamorous and exciting power boat racing during the 1920s. Courtesy of the Historical Museum of Southern Florida.

Indianapolis, Carl was totally in his element in the weeks leading up to the regatta. His daily mail was filled with exchanges of letters with men such as Charles F. Kettering, inventor of the self-starter and other automotive advances, and Edsel Ford concerning technical details of piston displacements, engine cooling systems, and the like.[33] Although Fisher was no engineer himself, his inquiring mind stimulated others to surmount gnarly problems in power boat engine design. One of his longtime friends and associates, championship racer and designer Gar Wood, allegedly claimed that Fisher "did more for the refining and developing of motor boats than anyone in the business."[34]

Carl and his friends also enjoyed venturing with their power boats far out onto the ocean. On occasion, Fisher organized races covering several hours, such as between Miami Beach and Key West. Jane recalled a race between these locations in about 1916. The contestants were Fisher, in his boat named the *Raven* and Detroit sportsman Charles W. Kotcher in the *Betty M.* It was memorable for Jane because she and two female friends were passengers, and the race was extremely close. After five hours of racing at top speed over open water, Fisher's boat reached the finish line at Key West just two boat lengths ahead of his rival. Jane recalled being "exhausted and drenched to our skins." But Carl was never happier: "We arrived in Key West soaking wet, to find ourselves met by a welcoming committee headed by Pete Chase, and were rushed off to a large reception in our honor. Flushed with victory and sunburn, and dripping with water, we listened to speeches and had our photographs taken clutching the silver cup."[35]

In some respects, Fisher's forays far out into the Atlantic Ocean resembled the elaborate western hunting expeditions and African safaris enjoyed by wealthy sportsmen in previous decades. Many aggressive, powerful men enjoyed using the fastest and most powerful machines, whether shooting the biggest guns to bring down dangerous game or trying to win high-speed races over miles of open water. Fisher, however, thoroughly analyzed the desires of vacationers, and he realized that most visitors to Miami Beach were of a considerably more sedentary bent. Many wealthy but physically soft men wanted to be surrounded by luxury while being presented with thrills and occasional challenges under carefully controlled conditions. Deep-sea fishing was an ideal sport for affluent, out-of-shape businessmen. They could sit comfortably in what amounted to a glorified director's chair while others maneuvered the boat, bought them food and drink, and baited their lines. There were hundreds of species of fish in the Atlantic Ocean, and expert guides could take these revelers to spots where they might land their favorites. Desk jockeys who seldom hefted anything larger than a fountain pen suddenly found themselves wrestling with huge marlins, sailfish, tarpon, even sharks. It sometimes took hours to reel in giant specimens weighing several hundred pounds. Seldom-used biceps and forearms burned and lower backs shrieked in agony. But strapping assistants could spell a tired angler, and many helping hands stood by to haul the flopping monster into the boat. Fatigue and sore muscles were forgotten when the happy, sunburned sea warrior, basking in applause from his wife and children, stood proudly next to his catch, suspended on a chain above the dock. The aches and pains of his struggle might last for a few days, but it was the experience of a lifetime, and the photographs and memories were indelible.

Fisher knew that lucky fishermen who caught the big ones would probably return season after season. He also sensed that they were ripe candidates for real estate sales, and he often personally accompanied high rollers out to the best fishing spots. He recalled making big real estate sales to prospects exhilarated and in a free-spending mood after an exciting day on the ocean. Many of his fishing expeditions revolved around pure friendship, though, with property sales a distant or nonexistent issue. Fisher and General Motors' top engineer, Charles F. Kettering, had been friends for years. One of "Ket's" few true leisure hobbies was fishing, and Fisher frequently used fishing stories to lure his friend to Miami Beach. In the spring of 1927 Carl described a recent fishing trip to Cuba: "I know at this time where there are more tarpon than any other place in the world. About four amateurs caught sixteen and lost at least thirty. . . . We had on tarpons so big they broke the lines and they jumped eight and ten feet into the air and it was impossible to gaff them."[36] In his mind, it was lunacy for any dedicated fisherman to resist the temptations of Miami Beach in winter.

Fisher had several close friends in the arts, including the poet James Whitcomb Riley. The two would occasionally spend the better part of an afternoon sipping highballs and exchanging ribald stories.[37] By most accounts, Carl was incredibly generous. On one occasion, Will Rogers saw an original Charles M. Russell painting hanging in the Fishers' living room. He offered Carl $5,000 for it on the spot. Carl good-naturedly refused the offer. A year later, Carl called his friend and invited him over for a "surprise." There, Rogers saw two nearly identical paintings side by side. Fisher had arranged for a gifted painter to copy the original. According to the story, he offered Rogers his choice, as a gift. After long deliberation, Rogers chose the fake. Fisher emphatically denied this account, claiming that Rogers knew all along that he was to receive the copy.[38] The larger point, however, is that Carl often went to extraordinary lengths to please his friends.

Jane recalled that although Carl was pleasant and usually gracious around her female friends, he was at his best and far more relaxed around men. He might take a group of cronies down to the Cocolobo Club, a small, private fishing resort he built in 1919 on Adams Key, twenty-eight miles south of Miami. Guests could stay in rustic, modest cabins, and a well-staffed clubhouse served meals.[39] Fisher thoroughly enjoyed practical jokes, and fishing trips offered him ample opportunities. Once he accompanied a group of friends on a bone fishing trip to Bimini on his yacht. His pals wanted to take out rowboats and seek bone fish; Carl declined to join them, telling them he had things to do on the yacht. Once they departed, Fisher heard gospel singers on shore. His curiosity aroused, he rowed ashore and found a church choir. An inspiration struck him. After services were concluded, Carl hired the entire congregation to go into the waters and net bone fish. Meanwhile, his luckless friends spent an uncomfortable day in rowboats under a broiling sun. In the late afternoon, they returned, tired, sunburned, and empty-handed. By Jane's account, they found her husband "lolling on deck, holding a fishing pole in one hand and holding an icy drink in the other, surrounded by Negroes who fanned him with palm leaves while they sang to the music of a jug band. 'Thought I'd show you sun-blistered rod and reelers how to fish in comfort,' he called down blandly."[40] Jane failed to recount whether Carl's chums were taken in by his trickery.

During the tourist season, Fisher could, if he chose, conduct business wearing a swim suit. Up in Palm Beach, in a throwback to customs of

Sun-worshipers could enjoy either the ocean or freshwater pools at Fisher's sumptuous bathing casino, the Roman Pools. Courtesy of the Historical Museum of Southern Florida.

earlier years, stuffy aristocrats spent much of their time going to formal parties, changing clothing, and sitting stiffly at tea tables under umbrellas, exchanging desultory gossip.[41] But Miami Beach was for a racier set. While some visitors enjoyed the sandy beaches, others preferred freshwater pools. Swimmers could avoid sand, if they desired. On cooler, breezy, sunny days when lying on the beach was uncomfortable, sunbathers could indulge their pursuit of the perfect tan by finding a nook next to a pool that was protected from the wind.

Fisher was acutely alert to what tourists wanted; almost everybody hoped to return home with a luscious tan. Earlier generations of Americans had considered creamy white skin a mark of status, proof that the individual did not have to engage in hard manual labor outdoors. By World War I, however, most of the employed nonfarming population worked indoors, either in factories or behind desks. Sporting a deep tan, particularly during winter months, informed others that one could afford the travel and leisure time usually required to obtain it.[42] Fisher was neither a sociologist nor a social critic, but he quickly developed a keen grasp of the chief wintertime attraction in the Sunshine State. Swimming pools were natural gathering places for almost every activity from serious exercise to casual lounging, and many visitors spent most of their time there. Other businessmen in Miami and Miami Beach, including the Collins clan, had built swimming "casinos" earlier, but nobody matched Fisher's swimming pool building in scale and opulence. One of his layouts, christened the Roman Pools, incongruously featured an enormous Dutch windmill located just a few steps from the pool. Besides being decorative, the windmill pumped water from two holding tanks into the swimming pools.

Fisher hired young, sun-bronzed, athletic members of both sexes as lifeguards or simply to act as scenic props. Consistent with the overall image he was trying to project at Miami Beach, he desired to maintain an aura of athleticism around his pools. Therefore, he hired nationally renowned divers and other water acts to entertain guests.[43] One "recruit" he didn't have to employ was his wife, Jane, who claimed in later years that she inspired the emergence of the bathing beauty in Miami Beach. Jane recalled that when the Roman Pools first opened, most women wore long black stockings, "bathing suits that would serve today for street dresses, and bathing shoes. Demure mop caps covered our long hair." But Jane grew weary of such confining attire. She was a good swimmer and "longed for greater freedom in the water. I found it in what I have been told was the first form-fitting bathing suit, with a shockingly short skirt that came only to my knees." Jane claimed that local ministers condemned her as "a symbol of the brazenness of the modern woman." Carl wholly approved: "By God, Jane, you've started something. Why, dammit, I've been trying for months to think up an idea for advertising Miami Beach."[44] Jane had made a significant fashion statement, and other female guests soon far surpassed her in sporting provocative attire. By the early 1920s, photographs of gorgeous women in swim suits considered revealing at the time were routinely used on advertising posters for Miami Beach all over the country.[45]

Nothing exemplified Carl's promotional flair more than his employment of elephants. During the 1920s he used several, the first of which was presented to him in about 1920 by fellow Hoosier Ed Ballard, former owner of Ringling Brothers Circus. Elephants enhanced the carnival

It seemed that everyone loved Fisher's elephant, Rosie, but she was a particular favorite of children. Courtesy of the Historical Museum of Southern Florida.

atmosphere enveloping Fisher's South Florida enterprises. His personal favorite was Rosie, who could be seen posing for publicity photos on golf courses, pulling children in a specially designed cart, or hard at work, pulling up tree stumps with her trunk. When President-elect Warren G. Harding visited Miami Beach early in 1921, Rosie appeared in wire service photos carrying his golf clubs. Such images generated marvelous publicity for Miami Beach.[46] In at least one case, however, Rosie cost Fisher a lot of money. A patron, either inebriated or simply sleepy, was riding in one of Fisher's streetcars. His window was open, and he happened to be holding a bag of peanuts in his lap. The car stopped next to Rosie, and the pachyderm, smelling the tempting target, apparently snaked her trunk into the window of the car just as the patron awoke. Startled at the vision of a huge gray trunk approaching his lap, the patron bolted from the car, fell down the steps, and broke his leg. He sued Fisher and won a large cash award.[47]

Such legal cases might have helped lead Fisher to drink, but it seemed clear that Prohibition was a more significant factor affecting his lifestyle.

Carl had never been comfortable with government regulation. His exchanges with military officials during World War I and occasional visits from Internal Revenue Service agents left a bad taste in his mouth. When national Prohibition went into effect in 1920, Carl was just beginning to position himself to receive the payoff for years of hard work and sacrifice at Miami Beach. He knew full well that the visitors he courted would demand their highballs. For Fisher, Prohibition not only violated his strong feeling that no government should tell him what to do, but it indirectly threatened his livelihood.

Carl did not simply tolerate rum-running into and out of Miami Beach; he became an active participant. Local politicians, realizing that free-flowing booze lubricated tourists' spending habits, were not prone to be spoilsports by insisting on enforcement. If the occasional blue-nosed Mrs. Grundy was offended, let her and her teetotaling family find a totally dry resort somewhere else. For his part, Carl wanted to ensure that both his house and hotel guests would be well supplied with liquor. That he required hundreds of cases of booze every year necessitated his personal attention to the matter.

He might have delegated the task of securing liquor to one of his managers, but Carl clearly enjoyed running risks and matching wits with Prohibition agents. Jane recalled that he built hidden wine cellars at their homes in Miami Beach and Indianapolis and kept them well stocked.[48] According to his longtime friend Gar Wood, a boat racer and designer of powerful engines, Carl enjoyed selling fast engines to well-known bootleggers so that they, too, could more easily circumvent the law.[49] In the early 1920s, Carl was basically dealing in shipments of a few dozen cases at a time; later in the decade, the booze was flowing so freely at his home and hotels that he arranged transfers of hundreds of cases each month. Albert Champion, president of the A. C. Sparkplug Company, helped Carl complete one transfer of 500 cases, packed in vinegar barrels and sent by boat; shipping cost $8 per case. Carl actively supported political organizations fighting Prohibition. In a letter accompanying a cash donation to the Association Against the Prohibition Amendment, Carl wrote, "The Prohibition amendment is, of course, a farce, and a greater one each day." A few months later, during the 1928 presidential campaign, he wrote to one politician, "You know I have always been a Republican but I am off the Republican party now on their Prohibition stand. I am for Smith on every angle."[50]

Fisher mastered the art of marketing vacations, entertainment, and leisure to others, but he seldom relaxed himself, at least in the sense of getting totally away from business. Although he may have preferred bathing suits, more often he was dressed in coat and tie, discussing important financial matters with bankers and lawyers or selling real estate to potential investors. Following World War I, his most time-consuming activity was building and managing his hotels. If he hoped to create a vacation paradise at Miami Beach, luxury hotels were indispensable. With one or two exceptions, Fisher had been unable to interest others in building hotels. Mrs. Tatum Wofford leased the Breakers Apartments at 23rd and Collins Avenue and converted it into a hotel. Within a few years, she had parlayed her initial investment into the brand new, exclusive Wofford Hotel, where she demanded an unheard-of rate of $25 per night. In 1916 Fisher had built a very modest hotel on Lincoln Boulevard. Not surprisingly, he named it the Lincoln, but it was hardly of stature befitting a great president. The hotel was an unpretentious two-story building containing only thirty-five rooms.[51] In fact, the Lincoln was so ordinary that he advised guests in advance not to expect too much. In preparing Mrs. Charles F. Kettering for a winter visit in 1917, he described it as "a very nice little thirty-five room hotel within a block of the seashore and opposite the golf links, which I built and fitted out on purpose to take care of friends in a pinch." He assured her that "if the hotel on this side isn't just what you want, we will get you over in town."[52]

Fisher entered a market ripe for development. By the onset of World War I, Miami had about 8,000 hotel rooms. These were, however, insufficient for the 10,000 to 15,000 tourists who were expected at the height of the 1917–18 season.[53] Postwar tourism would keep Miami and Miami Beach developers scrambling to catch up with demand. As late as 1922, Fisher informed one potential investor that Miami Beach still needed "a dozen high grade hotels."[54] Carl, with his millions, would have to lead the way.

In fact, Fisher announced the first of his magnificent hotels, the Flamingo, in 1919. Carl assumed some financial risk. He had spent a great deal of money dredging and reshaping the hundreds of acres of land at

Miami Beach, most of which he still owned. Hence Fisher was land-rich but cash-poor. He initially estimated the cost at $750,000, but he started building in an inflationary period, and the tab soon doubled. To enter the hotel business on a serious basis, Fisher needed to float bonds and attract other investors with deep pockets. Eventually, Fisher borrowed about $500,000 at 7.5 percent interest.[55]

Fisher showed considerable foresight in building the hotels at least one block from the beaches. He figured that construction of the hotels would greatly increase beachfront land values right next to the hotels. He and Jane had become enamored of the flamingo, the bird they believed exemplified the exotic lushness of the region. Carl hired a team of ornithologists to capture dozens of flamingos, in hopes that he could get them to nest permanently in man-made ponds next to the hotel; however, they quickly disappeared. Jane involved herself in decorating the lobby, which featured flamingo wallpaper and complementary bright colors. The decor in many rooms also featured flamingos in tropical settings. The hotel was eleven stories high at the center, topped by a dome of "jeweled glass lighted by varicolored floodlights," which was visible on clear nights from seven miles out on the water. Each of the hotel's two wings was five stories. The structure eventually contained 200 guest rooms. The breathtaking jewel of Miami Beach took about two years to build, officially opening the last day of 1920.[56]

When the Flamingo was completed and opened for business, fair-weather friends and casual acquaintances surrounded Fisher to offer congratulations. Many insisted that they had believed in him all along. But when deeply immersed in the hard work, he was basically alone, and problems compounded daily. In the spring of 1920 Carl upbraided the architects for enormous cost overruns.[57] He brought some problems on himself, however. After initial plans were approved, Carl and Jane Fisher's ambition to create a state-of-the-art facility induced them to add expensive extras. Fisher was so strapped for cash in the spring of 1921 that he offered to sell the hotel to New York financiers for $717,000, just over half of the funds he had invested in it.[58] Fortunately for Fisher, his offer was rejected.

Relying on recommendations of experienced hotel men, Fisher hired an extremely able manager several months before the Flamingo opened.

In this aerial view looking south, the Flamingo Hotel is in the foreground. In the distance, the viewer can see that Miami Beach was beginning to thrive by the early 1920s. Courtesy of the Historical Museum of Southern Florida.

Charles S. Krom, a graduate of Colgate University, took over the reins of the hotel and remained there for twenty-eight years.[59] Before the opening, Krom advised Fisher that they might be able to get as much as $60 or $70 a night for a two-bedroom suite with a bath, but he suggested that for the first season at least, they should let rooms go for as little as $15 per night, at least until they regularly attracted near-full capacity. Later, they would probably be able to increase rates for the best rooms to $30 or $40 per night.[60]

By the end of the 1921 fiscal year, Fisher could begin assessing the financial consequences of his decision to invest heavily in hotels. Although the Flamingo Hotel had not opened until the first of the calendar year, it earned $121,000 in net receipts over the first eighty-nine days of operation. His managers had charged an average of $15.40 per day per person on the American Plan. Fisher expressed optimism over its future, noting that during the height of the season in February, more than 200 potential guests had to be turned away for lack of space. Nevertheless,

Fisher still wanted to sell the hotel. As he put it in a letter to a potential buyer, "Running hotels is not part of our business. . . . We have a large amount of land to sell but we were forced to build the Flamingo." Fisher claimed that with the burgeoning tourism in Miami Beach, "we now need at least ten hotels with the capacity of the Flamingo."[61]

Fisher's long-range strategy for the development of Miami Beach was becoming clear. His overriding objective was to generate profits through enhancement of land values. Every other form of revenue was of secondary importance. By building hotels, golf courses, yacht basins, polo fields, swimming pools, and other amenities, he greatly increased the value of the rest of his real estate. Carl's entire fortune revolved around the long-range value of real estate. In 1919, Fisher unveiled a daring strategy for making unsold land more attractive. When lots weren't moving, rather than dropping his prices, Fisher announced that prices would *increase* a minimum of 10 percent every year. One of his real estate ads read: "If you wish to purchase property from us this season you may do so knowing the price will be advanced next year at least ten percent over the season. We try to give our customers an investment in a home site or business site that substantially and steadily grows in value."[62]

In hindsight, of course, Fisher's real estate ads can be viewed as gold-plated invitations for everyone to become an instant millionaire. Persons who did invest a few thousand dollars in his lots and held on for several years did become wealthy. At the time, however, there were few takers. Fisher stuck to his guns and raised prices, but the strategy did not appear to be working very well two years later.[63] As the 1921–22 winter season approached, Fisher still hadn't sold the Flamingo, nor were lots selling. In September 1921, one of his most trusted real estate managers, John H. Levi, described their unnerving scramble for cash. He informed his boss, who was back in Indianapolis, "Money is coming in very slowly to the Ocean View company." They were begging to borrow tens of thousands of dollars from people to whom they had loaned hundreds of thousands a few years earlier. "I had to get Ed Romfh to loan us another $10,000 to pay our September installment on the income tax, as Lummus could not loan us any more; and Ed loaned us that for only thirty days."[64]

That was the low point. Over the next few months, Fisher's accountants desperately juggled the books, devoting a major part of their energy to fending off persistent creditors. The boss, bored by financial details, tried to pass off such concerns as pettifoggery. To one Detroit banker who had just sent him a second notice of a past due account, Fisher resorted to sarcasm, calling him a "dandy little collector." He continued, "There isn't a chance, that I can see, for you to get this money until some time in the Spring." Fisher insisted that there were a large number of potential big sales that he was confident of closing during the 1921–22 winter season, "but in the meantime, I am doing some tall hustling to keep sufficient funds for pay-rolls, so I will appreciate it if you will lay off of me until I have some surplus cash."[65]

Throughout his career, Fisher was an inveterate gambler. Facing a situation that would cause most businessmen to practice caution, Fisher routinely rolled the dice. Even as he haggled over small short-term loans and struggled to meet his payroll, he raised venture capital to plunge even deeper into hotel building. As he explained to one potential investor late in 1921, "When we first built the Lincoln, it was our intention to build several hotels to cater to the very best class of wealthy patrons at the Beach, and from these hotels to sell some of these patrons residential property, in which we have been very successful." He was stretching the truth somewhat regarding the latter point. But Fisher perceived a symbiosis between his major building projects; each reinforced and fed off the other. He concluded that hotel availability at Miami Beach had not yet reached the critical mass required to put the vacation mecca over the top. He reiterated his appeal: "At the present time, we need at least ten hotels at the Beach the size of the Flamingo or larger." A year later, he had raised his estimate of necessary additional hotel capacity to a dozen. By then, he had determined that most other investors were too timid to build in advance of demand, so he would lead the pack: "It is our purpose to build hotels and sell them as fast as we can afford to do so."[66] In his long-range plan, his primary profits would be in residential land sales.

Fisher succeeded, at least concerning the first half of the equation. He expanded the size of the Flamingo by about sixty rooms and began building three new hotels: the Nautilus, King Cole, and Boulevard. These new facilities combined hosted about the same number of patrons as the Flamingo. Construction of the 189-room Nautilus began in 1923, the King Cole a year later. Construction of the Boulevard began in 1925.

Carl Fisher in his late
forties, at the height of
his influence. Courtesy of
the Historical Museum of
Southern Florida.

These hotels were strategically located nearby yet another Fisher-built facility, the brand-new Bayshore Golf Course.[67] The Boulevard was finally finished in August 1926, too late to affect the mid-decade boom. Land values near these new hotels quickly spiraled, even while they were under construction.

By the mid-1920s, other investors had jumped on board, and the Florida land boom was in full flower. Other resort builders rushed into the region to capitalize on the good times. On the Miami side of Biscayne Bay, George Merrick was building his fabulous Coral Gables community. A few miles north up the coast, Addison Mizner was masterminding the development of Boca Raton.[68] Miami Beach property leaped in value, and other hotel entrepreneurs entered the scene. The Pancoasts finally joined the move and constructed the exclusive 110-room Pancoast Hotel. Others committed on a far larger scale. Real estate developer J. Perry Stoltz originally came to South Florida to retire but soon got caught up in the craze and built the sumptuous Fleetwood Hotel during the 1924–25 season. Newton Baker Taylor (usually called by his initials N. B. T.) Roney, yet another high roller, announced plans in December 1924 to build the largest hotel yet in Miami Beach, the $2 million Roney Plaza, located at Collins Avenue and 23d Street. The latter facility opened in February 1926, barely in time for the bursting of the speculative land bubble, not just in Miami Beach but all of Florida.[69]

Few were thinking in negative terms about South Florida's future by the mid-1920s. Fabulous new hotels were opening, and the tourists were flocking to Miami Beach. By 1925 there were 56 hotels and 4,000 available rooms. Long-term guests could lease space in one of nearly 200 apartment buildings.[70] Visitors enjoyed virtually any active or sedentary form of warm climate leisure, and Fisher and his associates encouraged them to wallow in pleasure. If the hosts were so busy during the tourist season that they had little time for leisure themselves, the payoff was that profits were enormous. Some entrepreneurs probably experienced their greatest enjoyment when they sat down with glasses of scotch whiskey at the end of the day and totaled up their winnings. But not Fisher; he, too, enjoyed the whiskey, but he preferred the notoriety of being a celebrity. By the mid-1920s, Carl Fisher became a household name across the United States; some newsmen reported his net worth at as much as $100 million and wondered how he had grown so rich so fast. The handful of observers who knew him well, who fully understood the difficulties he had surmounted and the harrowing risks he had taken in the previous dozen years, may have justifiably argued that his good fortune was fairly earned. In fact, nobody had worked harder than Carl Fisher to turn Miami Beach into an adult fairyland.

10

Noonday Sun

Carl Fisher achieved dazzling success in Miami Beach. To be sure, he had enjoyed earlier triumphs. Some, like Prest-O-Lite, earned him great sums of money. Others, including building the Indianapolis Motor Speedway and hosting the famous Memorial Day races, brought him national, even worldwide fame, as well as the excitement of promoting state-of-the-art technology and huge crowd-attracting spectator sports. His leadership roles in the Lincoln and Dixie Highway Associations earned Fisher praise for performing a valuable public service and kept his name before the public, even if they brought him little or no additional wealth. But Carl's triumph at Miami Beach brought him unprecedented national attention and unimaginable wealth. The downside was that his enormous success at Miami Beach was apparent only after many years of struggle, and he did not retain his huge fortune very long.

When the good times finally arrived for Fisher and his associates in Miami Beach, they came with a rush. As late as 1920, land sales for Fisher's organization had been slow, roughly $500,000 for the year. Then the giddying climb commenced. By 1923 sales reached $6 million, and a year later $8 million worth of property changed hands. Growth, however, continued to spiral upward; in 1925 Carl and his agents sold $23 million worth of property. Many speculators were convinced there was no end in sight. Fisher had become a national celebrity. He was photographed with presidents and hobnobbed regularly with sports heroes and movie stars. Carl genuinely liked people, and he usually cooperated with reporters. He was both colorful and good copy; his pronouncements were often front-page news.

If there was a single event that put Miami Beach over the top, it may have been a visit by President-elect Warren G. Harding in the winter of 1921. Harding spent several days "bloviating" (Harding's own nonsensical generic term for indulging himself) at Miami Beach, and the entire South Florida region gained priceless publicity. Predictably, Fisher was at the center of complicated maneuvering to attract the accommodating politician, and when Harding finally arrived, he was almost constantly at his side.

Harding's campaign for the nation's top office and his landslide election in November 1920 had done a great deal to soothe the anxiety of a body politic that had been rubbed raw in recent years by the demands of arming for and fighting in World War I, the frightening loss of lives during the war, the influenza pandemic of 1918–19, controversy over whether to join the League of Nations, and the national Red Scare of 1919–20. Harding had promised a return to "normalcy" (another choice Harding malapropism), and he seemed to be helping achieve it even before he entered office. He was handsome, charming, and affable. His political mentor, Harry Daugherty, was initially drawn to Harding in part because he *looked* like a president. In stark contrast to that of the lame-duck president, Woodrow Wilson, who had been rendered largely ineffective for more than a year by a massive stroke, Harding's political style was collegial rather than confrontational. He enjoyed public rituals far more than serious behind-the-scenes deliberation over weighty matters of state.

Late in 1920, Fisher got word that Harding and his advisers were considering destinations for a vacation in a warm climate before his inauguration. Attracting personages of elevated stature for publicity purposes is at the heart of the resort business. Fisher sensed that dozens of rival resort entrepreneurs would be angling for a visit by Harding, but he figured he had nothing to lose in entering the bidding. He first offered Harding a free suite of rooms at the Flamingo, which he was rushing to completion even as he wrote. Should Harding visit, Fisher promised pure relaxation, away from newsmen and assorted grasping favor-seekers: "Every possible privacy and comfort will be yours, and no overdraft on your time and good nature permitted."[1] He added the lure of golf under sunny skies and "six hundred species of fish in the Gulf Stream adjacent to Miami Beach." But Fisher was not content with a simple letter of offer to Harding; he enlisted assistance from his influential friend at *National Geographic*, Jack LaGorce, who had connections with Harding's advisers. LaGorce contacted Harding's secretary, George B. Christian Jr., who advised him to be patient while his boss sorted out numerous invitations and requests.[2]

Biding his time was difficult for Carl, but he managed to restrain himself. In early January he received extremely encouraging signals from Harding's close associate, Ohio state senator William Miller. Miller advised Fisher that he had personally touted Miami Beach and that "I have the assurance of Mr. Daugherty . . . that [he] will use his influence to convince Mr. Harding that he ought to accept the invitation, if it is tendered."[3] A week later, LaGorce passed along discouraging news; he had learned via conversations with another Harding confidant, New Jersey senator Joseph Frelinghuysen, that although the president-elect planned to visit Florida, he would probably spend nights on a houseboat: "To sum the matter up, they deem it advisable not to accept any invitations on shore where in all likelihood they would be surrounded by people looking at them and interfering with their enjoyment in spite of all that could be done to protect them from it."[4] The next day, Fisher received a formal rejection from Harding himself: "My plans will not admit of such an enticing program. We are coming South soon and I am expecting to get a rather hurried glimpse of Miami and the Beach. We shall not be able to stay."[5]

Fisher's initial reaction was disappointment and disgust. He vented his frustration in a blustery letter to LaGorce: "This is the second time I have gone after a President and it is the last. From now on Miami Beach is going to be so hell-fired attractive that the Presidents and the rest of the near politicians will telegraph for accommodations. We certainly will never make another effort to get one of them here."[6] LaGorce responded a few days later, admonishing his friend not to take the rejection person-ally. He reminded Fisher that Harding had received dozens of similar invitations and that everybody was well aware of the enormous commer-cial value that would be generated by a presidential visit. He asked Fisher, "Would you personally accept such a thing from anybody, thus placing yourself under some kind of obligation—nay, I think not."[7]

Seemingly by magic, Harding's plans changed yet again. Perhaps Harding's fancy had been tickled by a personal visit to his home office in Marion, Ohio, by one of Fisher's most gifted assistants, a very attrac-tive secretary named Ann Rossiter. Fisher had instructed her to present his invitation "personally" if possible to the president-elect. In a detailed report back to her boss, Rossiter admitted that she had doubted she would get past Harding's phalanx of intermediaries. When she arrived at his office, there were "eight or ten [people] on missions of all kinds, waiting to see Mr. Harding. I was much surprised to be taken in away ahead of everybody else—this meant Senator Miller also. He gave us a full half hour." Rossiter concluded her otherwise businesslike report to her boss with an intriguing, if veiled, suggestion that Harding may have been influenced by her decidedly feminine appeal: "This personal call, personal touch, *or whatever you want to call it*, may not be without results" (emphasis added).[8]

Whether or not Rossiter's femininity influenced Harding, the presi-dent-elect visited South Florida for several days in late January, and Fish-er fully capitalized on his stay. The party arrived in South Florida a day ahead of schedule, and Carl was far better prepared to take advantage of the opportunity than were officials in Miami. Harding and his wife, Flor-ence, slept at a "cottage" at the Flamingo Hotel. Surrounded by photog-raphers, he golfed at Fisher's course. Surpassing Fisher's wildest hopes for generating unusual and riveting photo opportunities, Harding amiably posed with Carl's elephant Rosie, which was supposedly "caddying" for him. Harding took a swim at the Roman Pools and spent two days out on the water sport fishing with Carl and a few friends. Harding's vacation included a relaxing visit to Fisher's private fishing retreat, the Cocolobo Club, where he reeled in a sailfish. Carl's payoff was when Harding en-thusiastically "pitched" Miami Beach in a public statement: "Because of

A revealing picture of President-elect Warren G. Harding's visit to Miami Beach early in 1921. Harding, in bathrobe and slippers, shakes hands, while the nattily attired Fisher, at far right, waits to pounce on his prey. Courtesy of the Historical Museum of Southern Florida.

the attractiveness of Miami Beach, I hope to come here again. This beach is wonderful. It is developing like magic."[9] For Carl, Harding's endorsement was better than gold.

Harding was by nature a trusting, almost naive soul; he may have had little sense of the frantic maneuvering behind the scenes by various promoters to capitalize on his visit. Fisher had clearly stolen a march on his competitors. To the consternation of officials in Miami, Harding's gracious public comments focused on Miami Beach. Although Harding did make two brief visits across the bay, he spent most of his time with Fisher and his associates. Jane Fisher neatly summarized her husband's audacious coup: "Carl actually shanghied [sic] the President right out from under the nose of the pip squeak Miami reception committee. . . . The committee cooled their heels for hours along the inland waterway waiting for President Harding to appear."[10]

Harding's visit worked to the long-range benefit of the entire region, but Miami Beach reaped the most obvious rewards. As one astute analyst observed, "Carl's Miami Beach development was the first of its kind in Florida, the first to make something new, bright, expensive and fun out of what to most Americans had been nothing, a wilderness. Of all Florida resorts, Miami Beach was the best publicized and most important, it best reflected the spirit of the decade that later came to be known as the Roaring Twenties.... Carl and the twenties were made for each other. Its interests—sports, cars, movies, radio, common stocks, speculation, real estate, Florida—were his too: its circus atmosphere—ballyhoo, publicity stunts, movie stars, flagpole sitters—suited him exactly."[11]

Fisher's "kidnapping" of the president-elect had some long-term consequences he did not fully anticipate, however. Carl had figuratively left Miami officials with egg on their faces. As one observer noted a few days after Harding's visit, "Everybody is laughing at the way Carl Fisher put it over Miami. Miami had made great preparations for the entertainment of the President-elect, had gone so far as to procure guides and arrange all the essentials. When Mr. Harding got in sight of Miami and the highly decorated boats, ladies, etc., he shied off to the east. He never stopped shieing [sic] until he landed at the Lincoln Hotel."[12] According to one historian of Miami Beach, Miami officials never forgot the slight, and several of its influential men bore personal animosity toward Fisher for years.[13]

To his credit, Fisher soon realized that his coup had raised the hackles of Miami boosters, and he tried to make amends. He extended an olive branch through an offer to embark on a joint advertising campaign. In the late fall of 1921, Fisher was mulling over ideas for a huge outdoor advertising sign to be located at Fifth Avenue and 42nd Street in New York City. He wrote to his associate Thomas Pancoast, "I believe that this sign constantly standing out on rainy and stormy nights during the winter season would be of great value, as no doubt more people pass this corner than any other in the United States. . . . It would surely be a marvelous sign of great benefit to Miami and Miami Beach." He was trying to come up with the perfect slogan. "We could say 'It is June in Miami and Miami Beach.'"[14] Fisher asked Pancoast to pass along his offer to share both the cost of the sign and the benefits of the publicity to the Miami Chamber of

Commerce. When decision makers in Miami rejected the idea, Carl went ahead on his own. The sign eventually read, "It's always June in Miami Beach."[15] The flow of shivering, pasty-complected northerners to the sunny beaches in South Florida increased dramatically. Whether the sign contributed directly to the increase in business, sophisticated advertising executives considered the slogan inspired.[16]

By the early 1920s, Fisher had rediscovered his penchant for promotional flair which he had briefly discarded in the late 1910s when he used conservative appeals to attract sober-minded investors to his Alton Beach property. He had been persuaded, as he noted later, that "other rich men were somehow more refined." To his credit, he realized his mistake and quickly adjusted. Interviewed by a *Business* reporter in the early 1920s, Fisher stated, "I was on the wrong track. I had been trying to reach the dead ones. I had been going after the old folks. I saw that what I needed to do was go after the live wires. And the live wires don't want to rest."[17]

In past years Fisher handled a good deal of publicity himself, but by 1922 or so, activity at his sales offices was so frantic that he increasingly delegated these tasks to others. At times his publicists got carried away in their zeal to promote Miami Beach—and Fisher's property. Steve Hannagan, a graduate of Indiana University, had done excellent work promoting the Indianapolis 500 race, and Fisher brought him to Miami Beach in the early 1920s. He would eventually become a legend among public relations men. He could also be extremely opportunistic, even hard-boiled. When the yeast magnate Julius Fleischmann collapsed and died of a heart attack during a polo match, it was, by some accounts, Hannagan, not Fisher, who insisted that the dateline read Miami Beach rather than Miami.

For the most part, however, Fisher's extravagant promotional efforts fit the times nicely, and he handled the biggest ones himself. Perhaps nobody captured the spirit of Miami Beach and Fisher's role in its emergence better than the renowned humorist Will Rogers. Rogers had admired Fisher's land-building efforts in Miami Beach from the beginning. He labeled Fisher's dredges "all-day suckers." Concerning Fisher's promotional tactics, Rogers commented, "Carl rowed the customers out into the ocean and let them pick out some nice smooth water where they would like to build, and then he would replace the water with an island,

and today the dredge is the national emblem of Florida." Rogers always drew laughs with his punch line about Fisher training mosquitoes not to bite customers until land sales were final.[18]

It had taken Fisher, Thomas Pancoast, the Collins family, and a few much smaller-scale land developers years to build Miami Beach. Needless to say, before the boom in South Florida real estate, Miami Beach property development made virtually no impact on the national real estate market. Whether it was the hoopla surrounding Harding's visit, inspired outdoor advertising slogans erected at key locations, the syrupy promotional palaver written by publicists like Jack LaGorce and Steve Hannagan, or the attention attracted by story writers like Kenneth Roberts and such national icons as Will Rogers, Miami Beach was suddenly "in." Everybody, it seemed, wanted to be part of the action. Fisher was suddenly crowned as a marketing wizard; curious reporters swarmed around him, seeking "inside" stories on "how he'd done it." Jane Fisher doggedly insisted that her husband hated personal publicity, that he repeatedly deflected questions about his role to emphasize the quality of projects he was involved with and highlighted the contributions of others. Fisher was, indeed, surprisingly modest, but it is absurd to deny that he also reveled in being the center of attention.

In later years, some analysts suggested that Fisher had developed highly original strategies for marketing land, which helped explain his success. For example, Fisher built hotels ahead of actual demand, which in turn raised the value of the surrounding land so much that when it sold, Fisher got back the investment in his hotels plus a substantial profit.[19] Certainly Fisher employed such tactics, but they were not original to him. Railroad and steamship entrepreneurs and a host of other land speculators had been employing such tactics for decades before Carl Fisher appeared on the scene.

Without question, however, Fisher's hotels were focal points for his real estate endeavors. The aggressive promoter was acutely aware that happy and relaxed hotel guests were prime prospects for purchasing land for winter homes. This fact, however, created some internal tension in Fisher's emerging marketing organization. Above all, hotel managers wanted satisfied customers, which translated into repeat business, high occupancy rates, and bonuses or promotions for themselves. Keeping "business" away from the lobbies, restaurants, and lounge areas adjacent to swimming pools was one means of maintaining a relaxed, enjoyable ambience. Fisher's real estate salesmen, in contrast, salivated at the thought of cornering juicy prospects enjoying a relaxing meal or blissfully sunning themselves on the beach or next to a pool. More than one enthusiastic salesman pounced on unsuspecting guests before they even reached the registration desk. For the record, Fisher loftily mouthed platitudes about the right of hotel guests to be left alone. In practice, he let his real estate and hotel managers resolve the issue among themselves. Fisher's papers are sprinkled with sometimes caustic exchanges between hotel manager Charles S. Krom and property sales manager C. W. "Pete" Chase.[20] Although they occasionally squabbled over the presence of Fisher's salesmen, they were united in their determination to toss out agents representing rival real estate companies.

Fisher personally lured many friends and business associates to Miami Beach, drawing heavily from the "gasoline aristocracy" of Detroit and other nouveaux riches, largely from the Midwest. Whatever Fisher's scruples about "bothering" his hotel guests on the premises, he and his managers carefully screened guest lists for hot prospects. When a prominent guest arrived, Fisher might instruct his salesmen to leave him alone for a day or two, then send a free bottle of champagne to his room with a discreet note attached, offering to show him property if he was interested. This system occasionally backfired when prospects were identified only by name. On one occasion, Fisher's sales organization circled the name of a guest thought to be a "billionaire copper king." Fisher wined and dined him, took him out for a day-long cruise aboard the *Shadow J*," then finally got down to business. Fisher employed the personal touch, asking his prospect about the state of his business. "The honored guest puffed on his dollar cigar. 'Tell you the truth, Mr. Fisher, the haberdashery business isn't what it was. You've been mighty nice, and I'm going to send you a couple of neckties from my shelves.'"[21] Fisher had a robust sense of humor, and he enjoyed telling this story on himself for years.

Not all patrons were welcome everywhere in Miami Beach. By the late 1920s, many hotel and apartment building proprietors openly discriminated against Jews. Was Carl Fisher an anti-Semite? The evidence is mixed. Jane Fisher emphatically rejected the notion, pointing out that he had been engaged briefly to Emma Messing, a Jewish woman from Indianapolis. In addition, several of his good friends were Jews. They stayed in his hotels, bought his property, and often enjoyed meals at his home.[22] Others, however, analyzed the issue in more depth. Basically, they concluded that Fisher realized that the "wrong kind" of Jew would be bad for business. One Miami Beach resident crudely summed up Carl's attitude: "Fisher wasn't anti-Jewish. . . . He was anti-kike."[23] His business decisions and correspondence confirm this view. If the "wrong kind" of Jew wanted to buy, Carl would either instruct his salesmen to refuse to sell to them or steer them to less desirable or isolated plots. To one rude inquiry into the character of a recent buyer, Fisher replied that the individual in question was "a very high class type" of Jew.[24]

Even before Harding's early 1921 visit, Fisher and his managers noticed that property that had gone begging the previous season was beginning to sell. Early in 1920, Fisher informed one client that several homes in Miami Beach had sold for prices ranging from $30,000 to $60,000. After rattling off the well-known names of previous buyers, Fisher advised her, "If you have any idea of taking this Ocean front corner for a home site, I would strongly urge you to act promptly. . . . I just don't want you to be disappointed if the property you have your mind set on isn't available when you have decided to take it."[25] In May 1921, Fisher confided to one New York investor, "In spite of the financial depression in other parts of the country, Miami is still making considerable headway." This assessment included Miami Beach: "While our operating companies did not sell a great deal of land this winter, the actual sales at the beach and resales are probably 35% greater than last season's sales would total."[26] A year later, Fisher sounded even more confident as he summarized the 1921–22 winter season's sales: "I show a profit on my books at this time of about $9,000,000. . . . The future profit of this company can be fifteen or more millions of dollars according to the time taken to develop and sell it." Fisher saw no reason to be caught up in any frenzied sell-off. "The earlier it is sold the less profits it will make."[27] By the end of the 1922 season, Fisher sensed a speculative frenzy ahead; he was prepared to remain calm and deliberate before taking action.

By the 1923 season, Miami Beach was beginning to experience an unprecedented boom in which property values escalated dramatically.

In 1919 Fisher had instructed his sales force to increase the price of unsold land 10 percent per year. Other real estate developers had scoffed, telling him that he would never sell his property. Had Fisher stuck to his principle of advancing property prices *only* 10 percent per year, *he* would have been the fool. By 1923, prices seemed to be escalating that much every *month*. Traditionally, hotels had opened around January 1, after the Christmas holidays. In 1923, however, most opened weeks earlier. Fisher opened the Lincoln on November 1, and others were doing a brisk business by the first week of December. By the end of 1923, Miami Beach alone had twenty-one hotels, ranging in capacity from 15 to 250 rooms and capable of housing 4,000 guests per night.[28]

If Fisher urged his salesmen to stay out of lobbies in his hotels, he encouraged them to go after customers in other hotels. Undoubtedly, his competitors passed along similar instructions to their agents. By 1923 salesmen in their light-colored suits and straw hats seemingly outnumbered the tourists. They swarmed around Flagler Street in downtown Miami, and they sometimes came right to the edge of the water in Miami Beach. Wealthy, "retired" northern real estate agent J. Perry Stoltz ventured south in his yacht in the winter of 1923 and later described his experience: "I came down to Miami Beach only on conditions that I forget business altogether and not buy a thing, real estate or otherwise. I succeeded fairly well, except—when I went north in the spring, I found I was owner of 2,000 feet of bay front . . . between the bay and Alton Road."[29] Stoltz had little reason to lament his "slip." The property he purchased skyrocketed in value after he constructed the 350-room Fleetwood Hotel, a fabulous sixteen-story facility that featured a roof garden for dining and dancing under starlight.

In the mid-1920s, Stoltz, N. B. T. Roney, Addison Mizner, and George Merrick and hundreds of smaller-scale dreamers were pouring tens of millions of dollars into brand new developments, not just in South Florida but throughout the state and as far north as southern Georgia. Florida promoters launched a campaign to persuade state residents to mail 100,000 postcards before the start of the 1924–25 tourist season featuring "pictures and messages calculated to draw friends and relatives" to the Sunshine State. The Chamber of Commerce in West Palm Beach printed 50,000 publicity booklets featuring drawings of attractive youths enjoying winter play. Businessmen created the All-Florida Development Conference, whose grandiose purpose was to raise $200,000 to promote the state "throughout the world."[30]

Fisher's vision was finally becoming reality; big money was being invested in Miami Beach. Alfred I. du Pont had purchased property in 1922. Harvey Firestone, Roy D. Chapin, Harry Stutz, Albert Champion, and Frank J. Seiberling were among the many other important automobile men who moved in. Finally succumbing to Carl's relentless, if low-key, courtship, Edsel Ford also purchased extensive holdings at the beach, and he induced some of his Detroit pals to join him.

Miami Beach was booming, and there appeared to be some style as well as substance to its development. Not only were hotels and residences mushrooming, but the town was finally gaining a thin veneer of sophistication. In 1923 the Star Island Yacht Club opened. This club offered far more than boating after George B. Everart signed on as club manager. Everart had opened Maxim's in Paris and had run both the London Ritz and the New York Ritz. The Florida Art League hosted painting exhibits at the Miami Beach Chamber of Commerce Building, and there were both plans and cash pledges for a library, art museum, and natural history museum. After dark visitors could enter the casino at 23d Street to listen to the Miami Beach Casino Orchestra, which performed nightly.[31] Miami Beach was not Broadway, but in some ways local boosters were trying to compete with the resort's more sophisticated neighbor to the north, Palm Beach.

By the mid-1920s, families driving south passed staked-out subdivisions by the dozens, many of them miles from the closest human habitation. The vast majority of would-be tropical utopias never got off the ground; dreams of riches of thousands of small investors withered under the merciless sun. But there were dazzling successes. On the west side of Miami, George Merrick laid out an imaginatively designed community named Coral Gables, featuring a Mediterranean motif. In some respects, Merrick's development was aesthetically superior to Fisher's effort at Miami Beach because Coral Gables represented a more coherent organic community. Merrick may have stolen a page from renowned Kansas City,

Missouri, developer J. C. Nichols in hiring landscape architect Phineas Paist to design a community on a large scale in advance of development. Coral Gables featured gracious boulevards, many with curves and lined with mature trees. There were also "impressive city gates, plazas, fountains, neighborhoods full of Mediterranean villas, a zoned business center, even a university."

Ann Armbrister, a historian of Miami Beach, suggested that Merrick envisioned Coral Gables as a middle-class "suburban utopia." She quickly dismissed Carl Fisher, claiming that he "was no such cosmopolitan. . . . For his own child, Miami Beach, he did only what was necessary to sell it as a residential resort. He filled in the land, provided water and power, landscaped, built hotels and sports facilities to feather the city's nest, and then left it to grow itself."[32] Although there is some merit in her judgment, Armbrister ignored one critical variable. Merrick had full control over subdivision design at Coral Gables, whereas there were half a dozen or so totally independent large developers at Miami Beach. Even had he been so inclined, Fisher could not have maintained architectural integrity without stiff zoning laws and active cooperation from other developers.

Besides Fisher and Merrick, many aggressive developers were trying to capitalize on the Florida boom. About forty miles north of Miami Beach, Addison Mizner began an ambitious resort development named Boca Raton. Mizner announced plans for his project on April 15, 1925; in many ways, it mirrored Coral Gables in both magnitude and style. Boca Raton would be a carefully planned community, eventually housing several thousand residents. Spanish stucco was the dominant architectural style. Mizner imitated Fisher in announcing plans for immediate construction of a $6 million, 1,000-room hotel, two golf courses designed by Donald Ross, a polo field, swimming pools, and $1 million worth of other improvements. It would be "the world's most architecturally beautiful playground." He emphasized that he had endorsements and substantial investments from some of the nation's social and professional elite and even foreign royalty. Mizner's luscious advertisements claimed that sponsors of Boca Raton included Harold Vanderbilt, the Duchess of Sutherland, Wall Street investor Jesse L. Livermore, W. K. Vanderbilt, Colemen du Pont, Rodman Wanamaker, and many others. Mizner's development may have been sponsored by some extremely wealthy Americans, but it was not to be an exclusive playground for the rich. The town plan included residential sections for workers and an industrial district. Financial overcommitments and the collapse of the Florida land boom brought an abrupt end to building in Mizner's Boca Raton development, but he left a city plan that significantly influenced later development of the area.[33]

By the mid-1920s, several other prominent developers tried to horn in on the action at Boca Raton. Some planned to cooperate with Mizner in maintaining architectural integrity and coherent community design, but others offered aesthetic alternatives. George W. Harvey, a Boston real estate tycoon with substantial investments in West Palm Beach, announced in early June 1925 that he would build "Villa Rica," a 1,400-acre Spanish-style community within the boundaries of Boca Raton. Another West Palm Beach developer, A. W. Mathes, purchased $3 million worth of Mizner's land to develop his American Venice subdivision. Both projects fit loosely into Mizner's grand scheme. Yet Mizner also attracted competitors who expressed little interest in aesthetic integrity. A Chicago and Fort Lauderdale real estate agent named G. Frank Croissant trumpeted that he would build "Croissantania," just north of Boca Raton and west of the Dixie Highway, offering homes at prices "available to working men who could aid in the upbuilding of the entire community."[34] In Miami Beach, Boca Raton, and elsewhere, large developers were joined by hundreds of fly-by-night speculators who bought ten or twenty lots, some in remote locations. Obviously, many smaller developers hoped to capitalize on the massive publicity surrounding the Florida land mania without sharing promotional costs.

Although the Florida land boom was evident across the entire state, the center of action remained Flagler Street in Miami, where real estate offices lined both sides of the street and slick-talking salesmen dressed in dark blazers, light-colored pants, and straw hats hawked their wares to any passerby who appeared to have two dimes to rub together. Speculation was intense enough by 1923 and 1924, but by the 1925 season, the action resembled a feeding frenzy. Out in Coral Gables, thrice-defeated Democratic presidential nominee William Jennings Bryan was spending his declining years sunning himself beside a swimming pool, giving Sunday church sermons and speaking of the virtues of buying Merrick's real estate.

By early 1925, when the land boom was at its peak, downtown Miami and Miami Beach resembled a Middle East bazaar. Vacationers arriving by train were assaulted in the railroad station by "bird dogs," individuals on the lowest rung on the sales ladder of some real estate companies. They earned small fees by corralling prospects for real estate salesmen. Once vacationers collected their baggage and made it out to the street, they saw George Merrick's colorful busses offering free trips out to Coral Gables for a "once in a lifetime" opportunity to purchase one's dream home. Those unable to escape the clutches of the "bird dogs" soon found themselves face to face with one of the so-called binder boys, who were essentially novice real estate salesmen hoping to cash in on the boom. By 1925 thousands of these birds of passage had discovered Miami and Miami Beach.

The binder boys essentially sold paper options, not real estate. They trafficked in human greed. The buyer of a piece of property paid 10 percent of the negotiated price, promising to make future payments on a prearranged schedule. Most buyers intended to resell the same piece of paper for a higher price. For a time, many succeeded. Some properties changed hands several times in a single day. Men told stories of buying a lot for $10,000 over breakfast and selling the same lot before lunch for $15,000. A lot in downtown Miami that sold for $800 before the boom brought $150,000 in 1924. There was a tale of a man who parlayed two quarts of bootleg gin into $75,000.[35] Although reports of rising prices and huge profits were often inaccurate, highly exaggerated, or outright lies, in the climate of the moment few seemed willing to challenge the idea that South Florida's real estate boom would continue indefinitely.

The binder boys were the most visible middlemen in this bizarre boom, a stark symbol of its excess. They were distinguishable not only by their number but by their appearance. Often dressed in rumpled, slightly soiled linen suits or in golf knickers (which had the advantage of not needing to be pressed), they were on the same social level as carnival barkers, oozing a seedy air. They seemingly lived on cigarettes, coffee, donuts, and greasy hamburgers. If they didn't sleep on park benches or under bridges they might inhabit the cheaper hotels, three or four usually sharing a single room. But their "marks" were no more praiseworthy than the binder boys; *everybody* was out for the fast buck. In their frenzy not to miss out on "easy" money, many Americans were not particular about whom they dealt with.[36]

Sales techniques at subdivisions varied slightly, but one account fit many property auctions: "Some of the first-day sales were near-riots. When the Arch Creek section of Miami Shores was sold late in 1925, a crowd of buyers was waiting outside the office doors when they opened at 8:30 a.m. Two-and-a-half hours and $33,734,350 later, lots had completely sold out. Frantic buyers pushed checks and cash at salesmen; most paid little attention to which lots they bought, leaving it up to the company to decide. At 11:00 a.m. the sellers closed their doors to catch up with the bookkeeping. It took them five days to discover they were oversubscribed by more than $11 million."[37]

Through the summer of 1925 the boom continued unabated. To the uninitiated, it appeared that even the most simple-minded investor could make money simply by purchasing virtually any piece of land and then selling it to the next person in line. Naturally, the men at the top, those who understood the dynamics of property exchange and were experienced in sensing the rhythms of buying and selling, made the most money. Although Fisher never speculated in this manner, he benefited indirectly and became very rich. Estimates of his fortune at the peak of the boom ranged from $50 million up to $100 million. Nobody really knew, including Fisher. He had very little liquidity. His fortune was mostly on paper, and he was a lousy record keeper. Fisher sensed that he was "rich." Other than that, he didn't think about money carefully or often.

Possessing large wealth presented some problems for Fisher. Other than indulging in a few expensive hobbies, he had no particular interest in spending money. Wealth and fame attract parasites and sycophants, and many people clung to Carl Fisher. So did fund-raisers, and Carl gave generously to many charities, although his contributions were whimsical, not systematic. Perhaps because of his fondness for his valet, William Galloway, he made several contributions to black institutions, including Bethune-Cookman College and the Community Welfare House in Indianapolis, which housed "colored" women and children facing difficult circumstances.[38] Carl was also interested in giving former prisoners a second chance. He hired convicted felons, and he loaned funds to several so they could get a start in an honest enterprise. For years, he claimed that none of these human investments turned sour.[39]

Perhaps he was attempting to partially compensate for a lack of intimacy in his nuclear family. Both of his brothers had died in their thirties.[40] Carl had experienced an insecure upbringing, but he felt a filial duty toward both parents, even the father who had abandoned him when he was a child. Carl had maintained a proper, if somewhat distant, relationship with his mother. He certainly did not pamper her. Over the years, he sent her small sums of money on an irregular basis. Once his wealth became known, she often complained about needing more, and Carl usually responded dutifully. Predictably, Carl's father, Albert, also reentered his life at that point, writing long, ungrammatical letters to his son in which he described hardships and poor health. Carl unenthusiastically assumed the role of parent, responding with occasional cash gifts and hopes that his father would remain sober. In a pathetic yet revealing effort to rebuild a family that never was, he coaxed his parents to live together in a small house in Florida. The couple had never formally divorced. They resided together in peace, if not harmony, until Albert died in 1921. Carl evidently paid irregular visits to them, but their relationship appeared strained and uncomfortable.[41]

If Fisher's fortune was expanding in the mid-1920s, his marriage and personal life were in shambles. Jane had been an innocent, star-struck, fifteen-year-old, blithely unaware of most of his personal eccentricities, when she married Carl in 1909. Her husband thoroughly dominated the household, and he believed a wife's place was in the home. A good deal of Jane's youthful psychic energy must have been devoted to coping with some of Carl's crude personal habits. She recalled that during their courting days, he had "succeeded in hiding from me the fact that he smoked strong cigars and that he swore as casually as other men used ordinary speech."[42] When she moved into his bachelor quarters, the truth came out. Apparently, that was when she discovered that he chewed tobacco and insisted that spittoons be located throughout the house.

Carl and Jane Fisher toward the end of their marriage, in a light moment, wearing Christmas wreaths. Courtesy of the Historical Museum of Southern Florida.

Money apparently never caused tension in the marriage. Carl was hardly romantic or considerate on a day-to-day basis, but he occasionally dazzled Jane with enormous, unexpected presents. With the exception of his insistence on retaining his "manly comforts," he basically turned over management of the house and increasing numbers of servants to Jane. After they moved to Miami Beach, Carl spent less and less time at home, so Jane spent a lot of time by herself. Besides hosting elaborate luncheons, Jane enjoyed interior decorating and supervising landscaping around her houses, and her husband seldom complained about her expenditures.

They had very different notions of social life. Both were gregarious, and they loved entertaining at home, but Carl wanted Jane to be ready to entertain any number of people casually at a moment's notice. Jane preferred more formal, dressy functions, based on prearranged invitations. On occasion, Carl would show up in the midst of one of her fancy ladies' teas in dirty tennis shoes and shorts, smoking his cigar and reeking of sweat. His casual, constant swearing sometimes embarrassed her, and his social behavior was sometimes bizarre. At one "relaxed" dinner party, he picked up an expensive cut-glass goblet that one of their guests had given them as a wedding present and "threw it out the window at a cat fight. He was proud that he hit his target, oblivious to having broken the prize goblet."[43] Even when they did entertain formally as a couple, Carl followed his own schedule, sometimes simply walking out when the mood struck him. He could take only so much socializing while wearing a coat and tie. More and more often, Jane found herself making excuses for her husband's abrupt departures. Jane often appeared far more socially polished than her middle-aged husband. Their differences were even more pronounced when they visited other people's homes. They were a glamorous and wealthy couple, and they received many social invitations. Jane loved lavish parties and was usually eager to accept, but Carl detested them. On occasion, she managed to drag him to formal affairs, but it was clear that he seldom enjoyed himself. Jane found it virtually impossible to induce Carl to dress himself in what she considered appropriate attire. Although Carl loved expensive jewelry and occasionally lavished it on her, he feared that it might make her a target for robbery when they went out in public. Not surprisingly, as the years passed, they attended fewer and fewer functions as a couple.[44]

Carl's discomfort in other people's homes appeared rooted in the fact that he was not in control of the situation. Throughout his life, he repeatedly demonstrated a pattern of being uncomfortable, even sullen, in situations in which someone else was in charge. In the summer of 1914, Jane "tricked" Carl into taking her to Europe, but she noticed that he was bored and restless on the ship going over. Carl read the papers, and he knew that there were rumblings about the possibility of war. When a minor fire broke out on board the ship, he was convinced that it had been sabotaged. As soon as they arrived on the Continent, he seemed to be looking for a reason to terminate the trip and rush home. According to Jane, they were at an automobile race at LeMans when they learned that Germany had delivered an ultimatum to Russia. Carl informed Jane that there was a war on and that they must pack up and leave immediately. She was bitterly disappointed, but Carl was galvanized by the task of taking charge of getting them out of Europe and safely back to the United

States.[45] Later, Jane took numerous trips abroad, but Carl never joined her.

Like many men of his era, Fisher seldom, if ever, shared his inner feelings, and one may only speculate about his discomfort in not being in control. This may have been an outgrowth of childhood insecurities. His father's desertion of the family may have been a root cause. Young Carl had shortly thereafter sought to establish a degree of order in the household by getting a paying job. In business, Carl was almost always the dominant partner in any project he remained associated with for any length of time.

Carl and his young wife had experienced their share of marital difficulties during the 1910s, but Jane had given in to most of her husband's demands. To close friends, the Fishers appeared devoted to each other. The fall of 1921 brought a crisis that doomed their union. After twelve years of marriage, Jane finally became pregnant. Unfortunately, giving birth was an ordeal for Jane, who spent four days in labor in an Indianapolis hospital before doctors performed a Cesarean section on November 13, 1921. The couple delightedly welcomed the newborn, whom they christened Carl Graham Fisher Jr., but the father was as drained by the ordeal as was Jane. He had been appalled at Jane's suffering, and he allegedly lost nearly twenty pounds during her confinement. It was another situation he could not control.

Nevertheless, Carl Sr. soon recovered, and within days he was bringing friends by the score to admire his newborn son. Letters to friends and business associates during those happy days often mentioned Carl Jr. and how robust he was becoming. By Jane's account, some of her most intimate, close times with her husband occurred during the month that followed the birth of their son. Their joy soon turned to sorrow, however. A few weeks after his birth, Jane noticed that her baby wasn't feeding normally. One morning he appeared unusually quiet in her arms and cool to the touch. They called an ambulance to take the baby to the hospital. Jane recounted that she was too sick to go and that her husband rode in the ambulance with their son. The baby was diagnosed with pyloric stenosis, a blockage of the opening between the stomach and the small intestine. Doctors operated, but it was too late. The infant literally starved to death.

Both Jane and Carl were devastated, but they reacted in different ways. Jane recalled that "Carl came and went without speaking. I lay for weeks with my face to the wall. When he did speak it was with an anguish different from my own. 'I never want another. Never another baby, Jane.'"[46] Jane, by contrast, wanted desperately to try again.

If the couple had had professional counseling at this point, they might have saved their marriage. Carl's close attention to his wife and solicitousness during her confinement and bereavement reflected deep feelings, even if he found it difficult to verbalize them. His insistence that she not experience another pregnancy came from his desire to protect his wife from pain. In all likelihood, his fear surrounding virtually all aspects of childbirth, yet another situation over which he could exert no control, motivated his thinking. For her part, Jane knew how much her husband had wanted a son, and she must have felt that she had let him down. She may have felt a profound sense of guilt over the death of their child; if she had been more vigilant during his last feeding sessions, his life might have been saved. At the same time, she couldn't understand Carl's insistence that she remain childless.

True to his word, Carl stopped sleeping with Jane after Carl Jr.'s death.[47] Whether motivated primarily by a true desire for a child of her own or a desperate effort to save their marriage, Jane looked into adoption. It did not take her long to discover a likely candidate. In the spring of 1922 Mazie Rothay of Indianapolis offered her three-year-old son Clyde to Jane on a trial basis. Mrs. Rothay's background was somewhat dubious, at best. She claimed that she had lost her first husband during World War I and that she had remarried a few years later. She informed Jane that her second husband, a "traveling man," had deserted her and that he was not the boy's father.[48] Negotiations covered several months. Mrs. Rothay insisted that she was giving up her son only because she "personally" knew the Fishers' anguish over losing their son and realized that the wealthy couple could provide more advantages to her "baby." At the same time, she vacillated over whether she should cut herself off from the boy permanently.[49]

Several accounts claimed that when final legal papers were filed, Jane adopted the boy alone and that Carl refused to be a party to the transaction. These same accounts suggested that Fisher never grew close to the youngster and ultimately rejected the child, whom Jane had renamed John (nicknamed Jack, or sometimes Jackie).[50] Although there may be truth in these claims, in the short run, at least, Carl appeared very supportive; at least, he handled the business details. Over several years, Mazie Rothay continually requested adjustments in the adoption agreement, financial remuneration, employment references, and other forms of assistance. Ultimately, Carl set her up with a small pension.[51] In addition, he informed his lawyer in December 1922 that he wanted to be included in the adoption, that the only reason he had ever suggested it be done in Jane's name was that "I thought at first that she was so fond of the little fellow that it would be a compliment to have the adoption papers made out in her name, but she prefers it otherwise and this will be satisfactory to me."[52]

Whether or not Carl ever became attached to young Jack is immaterial. He was never comfortable showing his feelings. More important, adoption of a child could not cover up the couple's growing estrangement. From 1922 until 1924, Carl and Jane increasingly led separate lives. During the early years of their marriage, Fisher had engaged in several affairs, but he had conducted them in a fairly discreet manner.[53] By the early 1920s, he no longer hid his infidelities. For several years, Carl had been sleeping with his secretary, Ann Rossiter. After the death of his son, his conduct was more flagrant.[54] In an interview shortly before she died, Jane recalled that she had known her husband was a "womanizer" and that this had been "very difficult for a wife to take."[55] With money no longer a constraint, Jane felt free to spend lavishly, and she evidently found great enjoyment in doing so. Her social life became more and more glamorous; in future years, reporters would claim that during the 1920s, Jane had been the "queen of Miami Beach." In addition, Jane frequently traveled to Europe, either alone or with Jack. In the meantime, Carl was free to cavort with his friends of both sexes. Jane later recalled, "I went for society in a large way. Carl began drinking."[56]

In all likelihood, their decision to divorce was mutual. If there was ever a friendly, gentle divorce, Jane's and Carl's fit that description. In late November 1924, Carl signed a separation agreement, providing $500,000 in securities to Jane, plus $2,500 per month living expenses for life.[57] Just over a year later, they agreed to divorce formally. Ironically,

Carl's attorney determined that the easiest and least painful divorce would be through French courts: "Over there the grounds can be anything; that is, the French courts will grant decrees upon the general proposition that two people do not want to live together any more."[58] This suited Jane, who very much wanted to go to Paris; perhaps the thought that an extended stay in one of the world's most dazzling cities might deaden the pain of finalizing a divorce.

Symbolically, the breakup of the marriage marked the beginning of a downward spiral in fortunes for both Jane and Carl. For Jane, it was a series of disastrous marriages. Forty-three years after she left him, Jane recalled, "I couldn't do it. I divorced; I married again and again. I couldn't stay married to them because life was just too dull. It was too humdrum. You see, living with Carl Fisher was like living in a circus. . . . It was excitement, aliveness, that I never found again."[59]

Carl's compulsive need to control Jane continued even after their divorce. When Jane informed him that she intended to marry a much younger man she had met on the boat home from Paris, Carl wired back, "Jane, I'll be damned if I'll let you marry some stranger. You bring him down here I'll pay all his expenses—and I'll let you know if he's any good." Amazingly, Jane showed up with her new fiancé. Evidently, the young man passed muster, at least temporarily. Carl insisted on building a house for them in Miami Beach. When Jane protested that the house was far too large and elaborate, Carl replied, "Hell, why do you want to change anything when I tell you it's all right! Besides, it's practically finished. I'll have it all furnished, ready for you to move in to when you come down."[60]

For Carl, the divorce coincided with the beginning of the reversal of his fortunes. While he and Jane were married, he seemingly possessed a Midas touch. There were times when money was tight and he worried over paying bills, but for the most part one major triumph followed another. His decline after the divorce was probably coincidental because neither partner appeared emotionally devastated at the time. After the divorce, Carl achieved some minor successes, but his business affairs were marked mostly by discouraging reversals. After the mid-1920s Fisher's name gradually lost its magic. His decline would begin with the collapse of the Florida land boom in 1926.

11

Seeds of Doubt

As 1925 ended, anyone looking back at the previous quarter-century of South Florida's development must have been dazzled. If the first two decades of the twentieth century had brought major growth to the region, expansion over the most recent five years was staggering. The population of the region had multiplied by a factor of twenty since 1910 and had nearly tripled since 1920 to about 100,000 permanent residents. In 1920 there were less than fifty subdivision plats recorded; five years later the number approached 1,000. In 1920 there had been fewer than 10,000 real estate transfers; five years later the figure exceeded 174,000. In 1925 over $100 million in building permits were issued. Bank clearings in 1920 had been around $100 million for the entire year; five years later they passed $1 billion.[1]

On September 18, 1926, South Florida was struck by a devastating hurricane. Miami Beach was not spared, sustaining millions of dollars in property damage in a few hours. In the weeks following the disaster, a few rabid fundamentalist ministers across the nation insisted that God had enlisted nature to punish anyone connected to the Sodom-by-the-Sea. Just over three years later, some sober-minded analysts argued that the Miami hurricane of 1926 portended the precipitous collapse of the stock market. A few observed that money withdrawn from the Florida land bubble helped feed the runaway bull market of the late 1920s. In the self-castigating rhetoric of certain financial experts in the early 1930s, the speculative land bubble in South Florida embodied reckless and greedy American investors' thoughtless, naive faith in quick, easy money and endless prosperity. Even in South Florida's Shangri-la, they should have anticipated hard times.

In the seven decades since the wild speculative mania of the 1920s, virtually every serious analyst of the boom and bust, whether in securities or real estate, has focused on abundant warning signals that supposedly were obvious. At the national level, a few sophisticated financiers and public officials sensed the inevitability of a serious decline in stock prices, but they were either too timid or too selfish to sound effective warning. Intriguingly, although mired in personal problems, Fisher anticipated troubles in Miami Beach. Unlike many other investors, Fisher was not afraid to let his voice be heard. Even more, he attempted to intervene directly and personally when the land boom had grown out of control.

In hindsight, earlier weather conditions might have provided warning signals that a lot of property was exposed and that South Florida faced potential disaster. In mid-October 1924, two years before the devastating hurricane, Florida had been struck by a major storm system that caused serious flooding. There was little letup in rain for three weeks. Some highways in the interior of the state were under several feet of water. Fisher's property manager, Pete Chase, conducted a thorough inventory of property damage. His golf courses and polo fields were largely under water; a few trees had been uprooted and some advertising signs toppled. Beyond that, damage was minimal, and Chase voiced confidence that he and his men would have all facilities operating once they had a full day without rain. In contrast, many houses and some hotels in the Miami Beach area suffered significant flooding damage. In a relatively rare self-congratulatory letter, Fisher suggested to Chase that one of the chief reasons why their property came through the storm unscathed was that in addition to providing high-quality foundations for his structures, he had always urged his clients to build first floors at least three feet above ground level.[2] A few greedy subdividers and shoddy home builders suffered losses, and the storms of 1924 may have shaken out a few investors.

But most of the important developers, including Fisher, were unaffected and apparently unbothered.

Other warning signals were far more obvious and ominous, at least to Fisher. In the summer of 1925, as swarms of binder boys descended on downtown Miami and Miami Beach, Fisher challenged some of those he considered most responsible for encouraging rampant speculation. James Cox, former Ohio governor and Democratic candidate for the presidency in 1920, was a close personal friend whom Fisher had lured to South Florida. By the mid-1920s Cox had assumed control of the *Miami Daily News*. The paper was publishing thousands of real estate advertisements each week; one Sunday edition was the largest newspaper yet published. Although the paper was reaping a windfall from advertising, Carl felt that his friend was doing Miami Beach a long-term disservice, and he pulled no punches in letting Cox know his opinion.

Fisher's lecture to Cox included a general description of conditions: "If you are keeping in touch with the buying of Florida property you must know that literally millions upon millions of dollars is [*sic*] being shipped into Florida for the purchase of land, lots, apartment houses, etc." Fisher warned that much of it was outrageously overpriced: "Some of the property being sold in Florida will not bring as much money in thirty years as it is selling for now." He observed that "there is a tremendous amount of misrepresentation. There are an enormous amount of statements made that 'sharks' never expect to keep and also a great many statements are made by people who think they are going to do certain things but who fail to come thru." Fisher singled out numerous fancy hotel proposals that were nothing but hot air. On the basis of such dreams, land had been sold which would not be developed for years, and Fisher predicted disaster. "We are bound to have a big flare-back and Miami and Miami Beach are going to suffer as a result of some of the exploiting schemes that have been carried on around Miami and further North."

Fisher urged Cox to pull in his reins and think of the long-term good of the entire region. "Don't you think it would be wise for your reporters and your people to analyze some of the statements that are being made before you publish them? You have published in your paper, and so has the *Herald* and other papers, scheme after scheme which has never materialized and many people have invested thru the fact that a supposedly reliable newspaper publishes a statement of what some real estate dealer proposes to do. If you will check back thru your papers and look for statements that have not made good in the last two or three years, you will be amazed." Fisher closed with a prediction: "The situation has not been as bad during the past year as it will be during the next year."[3]

Fisher was not alone in his assessment of current real estate market conditions in the Sunshine State; savvy investors in other large real estate ventures in South Florida were beginning to hedge their bets. Yet thousands of others were still caught up in the frenzy, and many of them were gifted, intelligent people. Fisher's longtime friend and associate from the Dixie Highway days, Bill Anderson, editor of the *Macon Daily Telegram*, had driven down to Miami late in 1925. Reflecting on the current situation, Anderson pooh-poohed rumors of an impending smashup. He acknowledged that "a great many people refer to the Florida situation as a boom or 'bubble' and are expecting it to burst." But he was nevertheless dazzled by the achievements of the builders. During his drive he had observed that "the vast wilderness, sand beds and quagmires that you and I broke through on the first trip is now practically an unending line of buildings and paved roads." Anderson kicked himself for not having seen the light and for failing to buy into the action earlier: "My admiration for your ability as a developer and prophet is fully developed. If I had only had the good sense to visualize with you I would be riding around in a yacht instead of a Ford automobile."[4]

Anderson's letter, along with many other signals, sensitized Fisher to the potential damage that could result from continued unchecked speculation. Fisher was concerned about the general public, but when otherwise astute friends and associates fell under the spell of the speculative frenzy, he was moved to try to protect them. Carl increasingly focused his anger against the binder boys, whom he despised. In addition, he was infuriated because some advertisers working with these real estate salesmen used his name to advance their schemes. According to Jane, "The published announcement that Carl Fisher was interested in developing a new project was sufficient to sell land that ran into the millions. Carl fought back with full-page newspaper ads in which he emphasized: 'No dollar of mine will be invested in any Florida properties outside of Miami Beach.'"[5]

Obviously, speculation in real estate was getting wholly out of hand. In early October 1925, Fisher's sales manager, "Pete" Chase, had written to his boss about the "wild advances" in value of real estate in the previous few weeks. He noted that he had "sold Howard Lyons two of my own apartment house lots on the LaGorce Golf Course. When I charged Lyons $20,000 for these two lots, I felt I was making a fairly nice profit. Within three weeks these lots went to $50,000. I do not feel I undersold my lots at less than market price, nor do I feel that the sales department had one put over on it."[6]

In Fisher's view, the binder boys were chiefly to blame for the chaotic real estate market. The boss was not content just to write letters to newspapers lamenting their influence; he directly challenged the binder boys. Jane Fisher claimed that her then estranged husband almost literally ran the binder boys out of Miami single-handedly in 1925. This is a stretch, but Fisher undoubtedly helped curtail their activities. Although Fisher controlled little property in Miami, his real estate companies were involved in approximately half of all property transfers in Miami Beach. By the early fall of 1925 his companies had sold $23 million worth of property, and his real estate salesmen were basking in the rosy afterglow of huge commissions and the anticipation of unending prosperity.

No wonder they were jolted when Fisher marched into his office and instructed his sales manager to pull all of his property off the market! Fisher informed protesting salesmen that offering lots with as little as 10 percent down was shortsighted and dangerous. Henceforth, Fisher's salesmen were to sell land only to "serious" buyers, those who planned to develop property rather than simply turn around and sell it for a higher figure. They were instructed to raise the required down payment from 10 to 25 percent.[7]

Miami was unquestionably the center of the Florida land frenzy, and Fisher's highly publicized initiative sent warning signals to potential future land purchasers. All but the most naive potential investors had to sense that if one of the region's most powerful land developers was raising the "entry fee," it was going to be increasingly difficult in the future to expand the pool of buyers. That was what had stimulated the boom in the first place; investors had the sense that they were getting in early and that they could profit by selling to those who lacked their foresight. Other large investors sensed that the boom had peaked and it was time to get out.[8] On November 24, 1925, a few weeks after Fisher's announcement, Coleman du Pont resigned from the board of the Mizner Development Corporation, which was promoting Boca Raton. Du Pont's name was even better known than Fisher's in northern investment circles. Jesse Livermore, another prominent New York investor, had also been involved with Mizner's development and he, too, curtailed his involvement in Boca Raton.[9]

Long before the series of hurricanes that commenced in September 1926, there had been other signals that the honeymoon period in South Florida land speculation was over. For a variety of reasons, the frenzied building so evident in the first half of the 1920s was beginning to flatten out. Most of the construction material had to be brought in from distant sources, and Miami's rail and harbor facilities were inadequate to handle the volume. By late September 1925, the Florida East Coast Railway declared a temporary embargo on shipments into the area. It wasn't that railroad officials didn't want the business. The problem was insufficient storage space and railroad yard workers; some 2,200 rail cars were waiting to be unloaded. Miami's port facilities were equally overwhelmed; ships anchored for days outside of the harbor waiting to unload. In the midst of these difficulties, dock workers, earning just $0.45 per hour, realized their strategic advantage and struck for $0.60 per hour. Naturally, such business conditions were newsworthy, despite the frantic efforts of the Miami Chamber of Commerce and some prominent investors to downplay the problems.[10]

Fisher had no argument with legitimate land development and rapid construction. In fact, he did everything in his power to assist them. In Miami Beach considerable dock space was unused. Fisher either owned or controlled a good portion of it. He generously offered use of Miami Beach dock sites to Miami officials on a "temporary basis," until the congestion was relieved. Pete Chase thought that, in addition to committing a good deed, his boss would score a public relations coup: "Your offer of a temporary space would be hailed by the Miami merchants and the local public as an act of great kindness on your part . . . it will cost you nothing to do this, and gain you much support from the public, which support we will badly need before our Terminal propositions are taken care of."

Chase was referring to the fact that many public officials had resisted Fisher's initiative in constructing port facilities in Miami Beach over the previous dozen years, certain he was trying to steal their business. Chase concluded, "If we could announce that a half dozen ships were soon going to arrive at our terminal property, loaded with building material, and supplies, it would be a wonderful thing for us and for the community at large."[11]

Unfortunately, Fisher's civic gesture could not resolve Miami's infrastructure problems. By Christmas of 1925, congestion had gotten worse. Thirty-two ships were jammed into the harbor, and allegedly forty more vessels were headed for Miami. As a further complication, citrus growers had harvested an enormous crop requiring shipment north. In addition, some 1,800 telegraphers were on strike, which severely disrupted communications.

Two weeks later, the ultimate snafu unfolded. On January 10, 1926, the *Prince Valdemar*, a 240-foot vessel formerly serving the Danish navy, was being towed into Miami Harbor for conversion into a floating hotel. Unfortunately, the tugboat operators snagged the vessel on a sandbar. What might have been a minor mishap became a crisis when the tide went out and a wind gust caught the ship's masts. The vessel capsized, blocking entry into Miami Harbor. For nearly a month the ship cut off all delivery of goods into Miami by sea. The already overburdened rail network could not pick up any of the slack because rail yards all the way to Jacksonville, some 350 miles to the north, were jammed with goods headed for Miami. One developer, N. B. T. Roney, was trying to complete construction of his fabulous hotel, the $2 million Roney Plaza. All building ground to a halt for three months, and he missed most of the 1925–26 tourist season. Roney later claimed that the lost season cost him far more than the subsequent collapse in land prices.[12]

There were other warning signs that prosperity was shaky. The 1925–26 tourist season ended early; by mid-March 1926 hotels were far less crowded than they had been the year before. Fisher voiced concern that business at the Nautilus Hotel had dropped off significantly from the previous season. The hotel manager, George Krom, suggested that it was bad luck, combined with the fact that the pulse of activity in Miami Beach had been too stressful for some visitors: "You will appreciate the location of the Nautilus has caused us to have a clientele who desire quiet refinement. . . . The reason for this class of people not coming to Miami this year is due to the fact that numerous people who were here in Miami last summer returned North and reported a crowded overrun condition such that it was impossible to get decent accommodations and for such accommodations that were available, were charged exorbitant rates."[13]

Early in 1926 many other local businessmen noticed that the frenzied speculation of the previous tourist season had tapered off. To be sure, real estate trading remained brisk; almost 100,000 parcels of land would change hands that year. That, however, was barely over half the activity of the year before, and stories of speculators selling at a loss were frequently heard. Building permits for 1926 totaled $54 million, just over half the level for the previous year.[14] In addition, the local banking situation was increasingly worrisome. Growing numbers of banks throughout the state were failing, some because they had recklessly underwritten extremely shaky real estate loans during the saturnalia of speculation in recent years. While the *Prince Valdemar* blocked the harbor, shipping problems mounted. Negative news stories circulated, and it almost seemed as if South Floridians were psychologically prepared for an economic collapse.

Would the Florida land boom have imploded on its own without the hurricane of September 1926? It is difficult to imagine any other outcome; however, at the time few observers tied the bursting bubble to other causes. Both the hurricane itself and the damage caused were simply too spectacular. Many Americans, including some sophisticated business analysts, had not seen the cracks in the facade of prosperity before the hurricane. Almost immediately afterward, South Florida's economic collapse was swift and dramatic. Perhaps it was in some way comforting to attribute the reversal in fortunes almost exclusively to fickle Mother Nature rather than to human greed and stupidity.

Several popular accounts claimed that the hurricane caught residents of South Florida by surprise, but such was not the case. On September 15, three days before the first big hurricane struck, the *Miami Herald* carried a three-column, three-inch story headed "Miami Warned of 3 Tropical Storms at Sea." To be sure, the story appeared on page 16. It noted that there was one storm near Bermuda, another close to Nassau, and a third

near St. Kitts in the Bahamas. The weather bureau in Washington reported that the last-mentioned storm had "attained considerable intensity."
The following day one of the storms passed between Miami and Nassau,
bringing heavy rain to the Miami area. Two days later, news was more
urgent. The *Miami Daily News* carried a front-page headline that read
"Miami Warned of Tropical Storm," although a smaller readout just below opined that the brunt of it was headed for Nassau.[15]

Miami officials issued storm warnings at 11 a.m. on September 17,
but nobody was fully prepared for the storm that struck the area approximately fifteen hours later. In the dark early morning hours of September
18, a major hurricane lashed the South Florida region. Miami recorded
sustained winds of almost 100 miles per hour, and Miami Beach measured
bursts of up to 132 miles per hour. The latter community was particularly
hard hit, as huge tides of water rushed over the peninsula. According to
one eyewitness account,

> By 2 o'clock the wind, which had steadily increased, had reached a
> velocity of over a hundred miles per hour and some of the awnings
> were being torn off the building—tile from the roof was being torn off
> and pieces crashed down on the steps of the entrance to the building.
> A window gave way with a crash, and the onrush of wind into the
> room above shook the entire building, striking fear into hearts of the
> children and women. . . . By 3:30 or 4 o'clock in the morning, the
> vacuum caused by the terrific speed of the wind past the front door of
> the building had pulled the front door partly past the jams, and with a
> rope tied to the inside knob, three of us were required to keep it from
> being pulled and torn off entirely—another two hours would bring
> daylight—it seemed it would never come—seconds seemed hours,
> hours an eternity. It was five o'clock when we could feel relief—the
> roar of the storm was dying down some, and at six o'clock dawn began
> to break through, six-thirty daylight—most welcome sight I had ever
> seen—seven o'clock calm.[16]

Shattered residents slowly staggered out into the streets to look at the
damage or perhaps simply to escape the frightening claustrophobia experienced when shut up inside of structures that might come down on top of
them at any moment. What many did not know was that they were simply

in the eye of the hurricane and that the backside of the storm would soon sweep through with similar if not even greater intensity. Within an hour, the winds picked up again, and battered, bewildered residents hurried indoors to wait out the second half of the storm.

By the early afternoon of September 18, it was finally over. The great storm swept west, departing the western side of the state between Punta Gorda and Fort Myers. A *Miami Tribune* reporter ventured out into the wreckage and put his skills to good use in describing the scene:

> My first view of the storm's ravages at America's playground brought tears to my eyes. Beautiful Bell Isle is prostrate. The homes of Lee Rumsey, J. C. Penney and "Junior" Matthews withstood the gale but present a sorry sight with their shattered windows and ruined furniture. I am told the great pipe organ in the Penney home was damaged beyond report [repair?]. All royal palms are down. The Bay front area from the causeway to Carl Fisher's Flamingo Hotel is stark naked. Commodore Stolz's 100-foot yacht [*Fleetwood III*] is in ruins and partly sunk against the masonry of the causeway. The canal from Bell Isle to Meridian Avenue is half full of wreckage from the Mayflower Hotel, and the new Boulevard Hotel, of the Fisher interests, which was opened a month ago. . . . The glass dome is gone from the Flamingo and the furniture in the lobby and ground floors damaged. We proceeded through scenes of destruction to South Beach. Here is where the gale did its worst. It took the Coney Island of Miami Beach, twisted and gnarled it into an unrecognizable mass and flung it down on the sands. Hardee's and Smith's Casinos might as well have been under a barrage of heavy cannon for days. The Million Dollar pier is damaged. The South Beach Casino is tottering. . . . Charlie's Grill is a shell. The Ritz Restaurant is no more. . . . Not an apartment block, hotel or storage on South Beach escaped the ravages of the storm.[17]

If anything, the human toll was even more terrible than property damage, as 400 persons died and 50,000 lost their homes.[18] When the storm struck, Carl was up north supervising work on his next great project, an ambitious plan to develop a huge resort complex on the eastern tip of Long Island. According to Jane, when first told about the disaster, he quipped, "Hell, if it's going to cost me anything, I'm sorry I didn't see the show."[19]

Without question, the hurricane of September 1926 caught Fisher at a very awkward time. He was knee deep in yet another major project at Montauk, on Long Island, and he had very little liquid capital. Since he was trying to convince major investors to underwrite much of the construction costs, it was imperative that he appear financially rock-solid himself. Carl could ill-afford even a hint of being headed toward huge losses in Miami Beach. He obviously needed to minimize both the damage to Miami Beach as a whole and to his own property. Fisher made a hurried trip to Miami Beach shortly after the storm. He assured business associates that damage to his property was far less than he had feared, and he left the cleanup job to his managers. Three weeks after the storm, he informed his publicist and close friend Jack LaGorce that his total losses were about $400,000, approximately $200,000 of which would be covered by insurance. "Considering the wind velocity, we were probably very lucky."[20] To his former wife, Jane, at the time living in France, he claimed that the hurricane had exerted a cleansing effect by driving out the riffraff: "Don't worry about the hurricane. It will prove to be the greatest blessing to Miami Beach in the long run. Miami Beach will be more beautiful, bigger and better than ever before. After we get rid of this shyster boom trash there will be only hurricane-proof structures allowed to be built. Miami Beach will ride out all tides of time and change, and coming through this storm will only make her the winner and gainer in the end."[21]

Fisher was extremely concerned about overcoming negative reportage and salvaging the upcoming winter tourist season. In a letter to the publisher of the *Boston Herald* a month after the storm, Fisher observed, "We are rapidly cleaning up at the Beach. I am enclosing you a photograph of our Lincoln Hotel which was directly in the path of the storm, and also of the Nautilus, where we lost some foliage." Visitors could expect to experience the customary tropical delights because "our polo fields and golf courses suffered no damage except the loss of shrubbery."[22]

Even as Fisher downplayed the hurricane in referring to "high winds," his managers inventoried the damage. As Pete Chase noted, much damage was superficial, but the cleanup would take a good deal of time. A month after the hurricane, much work remained. "At the King Cole Hotel eight rooms in the east wing are badly soaked with water apparently caused by roofing paper blowing away. There is [*sic*] a number of bad leaks in the dining room caused by roofing paper blowing off. Plaster is off the dormitory rooms caused by roofing paper blowing away." Conditions were similar elsewhere. At the Boulevard Hotel, "About 100 rooms [were] partially water damaged by water coming through casements, damage consisting chiefly of wet rugs. About 50 rooms having boarded windows from recent storm have water damage consisting chiefly of wet rugs and some wet furniture."[23] Chase's report covered two full pages and provided long lists of tasks that were either unfinished or had not been started at Fisher's other properties.

If Miami Beach had been Fisher's top priority in the fall of 1926, it seems inconceivable that his hotels would still be in such disarray fully five weeks after the hurricane and just before the winter tourist season. Had he stayed in Miami Beach after the hurricane to supervise repairs on a full-time basis, his managers might have felt more of a sense of urgency to get things done. But Fisher was distracted by his big project in New York; he was experiencing cash flow problems, but he wanted to hide his worry. If he stayed in Miami Beach too long, investors might sense his mounting nervousness, a weakness they would surely exploit.

Thus Fisher tried to bluff through his concerns. He observed that, unlike the binder boys who had sold property to virtually anybody who would meet the initial down payment, he had sold property to more substantial investors who could meet their obligations. Fisher put up a brave front for both creditors and friends. Three weeks after the storm, he assured Jack LaGorce that "we have a great deal of money due and over due which will come in slowly as the season advances." In the same letter, however, he mentioned that he was considering selling the Indianapolis Motor Speedway and the Globe Realty Company, "which will help to bring money out of some other place than Florida."[24]

While Fisher tried to present a brave front, he was uncharacteristically edgy in the weeks after the hurricane. In a letter to one associate, Fisher lambasted "fly-by-nighters" who "havn't [*sic*] the back bone and guts to stick through a disaster." Yet Fisher also criticized the press for overplaying the damage. "We had an eighty mile wind in New York, and three people were killed, the same number as were killed in Miami Beach, and they didn't have a word to say about it in New York. At least the papers didn't use head lines about it."[25] Had Fisher really forgotten that more than a hundred times that number of people had been killed in South Florida just seven weeks earlier?

Fisher's occasional lapses into self-pity may have been influenced in part by sobering reports from his managers concerning business following the hurricane. In early January 1927 Charles S. Krom informed him, "It will be two weeks tomorrow since the Flamingo opened and as far as business is concerned, there just hasn't been any." He continued, "I have done my best to keep a stiff upper lip and create a spirit of optimism about the place." To make it appear that business was continuing as usual, Krom indulged in a time-honored yet dangerous practice of offering "freebies" to "worth while" or prominent people in the hope that their presence would attract paying customers.[26] As many hotel managers have discovered, once word got out that certain customers were staying for free, persons with the slightest connection to the gregarious Fisher began popping out of the woodwork, demanding similar favors.

The 1927 winter season was a disaster, and Fisher lost money. According to one source, the paper value of his holdings in Miami Beach dropped from $30 to $20 million.[27] Even worse, many of his supposedly dependable real estate customers failed to honor their debts. Although Fisher did not experience the reversals the binder boys did, he was definitely exposed. He still had an impressive fortune, but most of it was on paper. Savvy businessmen who had invested in his other projects sensed Fisher's vulnerability and approached the cash-flow situation gingerly. Roy D. Chapin, president of Packard Motors, inquired late in 1927, "How does it look for a full season at your hotels and for a profit out of them?" The implication was clear: if Fisher couldn't turn things around quickly, his image might suffer irreparable damage. Chapin continued, "The fact that the hotels did not make any money although they are important assets I think influences the attitude of the Guardian group because the difference between the loss shown this past year and a reasonable profit would make quite a difference in your income."[28]

The late 1920s brought partial recovery for tourism in South Florida. The stock market entered the most frantic upward surge of the huge 1920s bull market in late 1927 and early 1928. Despite occasional, temporary reversals, the prices of stocks had moved steadily upward from

1921 until the winter of 1928. In the words of one of the market's most prominent historians, John Kenneth Galbraith, in the spring of 1928, "the market began to rise, not by slow, steady steps, but by great vaulting leaps."[29] Industrial averages stood at 159 in 1925, zoomed to 300 in 1928, and added another 81 points between January and October 1929.[30] Profit-bloated speculators, breezily confident that the good times would never end, looked for ways to spend some of their profits, and tourism revived somewhat in 1928 and 1929.

Fisher provided an intriguing glimpse into his philosophy of resort management in a lengthy letter to one of his hotel managers in the early fall of 1928. During the mid-1920s, when the South Florida real estate market was in full bloom, he had prided himself in charging some of the highest rates in Miami Beach, at times as high as $40 per night for a double room. By September 1928 he mulled over whether to raise rates from $10 to $12.50. He was adamant about the need to make profits: "The rates at the King Cole have been universally low and the food and service have been universally good but there is a limit to what you can do in a place of this kind if you want to pay interest on the bonds." From now on, hotel managers were going to have to embark on an austerity program: "One trouble we have had for years is all of our hotel managers are competing with each other to see which one can get the best reputation on food and service at the complete expense of our organization." Fisher issued an ultimatum: "This situation is going to stop immediately. Every time you can eliminate a bell boy or a waiter you are contributing to a profit. . . . In other words, it is up to you to run this hotel this winter and make a profit out of it—otherwise, there will have to be a rearrangement of some kind."[31] On occasion, Carl revealed a lack of sophistication in his meddling with day-to-day affairs. Complaining of the high costs of some menu items at the Nautilus Hotel, he wondered, "Now what, for the love of God, does 'Lobster Thermidor' mean?"[32] The question undoubtedly left the head chef shaking his head.

In the flush years of the early 1920s, Fisher almost literally spared no expense to provide his hotel guests a dazzling "show." He casually spent tens of thousands of dollars trying to accommodate live flamingos at the hotel bearing that name. He allowed Jane to import authentic gondolas from Venice, along with Italian gondoliers. Elephants and other exotic

animals had wandered across his golf courses. After the hurricane, however, Fisher started pinching pennies. His belated attention to costs paid
off during the 1928 season. Charles S. Krom, manager of the Flamingo
Hotel, provided an encouraging report. "We had the finest class of people
at the hotel this year that we have ever had and I think our guests were
better satisfied and more contented than ever before." More important,
Krom reported that for the season ending in early 1929 the Nautilus
earned a net operating profit of $201,267.65. He had high expectations
for the future: "If general business conditions in the country continue to
prosper, I believe our business another year will be even better than it has
been in the past season."[33] During the same season, both the Flamingo
and the Lincoln Hotels posted profits of just over $70,000.

The collapse of the stock market in late October 1929 marked the
onset of the Great Depression, but its impact on tourism was not immediate. In April 1930, Krom reported another decent tourist season. Profits
actually increased slightly to $210,627.98. As he suggested to his boss,
"In view of the break in the market last fall I think we have reason to feel
pretty well satisfied." Krom wrote in detail about economies practiced
and efforts to convince guests to choose the European rather than the
American plan, noting that "we had less transient guests this year and I
think a somewhat older and more settled lot of people." Evidently, they
ate less, or they were satisfied with smaller portions. "Our bill for provi-
sions is $7,000 less than last year." One of the reasons was that the hotel
had hired "a much more economical chef." Fisher's other Miami Beach
properties were seemingly holding their own, although the tourist season
ended earlier than usual. Krom reported, "Our hotels were way ahead
until the tenth day of March when people commenced to leave here by
the thousands and we were forced to close the hotel very rapidly."[34]

By the spring of 1930, however, Fisher and his managers were clearly
whistling in the dark. The South Florida economy was imploding, and
the greater Miami region was hard hit. Between the peak of the boom in
1925 and the end of 1929, regional bank deposits declined 75 percent; the
number of building permits fell 90 percent, and their value plummeted
from $101 million to under $13 million. Bankruptcies increased 600 percent.[35] Carl's books at Miami Beach may have shown black ink in 1929
and early 1930, but some of his profit was realized by selling off assets.

As early as 1928, Fisher's managers in South Florida were entering pre-liminary negotiations with public officials to sell one or more of his golf courses to the city of Miami Beach. John H. Levi, president and treasurer of Fisher's Miami Ocean View Company suggested that the Flamingo links might bring in $1 million. Even if they had to take $750,000 for the property, it would be a good idea to reduce property tax liabilities.[36]

Over the next several seasons, Fisher and his associates vacillated over the disposal of land assets, particularly those originally set aside for recreation. Fisher wrestled with an uncomfortable dilemma. In the short run, it might be most practical to subdivide open space into lots for single-family homes. Prices for lots were dropping, however, and once recreational facilities were filled in, there would be fewer attractions for future hotel guests. Therefore, such a strategy would threaten future ho-tel revenues. But he had to keep cash flowing into the organization's coffers and allow it to meet current obligations. In February 1930, Fisher observed that interest in polo playing was evidently on the wane and that if he could not sell his polo fields, he might convert at least one of them into "an exclusive ladies' golf course."[37]

By the summer of 1930 Fisher's managers in Miami Beach were keep-ing an exceedingly close eye on local banking conditions, fearful that the organization might suffer irretrievable losses in the event of any bank failure. In response to rumors of potential troubles at the Bank of Bay Bis-cayne, accountant Paul Kunschik informed his boss that he had drawn the organization's account down to just over $300, an amount below which monthly service charges would be levied.[38] A few years earlier, at the height of the Florida boom, Fisher would undoubtedly have chuckled at such concern over savings of a few dollars per month service charges, but by the early 1930s such decisions seemed important.

At the end of 1931 Fisher had less than $2,000 in local bank accounts, and he was struggling to meet his payrolls. In mid-December he confid-ed to one of his Collins family associates, "We are up against a serious proposition here that must be straightened out quickly." Fisher noted that expenses were "going to consume us if we don't take immediate steps to put same in better shape than it is now." He requested employees to accept a portion of their salaries in land warrants rather than cash. Em-ployees accepting the warrants would receive a 5 percent bonus, Fisher claimed. "Now is the time to see just what employees will cooperate with us, and the quicker we find out the ones who are willing to go along with us, the better off we are." He candidly admitted that he faced deep trouble: "With the continued shortage of cash, and hoarding of cash in this country, we will soon be up against it, and won't be able to borrow our running expenses."[39] Fisher left no stone unturned in his efforts to extract every possible revenue dollar. In previous years, his golf course managers had been strict in enforcing rules concerning the age at which "junior" rates for children of guests would expire. With cash flows drying up and dwindling numbers of golfers showing up at the starter's window in the winter of 1931, Fisher advised them to cooperate with all but the most unreasonable requests by any paying guest. Specifically, he urged them to look the other way when guests tried to pass off aging offspring as "juniors."[40]

Fisher's former wife, Jane, with whom he maintained an uncommonly cordial, even loving friendship, commiserated with him late in 1931. "I hope these depression times will soon blow away. Like every one else we have lost—but there is no use crying about it. I have heard you say, 'It is not so difficult to make money as it is to hold on to it after you get it' and I am sure you are right." Jane tried to encourage her former husband, who in turn tried to keep a stiff upper lip. But the downward spiral continued. By the end of 1931, Fisher claimed "guests" could supposedly get rooms in "good" hotels in the area for just a dollar a night. In early January 1932, Fisher acknowledged that he was trying to sell his Miami Beach house and move into a smaller place to cut expenses. He confided to one business associate, "I am doing everything possible to keep afloat." Fisher added that his lawyers were strongly advising him against going into receivership "at this time, if it can be avoided."[41]

From 1932 on, Fisher sold off his Florida properties one asset at a time. As the 1932 winter season was winding down, Fisher, like thousands of other Americans facing far more desperate straits, worked out a barter system for exchanging of goods and services. Essentially, Fisher used property as his chief negotiating tool. In early February he wrote to one associate, "I have made several trades here this season, two lots for advertising in the two daily papers, six lots in the new sub-division for $12,000 worth of sidewalks, plumbing and street improvements; and by the creation of a small trust find, I have been able to use trust certificates and save about $3,000 in necessary cash layouts on personal interest accounts."[42] Six weeks later, Fisher tried to interest his friend Arthur Brisbane of New York City in buying his large home in Miami Beach, and his words conveyed a dispirited mood: "It is just a thought that you might want a house such as mine." After informing Brisbane that the place had cost $400,000 and he had a $125,000 mortgage, Fisher wrote, "Of course, I don't know why you would even consider such an investment at this time, but still you never can tell, and the only way I have been able to sell things in the past was to let a lot of people know what I had for sale."[43] One can hardly have imagined the confident "miracle-worker" of just a few years earlier being reduced to writing such sad appeals.

As the Depression approached its nadir, however, Fisher had long since dropped any pretensions of presiding over a limitless real estate empire. He was just trying to hang on. In December 1932 he informed an associate that he had instructed hotel managers to discontinue all advertising. By then, the hotel business was so poor that they were doing almost anything they could to attract any paying guests. He lamented to an investor in another of his properties that hotel rates were at all-time lows. Whereas his Lincoln Hotel had been able to charge as much as $40 per night in the mid-1920s, during the 1932 season its average rate had dropped to $5.49 per night. Fisher noted that this rate was a severe drop from the $8.72 per night average of the previous season, which in turn was a significant drop from the $16 to $21 per night the hotel had averaged between 1925 and 1930. Even at that, Fisher claimed that the Lincoln was doing better than some other famous hotels. For example, the fabulous Ponce de Leon in St. Augustine was charging daily rates as low as $4. Nevertheless, Fisher concluded gloomily, "I don't believe there will be 20 percent of the hotels in this entire district that will not be in the hands of Receivers or Bond Holders' Committees, unless we have a most unusual season."[44]

There was no magic in Florida or anywhere else in the winter of 1932–33, only despair and indecisiveness at both the regional and national levels. Franklin D. Roosevelt had been elected to replace the manifestly unpopular and seemingly helpless Republican incumbent, Herbert C.

Hoover, but nobody knew what the president-elect would do.[45] His pre-inaugural rhetoric sounded distinctly conservative, and few anticipated dramatic changes. In fact, January and February of 1933, just before Roosevelt took office, marked the lowest point in public confidence since the stock market crash of 1929. The nation had been wracked by three and a half years of economic decline. Fully one-quarter of the workforce was unemployed, and knowledgeable observers realized this figure excluded millions of Americans who had simply stopped even looking for work. Millions of families had used up their life savings and had exhausted their credit. Private charities were scraping the bottom of their barrels in forlorn efforts to stem the worst of the suffering. Despite President Hoover's earlier insistence that "nobody is actually starving," social workers knew better. As Inauguration Day 1933 approached, pessimistic observers believed the nation stood on the precipice of revolution.

In the early months of 1933, banks in Florida and elsewhere across the United States were failing. Fisher noted that what property was selling brought prices that were a fraction of those commanded in the mid-1920s. In late February, he informed one associate that he had run out of cash and that 60 percent of the employees still on his "payroll" had agreed to accept property deeds rather than cash.[46]

On the very day Franklin D. Roosevelt was sworn in as president, Fisher symbolically threw in the towel in Miami Beach. As he wrote to his close friend and longtime associate since the Dixie Highway days William Anderson, editor of the *Macon Telegram*, "We could have told a brilliant tale of Miami Beach success and the whole Greater Florida area here, if it had not been for the last crack on the chin. The Railroad trains cannot get people out of here fast enough to get back home, and see what it is all about." Although the collapse of the nation's economy seemed total and prospects for revival of the tourist industry remote, Fisher managed to maintain a sense of humor: "Some of these days we hope to get on the home stretch, and perhaps we may be running with hobbles, knee boots and blinders, but we may stagger out at the finish in the money."[47] As he typically did, Fisher put a brave face on his growing despair, but in just a few years he had lost an infant son, a wife, most of his fortune, and a good deal of influence. No longer was he viewed as the promoter with the Midas touch. He would, indeed, spend several more years promoting land and myriad other entrepreneurial initiatives in South Florida, but the size and significance of his projects steadily diminished. As the 1930s lengthened, Carl Fisher lost his position as a player in Miami Beach. By the end of the decade, his Herculean efforts to create a vacation paradise were a rapidly fading memory.

12

A Search for Greener Pastures

Miami Beach may have been Carl Fisher's largest and most renowned resort project, but it was not his first. At about the same time that he and Jane first visited Miami, Fisher entertained thoughts about developing summer resort areas in the North. Several factors, including timing and luck, influenced Fisher to make his first big commitment to resort development in South Florida. He could just as easily have developed land in the Midwest or dude ranches out west adjacent to the Lincoln Highway.

As in Miami Beach, Fisher's development of property in the North began modestly. In 1912 he bought land and built a summer home at St. Joseph on Lake Michigan. He purchased sufficient land to construct several homes or cottages. Typically, he did not consult Jane in deciding to purchase the Lake Michigan property. According to his wife, one evening he simply told her he wanted to take a "spin" in his automobile, and they drove all night from Indianapolis to St. Joseph so he could show her the property.[1] Fisher had good reasons for seeking lakefront footage. During the summertime he suffered from hay fever and catarrh. Various pollens in the air in Indianapolis caused him great distress. Lake breezes and cooler air provided some relief.

To fully understand Fisher's decision to promote northern resorts, it is useful to consider his mind-set at the outbreak of World War I. During his years as a manufacturer of automobile headlights and as one of the leaders of the Lincoln and Dixie Highway Associations, Fisher had developed close business and personal ties with many of the most powerful men in Detroit. Carl was nouveau riche himself, and he enjoyed hobnobbing with the energetic, free-spending parvenus of Detroit's gasoline aristocracy.[2] He would soon convince a good portion of the Detroit crowd to invest in property in Miami Beach. He convinced many of his automotive friends to test their machines at the Indianapolis 500 race. Although Fisher initially dreamed of helping Indianapolis challenge Detroit in producing automobiles, by World War I he realized that the Motor City would remain the center of the industry. For both business and personal reasons, it made sense for Fisher to develop one or more enterprises in Detroit.

Shortly after the armistice, Fisher announced plans to undertake a modest-sized resort development in the Detroit area. If he succeeded, he would be well positioned to meet the vacation and recreation needs of the automotive moguls on a year-round basis. In the summer of 1919 Ransom E. Olds, an important automobile producer, encouraged Fisher to invest in some of his property on Grosse Isle, located roughly fifteen miles south of downtown Detroit in the river connecting Lake St. Clair to Lake Erie. Fisher negotiated a $350,000 option to acquire up to 600 acres of Olds's property on the southern end of Grosse Isle.[3]

Two years later, he still held the option and was discussing possibilities of a big project with Detroit mayor James Couzens, a former high-level Ford Motor Company executive. Fisher was thinking of exclusive residential property with a resort atmosphere. "I am thoroughly posted as to what is necessary to do in developing this into the finest piece of residential property in the city of Detroit. I think after the property has been acquired, that the work can be well done for $1,500,000, which would include a small hotel, two good polo fields, some tennis courts, a small yacht club, and a first class swimming pool."[4] Fisher hoped to expand the project to a total of about 1,000 acres, mostly on the waterfront. The Grosse Isle property would pose challenges similar to those he faced in Miami Beach: swampy inlets would have to be dredged, bulkheads built, canals straightened. In addition, he was concerned that without constant maintenance, grasses would immediately grow back in dredged areas. Surmounting these problems would be expensive, but the area had enormous potential. Carl noted that there were already about $10 million worth of improvements on the northern half of the island, including fine homes, concrete roads, and a golf course. "But the most beautiful part of the entire property is undeveloped for the reason that the banks run into soft swale mud and grass." In the summer of 1921, however, Fisher was optimistic. As he pointed out to one prospective outside investor, if he acquired the additional land he was eyeing, "the two pieces of property will give about four miles of water front . . . this property will sell readily at $150.00 per front foot with the improvements I have in mind."[5]

Evidently, Fisher's timing was just a bit off, and he never followed through with his Grosse Isle project. Even as his interest peaked in the summer of 1921, Fisher realized he needed additional investors; he was too thinly stretched elsewhere to undertake the project himself. Although he envisioned profits of between $2 and $3 million, "most of which can be gotten back in three years," he admitted that his own funds "have been slack this year and may be the same for another year or two."[6] In 1921 and 1922 lot sales were beginning to pick up in Miami Beach, but the big payoffs were still in the future. Perhaps Fisher lost interest in Grosse Isle because he succeeded in luring dozens of automobile men and their families to Miami Beach.

Another contributing factor was that even residing on freshwater lakefront property during the hot summer months did not provide the physical relief Fisher needed. Just a month after writing his most enthusiastic letters to potential investors in the Grosse Isle project, Carl was turning his attention elsewhere. He casually informed another business associate that "[Jim] Allison and myself have been thinking for some time about getting a place on Long Island. As far as I am concerned, I must get out of this climate." He was still bothered by hay fever and catarrh, "conditions that entirely disappear on salt water."[7] Nevertheless, Fisher planned to take his time looking for Long Island property; he also considered property on the Connecticut shoreline.

A seed had been planted. By the mid-1920s, Miami Beach was a dazzling achievement, the talk of real estate investors and tourism industry experts around the country. But it was in the public eye only during the cold winter months. From early spring through late fall, South Florida receded into the background. Fisher loved being the center of attention and was addicted to intense, incessant action. He hated the lull of summertime, when few if any buyers visited Miami Beach. In late March or early April he usually left one or more managers in charge of Florida business and headed north for the summer and fall. He returned to South Florida only to attend to pressing business.

Fisher needed activities in the North to occupy him during the summer and fall. The Indianapolis 500 race interested him for many years, but the race was over by Memorial Day. Fisher and a few of his well-heeled sportsmen friends founded the Detroit Marine-Aero Engine Company, which built experimental motors for speedboats, placing star racer and engine designer Gar Wood in charge of operations.[8] But these endeavors were basically toys. Fisher turned fifty in 1924. Although he had done a lot of hard living, he remained ambitious and possessed vast amounts of energy. He still needed large challenges.

Revenues from the Miami Beach venture began mounting in 1923; by 1925 Fisher was raking in profits from land sales at a rate of over $1 million each month. A more cautious entrepreneur would have set aside a sizable portion of his winnings against the possibility of hard times. Fisher, however, possessed two serious flaws as a businessman. He was very uninterested in tedious record keeping. Reviewing accounts was one of his least favorite activities. He put these duties off until the last possible minute, and sometimes he treated his accountants like meddlesome spoilsports. In addition, in the midst of his great Miami Beach success, Fisher succumbed to hubris. Newspapermen and business writers for numerous publications portrayed him as a modern-day Midas. Carl publicly dismissed such flattery; he even anticipated the impending collapse of the South Florida real estate bubble. Certainly he was more shrewd than many of his contemporaries, but he seldom took positive action to protect his investments. Instead of diverting at least a portion of his fabulous profits into safe investments, he extended himself even further into the real estate market. In retrospect, the commitments he made in the mid-1920s to a new vacation paradise in the North precipitated his devastatingly rapid economic downfall.

Fisher and Jim Allison may have discussed acquiring property on Long Island as early as 1921, but neither followed through until the next year. Carl leased property on Long Island in late June 1922, occupying a cottage owned by the Philadelphia du Ponts through September.[9] It was located on the north shore of the island at Sands Point, no more than twenty miles from mid-Manhattan. Carl and Jane were still together, and evidently they found the sea breezes much to their liking. Within weeks, Fisher was dickering with real estate agents over acquiring larger tracts of land in the vicinity for possible development. In August 1922 he inquired about the 100-acre Cornwell estate, located close to the du Pont home; evidently Carl considered constructing a hotel.[10]

Fisher abandoned plans for a hotel on the north shore of Long Island, but he did purchase land for a modest-sized real estate development. In 1922 he began building the Bayview Colony near Port Washington, including a small shipyard for the Purdy Boat Works, where he and his friends could tinker with their yachts and speedboats. There were forty-five choice restricted home sites. Most of the lots cost between $8,000 and $10,000, although a handful were offered at prices up to $50,000. By the spring of 1925, over half of the lots had been sold; several homes were occupied, and more were being built.[11] Unfortunately from Fisher's viewpoint, sales and development stalled in the late 1920s. By early 1930, Fisher was trying to dispose of Bayview at fire sale prices.[12]

By then, Fisher was concentrating most of his attention on a far grander scheme for Long Island. By the mid-1920s, the area was experiencing an unprecedented boom. The rich and famous had discovered Long Island at least a generation earlier. Aristocrats like Theodore Roosevelt had built rambling homes, but the developed areas of Long Island were relatively close to New York City. Roosevelt's Sagamore Hill, for example, located in fashionable Oyster Bay, was about twenty-five miles from Manhattan as the crow flies. New transportation technology helped make Long Island more accessible for the affluent upper middle classes, if not yet for the masses. Public works impresario Robert Moses was rapidly extending modern motorways to Long Island. Novelist F. Scott Fitzgerald's acclaimed work *The Great Gatsby*, set on Long Island, appeared in 1925. Readers imagined themselves living like Jay Gatsby or even Nick Carraway, on the fringes of high society. To some of the aspiring upper middle classes and nouveaux riches, awash in their recent Wall Street winnings, an address on the "right" part of Long Island became an important status symbol.

Naturally, land speculators had snapped up tens of thousands of acres of available property, and prices close to New York City had skyrocketed by the early 1920s. Fisher's fertile imagination worked overtime in 1923 and 1924. As profits from Miami Beach soared, he dreamed of a northern resort to rival or even exceed Miami Beach in size and scope. It quickly became apparent to him, however, that if he intended to build a truly monumental project, it would have to be far out in the wilds of eastern Long Island. Fisher and his real estate agents combed the area for a suitable location. An agent finally showed him a large piece of property far from New York City. By the spring of 1924 Carl was bubbling with excitement over possibilities of developing Montauk Point, located at the very tip of Long Island on the south side of Block Island Sound. If developed, the property would appeal strictly to vacationers, not commuters, because it was more than 100 miles from Manhattan. If it was developed as Fisher imagined, complete with adequate transportation facilities, a prosperous businessman might find it attractive to settle his family there for the summer, then take a train out to join them on weekends.

Contrary to accounts claiming that Fisher jumped into the Montauk project without much thought, available evidence reveals considerable deliberation. In late April 1924 Fisher described his "discovery" to one of his managers in Miami Beach: "We looked over the Montauk property Saturday. There are 12,000 acres and some twenty-five miles of water front, including some beautiful inland lakes, and it is the most beautiful piece of property I have ever seen for development work." Fisher discovered that in the early 1880s Austin Corbin, president of the Long Island Railroad, had imagined building lines all the way out to Montauk Point and turning it into a major commercial port. Passengers might disembark from ships at Montauk and take fast trains into New York City, thus cutting several hours off their journeys to and from Europe. Corbin had been killed in a carriage accident and never carried out his plan. Fisher confided that high-level executives for the Pennsylvania Railroad were encouraging him to revive Corbin's plan. Several financial houses in New York were also urging Fisher to take the plunge.[13]

Fisher informed his manager in Florida that he wouldn't be stampeded into precipitous commitments, stating that he had "decided to let the matter drop entirely for at lease one more year."[14] A few weeks later, however, he was boosting the idea to his gasoline aristocracy friends in Detroit; he clearly imagined enlisting their participation in Montauk, just as when they had followed him to Miami Beach. To Packard Motor Company president Roy Chapin, Fisher crooned almost precisely the same words he had written to his Miami manager: "The Montauk property is the last piece of big property to be had in this country, and it [is] by long odds the finest location I have ever seen." Carl imagined selling 12,000 acres at prices comparable to current lot prices at Miami Beach.[15]

More cautious friends and associates tried to talk Fisher out of the idea. When Jack LaGorce told Carl that he did not need more money and might be wise to think twice about Montauk, Fisher replied angrily, "Damn your soul, who said I'm building Montauk for money. What the hell do I care about money! Miami Beach is finished and there's nothing left for me to do there."[16] Yet he did hesitate. At Carl's urging, his Miami Beach partner Irving A. Collins visited the site in the spring of 1925. Upon returning home, Collins wrote thanking Fisher for the tour but urging caution: "I understood that you were going to give it the go-by some time ago, and I hope it is not too late for you to retire gracefully from the proposition." Collins knew his partner well, warning prophetically that if Fisher induced others to invest, he would feel personal responsibility far in excess of the proportion of the capital he invested. In addition, Collins believed that although the project was too far from New York City to encourage commuters, it was "too close for exclusive residence[s]." Like LaGorce, the conservative Quaker asked his erstwhile partner why he was considering it: "From a monetary standpoint you do not need it, and why do you do it?" Finally, Collins injected anti-Semitism: "It being so close to New York the Jew element will enter into it much to your disgust."[17]

But Fisher had crossed the Rubicon: he was determined to proceed. He replied immediately to Collins's warning: "I am going to get a crowd together and go ahead with Montauk." In making his commitment, Carl revealed both his greatest strengths and weaknesses as a businessman. He simply could not stand still. As one shrewd observer noted, "Like a child, he had some inner imperative to grow upward and outward, to do bigger, better, faster, more wonderful and dangerous things each year."[18] Fisher ignored Collins's anti-Semitism while responding to his partner's other caveats point by point. He called the location ideal and discounted other risks. He claimed that he would invest no more than $1 million of his own funds and that he would not go ahead unless others invested $6 million. He confessed that he felt a real need to "see a place every two or three weeks where the steam shovels are throwing dirt and the buildings are going up." But he assured Collins that he was "sure that Montauk [would] be a success. The people who [would] conduct Montauk [were] all bold business men with money and with brains and with vision."[19] He also intimated that he would let others do most of the work. By the early summer of 1925, more than a year after Fisher had first viewed the property, he had put together a syndicate of thirty-four original subscribers. They finally committed to purchase the site. Given the soaring prices on some of the land parcels closer in to the city, Carl and his associates considered the $2.5 million paid for nearly 10,000 acres a bargain.[20]

By late summer 1925, Fisher was knee deep in plans for Montauk. In retrospect, his overconfidence had a negative influence on his performance in building and promoting the development. He underestimated the physical challenges awaiting him. At Miami Beach, he had spent $2,000 per acre just to *create* land; at Montauk, the ground needed only to be cleared and graded. The task paled in comparison to building the Lincoln Highway. In a letter to his old road-building associate Henry B. Joy, Fisher acknowledged that Montauk was a "three year job," but he was convinced the basic framework for a fabulous resort could be established with $7 million.

Seventy-five years ago, $7 million went a lot farther than it would today. Fisher believed that sum would provide two large hotels and one smaller hotel, two casinos (one for swimming, the other for gambling), two polo fields, three golf courses, thirty miles of interior roads, between thirty and forty houses, and dredging an opening from Lake Montauk to the ocean. Selling property should be easy; Fisher noted that his organization had "made more than $100 million dollars for our customers in Florida and these same people would buy millions of dollars worth of Montauk." Fisher urged his old partner to take a piece of the action. At the end of his pitch to Joy, he crowed, "I have an organization that could just play with this property as compared to the work down south. The job at the beach was ten years work—this could be easily finished in three."[21]

There were significant flaws in the execution of his development plan. In Miami Beach, Fisher and several experienced partners had shared the risks of carving out a 3,000-acre tropical paradise. Despite his disclaimers, at Montauk, Carl ended up in full charge, and the proposed development covered three times as much space. Irving Collins was not restrained in telling Fisher he was crazy to take on such a huge task; unfortunately, men closer to Fisher, particularly those on his payroll, did not sound warnings. Some were clearly in awe of their boss. After his stunning success at Miami Beach, which flew in the face of "prudent" advice, they may well have believed Fisher could succeed in anything he attempted. Whatever the reason, Carl was surrounded by sycophants during the critical weeks and months when commitments were made. Timing of his commitments was equally unfortunate, many being made in the months and weeks immediately preceding the great hurricane in September 1926.

Earlier that summer, Fisher had asked two of his property managers to assess his competition by surveying other real estate developments on Long Island. Joseph C. Copps spent a week studying potential rivals before submitting his report. He divided Long Island into several sections and analyzed the types of real estate developments in each. Copps discovered that the largest and "most active" project was Idle Hour, a 260-acre subdivision created from a portion of a large estate formerly owned by William K. Vanderbilt. Another investor had purchased 1,400 acres near Southampton. Copps opined that the owner was waiting to see what Fisher would do before committing himself. A third development on the North Shore near Oyster Bay supposedly encompassed the huge Van Austin estate, constituting 6,000 acres. Copps didn't think much would come of it, however, since, in his opinion, "this [was] run by 'Binder boys.'" Finally, Copps mentioned a small project in the "Jewish District" between Amityville and Oakdale. He labeled a 400-acre tract "apparently a mediocre attempt by 'Jewish Boys' to duplicate some of our Fly-By-Night Florida Developments." He concluded: "Montauk Beach has no competition on Long Island, nor is there any development that can be used as a comparison. . . . There is not a solitary development on Long Island today offering permanent improvements such as we plan in the form of hotels, clubs, golf courses, bathing casinos, etc."[22]

Such words were just what Fisher wanted to hear. What neither Fisher nor his managers took sufficiently into account was the variety and number of mature amenities already on Long Island *before* they arrived. There were numerous yacht clubs, golf and tennis clubs, and other private resorts catering to virtually every popular outdoor activity. Perhaps Carl could be forgiven for discounting old institutions and tradition. He had built a national reputation and a huge fortune creating new attractions and facilities for first-generation consumers: roads for new automobile owners, racetracks for a new generation of sports fans, and vacation retreats for people with new money. In the mid-1920s he was trying to attract the Detroit crowd to a new summer resort in the East. Perhaps, in his mind, they would be joined by the nouveaux riches from the brokerage houses on Wall Street. In the summer of 1926 few, if any, anticipated the end of the unprecedented bull market. Undoubtedly, Carl's optimism concerning Montauk made sense to many observers.

Fisher planned to make the Montauk development a "class" operation in every respect. At one point he worried about the impression the very location of his sales office in New York City might convey. When he learned that his representatives were negotiating to lease sales office space on the ground floor along 44th Street, he voiced distress. Fisher complained that ground-floor offices invited "dirt, dust, smells, crowds on the sidewalks and, the worst, the inquisitive idler who stops in to take up your time. We don't want this class of people at Montauk. . . . The people who are interested in our property will come to 57th Street, get in the elevator and come up to our offices where the atmosphere will be cool and pleasant and where we can have maps on the wall with a good view. . . . We are not in the 'wrap-it-up and take-it-home' business."[23]

One writer claimed that when the great hurricane struck Miami Beach on September 17, 1926, Fisher "immediately put Montauk on the back burner."[24] Such was not the case. Just a week before the Florida disaster, Fisher had assured his reluctant partner Irving Collins that interest in Montauk among his friends and business associates in Detroit was so intense that he and his sales force couldn't accommodate all of the visitors:

"Nearly everyone in Detroit knows something about Montauk and our greatest trouble now is to get some place for the people to eat and sleep."[25] Despite the hurricane and the consequent distractions it caused, Fisher remained bullish regarding Montauk. He was more concerned about the hurricane's impact on his associates than any losses he might suffer. Many of these individuals had made a lot of money with Fisher in Miami Beach, and he was confident they would weather temporary reversals. By the fall of 1926 almost three dozen subscribers had invested in the new project. In a personal sales pitch seven weeks after the hurricane to Harvey S. Firestone, founder of the Akron, Ohio, tire company, Fisher acknowledged that the "cyclone" had damaged some of his associates and had slowed down collections on money owed to him. But it had not diminished interest in Montauk. Fisher claimed that his agents had sold $700,000 worth of Montauk property in the past two months "without any advance campaign or particular effort to sell." Carl informed his friend that property was selling for about $11,000 per acre and urged him to get in on the ground floor: "A $100,000 to 200,000 investment in Montauk will give you tremendous returns in from seven to eight years."[26] Such aggressive appeals do not sound like an entrepreneur trimming his sails.

Fisher vigorously promoted Montauk in the winter of 1926. As in Miami Beach, he wanted savvy and aggressive salesmen and actively recruited "live-wires." He urged one prospective employee to spend the winter in Detroit lining up prospects, then bring them to Montauk in the late spring or early summer to close sales and reap handsome commissions.[27] Some of Fisher's associates were equally caught up in the excitement of being in on the ground floor of an exciting new opportunity. W. A. Kohlhepp was so convinced of Montauk's future that he determined weather was no deterrent in showing the property to prospective investors. In mid-December, he arranged a train trip to Montauk for a dozen or so bankers, lawyers, and representatives of major real estate companies. In a long memorandum to his boss, Kohlhepp described the excursion in detail. Before they set out, he phoned Montauk and was informed that the weather was clear. By the time the group completed a two-hour-and-forty-minute train ride, a winter storm had blown in, and the prospective investors slipped and stumbled as they climbed over sand dunes and rocks to inspect the property. Despite the obstacles, Kohlhepp declared the all-day trip a success, claiming that "the entire crowd seemed to be in splendid spirits and were quite enthusiastic over the development." He added a portentous afterthought: "Of course, if we had had a good clear day, their enthusiasm would have been much greater."[28]

Fisher's enthusiasm was boundless, and he sincerely believed potential investors could not lose. In advising E. W. Preston of the *Boston Herald* about future prospects at Montauk, he suggested the newspaperman invest in a hilltop site: "I am satisfied that the hill tops we are selling now for 30,000 to 40,000 will easily bring 100,000 in the next three years." Fisher planned to follow the same marketing strategy that had succeeded so well in Miami Beach. In the early 1920s, he had raised prices even when property had not sold at lower prices, thereby creating an aura of success. At Montauk, he would provide a slightly different twist. Once total sales reached $1 million he would raise lot prices 10 percent; after they reached $2 million he would advance prices another 10 percent. After that, all bets were off, but Fisher expressed little doubt that future prospects were dazzling: "From time to time we will increase the prices as the market warrants."[29]

At the end of 1926 Fisher was aglow with dazzling plans. In addition to the hotels, private homes, yacht clubs, and golf courses, there would be the Montauk Club, the focal point for all recreational activities at the resort. Fisher confidently planned to sign up 1,000 members, each paying a $1,500 initiation fee. In addition to golf, polo, tennis, both indoor and outdoor swimming, an automobile racetrack with a small grandstand, yachting, fishing, and more leisurely activities on the many miles of beachfront, members would be able to enjoy equestrian activities, including organized hunts. For hardier souls who visited during the winter, there would be ice skating, tobogganing, and a wide choice of indoor activities, including various performances at a large auditorium, an aquarium, and year-round casino gambling. Fisher stressed the summer attractions, informing one investor, "Certainly this will be the largest all around outdoor club in the world. No other club can touch what we offer." Toward the end of his sales pitch, he hiked the number of potential members to 2,000, each of whom would pay initiation fees of $2,000 *plus* fees for everything they used.[30]

Fisher's associates in Miami Beach and Detroit had no doubt regarding the seriousness of his commitment, even if they questioned some of his initiatives. If Montauk had Fisher's name attached to it, most reasoned, it must be given every chance to succeed. If Montauk offered tennis, it must host top-notch tennis tournaments, rivaling those held at Forest Hills. A Miami associate informed Fisher that he had engaged in serious talks with tennis star Bill Tilden about a possible connection with Montauk. Tilden was also interested in theater, and he considered being connected to Montauk on several levels, including "becoming affiliated in the sale of property."[31]

Long after the Florida hurricane, Fisher remained convinced that Montauk would succeed, or at least that was the impression he conveyed in public. Carl also assumed that everyone living in and near Montauk would be as thrilled with the project as he was. There were already a few dozen people living in the area before he bought huge tracts of land. Most sold out to Fisher, but there were a few "old salt" die-hards who insisted on living as they had before, practicing their crafts as they pleased. Some were fishermen, who, in Fisher's view, occupied a somewhat dilapidated fishing camp. As Fisher saw it, he was doing them a huge favor in creating large markets for their catches. Thousands of summer residents would soon be prowling local markets, snapping up fresh fish. In return, Fisher expected gratitude, and he believed the fishermen, almost like movie "extras," should be willing to blend unobtrusively into the scenery and make colorful entrances when needed: "All we expect of the Fishing Village is their co-operation in cleaning the place up." In a letter to the congressional representative from the Montauk district, Fisher revealed a level of arrogance seldom witnessed by his closest friends and associates. Surely the fishermen should be willing to move their village if it would improve his grand design for Montauk. He would agree to sell them small lots at modest prices, or he would "build some small houses and rent them at reasonable prices."[32] Any notion that the fishermen and their families might not be delighted by the chaos of dredges and bulldozers invading their formerly isolated, peaceful village appears to have wholly escaped the driven developer.

Despite economic reversals at Miami Beach, construction at Montauk continued through 1927, and Fisher and his salesmen proudly showed visitors new additions. Confirming their faith in the future of the development, officials of the Long Island Railroad announced plans in April to extend lines all the way out to Montauk and build a station there. Until then, the end of the line had been in Amagansett, twelve miles to the west; visitors had to secure alternative means of covering the final leg of the trip. The extension and railroad station would be completed by June 1927, in time for the summer season. Fisher's dream of offering Montauk as a viable eastern terminus for major shipping lines briefly gained credibility because the Long Island Railroad was directly hooked up with the Pennsylvania Railroad. Railroad officials promised amenities such as direct Pullman service between Pittsburgh and Montauk, as well as easy connections between the resort and Philadelphia, Baltimore, and other major cities. To complete the development of Montauk as a major eastern harbor, all Fisher needed to do was dredge a deep-water channel from Block Island Sound into Lake Montauk, then construct dock facilities for up to fifty ocean liners.[33]

On the surface at least, construction activities were impressive. In the spring of 1927 Fisher's pride and joy, the Montauk Manor, neared completion.[34] The hotel was a massive 200-room facility in Tudor style. There was also a six-story office building, where salesmen could catch up with their paperwork and visitors could keep up with business affairs "back home" while their families enjoyed leisure activities at the resort. True to Carl's word, the Montauk Yacht Club was constructed, a golf course laid out, and polo fields built. There were stables for horses, a church, boardwalks for strolls along the beach, and many other amenities. Fisher also built several expensive homes overlooking Lake Montauk, with magnificent views out over Block Island Sound and the Atlantic Ocean. By the summer of 1927, Montauk appeared to be a promising investment opportunity.

In the spring of 1927 Fisher gushed with enthusiasm about his development's future. In a long letter to the president of the Pennsylvania Railroad, he envisioned attracting major conventions, which would greatly increase railroad patronage. Montauk might not be ready to host a big gathering quite yet, but with another major hotel or two, it could accommodate very large meetings. He recalled a discussion with an official from the American Medical Association about hosting between

Fisher's sumptuous Montauk Manor, which opened in 1927. Courtesy of Montauk Library, Montauk, N.Y.

4,000 and 5,000 people. Doctors themselves might be satisfied with hotel rooms and banquet halls, but their families wanted recreational facilities. In Fisher's opinion, "Nobody wants to go to New York in the summer time to a convention, and nobody wants to go to Chicago, so that leaves it up to Atlantic City." That resort facility, however, had many "negatives," some of which Fisher stated in crude terms: "Atlantic City is becoming more and more obnoxious to the good class of people. First, the Negroes bathe all over the Beach and there is no way to stop it. Negroes in Atlantic City practically control politics." Furthermore, Fisher charged, hotels there allegedly gouged visitors; neither its climate nor its scenery matched Montauk's. Fisher was so intoxicated by his resort's future that he claimed that "in a few years Montauk will *be the one great convention city of the world*" (emphasis added).[35]

In the summer of 1927 the Montauk Manor hosted a few small conventions, but the results were not always satisfactory. Within two weeks after the hotel opened, Fisher heard rumors that the Montauk Manor had been the site of wild parties, overrun by loud drunks. Carl acknowledged that his organization did have "a great many friends who should be protected to a certain point," but that if they became too disorderly, they would have to be thrown out. Fisher instructed his managers to refrain from supplying free liquor to anybody. He did not want the hotel to "have a very bad and rough name." Even more surprising, at one point Fisher suggested to one of his managers that it might be wise to refuse to host conventions in the future. "This is quite a disappointment to me because I thought Montauk was the natural place for conventions to be held in America and that eventually as our hotels grew in size and number we would have an enormous number of people coming to our conventions."[36] In reply, the manager assured his boss that the disturbances had not been caused by conventioneers but by members of another private group.[37] Evidently reassured, the boss went back to his strategy of promoting conventions. A month later Fisher wired another executive wavering over choices of future convention sites, claiming that "Montauk beats Colorado in every way." He noted that in mid-July it was 90 degrees in New York, but that at Montauk "we were wearing light wool sweaters on the golf course [with] a continuous breeze like nothing you have ever seen any place. . . . Hope not too late to change your mind."[38]

By the end of the 1927 season, Fisher's property managers at Montauk were under tremendous pressure to sell lots. Just as at Miami Beach, however, they had to walk a fine line between creating a general atmosphere of calm relaxation and closing a large volume of sales. Some guests observed that salesmen were too pushy, that "knockers were whispering about salesmen at the hotel." With relatively few of the resort's proposed attractions yet finished, salesmen had a tough sell. One manager informed Fisher that it was equally difficult to find men either able or willing to take up the task; of 176 prospective salesmen interviewed, only one had been hired.[39]

A few of Fisher's friends and longtime business associates reinforced his enthusiasm for Montauk. Former Ohio governor and Democratic presidential nominee in 1920 James M. Cox visited Montauk early in the summer of 1928 and waxed poetic concerning its attractions: "The whole topographical picture reminds me of Scotland. There is nothing quite like it in this country. . . . When your golf courses are completed . . . then, I think that Montauk can be described to the golfers of this country, if not actually christened as the Glen Eagles of America. . . . I can conceive of nothing which would do tired nerves as much good as the heavenly silence of the dawn and eventide at Montauk."[40] In the same letter, Cox expressed interest in investing in the project. Fisher replied immediately, urging his erstwhile friend to invest, not so subtly reminding Cox of his own past triumphs: "Ten thousand dollars in the Prestolite in the early days would have returned a profit of over $2 million and I think it is safe to say that $10,000 in Montauk will easily make a million over a period of ten years."[41]

Cox's references to a Scottish appearance at Montauk referred to one of Fisher's more imaginative promotional ideas. At the end of the 1926 summer season, Fisher and his associates mulled over future improvements and attractions. Someone came up with the idea of trying to attract the International Sheep Dog Exhibition, held annually in September.[42] In September, good weather usually prevailed on the eastern end of Long Island. Whether or not they landed the show, they figuratively eliminated some of the sand dunes from their image of Montauk in the future, replacing them with grass-covered fully sodded hills and fields.

Despite all of the dredging and construction occurring at Montauk in 1927 and 1928, in some respects it was still a very rustic environment. A profusion of wildlife remained. Foxes, even weasels and muskrats might lend charm to the place, but the skunks, gigantic turtles, and eels were drawbacks, at least in Fisher's mind. In a joking mood, he wrote to one associate, "We have snapping turtles in the lake that would snap a leg off.. . we have turtles that would drag down an eight pound dog." Fisher stated that he had hired a game warden. "We have bought him a sieve and he is going to clean out the lakes. We have eels there weighing 25 pounds; we also have turtles weighing 25 pounds." Once the property was cleared of the "wrong" types of wildlife, preferred species would presumably return in abundance: "This will give us a big chance to have a lot of ducks and all sorts of bird life at Montauk in the spring."[43]

Profound changes appeared in Fisher's prospects at Montauk in the next two years. Just before the 1930 season, Fisher wrote to his old friend Jack LaGorce that he had recently read about a Mongolian jackass that could run forty miles per hour. He inquired about the possibility of importing one of the animals and keeping it at Montauk. LaGorce replied, "Your interest in wild asses doesn't surprise me for God knows you have had enough contact with them!" He continued his commentary on

Fisher's growing menagerie: "Haven't you got enough white elephants on your hands without adding what Kipling describes as a 'Devil, an ostrich, and an orphan child in one'?"[44]

By mid-1930, Carl Fisher may have felt that *he* was the jackass for ever having taken on the Montauk project. His Long Island dream was collapsing all around him. The project was hemorrhaging money. Had it been only his own funds, he could have lived with it, but he had drawn many of his close personal friends and associates into the project. Some of his younger protégés, confident in their boss's reputation as a miracle man, had invested most of their life savings in Montauk, and Carl felt a strong moral responsibility to try to help them retrieve their funds. By the summer of 1930, he was losing control of Montauk, and he was staring failure squarely in the face.

Why did Montauk fail? In retrospect, the enormous obstacles blocking Fisher's dream of creating a second vacation paradise on the eastern tip of Long Island appear almost painfully obvious. Uncertain and often downright nasty weather made the region suitable for leisurely, pleasant vacations for only a few brief months each year. More conservative advisers had urged Fisher to exercise caution before committing millions to the project at Montauk. In all likelihood, it would be years before he could realistically expect profits. Still, some of his partners who advised Fisher against overextending himself at Montauk invested in the project.[45]

In the mid-1920s, Fisher appeared immune to fears of failure. If he was touched by hubris, it was understandable; his career was at high tide. He had repeatedly achieved the "impossible"; surely he could establish a leading resort on the eastern tip of Long Island. If he was immune to cautionary advice from partners, it would have taken an extremely secure and strong-willed subordinate to make Fisher listen to reason. Perhaps more important to Fisher loyalists, another viable resort community meant more sales and managerial jobs, broader opportunities for professional advancement, and greater chances for lucrative real estate "side deals" of their own. No wonder they told the boss what he wanted to hear.

In retrospect, personal qualities that served Fisher well during boom times helped trap him in hard times. During most of his life, money burned a hole in his pockets. Although some observers guessed that at his peak in the mid-1920s, Fisher possessed a fortune approaching $100 million, most of it was nonliquid paper. Since he was a poor record keeper, Fisher probably had only a vague sense of how much he had at any given moment. More to the point, throughout his career, Fisher habitually reinvested money as fast as or even faster than he made it. When he made large financial commitments at Montauk, Fisher expected to meet his obligations through receipts of money owed him for various real estate transactions at Miami Beach. Even before the hurricane of September 1926, some investors were slow to pay. Within weeks after the disaster, these troubles were chronic. In early December, Fisher reluctantly informed Howard Coffin, a Detroit auto man and longtime friend and Florida real estate partner, that collections were already a problem: "We are finding it very difficult here, to press the great many people who owe us large sums of money. We will just have to be content and give them time to pay."[46] In hindsight, it might have served his interests better had he demanded prompt payment.

By early 1927 Fisher was for the first time nervously approaching eastern bankers and brokers, looking for short-term loans to meet expenses. They were more sophisticated and more hard-nosed than some of his associates in Detroit, Indianapolis, and South Florida. Richard Hoyt, a managing partner of Hayden, Stone & Company, frankly assessed the shortcomings in Fisher's initial financing and overall investment strategy. He urged Fisher to spread risks by expanding his partnership base. As for participation of his own firm's clients, Hoyt expressed firm reservations: "We, of course, are dealing with an established clientele, and we cannot get away from the fact that at the moment the collapse of the Florida real estate values has greatly shaken the confidence of the public in this sort of enterprise." He concluded, "We have probably the most extremely unfavorable conditions that can be imagined at the present time to attempt to sell any securities based on Florida real estate or upon a similar project which you are undertaking at Montauk Point." Evidently, in seeking investment capital, Fisher pressed the point. In a follow-up letter three weeks later, the broker emphatically underscored his warning: "Any plan to raise a small amount of money to carry on over the next few months is entirely uninteresting to me, because I feel it would lead to an inevitable financial jam within twelve months." He continued, "It would be far better to stop spending money now than get more money and more people involved and then have a jam." Three weeks earlier, Hoyt had urged Fisher to add partners, yet he advised his own clients to avoid Montauk.[47]

Fisher followed Hoyt's advice, at least in part; in early 1927 he tried to recruit more investors. At the same time, he needed to extinguish brush fires among those already committed. He did not always do so effectively. Irving Collins had entered Fisher's combine hesitantly; not surprisingly, he was one of the first to become skittish when storm clouds gathered. Replying to a letter in which Collins asked for more input in managerial decisions, Fisher demurred. He noted that Collins had already exerted a good deal of influence at Montauk, including a decision to close down the Montauk Manor during bad-weather winter months. Fisher testily reminded Collins that he had personally invested most of the money: "I do not care to put a large sum of money into Montauk and a large amount of my security back into this to have any Board of Directors make decisions for me as to what I should do with my own money."[48]

Fisher was still courting Hayden, Stone, trying to recruit sophisticated eastern investors with deep pockets who would stick with the project over the long haul. For the project to make an impact, Carl sensed he needed to develop financial bases outside Detroit, Indianapolis, and South Florida. He realized the need to demonstrate financial responsibility and reassured Hoyt that he was working hard at "cleaning up [his] financial obligations at Montauk" and that future development "would proceed at a slower pace." Unfortunately, by the early spring of 1927 his Detroit associates were also becoming nervous. Millions of dollars were going in, but nothing was coming back out. Perhaps trying to boost his friend's spirits, Roy D. Chapin of Packard Motors recounted an encouraging conversation with the president of the Pennsylvania Railroad, in which the latter supposedly expressed full confidence in the venture. Chapin, however, was concerned about finding sources of cash for future development. He worried about slow payments on outstanding Florida property debts: "The attitude of everybody here is that Florida is going to take some years to come back."[49] Chapin believed the fates of the two resort areas were inextricably intertwined.

Fisher knew that Chapin was right. He would have to raise funds from other sources. He might rely on banks and brokers for some of it, but his only sure sources were his own possessions. In the spring and summer of 1927 Carl commenced a fire sale of his assets. To potential lenders, he naturally tried to convey the impression that he was doing so in an orderly manner. In mid-April he informed the president of the New York Trust Bank that he had "three large deals on now, one of which [had] been completed." Fisher sold his house at Sands Point, on the north side of Long Island, for $400,000. He also mentioned "tentative deals" to sell the Bayview Colony at Port Washington on Long Island for $350,000 and the Flamingo Hotel in Miami Beach for $1.5 million. Sizable portions of all three sales would be cash, and Fisher knew right where it was going: "I would like to put most of these monies into immediate development of Montauk, especially the harbor, and the dredging of the harbor will provide us with two additional polo fields."[50]

By the summer of 1927 Fisher had reached a critical juncture on the Montauk venture. His margin for error was uncomfortably thin. But even when objective men pointed out cracks in the facade, Fisher remained blinded by his experience at Miami Beach. He had poured money into that project for a decade before the payoff came; everybody had told him at the time that he was crazy. Why wouldn't Montauk fit the same mold?

In June 1927 one of his more insightful sales managers at Montauk tried to explain why not. J. G. Caffrey pointed out crucial differences between the two communities. He was on shaky ground in claiming that Miami was "the only real winter resort in the United States," but several other observations appeared on target. Caffrey pointed out that Miami Beach had benefited enormously from advertising paid for by Miami and other Florida interests, including George Merrick's enormous promotion of Coral Gables. Although he did not want to "discount the fact that you were the pioneer and courageous enough to start the procession," no such ideal situation existed on Long Island. "Long Island, for practically 100 miles, is covered with beautiful homes and wonderful resorts and for that reason the competition is so much greater than that confronted by Miami with respect to other Florida cities that there is no comparison."[51]

Fisher may have overlooked the wisdom in Caffrey's observations be-cause the chief purpose of his sales manager's communication was to point out the difficulties of recruiting and retaining first-class salesmen. Although Caffrey ritualistically paid homage to Montauk's unique, rustic charms, he also observed that salesmen incurred high costs in getting to and from Montauk and meeting prospective clients there, "so far removed from the monied centers." He insisted that to be competitive in the job market, "to build up their enthusiasm and give them sufficient financial support which will inspire them to produce business," the organization had to raise commissions from 7.5 to 10 percent. Otherwise, the Montauk Beach Development Corporation would "never attract competent, motivated salesmen."[52]

By mid-summer 1927, both men were showing the stress of disappointing sales in the midst of mounting costs. Fisher complained to Caffrey that he had received reports of salesmen pursuing prospects into the hotel, drinking on the job, and generally behaving in a far too familiar, pushy manner with the guests: "In fact, a cleanup is necessary on the whole property out there. I hold you responsible and you have muffed the job."[53] Fisher hardly ever berated subordinates in such a curt manner, even in private communications. Caffrey resigned a month later. Fisher wanted his new sales manager to make immediate changes. For starters, his new man should get rid of all stenographers on the payroll and hire new ones. The current group had been laxly managed and had gotten used to spending evenings at the hotel dancing and generally mixing with guests. Fisher worried that at best such "familiarity" would exert a negative effect on work habits; at worst, it could lead to a highly publicized scandal.[54]

By the fall of 1927 it appeared to some men close to Fisher that he was obsessed with Montauk. Carl had gradually lost interest in automobile racing over the past decade, so he and Jim Allison sold their interest in the Indianapolis Motor Speedway to a group headed by Eddie Rickenbaker for "an undisclosed amount of cash plus 6.5 percent first mortgage bonds worth $700,000."[55] The transfer took place on August 15, and Fisher immediately plowed his portion of the proceeds back into Montauk. In October, Fisher's former Lincoln Highway associate Henry B. Joy confided his reservations about investing any additional capital in another partnership involving Fisher: "I do not feel like paying any debts to [another joint venture] because it just goes into the Montauk Company's maw. They now take everything that anybody pays in."[56] Joy by no means accused Fisher of dishonesty, just imprudent decisions.

By the winter of 1927, Fisher's mood swings concerning Montauk resembled those of a manic depressive, vacillating wildly between extreme enthusiasm and deep despair. Occasionally he manifested both emotions simultaneously. In November 1927 he had to decline a request from an old associate from the Community Chest in Indianapolis. Fisher observed that the chief reason was that he was scrambling to make ends meet at Montauk: "I am writing letters as fast or probably faster than you are, trying to collect notes that are due and quite a number that are past due, also trying to clean up some sales that have been dragging here at Montauk for the past six months." Yet he insisted in the same letter that "we have a good tail hold on a wonderful development with enormous possibilities." He had already poured in $7 million, and with another $3 million he hoped to place the organization in a position to pay dividends. Carl took heart in the fact that during the summer of 1927 the hotel had hosted 4,000 overnight guests and 20,000 people had visited Montauk. He noted that ten salesmen had sold $2 million in property.[57]

What Fisher failed to mention was that he had personally closed the key sales; he was virtually carrying the project on his own broad back. A telling indicator of his stress was that he complained repeatedly about the lack of gumption among his salesmen. He admitted that "you have to have the goods when you sell anything from peanuts to elephants," but he insisted that "we have the goods at Montauk." If he could find just six or eight aggressive and hardworking salesmen, Fisher was convinced they would carry the project farther and faster in future seasons.[58] Increasingly, however, pessimism crept into Carl's thinking. Even though she visited her former husband infrequently, Jane noticed it: "Never before had I seen Carl harried by anxiety. Many times when Miami Beach had seemed a bubble that must break, I had seen Carl grim and fighting mad, but never worried like this.[59]

During the next two seasons, Montauk became an increasingly hand-to-mouth operation. At the close of 1927 Roy Chapin observed that it was critical for Fisher to get construction moving quickly early in the

1928 season so that Montauk might continue to appear forward moving, a "hot" property and attractive real estate investment. Unfortunately, in feeling about for loan money for the project, Chapin discovered that interest rates were high, "more costly than later in the year."[60] In the spring of 1928 Fisher hoped that Congress would help underwrite the development of Montauk as an international port. Fred A. Britten (R.-Ill.), a friendly congressman from Illinois, was initially enthusiastic and supportive. In February 1928, Fisher provided Britten with ammunition for use with his colleagues, claiming that "over the past twenty years the best engineers in America and England and France have decided that Montauk is the best landing port on the American continent."[61]

But the turnaround Fisher had anticipated did not come in 1928. Development continued, but at a desultory pace. Longtime friends and associates who had pleaded to be allowed to participate in the project two years earlier nervously inquired about the safety of their investments. Taking stock of the situation in January 1929, Fisher wrote an unusually frank letter to Pennsylvania Railroad executive George LeBoutillier, who was still promoting Montauk as an international port. Fisher stated that to keep the project moving forward, he would have to sell $2 million more in property "to take care of minimum figures this year."[62] If sales fell short of that goal, the principal investors would have to pledge more capital. A few weeks later, Carl uncharacteristically assumed the mantle of victim: past difficulties were caused largely by a string of incompetent or less than energetic managers and sales personnel. After describing the shortcomings of a series of unmotivated managers, Fisher figuratively patted himself on the back: "By taking them out of any control at Montauk I undoubtedly saved several hundred thousand dollars in expense."[63]

This letter provided a striking insight into the effect the unrelenting strain of nursing Montauk along was exerting on Fisher. In virtually all of his dealings with associates involving Prest-O-Lite, the Indianapolis Motor Speedway, the Lincoln and Dixie Highways, and the development at Miami Beach, Fisher had almost invariably highlighted the initiatives of associates while minimizing his own contributions. Former associates observed that his generosity of spirit was a vital ingredient in his organization's high morale. Men enjoyed working for Fisher. He might occasionally snap at subordinates for being slow to take action, but he almost invariably softened his criticisms, often later in the same communication. His patience and faith had been severely tested before, particularly during the lean years at Miami Beach. Now, in the late 1920s, his elasticity was diminished; by slow degrees, he was beginning to feel sorry for himself.

Paying close attention to costs had never been one of Fisher's long suits. He appeared bored with columns of figures, and he had never been particularly interested in money for its own sake. Carl had never included "detail men" among his intimates; rather, his close friends were publicists, tinkerers, and big idea men such as Jack LaGorce and Jim Allison. Accountants particularly bored him. By the end of the 1929 season at Montauk, however, it was obvious that someone was going to have to take a hard look at the financial figures. It is uncertain who ordered a general audit of the Montauk Development Corporation. It might have been Fisher himself or investors who wanted hard answers regarding future prospects for the project before committing additional resources. As the richest and most prominent investor in Montauk, Carl was clearly the most vulnerable to lawsuits. He periodically experienced visits by agents of the Internal Revenue Service; conceivably, the audit was undertaken because of pressures from the government for complete and detailed financial disclosures.[64]

Whatever the reasons for the audit, those examining the books in the late summer of 1929 were incredulous at what they found. Bookkeeping for Montauk had been inordinately casual and appallingly sloppy. The initial payouts had been made in December 1925, but cash disbursement books and vouchers went back only as far as August 1926. After sifting through what records they could find, accountants discovered that expenditures exceeded receipts by over $4 million. They discovered that "estimates for work performed were made without any audit being made of them." There was a treasurer, but he split time between Montauk and Florida. Hence, even for some large expenditures, there were no countersignatures. The corporation used thirteen different banks: "There were many transactions of funds from one bank to another and frequently the recorded information covering the transactions was very meager."

Payroll data were similarly incomplete, even suspicious. The accountants could not audit the payroll for the simple reason that "no record of employees or rates of pay were on hand." They did uncover several cases of questionable ethics. One E. V. Conway, auditor and assistant secretary of the development company since 1927, had raised his own salary from $300 to $350 per month. "Mr. Conway, when questioned regarding the misappropriation of funds, could give no reason for his action other than he thought he was worth more than he was receiving and raised his salary check accordingly."[65] Considering the typical dry-as-dust language of accountants and auditors, these judgments of Fisher's lax fiduciary management were devastating.

The auditors' uncomplimentary analysis of the Montauk Development Corporation highlighted many of the mistakes that had been made to date. In addition, timing and market conditions dealt the organization blows from which it could not recover, even had management been vigilant. By the fall of 1929 Fisher must have known that his pet project was in deep trouble. Just days before the spectacular collapse of the stock market in late October, Fisher insisted to his railroad partner George LeBoutillier, "Don't think for a minute I have changed my mind on Montauk and that I am going to quit on the job if there is any way of avoiding same."[66] Within weeks of the crash, Carl realized that almost all of his investors had suffered grievous financial losses. Although Fisher himself was not a serious speculator in stocks, he clearly understood that reverses there had grave implications for his organization's future. Two weeks after October 29, better known among economists and historians as Black Tuesday, he confided to one stockholder, "The financing of the Company is entirely on my shoulders now."[67]

Late 1929 and early 1930 brought an avalanche of business failures and foreclosures nationwide. Like thousands of other business moguls, Fisher needed to unload property. At the outset at least, Fisher was optimistic; or at least agents representing him were. New York real estate developer Ernest L'Ecluse informed Fisher in early January 1930 that several deals were in the works involving "disposing of Montauk as a whole." He was working with another real estate agent, Amos Lamphear, who represented a combine identified solely as "the Deering people." L'Ecluse quoted them a price of $10 million. If that deal didn't go through, L'Ecluse mentioned possibilities of a sale to William K. Wrigley Jr. Apparently, a representative of Wrigley believed that "development by him would give him the most prominent piece of recreational property on the Atlantic Seaboard and with his Catalina Island operations, should give him all the publicity that he could possibly hope to get." The agent assured Fisher that he was offering Montauk in a very discreet manner only to selected clients. He did not want to give the impression that he was conducting a fire sale. Fisher simply responded that he hoped that "either of these deals may go through."[68] Clearly he was interested in unloading Montauk; by then, he wasn't particular about who bought it.

L'Ecluse's initial optimism proved unfounded. When he reported to his client two weeks later, there was no mention of any "Deering group" or Wrigley. Instead, the agent was attempting to interest one James B. Regan in purchasing Bankers Trust Company paper representing most of Fisher's personal liability at Montauk. By then, Fisher and his associates had evidently indicated their willingness to abandon the dream of maintaining any grand design at Montauk and conceded the need to break the development into virtually any configuration of parcels that could be sold. Unfortunately, anyone expressing interest in buying anything in the spring of 1930 was besieged by prospective sellers. L'Ecluse reported in early March that former Democratic Party chairman John Raskob and 1928 Democratic presidential nominee Al Smith were assiduously courting Regan as a potential investor in the newly opened Empire State Building. In early April, Regan actually made an offer to take over some of Montauk, but under conditions which Fisher felt were unconscionably one-sided.[69] Fisher wanted to sell, but he refused to sacrifice his property. In the spring of 1930, he was still able to meet interest payments; he could hang on a while longer.[70]

Occasional side issues offered rays of hope. In late April 1930 Robert Moses, head of the Long Island State Park Commission, announced the near completion of plans to build a parkway covering the entire length of Long Island, terminating at Montauk Point. Moses was a shrewd, powerful politician who usually got what he wanted.[71] He found Fisher and the officers of the Montauk Development Company easy to deal with, and he was impressed with Fisher's vision.[72] Fisher's concept of linking rail and highway access with real estate development at Montauk was in many ways parallel to his vision of Miami Beach. If and when the parkway was built, automobile travel from New York City to Montauk would be far easier. Montauk would be considerably less isolated, and property values would presumably advance accordingly.

Unfortunately, warmer temperatures in spring and summer of 1930 failed to heat up prospects for sales at Montauk. In fact, the new year brought little but troubles. In May, the Board of Directors had to send stockholders their annual message. After dutifully listing the minor improvements made to certain clubs and other facilities, they candidly admitted that real estate prospects were bleak: "Due to the enormous activity of the stock market and the unusual opportunities for profit offered through stock speculation, there was very little, if any, public interest displayed in the purchase of real estate during the past two seasons."[73] In mid-July, the developers received another blow when a New York newspaper broke a story about big-time gambling at the Montauk Manor. A reporter had visited the hotel on a Saturday night and described the scene: "The games are played often for high stakes but in the main the patrons themselves govern the amount they will play for. Men and women drift in from the opposite side of the building, play a few hands, win or lose, and return to the dining room for more dancing. This continues until 1 a.m. or later when the club usually closes for the night. Saturdays it remains open longer."[74]

If Fisher responded to the raid on the gambling casino at the Montauk Manor, there is no record. He certainly knew about it, as did virtually anybody with any money and social standing on Long Island. For many young and affluent couples, a Saturday night gambling at the Manor was a favorite pastime.[75] It is even possible that Fisher appreciated the newspaper write-up because by the summer of 1930 Montauk needed all the publicity and almost any patrons it could attract. By then, Fisher was less cautious in expressing his despair. He admitted to his old friend New York newsman Arthur Brisbane that his efforts to locate a corporate buyer had been unsuccessful, and there were no viable prospects on the horizon. To another Wall Street money man, Fisher uttered a lament he would not have dreamed of in his halcyon days: "You cannot sell real estate to people who don't want it." That winter, he was so fed up with the whole mess that he would make no effort to be reelected as a board member. Fisher informed Irving A. Collins that he would be "glad to be relieved of the responsibility."[76]

Despite Fisher's discouragement over prospects at Montauk, he pursued any possibility of its economic resuscitation, however remote. When prospects had appeared bright in the mid-1920s, Fisher had discussed possibilities of creating a new seaport at Montauk. In the late fall of 1930, the idea resurfaced. Fred A. Britten, chairman of the House Committee on Naval Affairs, once again became intrigued by the concept. Fisher had courted Britten, a fellow "boat man," for some years, sending thoughtful little gifts and other tokens of esteem. Britten now claimed he wanted to "do something" to help Montauk. The two men worked up a plan to persuade the navy to conduct major maneuvers off the shoreline at Montauk the following summer. Presumably, thousands of visitors would enjoy the show; top-ranking naval officers and guests could be royally entertained; and Montauk would receive a big publicity boost. The more he thought about the idea, the more enthusiastic Britten became. He mentioned that for the first time in history, naval maneuvers would be visible from the shoreline, and he believed there were fully one million excellent viewing sites.[77]

True to his word, Britten reached agreement with the chief of naval operations to conduct a full week of maneuvers in mid-August 1931. Elaborate plans were finalized. The much anticipated week arrived, and the maneuvers were carried out. Several thousand visitors did take trains or drive out to Montauk to observe the show. A few dozen naval officers stayed in the hotel; the appropriate banquets featuring big meals were enjoyed by dignitaries and ordinary visitors. But when it was all over and the last guest had departed, not much had changed at Montauk.[78] By the early 1930s it would have taken far more than military fireworks to revive the moribund development.

The year 1932 was one of the worst in the history of the nation, marked by the single most desperate year of the Great Depression. President Hoover suffered an agonizing final year in office, attempting without success to find some solution to the deepening financial morass. The erstwhile engineer and "wonder boy" of American politics, Hoover had never experienced failure at any point in his illustrious career. In November he suffered crushing rejection in his bid for reelection. Fisher, born in 1874, the same year as Hoover, had been similarly blessed in never experiencing a major failure up to that point in his life. Fisher's reversals, if less critical to the nation as a whole, were no less devastating from a personal standpoint. Despite his best efforts, he ultimately had no choice but to stand aside and let Montauk fall into receivership.

In early January, the Montauk Beach Development Corporation formally announced to its stockholders that the end was near. Writing on behalf of the directors, Parke G. Haynes observed that "the income of the corporation has diminished to a point where it is not sufficient to provide for even a substantial portion of the corporation's ordinary expenses, to say nothing of interest and principal installments on mortgages and bonds." The statement included acknowledgment that had it not been for Fisher's desperate efforts to infuse new capital into the organization, "we would, in all probability, have found ourselves two years ago facing the same situation which we are facing today." For his part, Fisher put on a brave face and hid his feelings. At times, he appeared almost detached from the process. In mid-March he noted laconically to one associate that "any one of half a dozen different plans we have had to re-finance Montauk seem to be impossible at this time to put over." A few weeks later, he expressed hope that the property at Montauk could be divided up into hundreds of small lots and sold off piecemeal for modest homes.[79] Fisher's grand design for a beautifully planned, elegant summer resort had come down to that!

The official announcement of final default of the Montauk Corporation came on June 3, 1932. The receivers had to wait until the last of the bonds defaulted. All told, there was at least $3.7 million in outstanding debt. The announcement understated the obvious in pointing out that "there is a probability that the liquidation of assets will leave little, if anything, to the stockholders."[80]

Corporate legalese might shroud Fisher's personal feelings, and in communications with old friends and business associates, he tried to maintain an upbeat attitude. But Jane Fisher and others close to him believed it hurt him deeply to have "failed" his friends. True, he had warned many associates against gambling too much on Montauk, and he bore no legal obligation to protect their investments. Nevertheless, Carl felt an enormous *personal* stake in the fate of his northern resort venture because he was sure that he had let his friends down. Some, even those who had lost heavily, tried to cheer him up. Tom Milton, a former Indianapolis 500 winner, magnanimously insisted that he still felt it had been a "privilege to be allowed to buy any of the stock and also that had normal times prevailed it would have been just as good an investment as Miami Beach was." He urged his mentor not to bear "moral responsibility you are assuming for conditions over which you could not possibly have any control."[81] Fisher was deeply touched by such generosity and unselfishness, but when Montauk failed, his self-image suffered a serious, irreversible blow.[82]

Despite his acknowledgment that Montauk had failed, in unguarded moments Carl fantasized that somehow, in some way, it could be revived. In the spring of 1933 he claimed that a good number of small-time investors "still have faith in Montauk." Fisher hoped he could help them make contacts that would enable them to resume development at least in a small way. Two years later, Fisher was still spending time at Montauk, at least in the summertime. In August 1935 he wrote to his second wife, Margaret, that he was staying in a cottage and doing a good deal of the maintenance work himself: "I have blisters from a rake, but bot [*sic*] a new scythe blade and have to cut weeds. . . . Paint floor of porch tomorrow." But just days later, Fisher seemingly abandoned pretenses. In a second letter to Margaret he wailed, "I won't live here next year—it's dull and *gloomy*" (emphasis in original).[83]

By then, Fisher could no longer delude himself about Montauk's future. Most of the home sites had never been developed; they were overgrown with weeds. The empty seven-story office building stood like a grain silo amid sand dunes near the waterfront. A local reporter visiting the desolate site in late November 1935 wrote that it rose "so absurdly out of the sand dunes that motorists often stop and stare at it with their mouths open."[84]

In about 1938 Lindsey Hopkins of Atlanta gained control of the property at Montauk and hired Alfred Barton to assume management of the site and explore its possibilities. When Fisher learned of the transaction, he persuaded Barton to visit him in Florida to discuss their plans. By then, Fisher was in poor health and did not have long to live. Barton recalled that Fisher was well aware that control of the project was out of his hands, but even as an observer he remained fascinated with its future prospects.85 His never-ending love affair with the development that had ruined him financially exemplified his approach to life. As long as he had ongoing projects to work on or new proposals to make, it really didn't matter much to Fisher whether he had much money in his bank accounts.

13

Twilight of a Career

Thirty years ago, one astute historian of Miami Beach proclaimed that Carl Fisher and the 1920s were "made for each other."[1] This pithy comment stuck, and almost everyone recounting any details of Fisher's life and achievements has repeated it. Without question, it contains large elements of truth. Fisher was expansive, optimistic, and daring. He masterminded new forms of promotion and publicity, significantly advancing the art of ballyhoo, so intimately associated with the Roaring Twenties. In other respects, however, Fisher was far removed from some of the most important shifts affecting American free enterprise during those years. Large corporations were aggressively "modernizing" their organizational structures and rationalizing their managerial systems. While many forward-looking "New Era" businessmen joined industry-wide associations, achieved new levels of standardization, and in some cases pooled information, all under the benevolent eye of Herbert Hoover's Department of Commerce, Fisher was uninterested in and perhaps even unaware of these trends.[2] He was a big idea man who loved interacting with people in the great outdoors. Fisher was temperamentally unsuited to paying close attention to tedious details and disciplining himself to complete endless hours of dull, indoor work. Fisher was happiest when he felt free to let his imagination run rampant, to conceive of enormous projects; others could handle the mundane details. Fisher was more than willing to troubleshoot on an occasional basis, but he sought and rewarded reliable executives to manage his investments on a daily basis without requiring too much of his time checking details.

If Fisher was in many respects comfortable in the business climate of the 1920s, he was completely out of his element in the 1930s. Following the collapse of the stock market, the corporate economy experienced a four-year-long rapid downward spiral; the "miracle men" of the Jazz Age, with few exceptions, experienced a collective, shattering loss of confidence. Large corporations felt themselves under attack from every side. Their carefully cultivated public images seemed ruined, and their newly minted public relations departments worked overtime to try to contain the damage. New government regulations, beginning under the luckless Herbert Hoover but vastly expanding under the New Deal after Franklin Roosevelt's inauguration, created new levels of complexity. Many self-assured entrepreneurs of the 1920s felt uncertain and confused in the 1930s.

If big businessmen, supported by large organizational structures, were operating in dark shadows during the depression, small businessmen and individual entrepreneurs experienced almost total eclipse. New government bureaucracies such as the Reconstruction Finance Corporation might assist large businesses, but they provided little hope for the small entrepreneur. Although some new enterprises were founded and a handful of big businesses such as radio and the movie and liquor industries flourished, the 1930s were generally a bad time for bright innovators with imaginative ideas but little capital. There was very little venture capital around; the few Americans and large institutions with money to invest sought blue-chip stocks rather than risky propositions.[3]

As the 1920s ended, Carl Fisher's fortune was quickly evaporating. Without question, the devastating hurricane in South Florida in September 1926 marked the critical turning point in Carl Fisher's career. Before then, virtually everything he touched turned to gold; he appeared blessed with the Midas touch, and fortune-seekers flocked to him. After the hurricane, Fisher seemingly lost his magic overnight. He made a series of decisions and commitments that turned out badly and from which, ultimately, he could not recover. As Miami Beach historian Howard Kleinberg astutely remarked about Fisher, "Miami Beach was but one of many fantastic obsessions in a life led close to the edge of disaster."[4]

Others tried to provide more rational, coherent reasons for many of Fisher's commitments during these turbulent and stressful years. In her fawning, fond biography of her former husband, Jane Fisher claimed that immediately following the hurricane, "All work stopped on Montauk. The thousands of workmen dropped their tools and stopped the dredges. Carl hurried back to Miami Beach to throw everything he possessed into the salvaging of the Florida city. Montauk would be sacrificed that Miami Beach could be saved."[5]

This clearly represented wishful thinking. If Fisher had, in fact, pursued such a course of action, he might have preserved the bulk of his fortune. Initially, however, he downplayed the significance of the damage to Miami Beach in general and his own investments in particular. It was almost as if he believed he could turn the clock backward by sheer force of will. He enlisted the aid of his old friend, publicist Jack LaGorce, in attempting to minimize the effects of the storm and to convince Americans that a vacation in Miami Beach during the winter of 1926 was still a wise choice. Perhaps Fisher read so many of LaGorce's syrupy releases that he began believing them. Even more important, although Carl had temporarily suspended work on Montauk after the Florida hurricane, he soon resumed building. In the spring of 1927 he sank another $5 million of his personal wealth into Montauk. By the late 1920s, between Montauk and Miami Beach, Fisher was spreading himself far too thin.

Although Fisher discounted it publicly, the hurricane dealt him his first serious financial blow. Bankruptcy at Montauk nearly finished him. Fisher's very loose, unstructured organization, at one time during the peak years at Miami Beach numbering dozens of salesmen, property managers, and publicists, quickly withered away. During the late 1920s and early 1930s, Fisher was hounded by creditors, and he spent much of his time worrying about selling off his tangible assets to meet their demands. His vision narrowed; he now involved himself in micromanagement of his dwindling list of assets. Hotel managers in Miami Beach who had formerly consulted him only on issues involving expenditure of tens of thousands of dollars worth of decorations now found the boss dithering over profit margins on various lunch menu offerings or bargains that might be obtained by purchasing paper doilies in bulk. Carl was clearly out of his element engaging in such mundane matters; he found it increasingly hard to concentrate.

Although Fisher's financial stake in both Miami Beach and Montauk rapidly shrank in value during these years, he still divided time between South Florida and Long Island. Following liquidation of Montauk, he had few remaining financial interests in the North. By the early 1930s he had sold his sumptuous homes in both locations, moving to far more modest quarters. He was little bothered by his diminished lifestyle; in fact, it seemed to suit him.

What must have disturbed him far more was that as hard times continued and the depression deepened, he had fewer and fewer important matters to occupy his time. In earlier years, the sheer size of his fortune and the strength of his reputation induced other promoters to approach him with their proposals and ideas. By the early 1930s, most of Fisher's fortune was gone; far worse, his image of invincibility was shattered. Under different circumstances in a booming economy, he might have borrowed large sums of money and resumed his career as a promoter. In the depression, he found few businessmen willing to take chances. In the 1910s and early 1920s, Fisher had been able to borrow millions. By the early 1930s, when he approached bankers seeking small loans for his projects, he watched their attention wander, eyes glaze over, and jaws set. In correspondence with friends and business associates, Carl tried to make light of his troubles, but his diminished stature in the eyes of financiers must have hurt far more than he admitted. In an uncommonly sensitive response to his greatly altered circumstances, his former business associates, members of the Collins and Pancoast families, discreetly set him up with a nice office in Miami Beach and a modest annual stipend sufficient to finance his basic needs.[6]

From World War I through the 1920s, Fisher had been a key decision maker in Miami Beach. As his fortune diminished, so did his influence. Nevertheless, there were a few occasions when he tried to reassert his influence. In 1927, legendary Chicago gangster Al Capone had purchased a home in Miami, and he spent a considerable amount of time in the city. Following the St. Valentine's Day Massacre in 1929, however, federal

Notorious Chicago mobster Al Capone (*center*) returned to Miami Beach in the early 1930s. Although Fisher's influence was by then on the wane, he played a key role in making Capone's stay in the region as uncomfortable as possible. Courtesy of the Historical Museum of Southern Florida.

authorities hounded him incessantly and finally managed to convict him on a concealed weapon charge. He spent ten months in prison. Miami leaders hoped they had seen the last of him, but Capone made known his desire to return to Miami after his release from prison. Several civic leaders publicized their desire to prevent his return, or at least cut it short.

Fisher had recently revealed a strange, proto-fascist attitude toward controlling newcomers venturing into the state. In a letter to his friend and longtime newspaper editor James M. Cox, Carl fantasized about establishing an office that would "register all of the people coming into the state of Florida, and take their finger prints, each person to have an identification card from the Mayor and Chief of Police of their home town before they be allowed to enter the state." A few lines farther, he revealed his basic intention: "Even if the programe [*sic*] is not carried thru to a complete success at first, it would scare thousands of crooks away from the state."[7] Carl evidently never pondered the potentially appalling by-products of such a massive assault against civil liberties.

Jane Fisher claimed that her husband took the lead in standing up to Capone, that he was one of the few men with the courage to look Capone straight in the eye in a courtroom and tell him he wasn't wanted.[8] Local reporters noted that during Carl's testimony, Capone "sat for five minutes and glared at the witness with all the intensity of an infuriated beast." Carl allegedly "returned stare for stare."[9] Yet other accounts discount Fisher's influence in making life hard for Miami's least welcome newcomer. Howard Kleinberg reported that Fisher did assign a "security man" to keep a full-time watch on Capone and report his every move but claimed that Carl's civic outrage was motivated largely by the fear that the Chicago gangster might horn in on his *own* illegal liquor dealings. Kleinberg further suggested that Fisher had actually been a major contributor in creating the morally loose ambiance that attracted Capone to South Florida in the first place.[10] Kleinberg's assessment is somewhat persuasive; Fisher had always been a staunch opponent of Prohibition in both thought and action. But Fisher and his rum-running boat captains had never engaged in gunplay or violence, and he was genuinely concerned that the presence of Capone could permanently scar Miami Beach's image.[11] Civic leaders like James Cox, owner of the *Miami Daily News*, took a more active daily role in hounding Capone. Constant newspaper scrutiny of his activities, as much as anything else, helped rein in the gangster. In comparison, Fisher's contribution appears relatively minor.

Gambling had come to Miami Beach not long before Capone. Fisher had been aware of it, but he had always been on the fringes. As late as 1928 he approved of its being introduced only into very "select" locations.[12] Jane Fisher recalled sadly that after he sold the Shadows, their former home in Miami, it was converted into a gambling casino. She almost could not bear to visit, but she eventually went for a look. "I went slowly up the stairs to Carl's room. . . . Final triumph of the gambling interests was in Carl's bedroom. A roulette wheel was standing where his bed had once stood under the pictures of Lincoln and Napoleon."[13]

Fisher was quickly becoming an anachronism in the city he had done so much to build. Increasingly, his communications took on a softer,

reflective, even resigned tone. Following a dismal season in South Florida during the winter of 1932–33, he wrote to his old Dixie Highway
associate, William Anderson of Macon, Georgia, "We could have told a
brilliant tale of Miami Beach success and the whole Greater Florida area
here, if it had not been for the last crack on the chin."[14] Even then, when
communicating with associates and cronies, he tried to sound optimistic
regarding the future.

Although the hurricane of 1926 marked the beginning of the rapid
decline in Fisher's fortunes, he was involved in one significant venture in
his later years. Late in 1926 Fisher was a moving force in the development
of large diesel engines. It was a natural fit. He had owned yachts for many
years, and he had always been fascinated with motors, large and small.
Thus he was naturally interested in any invention that promised greater
power, speed, and efficiency with less noise.

Fully to understand Fisher's involvement in this key enterprise, we
must backtrack a bit. One of Fisher's good friends was Charles F. Kettering, the renowned inventor of the electric self-starter, a revolutionary breakthrough for automobiles. The two men had known each other
since Fisher's years with Prest-O-Lite as a headlamp manufacturer. With
the self-starter, soon mass-produced by Delco, Kettering made an even
larger splash in the automobile industry than Fisher had. Introduced as
an optional feature for the 1911 Cadillac, the self-starter had swept the
industry by the mid-1920s. No longer did automobile owners have to risk
life and limb with the awkward, dangerous hand cranks. Kettering was
originally from Dayton, Ohio, but by the 1920s he had become an insider in Detroit's gasoline aristocracy.[15] Kettering liked yachts and warm-
weather vacations. Along with many other automobile men, he and his
family became regulars during the winter seasons in Miami Beach. His
yacht, the *Olive K*, named for his wife, was powered by a diesel engine.
According to his biographer, it literally became a "floating laboratory."
During vacation jaunts with family and guests, "Ket" disappeared into the
engine room for hours on end to tinker with motors while others enjoyed
fresh air and sunshine.[16] On more than a few occasions, Fisher joined his
friend below the decks. Fisher's fanciest yacht, the 150-foot-long *Shadow
K*, was also equipped with an experimental diesel engine.

The diesel engine, originally conceived by Rudolph Diesel, had been around since the 1890s. Diesel had predicted that his compression-ignition power plant would "revolutionize the power field," even replace the steam engine.[17] To a certain extent he was right. Diesel engines were used for stationary power in factories, merchant ships, and switching locomotives. A major drawback was that they were exceedingly heavy and dirty. If they were to have a significant future in transportation other than powering ocean vessels, lighter, cleaner, more flexible diesel engines had to be designed. As head of General Motors Research Corporation in the 1920s, Kettering acquired the corporate backing to pursue this objective.

Fisher helped channel Kettering's research in diesel engines. During summers in the North, Fisher had become familiar with boat manufacturers and engine designers throughout the region. He was deeply impressed by O. D. Treiber, who was then conducting diesel design research at his engine shop in Camden, New Jersey. Like many inventors, Treiber had a wealth of ideas but little capital. When he and Fisher met in the mid-1920s, the latter had money. Carl became Treiber's most influential financial backer and introduced him to friends in the automobile business.[18]

By early 1927, Kettering was searching intensely for new concepts in diesel engine development, and he sought out Fisher for leads.[19] Carl replied immediately. As he saw it, the timing couldn't have been better. He described Treiber as "the smartest man in the Diesel Engine game in the United States." Fisher admitted that he had suffered a significant financial setback because of the recent hurricane and was feeling pinched for investment capital. Perhaps Kettering, through General Motors, could take up some of the slack. Carl advised his friend that Treiber was in the process of negotiating custom orders from various sources. In Fisher's view, the potential for diesel engine development was unlimited. He wrote to Kettering: "You would be surprised to know the tremendous interest there is in railroads, street car lines, bus lines, and all other power company plants in connection with oil burning Diesel motors." He urged Kettering to spend a day with Treiber exploring ideas.[20]

Kettering followed his friend's advice and met Treiber. The latter was struggling to put together his own corporation. Treiber was definitely a small-time operator; his corporation was originally capitalized at a mere $35,000. Kettering sensed that Treiber knew even less than Fisher about cost accounting or profit and loss statements. The businessmen who met him and interviewed him sensed his naiveté regarding matters of money.[21] Nevertheless, Kettering was sufficiently impressed with his engineering skills and theories to consider underwriting some of Treiber's stock offering.[22]

Fisher was impressed with Treiber's potential for making significant long-term contributions to the advancement of diesel technology, but he had more immediate, selfish concerns as well. Treiber was under contract to build three boat engines for Fisher; although Carl had, according to his own calculations, poured $225,000 into Treiber's coffers by July 1929, none of the engines were yet finished. Naturally, Fisher was worried that the engineer might go bankrupt before delivering any of the engines.[23] If Treiber received substantial backing from General Motors, Carl's personal concerns would be eased.

Fisher was torn between conflicting desires. He fretted over Treiber's inability to manage costs. Much as he wanted General Motors to assume the bulk of financial responsibility for Treiber Diesel, he felt bound by honor to report the situation truthfully to Kettering and his associates. Carl provided a straightforward statement regarding Treiber's inability to handle significant sums of money. He also expressed worry that if General Motors did in fact take over the company, completion of Fisher's engines might become a very low priority. For Carl, the best of both possible worlds would be for Treiber to concentrate on finishing his engines, then be absorbed by General Motors.[24]

Even as he wrote, Fisher could sense Kettering's interest in Treiber Diesel ebbing. Within days of presenting his take on the situation to Kettering, Carl was courting other potential investors with deep pockets. Significantly, he painted a somewhat different picture of Treiber's operation to others. To Dan J. Mahoney of Dayton, Ohio, Fisher wrote: "They are making money and the prospects of the company are just staggering. They are selling engines on their merits to the hardest boiled buyers of engines in America, and the patents Treiber has, if they can be made good, are worth millions." Fisher acknowledged that Treiber was no businessman, that he was signing contracts for huge jobs far into the future, where estimating costs was hazardous at best. But he assured Mahoney that the designer's upside potential was enormous. Fisher conceded that he had originally intended to finance Treiber himself, but Montauk was draining too much of his capital. He concluded, "I do want this company to be a success and I am perfectly willing to let somebody else take a lot of the profit out of it."[25]

By then, Kettering and General Motors were seriously examining designs offered by other diesel engineers. In late August, Kettering informed Fisher that he was enormously impressed with the new engines delivered by the Winton Company. In contrast, his new assessment of Treiber's designs was not flattering: "From my standpoint, the present Diesel engines that Treiber is building I would not have as a gift." Three weeks before the stock market crash of October, Charles E. Wilson, vice president of General Motors, formally canceled negotiations with the Treiber Corporation.[26]

Treiber Diesel had been just one of numerous companies General Motors had consulted regarding development of a promising new avenue of technology. After 1929, the corporation considered diesel power so promising that it earmarked significant internal funding for experimentation. Once this basic commitment was made, neither Kettering nor General Motors needed the assistance of independent contractors. Kettering, of course, achieved enormous success and acclaim for engineering huge advances in diesel engines during the 1930s and 1940s. The diesel engines General Motors produced for locomotives and ships helped keep the automobile giant alive during the grim years of the depression.[27]

In contrast, Fisher was left with the unappealing task of trying to drum up interest in a gifted but improvident designer during the worst financial crisis in American history. It was a hopeless task. In late 1929 and early 1930, Fisher approached one financier after another, touting Treiber's potential, trying to convince them that a small investment in the company would help them recover from their own recent losses.[28] Finding no success in eastern financial circles, he approached some of his more prosperous friends and business associates. Occasionally, his encomiums sounded almost delusional. In a late December 1929 appeal to Eddie Rickenbacker, who had purchased his interest in the Indianapolis Motor Speedway two years earlier, Fisher insisted, "If some of our patent claims can be made to stand, we are in a position with sufficient factory facilities to dominate the Diesel engine business in America." Later in the same letter, however, Fisher appeared more down-to-earth concerning Treiber's prospects: "If you are not interested, please consider the matter confidential and forget it as I don't want to peddle this business around any more than necessary."[29]

By the summer of 1930, Fisher finally admitted to himself and others that he had backed a losing horse. In a long letter to his protégé former race car driver Tom Milton, in which he summarized his experience in the industry, Fisher observed, "There is a tremendous demand for diesel engines and I think Treiber is one of the best posted engineers in this business; in fact, he is two or three years ahead of most other engineers." His failure boiled down to the fact that Treiber was a poor businessman: "If we could only keep him locked up in a cage where he would do all the designing work and submit it to some real engineers to build, then we would be going."[30] Unfortunately, the end was near for Treiber Diesel; in September 1930 creditors forced the company into receivership, and a reorganization effort proved futile.[31]

Fisher's effort to become a force in diesel engine development was his last fling in a truly pathbreaking industry. From the late 1920s forward, most of his promotions were local, centered on South Florida and Miami Beach. At the end of World War I he had imagined South Florida as a center for international commercial and passenger aviation. A decade later, significant strides had been made in the development of passenger aircraft. By May 1929, Fisher was in the thick of efforts to establish Miami as a major hub for service to the Caribbean, even South America. He offered to donate land on Virginia Key, in Biscayne Bay, to the city of Miami in an effort to attract Pan American Airlines. He publicized his offer in a letter to his longtime sidekick John Levi, who was becoming a force in Miami politics.[32] Fisher's offer was by no means disinterested philanthropy. Local property values had plunged following the hurricane of 1926. Fisher still held considerable property there, and well-publicized advances in airline service might help revive the regional economy and reverse the slide in prices of real estate. Although Fisher was visionary in anticipating the city's future in aviation, he would reap none of the long-term financial benefits.

Following the collapse of the Florida land boom and his misfortunes at Montauk, Fisher became involved in a series of minor promotional efforts, each seemingly less significant than its predecessor. Carl had always been interested in promising inventions, and by the late 1920s he had submitted several of his own ideas to the United States Patent Office. As he noted in a letter to one associate in the summer of 1929, "This is really a small side line I am just dipping into for amusement."[33]

It is difficult to determine precisely when Fisher's interest in marginal projects began, but during the spring of 1928 he began promoting a device called the Aerocar. Designed by one of the most innovative minds in aviation production, Glenn Curtiss, the Aerocar was essentially a glorified trailer, which could be hitched up behind an automobile. Every summer, millions of Americans took to the road, hauling an amazing array of homemade campers behind their Model Ts, Buicks, and Dodges. Automobiles were being built with more powerful engines which were capable of pulling significant loads. By the late 1920s, designers and manufacturers of inexpensive, practical trailers imagined reaping fortunes.[34]

Fisher waxed enthusiastic about the Aerocar, and he proposed to be in on the ground floor promoting it. Carl envisioned hooking up again with his old friends and associates in the automobile business. In a gushing letter to Roy Chapin, he trumpeted the device's advantages: "Glenn Curtiss has the greatest trailer that was ever made in America. It is the cheapest thing built, it is absolutely noiseless. . . . This trailer is going to revolutionize touring in this country." How did Fisher fit in? In his view, he was the obvious choice to sell it to America. "Glenn built this trailer for advertising purposes; he never had any idea at all, I don't believe, that anybody wanted to buy one. . . . I am doing my very best to get Glenn stirred up to the enormous possibilities of this trailer for touring and for light delivery work."[35] Fisher fantasized about selling nearly one million of them!

During the late summer and early fall of 1928, Fisher enthusiastically touted the Aerocar's potential uses. New York newspaperman Arthur Brisbane evidently shared his fascination and ordered one as soon as he experienced his first ride. A major obstacle was that there was nobody around to manufacture the vehicle in volume at a low price. Moving from brochures and engineering drawings to efficient, large-scale production is an enormous step. Fisher had to lobby hard with the directors of the quickly organized Aerocar Corporation to support the concept of producing them in quantity.[36] By late September, Fisher was deeply involved in discussions with the Briggs Body Corporation in Detroit regarding production of several different types of Aerocars. Carl imagined turning out thousands of units serving various needs: mobile operating facilities for surgeons in wartime ambulances; "opera cars" complete with drawing rooms, dressing rooms, and bridge tables; traveling salesmen's showrooms; open-roofed sunshine cars—"In fact, the field is almost unlimited."[37] He also hoped to equip them with refrigerators and other amenities.

Business associates and other promoters didn't respond to the Aerocar as enthusiastically as Fisher hoped. In the spring of 1929 Kettering stated lukewarmly, "I have not got quite the vivid imagination that you have, where this will revolutionize transportation, but I can see where a nice business might be built up, making and selling this."[38] A year after his initial association with the Aerocar, Carl was promoting the vehicle on a very small scale, offering demonstrations to any interested sponsor. Exploiting his inside connections at the Indianapolis Motor Speedway, he arranged to display the Aerocar at the parade preceding the 1929 Memorial Day race.[39]

In the late summer of 1929, Fisher and the handful of men interested in the Aerocar finally established a small manufacturing plant in Opa-Locka, Florida. The site was just a few miles northwest of Miami; however, the "factory" turned out only a few dozen units. The stock market crash occurred just weeks after the Opa-Locka plant opened. Many Americans taking to the road were hard-pressed to provide gasoline for their tanks. Few of them possessed the means to spend hundreds of dollars for luxurious trailers; rather, they strapped most of their belongings to the roofs of their increasingly dilapidated vehicles. By the late summer of 1930 Fisher realized that his dream of a trailer empire was dying. He mused to Tom Milton, "I don't know what we are going to do with the Aerocar, and it really doesn't make a damned bit of difference to me because I have plugged along with it and I have other work to do. I still love the Aerocar and would not give it up for anything I have ever ridden in."[40]

Despite these philosophical words, Fisher was still stubbornly holding onto his dream a year and a half later. He had experienced a ray of hope in the summer of 1931 when General Motors borrowed several units for test runs. The company even requested extensions of time for tests, briefly raising his spirits. In the early fall, they returned the vehicles without comment and placed no orders. Carl insisted to Roy Chapin, who, perhaps out of sympathy for an old friend, had bought a few shares of stock in the company, that although Aerocar hadn't made any money yet, he still believed prospects "grow better daily, and my stock in the company is not for sale." In fact, Fisher claimed, if he had extra cash to invest, he would "be very glad to purchase all of the outstanding stock on the same basis as yours has been purchased."[41] Fisher was clearly whistling in the dark at that point. The Aerocar Corporation was organized at the wrong time and never had a chance. Like hundreds of other small companies, including many promoting good ideas, Aerocar vanished without a trace during the depression.

Fisher responded to the stock market collapse like many of his fellow entrepreneurs, initially discounting its seriousness. But as his personal fortune shrank, then vanished, during the next few years, he was forced to confront his own diminished circumstances. For one of the first times in his life, Carl began thinking seriously about how less affluent Americans lived; this led him to consider some solutions to their housing needs. He never mentioned the source for his inspiration, but he may have been responding to some of the more idealistic ruminations of national planning advocates who were beginning to shape Franklin Roosevelt's New Deal.[42] In the spring of 1933 Carl unveiled designs for cheap prefab houses suitable for Americans of modest means. At first, he didn't really focus on providing them for poor people. The primary building materials would be steel and asbestos, and costs would range from $1,000 all the way up to $10,000.[43] Fisher claimed they could be constructed on small plots of land, costing as little as $25 to $30 per acre in some areas. His initial target market niche was decidedly middle class. According to Fisher, they would appeal to "retired businessmen or ex-Army officers, school teachers, ministers, and others who want a small home, where they could live outdoors a big part of the year, and help support themselves with small gardens."[44]

Fisher toyed with the concept of prefab housing for the next two years. Although he spent only $5,000 on his own experiments, he imagined himself rivaling the Johns-Manville Company in commitment to testing different home designs and combinations of building materials. For potential markets, Fisher was still thinking largely of retired, middle-class northerners with sufficient means to move to Florida and buy modest cottages built on cheap land. The big appeal of the houses would be that they were "practically indestructible, and certainly fire-proof, vermin-proof, and proof against the continuous sunshine."[45]

By the summer of 1935, Fisher had adjusted his image of potential dwellers in prefab houses. New Dealers had just begun to construct tiny amounts of government housing in various experimental configurations, from private dwellings to apartment buildings, most intended to house poor people.[46] Surveying the housing situation in Miami, Fisher noted that many thousands of poor people were living in shanties. He proposed building several thousand homes, primarily for the "colored population," constructed out of sand and coral rock building blocks. To make them fireproof and bug proof, they would have concrete floors. The roofs would presumably be constructed of colored asbestos shingles. Upkeep and maintenance costs would be minimal. When the units changed hands, the insides could be hosed down and a new coat of whitewash applied, both inside and outside, "to make them sweet and clean."[47] Fisher argued that there was probably $5 million worth of dilapidated housing in the Miami-Dade region; thus there was a huge potential market for this new housing.

By the mid-1930s, Fisher no longer had the means to build houses; he was simply interested in such designs, and he hoped his ideas and suggestions would reach the eyes and ears of better-positioned decision makers. Fisher's ideas probably never reached the consciousness of New Dealers in Washington, but he still possessed sufficient local visibility that it was wise for public officials to respond. The chief of Miami's Division of Buildings complimented his proposals as "very practical, indeed, and particularly when such houses are to be occupied by persons with low hygienic standards of housekeeping."[48] He did not subscribe to Fisher's scheme of stark building-block walls, preferring instead stuccoed exterior walls and conventional, plastered interior walls. Nothing further was heard about Fisher's housing ideas, however, and he evidently dropped the matter.

Early in 1935 Fisher became intrigued by another enterprise: outdoor advertising signs. In the mid-1930s most outdoor signs were inanimate painted advertisements on wooden blocks attached to telephone poles, posters or metal signs in windows or on buildings, or larger appeals paint-ed on the sides of barns. In recent years, promoters had experimented with blinking neon lights and electric-powered signs with moving parts. Fisher was captivated, and he hoped to play a role in the industry's emer-gence. In February he urged Tom Milton to come into the business with him, declaring that it was a sure-fire growth enterprise. Milton, however, demurred; he currently had a salaried job in Detroit and was reluctant to take any chances in the middle of the depression: "If I were alone or if the closing of the banks here had not so crippled me I would be in a fine position to take a chance on something that held promise but under present circumstances I must hang on to what I have."[49]

Fisher kept pressuring his former protégé. In November, he informed Milton that he had applied for patents for window signs, "especially with heads of human beings and animals, to be illuminated from the inside—flashing or fixed." Carl was particularly intrigued with signs with eyes that seemingly moved with the viewer so that one aware of the sign felt he was being constantly watched. Fisher was convinced there was a great future in the business, and he once again urged Milton to join him in pro-moting the idea: "Then you won't have to work for anybody any more."[50] Eventually, Fisher accepted Milton's decision to stay out of it; their future correspondence avoided the subject of outdoor advertising.

In promoting outdoor advertising signs, Fisher contacted individuals with experience in the business and received discouraging feedback. Es-sentially, they told him that he had gotten into the game too late. Frank Horuff, a manager for the Indiana Amusement and Vending Machine Association, did some investigating for Fisher and reported, "From what I find, what you are trying to do, that field has been fully covered." He urged Carl to stay clear of the business: "It is hard to get into the other man's game, unless you can outsmart him with something that is newer, better or at a less price."[51] Horuff's warning did not completely discour-age Fisher. Late in 1935 and early in 1936 he erected a handful of inno-vative electrically powered outdoor signs on buildings in Miami Beach.[52] Like most of Fisher's other initiatives in the 1930s, little more came of it.

However discouraging his prospects, Fisher's mind never slowed down, and he never lost his enthusiasm for new projects. In his final years, Carl came up with many additional schemes, some designed to make money. In the spring of 1936 his thoughts once again turned to the past, especially the excitement of the Indianapolis 500 motorcar race. Fisher imagined bringing similar spectacles to South Florida. He tried to interest the Indianapolis track's new owner, Eddie Rickenbacker, in developing a major racing oval in Miami: "I have thought for the past two years [about] the subject of a speedway down here, where you could build a speedway for less money than at any other place in the United States." Fisher presented an image of bored tourists looking for excitement, warm-weather climate, and year-round racing. He even had the spot picked out and offered to help broker the deal.[53] But Rickenbacker had his hands full with Indianapolis and other enterprises and gently declined Carl's offer.

In yet another promotional effort, Fisher announced that he had been issued a patent for a combination of silica sand and rubber that allegedly provided "a tough semi-skid proof material for rubber soles on shoes, rubber belting, rubber hammers and all other types of rubber surfaces."[54] Not surprisingly, considering the heat and humidity that blanketed South Florida for much of the year, another promising business that interested Fisher was air conditioning. Early in 1936 he applied for and received a patent for a device known as a Solar Operated Refrigerating System. The problem would be manufacturing and marketing, which required huge amounts of capital. Unfortunately, his appeals for marketing and technical support, to say nothing about investment capital, fell on deaf ears.[55]

Without question, Fisher was aware of his diminished clout; more and more often he sat in his office waiting for his telephone to ring. As the 1930s lengthened, so did the intervals between incoming calls. He had to sell personal possessions, including household furnishings and valuable paintings, to meet living expenses, and in 1935 he declared bankruptcy. Except on rare occasions, Fisher didn't feel sorry for himself. He remained personally popular, and many of his former business associates dropped by when they had time. In his last years, several of his smaller projects were conceived primarily in an effort to help him and his cronies enjoy a good time. In the late 1930s Carl tried to organize several small boating clubs. In the late 1910s he had built and enjoyed the facilities at

Toward the end of his life, Carl Fisher had less to do and far more time for leisure. Courtesy of the Historical Museum of Southern Florida.

the Cocolobo Club, located an hour or so by boat south of Miami. Fifteen years later, he and a few friends organized the Caribbean Club in Key Largo, a fishing club, with about one hundred members and a few modest buildings.[56]

By the late 1930s, Fisher realized that he was an anachronism; his time was drawing short, and he had little to live for. Although frequently invited to civic banquets and other public events, he was no longer an important player; more and more often, he heard about key decisions only after they were made. Carl had been concerned over his health for years, and by mid-1938 he was hearing little but bad news and dire warnings from his doctors. As war clouds loomed over Europe and the Pacific Ocean, an era was ending. Fisher, too, was merely waiting for the end.

14

Taps

As both his fortune and his influence waned, Fisher's visits to his office in Miami Beach became less regular. When he did go there, he had little to do. He would eagerly scan the morning mail, hoping for some encouragement regarding one or another of his minor promotional ideas, but often there was no mail or only advertisements. Sensitive to their former partner's diminished circumstances, the Pancoast family provided him with a secretary, and the younger men in the organization occasionally dropped in to ask his advice concerning sale or development of Miami Beach property or other business matters. Carl was flattered to be consulted; for a few moments, at least, he could feel like a player again.

Much of his time in his office was spent on the telephone talking to old friends or dictating long, gossipy letters to them. He reminisced about experiences shared long ago. In typical Fisher fashion, he tried to buck up the spirits of friends whose fortunes had fallen even further than his own. Carl retained his sense of humor and could still insert the needle when he thought the occasion warranted. His former racing friend Barney Oldfield was trying to write his autobiography and sent Fisher a chapter about his racing experiences at Indianapolis. Oldfield had described breaking a certain speed record. Fisher wrote back, chiding his friend for certain omissions: "You left out the fact that you had had a few drinks. . . . Of course, if you have tried to dodge the fact that you were drunk a good deal of the time, or at least in a hilarious mood a good part of the time . . . you spit in the eye of a great many of your friends."[1]

Fisher's sensitivity to other people, at least other males, never deserted him. He maintained a remarkable ability to see the other person's point of view. When John LaGorce expressed deep disappointment that his young son had dropped out of college and had gotten married, Carl reassured him it was not the end of the world: "I think the kid is all right. He shows he does not give a damn for your opinions or advice, which is another good indication . . . I think you are a plain damned fool to worry about the situation. The boy is all right, let him alone and let him go to work."[2] Carl also formed some meaningful new friendships. Although he remained indifferent to organized religion his entire life, he formed a close friendship with an influential local Catholic priest, William Barry. During his heyday, Carl had donated generously to Barry's endeavors, including valuable land for an addition to a church in Miami Beach. Although Fisher's fortune vanished, Barry remained close to the former tycoon. The two men also enjoyed very earthly pleasures, including prizefights, movies, and ice cream. Jane recalled, "Father Barry urged ice cream upon Carl as a sweet substitute for Scotch."[3] Although Barry maintained no hope of converting Carl to Catholicism, the priest often left "meaningful" books on Carl's bed stand.

Fisher had more opportunity to read them because he spent increasing amounts of time at home. As the 1930s progressed, there were many mornings when he either felt lazy or too poorly to put on a facade and make an appearance at the office. As long as his eyes held out, Fisher enjoyed reading. He had long been an ardent admirer of both Lincoln and Napoleon, whose framed pictures adorned his bedroom.[4] His reading tastes ran to biographies, history, and fiction, mostly mysteries. Fisher had an extraordinary range of interests and was a voracious reader. In the summer of 1930 he requested forty-one books in a single order. They included H. G. Wells's *Outline of History*, biographies of Jefferson Davis, Emile Zola, Cleopatra, François Villon, General John Burgoyne, and Rasputin. In addition, he asked for a history of famous trials, books on gardening, philosophy, psychoanalysis, chemistry, opera, and religion.

He topped off his order with a dozen or so mysteries.[5] Although he had journeyed to Europe rarely and had seldom enjoyed his experiences, he loved reading European history. Fisher was particularly mesmerized by the history of Elizabethan England, claiming at one point that one of his "great uncles" had been beheaded in 1534 for getting "mixed up into the politics of Henry VIII and the times."[6]

Although he lacked formal education, Carl Fisher possessed a good mind which he exercised regularly. Robert H. Davis, editor of the *New York Sun*, wrote to him: "You have a discriminating taste for good books and I place you among the very few of my friends whose selections are worth reading." Davis continued that he was bombarded with unwanted volumes: "Bartenders, embalmers, and shooting gallery proprietors send me with high recommendations certain books that I am supposed to absorb. Ninety percent of them are rubbish. . . . The best books clubs are responsible for much of it."[7] If Carl's reading tastes were eclectic and "undisciplined," they were nevertheless impressive for a man with a sixth grade education. Throughout his life, Fisher never stopped educating himself.

Unfortunately, in his final years Fisher paid far less attention to his body than to his mind. During his first six decades, Carl was inconsistent in caring for his health. In his youth he had been nicknamed "Crip" because of his physical clumsiness and his tendency to fall down. In school, he had been unable to see the blackboard at school clearly, and he had been an indifferent student. Some considered him the dumbest lad in his class. Neither he nor his mother had connected his inability to concentrate on his studies with poor eyesight. Carl, an uncomplaining sort, may simply have assumed that the rest of humanity saw the world with equally fuzzy vision. After all, his friends and rivals on the bicycle and race car circuits also talked of seeing the landscape as little more than a blur. He did not consult an eye specialist until age thirty-one—after he retired from race car driving.[8]

As a young man, even well into his middle age, Fisher had a short, stocky, sturdy body, which he taxed to the limit. He worked and played hard. His first wife, Jane, complained that he was constitutionally incapable of relaxation. Fisher was a vigorous sportsman, and he *attacked* every new sport he attempted. In 1921 one old friend witnessing the forty-seven-year-old riding a polo pony and competing against far younger and more experienced players commented to Fisher that "I know that you want to keep young and hard, but when you play polo you play it from your toes to your ears and with a strenuousness that everybody could see." He urged Fisher to take care of himself, adding, "If you don't, some day there is going to be an explosion in your physical boiler and then you will be forced to do what I am anxious to see you do voluntarily."[9] That same year Carl's personal physician warned him about his diet; among other disturbing signals, his blood sugar was far too high.[10]

Fisher thumbed his nose at suggestions that he slow down. He refused to be treated like an old man, and he instinctively distrusted doctors. Carl informed his physician that he was not about to "follow any suggestions you make unless I know exactly what you are trying to do. Because you hand me a bottle of pills with the suggestion that I eat one every hour or so, doesn't mean that I am going to do so. I want to know the why and wherefore of every step that has been made in this matter."[11] Carl talked a good game; perhaps he unconsciously hoped that *sounding* conscientious about what he put into his body could substitute for lack of willpower. His doctor, however, was not fooled. He was particularly concerned that Fisher ate large quantities of salted peanuts, roasted in oil. Late in 1921 his physician warned Fisher that his blood sugar was so high that he was a borderline diabetic.[12]

Fisher affected a casual attitude toward his health, but he experienced frequent bouts of anxiety about his physical well-being bordering on hypochondria. As he observed to one associate in the summer of 1921, his interest in acquiring property on Long Island was motivated at least in part by health concerns. Carl could no longer stand summers in Indianapolis: "As far as I am concerned, I must get out of this climate as I have the devil's own time with hay fever and catarrhal conditions that entirely disappear on salt water."[13] Two years later, he had a scare concerning a heart condition, which he dealt with in typical Fisher fashion: "After fooling around with about one dozen of the noted heart specialists in this country—all of whom advised me that I had an athletic heart and must give up athletics and a lot of other bunk, I ran into Dr. Walden." Fisher claimed that the good doctor "entirely cured me in ten days" through a strict diet of meat and grapefruit juice.[14]

This remark was highly revealing of Fisher's attitude toward his health. For the remainder of his life, whenever health issues came up, Carl placed faith in quack cures, often through fad diets that required dramatic modification of his eating patterns. Invariably, he lost enthusiasm for the regimen after a few days or weeks at the most and returned to his self-destructive behavior. Occasionally, other afflictions unrelated to his heretofore self-indulgent diet bothered him. Late in 1923 Fisher suffered from neuritis, and he received considerable relief from daily massages. He informed his friend James Cox that if he experienced further flare-ups of neuritis, he would jump the next train to take advantage of the well-known cures offered at Hot Springs, Arkansas.[15] In the summer of 1926, shortly after Jane left him and departed for Paris, Carl complained to her in letter, "I am having trouble with my eyes, a blood vessel snapped in one, and I have spots over that eye which makes it very difficult for me to read."[16]

Fisher frequently gave health advice to others, almost none of which he followed himself. In hindsight, his eating and other oral habits were appalling. He informed one friend that some of his health troubles were rooted in his diet, which up to then had included far too much "white bread, grease, onions, and other perfectly indigestible food—including every so often the swallowing of an end of a cigar."[17] Considering his large daily intake of cigars and regular ingestion of bits of tobacco, that was not surprising. In 1929 Fisher admitted that he had smoked cigars "continuously" for the last fifteen years, consuming anywhere between fifteen and twenty-five per day. In typical fashion, he made light of their effect on his health: "I am now smoking a ten-cent cigar which is probably about one half cabbage and the other half turnip, but the strain on my heart is not as great as it would be with the Cuban cigars."[18]

Through the 1920s Fisher had occasionally complained about health problems. By the next decade they became a constant worry. The fundamental problem was that he was drinking far too much. After he and Jane were divorced in 1926, Fisher began living openly with his secretary, Margaret Collier, who had been his lover for years. Carl finally married Margaret in 1927. Evidently, she liked the bottle as much as Carl, so married life did nothing to curb his appetites. During the first years of their marriage, Margaret reveled in the whirl of parties and expensive evenings out on the town.[19] Margaret's health, however, was never strong. Friends cautioned Carl that the strain of entertaining guests was taking its toll on her. In November 1930, John LaGorce and his wife entertained Margaret when she was in Washington, and they were shocked at her appearance.[20] Margaret was hospitalized on several occasions, and she and Carl spent increasing amounts of time apart. By several accounts, their marriage was unfulfilling, if not sordid; both apparently, were unfaithful.[21] Clearly, neither was capable of providing the nurturing the other needed.

By the early 1930s, Fisher's waistline was expanding even as his bank account was contracting. In a mildly complaining letter to LaGorce in 1933, Fisher mentioned that he had ordered a "Weil Health Belt," a sort of corset to hold in his bulging stomach. In the same letter he made light of his plight: "I want to tell you about my last shot of bad luck. Just when the price of beer is down to my price [Prohibition had just been repealed], without grumbling, my Doctor tells me I must quit drinking beer."[22]

By 1934 his doctors confirmed that Fisher was a diabetic and would have to take insulin regularly.[23] The same year, Fisher was experiencing back trouble so intense that he was confined to bed most of the time. Early in 1935 he wrote to his doctor that he had devised his own remedies for his illness. Until recently, his back pain had been so severe that he was able to sleep only an hour or two per night. Nevertheless, the previous evening he had eaten a large plate of chop suey, washed down with two glasses of scotch. He boasted that he got a full night's sleep and woke up feeling great. This, according to Fisher, would constitute his future regimen![24]

By then Fisher was figuratively playing Russian roulette with his health. Doctors frantically advised him to curb his appetites and strictly limit his intake of certain foods and alcohol. He made a mockery of such advice, complaining to his primary physician that one diet made him so hungry that he couldn't resist consuming steaks and fried potatoes instead. He confessed to his physician that he was still drinking "four or five bottles of beer a day."[25] How much more he may have been drinking was anybody's guess. Margaret, in delicate health herself, was spending increasing amounts of time away from him visiting friends or "recovering" in sanitariums. Fisher was living largely alone, tended by "a very bright colored boy" who did his grocery shopping and attended to his routine physical needs, including giving him his insulin injections.[26]

Fisher's former wife, Jane, who still visited him occasionally, vividly described his dramatically reduced position in Miami Beach: "Through its streets Carl moved slowly, hardly known by the new crowd whose cars flashed through the streets he had built. . . . He walked ponderously, greatly weighted now, to the cash-and-carry market to select vegetables and groceries and have them carried home by a little colored boy in pace with his slow steps."[27]

For those close to him, the experience of dealing with his deterioration was extremely stressful. Carl sometimes vented his frustration against bankers, the Internal Revenue Service, and other institutions in letters to Fred Humpage, who had loyally shouldered much of the legal and financial paperwork for years. Humpage practiced inordinate consideration and tact in responding to his boss's explosions, which revealed how forgetful and sadly confused the former mogul had become by the mid-1930s.[28] Years after Carl's death, some former friends and associates described him as acutely depressed in his final years. Rose Weiss, a colorful fixture on Miami Beach, recalled him lamenting, "I wish I was the Carl Fisher of yesterday . . . I am absolutely alone and lonely."[29] Walter Dennis Myers, an Indiana lawyer who defended him in several lawsuits with women, visited Carl in Miami Beach and claimed he stated, "I'm a beggar-dead broke, no family to fall back on . . . I used to be able to make dreams come true. Can't do it any more. I'm only a beggar now. The end can't be far away."[30] Somehow, these accounts emphasizing self-pity appear highly uncharacteristic of Fisher. If he occasionally gave in to despair, he far more frequently discounted his problems and afflictions.

Considering how Fisher abused his body and ignored doctors' advice, it is astonishing he lasted as long as he did. By 1936 or 1937, his system was so severely damaged that he was retaining vast amounts of liquids. He had to visit the hospital weekly to have twenty pounds of fluids "tapped" from his stomach.[31] He was suffering advanced cirrhosis of the liver. When he swelled up, he had a very bloated appearance. Sadly, Fisher had to have two rows of buttons on his suit jackets, one for when he was swelled up, the other for after he had been "drained."

By early 1938 knowledgeable consultants were unanimous in their opinion that he wouldn't live much longer. One physician, a family friend who had advised Fisher on health issues for two decades, recounted his battles with his body over the past several years, expressing amazement that he had recently survived a severe bout with pneumonia, along with his perilous liver condition. The doctor lamented to Margaret: "I wish you and I could do more for Carl but there is so little to do now. I only wish he had done some of the things I asked him to do so many years ago when there was some chance to help him and try to ward off the things now present."[32]

Fred Humpage told Margaret that doctors had informed him that the only thing keeping Fisher going was an "exceptionally strong heart." The frequent "tapping operations" were draining huge amounts of fluids and had to be exacting an enormous toll on his strength. In August 1938 the most optimistic doctors gave Fisher no more than a year to live; some thought he would be dead within a month.[33]

In his customary way, Fisher tried to make light of his situation. He described one "tapping operation" late in the summer of 1938: "The new opening sealed up immediately, but she 'busted' open on me day before yesterday—almost blew my suspenders off." In a letter to Jane, Carl discounted reports of his imminent demise: "I know there are a lot of reports circulating that I am dying, and some that I am already dead and buried. I have felt very good in the last three weeks as compared with the previous seven months." Fisher claimed that he was following the doctors' orders and that he didn't drink any more, but he kept a little "Mountain Dew" so that his visitors could enjoy an occasional nip. "I let the tears from my eyes roll into a cocktail of tomato juice and listerine, diluted with some Vitamin Bs in capsules, and wild goose liver oil. If you get cirrhosis of the liver, try this remedy. It won't do you a d—d bit of good, but it is terrible punishment."[34]

Such superficial cheerfulness was sheer bravado. Those who visited him frequently in his last year claimed that he had basically given up, that he was indulging his appetites indiscriminately, and that he was drinking himself to death. Jane recalled her last visit in the spring of 1939: "He was in bed. His once powerful body was misshapen under the covers and his once always-smiling face was wreathed with suffering. The dimples that had become his insignia of determination, as well as of laughter, had

Carl Fisher in his early
sixties; the signs of hard
living were evident.
When this photo was
taken in about 1938,
he had only a year to
live. Courtesy of the
Historical Museum of
Southern Florida.

become lines of pain." Jane had her own troubles, as dark clouds already shrouded her third marriage. They tried to cheer each other up, but Jane found the effort excruciating: "The poison seeping into his once vital body drove him into outbursts that made him lash out against whoever might be nearest to him in such moments. Added to this anguish was the humiliation of failure."[35] When Jane left, she sensed that she had seen him for the last time.

Nevertheless, the end came suddenly. In July 1939, as the Miami Beach Chamber of Commerce prepared to celebrate its nineteenth "birthday" with a banquet, another pioneer, Tom Pancoast, extended an invitation to Fisher. Although touched by Pancoast's thoughtfulness, Fisher initially declined: "You fellows at those luncheon parties live too high for me. I am on a diet, mainly of pretzels and bird seed, and some of these I have to take with a high pressure gun."[36] At the last moment, he changed his mind and made an appearance. After the lunch, Pancoast quickly penned a note, thanking Fisher for making an effort to come: "Of all the people who attended the birthday luncheon yesterday . . . I felt more honored by having you present than anybody else."[37]

The letter never reached Fisher. On the morning of July 15, he suffered a gastric hemorrhage. Friends rushed him to the St. Francis Hospital in Miami Beach, which his old friend Jim Allison had built. They also sent telegrams to those close to him. Margaret was in New York and could not get home in time to say good-bye. Nor could Jane. At 4:52 p.m., Fisher breathed his last. Three old friends, Fred Humpage, Dan Mahoney, and Frank Katzentine, were in the room, along with his doctor, Frank Voris.[38]

Carl Fisher had lived an extraordinary life. Always willing to take risks, he had gambled and won for almost six decades. He lost a big hand at Montauk, and thereafter his luck had turned sour. As Howard Kleinberg astutely observed, his last rolls of the dice produced nothing but snake eyes.[39] Yet he was philosophical about his reversals and, for the most part, refused to feel sorry for himself. What hurt most was his sense that ultimately he had failed his friends. Carl felt personally responsible for their financial losses and wished Montauk had turned out differently, for their sakes. This apparently did not translate into deep feelings of personal guilt. Encouraged by his good friend William Barry to take up religion and convert to Catholicism, Fisher demurred, explaining that he had nothing to be ashamed of.

Fisher packed an enormous amount of excitement, achievement, adventure and fun into his sixty-five years. As his life fizzled out, he must have sensed that he had seen more and done more than almost all of his contemporaries. Like a meteor streaking across the sky, Fisher's life was fast-paced, comparatively brief, and dazzling.

Flags in Miami Beach flew at half-mast. Following a lavish funeral in Miami Beach, Carl's body was cremated, and the urn carrying his ashes remained in Miami Beach until 1943, when they were sent to Indianapolis and buried in a mausoleum at Crown Hill Cemetery. The burial site was the only property he still owned there. Two years after his funeral, a far smaller number of friends and former associates gathered at a small public park at Alton Road and Fiftieth Street in Miami Beach, where they dedicated a rather strange bronze bust, set amid a pedestrian concrete monument. By 1941 his old friend John Levi was mayor of Miami. Levi provided the inscription carved into the Fisher memorial: "He carved a great city from a jungle."[40]

Epilogue

Although he promoted various projects until the end of his life, Carl
Fisher may have sensed that the world had passed him by. When he died
in 1939, newspaper columnists in Miami Beach, Indianapolis, and a few
other cities wrote lengthy, adulatory obituaries; some of them were an-
alytical as well. Dignitaries in Miami Beach acknowledged his passing
with appropriate ceremonies and expressions of sorrow. The vast majority of Americans, however, soon forgot him. Carl's fantasy world and their
harsh realities were entirely incompatible. As they slowly emerged from
the Great Depression, most citizens were absorbed by their own problems, and a new and frightening set of challenges loomed on the horizon.
Fisher symbolized a carefree, bygone era. Fun, it seemed, was passé.

Did Fisher leave a lasting legacy, or did it quickly crumble? Without
question, his former wife, Jane, remained his most loyal supporter. In a
valiant effort to keep his memory alive, she arranged for publication of
a fawning biography eight years after Carl's death.[1] His once formidable
fortune had all but vanished. Fisher had been a notoriously sloppy re-
cordkeeper, and accountants had a nightmare trying to sort through his
papers; various computations of his net worth at his death range between
$55,000 and $141,000. In contrast to Jane's effort to maintain Carl's rep-

utation, his widow, Margaret, appeared interested in little but extracting what she could from his withered estate. Fourteen years after his death, she was still wrangling with estate lawyers over the last few dollars.[2]

In Miami Beach, dozens of exquisite art deco buildings remained. Although Carl was not responsible for all of them, many of the structures (some designated as historical landmarks) remain, standing provocatively in their shimmering pastel coats of paint. Strolling down side streets in South Beach, just off Collins Avenue on a balmy winter afternoon, one can see the sights and almost hear the sounds of seventy-five years earlier: the murmur of cocktail party conversation amid the tinkle of martini glasses, the shrieks and laughter of flappers being tickled by smitten "Valentinos," the smooth roar of Stutz Bearcat, Marmon, and Packard engines. One can almost picture Fisher, dressed in his linen suit, white shirt, and brightly colored necktie, topped off with his trademark floppy hat, presiding over the festivities with a benign, somewhat bemused look on his face. Elsewhere in Miami Beach, fewer vestiges of Carl's creation are visible. Farther north, the giant high-rise hotels on the beach stand shoulder to shoulder. On the bay side, a few of the most dazzling homes built by Carl's high-roller friends in the 1920s remain, but most have been torn down and replaced by more modern, sumptuous dwellings. Only a few old-timers remember Carl Fisher or his hotels, which were demolished decades earlier.

As one drives across the country, vestiges of the Lincoln and Dixie Highways have all but disappeared. Souvenir hunters removed the last of the Lincoln Highway signs decades ago. Massive new interstate highways now manage one hundred times the volume of traffic that the modest, two-lane transcontinental roads carried seventy years ago. As you drive along Interstate 80, if you look carefully, you might occasionally see unused strips of asphalt paralleling the modern road. Some of that crumbling surface was originally part of the Lincoln Highway. Small patches of deserted highway formerly maintained under the name of the Dixie Highway can also be seen in the South. But for the most part, Fisher's big dream now resides in a few historical photo books, monographs, and the diaries of automobile pioneers.

In Indianapolis, the most permanent of Carl's creations still stands. The Indianapolis Motor Speedway still hosts the Memorial Day race, which has grown bigger and even more important over the years. Undoubtedly, Carl would be dazzled by the speed of modern racers, the value of the prizes, and the size of the crowds, but most other aspects of the race would seem familiar. The speedway itself has gone through several changes in ownership since Carl sold it to Eddie Rickenbacker in 1927. Although the track has been resurfaced numerous times, much of the foundation of bricks installed almost ninety years ago remains.

It would be unrealistic to suggest that Fisher belongs in the first rank of American entrepreneurs. He did not revolutionize an industry, like Carnegie, Ford, or Rockefeller. Nor did he almost single-handedly invent a wholly new area of enterprise, like J. P. Morgan or Bill Gates. Unlike Alfred P. Sloan and other "organization men," he was almost totally uninterested in developing complex corporate hierarchies and sophisticated business procedures. Without question, Fisher was happiest and most creative when he was promoting his projects, but earlier entrepreneurs had devised marketing skills he applied. Phineas T. Barnum's tactics were at least as audacious, if no more spectacular than Carl's stunts. Fisher clearly grasped the fact that, as the twentieth century unfolded, large numbers of his countrymen possessed new wealth and that there was a huge potential market in devising new ways for them to *enjoy* their fortunes. As Cindy S. Aron and others have shown, vacations were not new for Americans in the early twentieth century. Fisher, however, thought in terms of *extended* vacations, long-term relaxation.

Only at the very end of his life did Fisher conceptualize the concept of retirement; and even then, he really didn't think in terms of discrete communities for retirees. Even had he done so, by the mid-1930s, he no longer possessed the capital or clout to do anything about it. Most elderly Americans were struggling to keep hold of the older homes they had, not thinking about entirely new settings and lifestyles. Had Fisher maintained his health and enthusiasm for development, and had he lived into the postwar era, he might well have served as a link to retirement community developers such as Del E. Webb and Ross W. Cortese.[3] Fisher's career resembled the life cycle of a comet: rising quickly, shining brightly, then falling swiftly.

Notes

Introduction

1. McCullough quoted in *Mr. Miami Beach*, PBS video, first aired February 2, 1998.

Chapter 1. A Shaky Foundation

1. William G. Alexander to Carl G. Fisher, July 20, 1925; Alexander to Margaret Fisher, April 18, 1938, both in box 4, Fisher Papers.

2. Alexander to Fisher, April 18, 1938, ibid.

3. For a superb treatment of the early settlement of river towns along the Ohio River, see Wade, *Urban Frontier*.

4. Amos M. Fisher to Dr. William G. Alexander, January 21, 1926, box 4, Fisher Papers.

5. Untitled, mimeographed manuscript dated January 24, 1926, ibid.

6. Amos Fisher to Alexander, January 21, 1926.

7. *Encyclopedia Americana: International Edition*, 15:62; Peckham, *Indiana*, 36–37.

8. Madison, *Indiana Way*, 81–85.

9. Peckham, *Indiana*, 65–67, 68, 70, 73.

10. Carl Fisher to Frank B. Shutts, October 21, 1921, box 4, Fisher Papers.

11. State constitutional provision quoted in Peckham, *Indiana*, 138.

12. There is some uncertainty concerning Carl's order of birth. In his recent book, Jerry Fisher, a distant relative, claimed that Carl was the oldest of the three brothers (*Pacesetter*, 1), but he provided no documentation. Polly Redford claimed

that Carl was the second-born son. See Redford, *Billion-Dollar Sandbar*, 45. Jane Fisher provided the information that he was the second born in an oral history interview several years earlier. See Redford interview of Jane Fisher, April 4, 1966, Special Collections, Richter Library, University of Miami, Coral Gables, Florida.

13. Redford, *Billion-Dollar Sandbar*, 45.

14. Ibid.; Peckham, *Indiana*, 104–6.

15. Fisher, *Fabulous Hoosier*, 33; Redford, *Billion-Dollar Sandbar*, 45–46.

16. Fisher, *Pacesetter*, 7.

17. Riggs, "Carl G. Fisher," 68.

18. See, for example, Fisher, *Fabulous Hoosier*, 33; Jane Fisher interview by Polly Redford, April 4, 1967, Oral History Collection, Special Collections, Richter Library, University of Miami.

19. Fisher, *Fabulous Hoosier*, 33.

20. Redford, *Billion-Dollar Sandbar*, 48.

21. Several scholars perceived direct links between bicycle enthusiasts and the Good Roads Movement. See, for example, Mason, "The League of American Wheelmen and the Good Roads Movement," and Hugil, "Good Roads and the Automobile in the United States," 332–40.

22. Tarkington became a lifelong friend. Decades later, he routinely visited Fisher at his home in Miami Beach. See Fisher, *Fabulous Hoosier*, 69–70.

23. There is a long story about the history of the Zig-Zag Cycling Club in the February 7, 1931, issue of the *Indianapolis News*.

24. Ibid.

25. Redford, *Billion-Dollar Sandbar*, 47.

Chapter 2. Cracking the Door of Opportunity

1. Redford, *Billion-Dollar Sandbar*, 45; Boomhower, "Carl G. Fisher," 24.

2. Fisher to W. W. Atterbury, April 26, 1927, box 2, Carl G. Fisher Papers.

3. Redford claimed that he was thirteen when he took the railroad job. Fisher recalled that he had been fifteen. See Redford, *Billion-Dollar Sandbar*, 45; Fisher to Atterbury, April 26, 1927.

4. "Drummer" was a contemporary term describing commercial men in general but most commonly traveling salesmen.

5. Fox, *Illustrated History of the Indianapolis 500*, 451.

6. Fisher to Atterbury, April 26, 1927, box 2, Fisher Papers.

7. Redford, *Billion-Dollar Sandbar*, 47.

8. *Indianapolis Times*, December 7, 1944.

9. Ida Fisher to Earle Fisher, May 8, June 8, 1898, Fisher Papers.

10. For a brief history of bicycling, see Alderson, *Bicycling*. See also Palmer, *Riding High*, and Smith, *Social History of the Bicycle*.

11. Nash, *Magic of Miami Beach*, 94.

12. Background on Fisher's bicycle racing activities was gleaned from an obituary in the *Miami Herald*, July 16, 1939.

13. Pope, the leading figure in bicycle marketing in the United States, had imported the best British bicycles early in his career, but in 1878 he began producing the much esteemed "Columbia" safety bicycle, which ultimately made him a rich man. See Rae, *Road and Car,* 28–29.

14. Ibid.

15. *Miami Herald,* July 16, 1939; Fisher, *Pacesetter,* 16.

16. Rae, *Road and Car,* 29.

17. Fisher, *Fabulous Hoosier,* 36.

18. *Indianapolis Sentinel,* July 1, 1898; *Indianapolis Star,* July 1, 1959.

19. Fisher, *Fabulous Hoosier,* 37.

20. See Bush, *Lord of Attention,* especially chap. 1. Bush writes, "Crowds were becoming ever more aestheticized, celebratory, and apolitical. The participatory, theatrical, and consumer oriented crowd was often seen to be filled with exciting personalities; fashionable, modern, and fun to be with, the individuals composing these crowds were perceived to be less serious than their parents and more reliant on peer approval. After all, it was P. T. Barnum's world more than that of the educated remnants. By the 1890s Americans lived more and more of their lives in commercialized crowds. Circuses, sports events, and revivals were becoming highly organized and widely accepted as adjuncts to the social order" (28).

21. Fisher, *Fabulous Hoosier,* 37.

22. Ibid., 37–38.

23. Deborah Markisohn to author, April 14, 1997.

24. Redford, *Billion-Dollar Sandbar,* 49–50. In all likelihood, she took the story from Al Bloemaker. According to Bloemaker, it was a two-and-one-half-horsepower De Dion motor tricycle, costing $650 (*500 Miles,* 19).

25. Bloemaker, *500 Miles,* 19.

26. *Indianapolis Star,* July 3, 1912.

27. Boomhower, "Carl G. Fisher," 25.

28. Bloemaker, *500 Miles,* 21.

29. Fox, *Illustrated History of the Indianapolis 500,* 454. Fisher's speed record was fleeting, and he had to compete for attention with a great many other drivers. The "mile-a-minute" standard, or something very close to it, was being achieved by other drivers under different conditions. On October 25, 1902, Barney Oldfield had tested Henry Ford's famous "999" racing car over a five-mile time trial, which he completed in less than five and a half minutes. On December 1, 1902, Oldfield raced a mile in one minute and 1.2 seconds. See Nevins, *Ford,* 218.

30. By 1904, automobile speed records were being established and quickly broken at all different lengths, on a variety of different surfaces, by many different classifications of vehicles. Fisher's "record" was little noted and certainly not long remembered. In the same year, his pal Barney Oldfield drove Ford's "999" monster over ninety miles per hour on frozen Lake St. Clair, Michigan. In Ostend, Belgium, M. Rigolly drove a Gabron-Brille 103.55 miles per hour, the first land vehicle to exceed 100 miles per hour. See McShane, *Automobile,* 31–32.

31. Riggs, "Carl G. Fisher," 70.

32. Ibid., 69.

33. Fisher, *Fabulous Hoosier,* 41.

34. Collier and Horowitz, *The Fords,* 59.

35. For full biographical treatment of Durant, see Weisberger, *Dream Maker,* and Gustin, *Billy Durant.*

36. *Miami Herald,* July 16, 1939.

37. Riggs, "Carl G. Fisher," 70–71; *Miami Herald,* July 16, 1939.

38. *Indianapolis News,* October 31, 1908.

39. Fisher, *Fabulous Hoosier,* 44.

40. In the days following his ascent, stories appeared in the *Boston Transcript, Brooklyn Eagle, Chicago Daily News, Chicago Record-Herald, Detroit Times, Los Angeles Times, Philadelphia Inquirer, St. Paul News, St. Louis Post-Dispatch,* and *San Francisco Call.*

41. *Indianapolis News,* December 22, 1908.

42. *Indianapolis Star,* June 6, 1909.

43. Kimes, "Rise and Fall of the Empire Automobile," 72.

44. Ibid.

45. Ibid., 73.

46. Phelps, *Indiana in Transition,* 316.

47. For an excellent account of Studebaker's life cycle, see Critchlow, *Studebaker.*

48. Peckham, *Indiana Way,* 182. Another source claims that Indiana had one hundred manufacturers of automobiles by 1909 but that only sixteen lasted for more than fifteen years. See Huffman, "Indiana Autos," 35–51. For more analysis of why Detroit became the center for automobile production, see Rae, "Why Michigan?" in Lewis and Goldstein, eds., *Automobile in American Culture,* 1–9, and May, *Most Unique Machine.*

49. I owe thanks to my friend and colleague Mark H. Rose for this insight.

50. Kimes, "Rise and Fall of the Empire Automobile," 77.

51. F. H. Akers to Fisher, April 28, 1919; Fisher to Akers, April 30, 1919; Fisher to J. G. Vincent, September 4, 1919; Fisher to Akers, June 22, 1919; all in box 1, Fisher Papers.

52. For an example of this type of nettlesome correspondence, see H. H. Batchellor to Fisher, December 31, 1920, box 1, Fisher Papers.

Chapter 3. The Initial Fortune

1. During several decades following the Civil War, Henry Adams, a direct descendant of Presidents John Adams and John Quincy Adams, had developed a reputation as a gloomy commentator on contemporary society, including national politics, the advent of new and in some ways threatening technology, and many other trends. For one of the most brilliant and disturbing of his commentaries, see Adams, *Education of Henry Adams.* In recent years, several prominent historians of technology have emphasized that early twentieth-century Americans had enormous faith in techno-

logical "fixes," even technological utopias. See Smith and Marx, eds., *Does Technology Drive Progress?*

2. Tichi, *Shifting Gears*, 25.

3. For two excellent accounts of automobile travel, see Berger, *Devil Wagon in God's Country*, and Belasco, *Americans on the Road*.

4. Fisher, *Fabulous Hoosier*, 47.

5. Jane Fisher provides the $10,000 estimate. See ibid., 48. Another source claims the cash outlay was $2,000; see Riggs, "Carl G. Fisher," 69. Jane Fisher may have confused the partners' original investment with the value of stock in the initial public offering. When Fisher and Allison filed incorporation papers in September 1904, they offered 200 shares at $50 apiece, a total of $10,000. See Prest-O-Lite Incorporation Papers, September 6, 1904, Indiana State Archives, Indianapolis.

6. Prest-O-Lite Incorporation Papers.

7. Fisher, *Fabulous Hoosier*, 48; Prest-O-Lite Incorporation Papers.

8. *Indianapolis News*, May 12, 1948.

9. Ibid., June 8, 1908.

10. Ibid.

11. Ibid.

12. Ibid.

13. *Indianapolis Sun*, June 16, 1908.

14. Redford, *Billion-Dollar Sandbar*, 51.

15. *Indianapolis Star*, December 7, 1911.

16. *Indianapolis News*, December 13, 1911.

17. *Indianapolis Star*, December 31, 1911.

18. For a superb biography of Kettering, see Leslie, *Boss Kettering*. For Kettering's work on self-starters, see pp. 46–51.

19. In fact, just two months after the building collapse in December 1911, the city council passed an ordinance once again permitting Prest-O-Lite to operate within city limits, as long as basic safety precautions were followed. See *Indianapolis Star*, February 10, 1912.

20. In two newspaper interviews published fifty years after these events, Trotter claimed that he owned the Speedway Realty Company which set up the actual town. See ibid., May 27, 1962, February 16, 1966.

21. "HiStory of Speedway," undated newspaper clipping (ca. 1966) located in Speedway Public Library, Speedway, Indiana.

22. For details about the new plant, see *Indianapolis Star*, May 25, 1913.

23. McCarthy, "The Man Who Invented America's Playground," 66.

24. Mimeographed, untitled, undated statement by Carl G. Fisher, box 1, Fisher Papers. See also Fisher's extensive obituary in the *Miami Herald*, July 16, 1939.

25. Fisher, *Fabulous Hoosier*, 64–65.

26. For details, see *Miami Herald*, July 16, 1939. See also Fisher, *Pacesetter*, 32–33; Redford, *Billion-Dollar Sandbar*, 52, 61; McCarthy, "America's Playground," 66; Boomhower, "Carl G. Fisher," 26; and Riggs, "Carl G. Fisher," 69.

27. Fisher, *Fabulous Hoosier*, 52.

28. Redford, *Billion-Dollar Sandbar*, 52.

29. Ibid.

30. Fisher to Messing, December 1, 1938, and Messing to Fisher, December 19, 1938, box 16, Fisher Papers.

31. Walter Dennis Myers, "Recollections," undated manuscript, p. 219, Myers Papers, Indiana Historical Society, Indianapolis.

32. *Indianapolis Star*, October 6, 1912.

33. Case #88,446, Superior Court, Marion County, Indiana, undated mimeographed manuscript, box 16, Fisher Papers; for newspaper accounts of the trial, see *Indianapolis Star*, January 28, February 2-4, 1913.

34. Fisher, *Fabulous Hoosier*, 2.

35. Ibid., 3-4. Jane failed to mention whether she first called the fire department.

36. There is an extensive body of literature on gender relations and the expectations from each other that men and women had. Good starting points include Bederman, *Manliness and Civilization*; see also Coontz, *Social Origins of Private Life*.

37. Fox, *Illustrated History of the Indianapolis 500*, 463.

38. Fisher, *Fabulous Hoosier*, 6.

39. Ibid., 5.

40. Ibid., 9.

41. Riggs, "Carl G. Fisher," 73.

42. At the trial three years after they were married, Jane Fisher took the stand and swore, under oath, that her future husband had been with her from 7 p.m. until about midnight on the eve of their nuptials. This is almost certainly false. In her book, *Fabulous Hoosier*, published thirty-five years after the lawsuit was settled, Jane wrote of Fisher's strange phone call to her and his sending Galloway to speak with her. It is difficult to avoid the conclusion that Fisher and his lawyers talked her into committing perjury.

43. Fisher, *Fabulous Hoosier*, 10.

44. Ibid., 10-11.

45. Ibid., 12-13.

46. An architectural editor for the *Indianapolis Star* conducted readers through a tour of the house, providing rapturous commentary. See *Indianapolis Star*, Women's Section, February 2, 1913.

47. Ibid., 16.

48. Redford, *Billion-Dollar Sandbar*, 52-53.

Chapter 4. Building a Brickyard

1. For broader cultural advances, sophisticated Americans were still looking to Europe for their cues. Although late nineteenth-century artists, writers, and intellectuals were busy developing an indigenous cultural framework worthy of international recognition and respect, most American intellectuals still looked anxiously across the Atlantic for affirmation for their efforts. Most wealthy Americans still regarded

the grand tour of Europe as a rite of passage in their emergence and acceptance into polite society. From machinery to public policy, Americans borrowed much from Europe's older civilizations. For a recent, brilliant treatment of many of these concepts, see Rodgers, *Atlantic Crossings*.

2. Fisher, *Pacesetter*, 43.

3. Fox, *Illustrated History of the Indianapolis 500*, 159.

4. Fisher, *Fabulous Hoosier*, 41.

5. Riggs, "Carl G. Fisher," 70.

6. Quoted in Fox, *Illustrated History of the Indianapolis 500*, 159–60.

7. Riggs, "Carl G. Fisher," 70.

8. Cavender, "He Planned the Track," *Indianapolis Star Magazine*. May 27, 1962, 26.

9. Riggs, "Carl G. Fisher," 70; History Committee, *Story of Speedway*, 65. More than a half-century later, Trotter recalled the price of the original piece of land for the track as $100,000 rather than $80,000 (see Cavender, "He Planned the Track," 26).

10. Riggs, "Carl G. Fisher," 72.

11. Ibid., 72–73; see also Boomhower, "Carl G. Fisher," 26. The most detailed accounts of the races themselves are in Bloemaker, *500 Miles*, 54–66.

12. Taylor, *Indy*, 14–15.

13. Fisher and Allison had not yet sold Prest-O-Lite to Union Carbide, and both men had limited access to capital.

14. Fox, *Illustrated History of the Indianapolis 500*, 10, 462; Bloemaker, *500 Miles*, 71.

15. Fox, *Illustrated History of the Indianapolis 500*, 10. See also Taylor, *Indy*, 15–17.

16. Certainly Fisher and his associates tested the track thoroughly. In late May 1910 they staged a series of forty-two separate races over three days. There was another series of races on July 4, yet another in early September. See Taylor, *Indy*, 17.

17. Fisher, *Fabulous Hoosier*, 20–21.

18. Kleinberg, *Miami Beach*, 35.

19. Fox, *Illustrated History of the Indianapolis 500*, 462; Riggs, "Carl G. Fisher," 74.

20. Fisher, *Fabulous Hoosier*, 53.

21. Fox, *Illustrated History of the Indianapolis 500*, 11.

22. Taylor, *Indy*, 36.

23. Fisher, *Fabulous Hoosier*, 59.

24. Fox, *Illustrated History of the Indianapolis 500*, 11. Al Bloemaker provides more details of Mulford's crew helping nurse the balky racing machine around the final laps. See *500 Miles*, 106–8.

25. Bloemaker, *500 Miles*, 107–8.

26. Fisher, *Fabulous Hoosier*, 53–58.

27. Ibid., 59.

28. Fox, *Illustrated History of the Indianapolis 500*, 11–12.

29. Slauson, "Making a Sport of Speed," 630.

30. Fisher to Howard E. Coffin, July 16, 1917, box 1, Fisher Papers.

31. Redford, *Billion-Dollar Sandbar*, 107.

32. Fisher to LaGorce, March 28, 1917, box 1, Fisher Papers.

33. Fisher to George Bumbaugh, April 9, 1917, box 2, Fisher Papers.

34. Fisher to City Council of Eaton, August 23, 1917, ibid.

35. Two letters from Fisher to Coffin, both dated July 16, 1917, both in box 1, Fisher Papers.

36. Fisher to Coffin, September 22, 1917, ibid.

37. *Philadelphia Sunday Magazine*, September 8, 1918.

38. Fisher to Colonel E. A. Deeds, undated letter, ca. May 1918, box 2, Fisher Papers.

39. Fisher to Deeds, May 7, 1918, ibid.

40. Fisher to Carl H. Eigenmann, July 26, 1918, Eigenmann Family Papers, Special Collections Department, Lilly Library, Indiana University, Bloomington.

41. Redford, *Billion-Dollar Sandbar*, 111.

42. Robert K. Murray has written an excellent study of the phenomenon, *Red Scare*. For more modern, if partial, treatments, see Bennett, *Party of Fear*, chap. 11; see also Higham, *Strangers in the Land*, 222–33, 254–63, and Klingaman, *1919*, 94–100.

43. Fisher, *Fabulous Hoosier*, 102.

44. Ibid., 106.

45. Fisher to C. Harold Wills, October 16, 1919, box 1, Fisher Papers.

46. See Fisher to Antonio Giraudier, Jr., March 25, 1920; Fisher to James A. Allison, March 27, 1920; and Fisher to Allison, June 29, 1921, all in box 8, Fisher Papers.

47. Recently, the topic of vacationing in the United States has attracted a great deal of attention from historians. Although the literature is extensive, those interested in pursuing the subject might start with Aron, *Working at Play*, and Rothman, *Devil's Bargains*.

48. Fox, *Illustrated History of the Indianapolis 500*, 12.

49. Allison to Fisher, June 14, 1923, box 1, Fisher Papers.

50. Riggs, "Carl G. Fisher," 80, and Fisher to Elmer Stout, September 4, 1928, box 8, Fisher Papers. See also Fisher, *Pacesetter*, 308.

51. See, for example, Fisher to Rickenbacker, March 1, 1929, box 15, Fisher Papers.

52. Riggs, "Carl G. Fisher," 74.

53. Fisher to Albert Judson, October 17, 1919, box 8, Fisher Papers.

54. Fisher to Antonio Giraudier, Jr., March 25, 1920, ibid.

55. Fox, *Illustrated History of the Indianapolis 500*, 468. See also Fisher, *Pacesetter*, 304–5.

56. Fisher to T. E. Myers, August 15, 1935, box 12, Fisher Papers.

57. Fisher to E. V. Rickenbacker, May 5, 1936, box 15, Fisher Papers.

58. Fisher to Rickenbacker, May 22, 1936, ibid.

Chapter 5. Roads Worthy of a Nation

1. See Hughes, *American Visions*. In chap. 2, "The Republic of Virtue," Hughes develops this theme.

2. Quote in Sears, *The American Heritage History of the Automobile in America*, 66.

3. See Mason, "The League of American Wheelmen and the Good Roads Movement," and Hugill, "Good Roads and the Automobile in the United States," 332–40.

4. McCarthy, "Lincoln Highway," 33. The most authoritative study of road building and government policy in the late nineteenth and early twentieth centuries is Seely, *Building the American Highway System*.

5. For more background on the early years of road building, see Seely, *Building the American Highway System*, and Rae, *Road and Car in American Life*, 36–39.

6. Lincoln Highway Association, *Lincoln Highway*, 6.

7. Hokanson, *Lincoln Highway*, 52.

8. Boomhower, "Carl G. Fisher," 27; McCarthy, "Lincoln Highway," 32.

9. McCarthy, "Lincoln Highway," 32.

10. Cashman, *America in the Gilded Age*, 24.

11. Fisher, *Fabulous Hoosier*, 69.

12. McCarthy, "Lincoln Highway," 33. For an in-depth analysis of the early politics of road building, see Seely, *Building the American Highway System*.

13. McCarthy, "Lincoln Highway," 33.

14. *Indianapolis Star*, October 24, 1912.

15. Ibid., November 6, 1912.

16. McCarthy, "Lincoln Highway," 33–34.

17. Couzens letter quoted in Hokanson, *Lincoln Highway*, 8. In a further effort to sway Ford, Fisher solicited an endorsement letter from President William Howard Taft. Disappointed but not discouraged by Ford's initial rejection, Fisher continued to press him to change his mind over the next several months. His efforts never bore fruit. See Fisher, *Pacesetter*, 83–84, 87.

18. Ford's strange mixture of generosity toward workers yet savage repression of union organization, farsighted awareness of the need to build autos for the masses yet refusal to adjust marketing appeals as the industry modernized, and many other paradoxes have challenged generations of Ford's biographers. As two of his more astute biographers note, "Few of these writers, popular or scholarly, have understood the degree to which writing about the old man is like handling mercury. He was like a fox—back-tracking, sidestepping, and covering his trail. During his life he gave writers only a whiff of what he really was. After his death, family members kept their counsel, fearful of rattling the skeletons he had left in the Ford closet" (Collier and Horowitz, *The Fords*, 437).

19. McCarthy, "Lincoln Highway," 34. Historian Mark Wolfe attributes the name "Lincoln Highway" to Frances McEwen Belford of Denver, who persuaded U.S. Representative Edward T. Taylor to introduce a bill in Congress "establishing the Lincoln Memorial Highway from Boston, Massachusetts, to San Fransisco, Califor-

nia." Although the bill never made it to the floor of Congress, Wolfe notes that "the idea was planted." See Wolfe, "How the Lincoln Highway Snubbed Colorado," 3.

20. Fisher, *Fabulous Hoosier,* 71.

21. For a fascinating examination of the early twentieth-century power elite in Detroit, see Davis, *Conspicuous Production.*

22. Redford, *Billion-Dollar Sandbar,* 74–75.

23. Ibid., 75.

24. Hokanson, *Lincoln Highway,* 9

25. Ibid., 151; McCarthy, "Lincoln Highway," 35.

26. McCarthy, "Lincoln Highway," 36.

27. Fisher, *Fabulous Hoosier,* 75.

28. Ibid., 73.

29. Lincoln Highway Association, *Lincoln Highway,* 39.

30. Fisher, *Fabulous Hoosier,* 74–75.

31. Ibid., 76–77.

32. Hokanson, *Lincoln Highway,* 12.

33. Lincoln Highway Association, *Lincoln Highway,* 49–51.

34. *The Address to the Conference of Governors at Colorado Springs, Colorado, August 26, 1913, on the Lincoln Highway,* pamphlet issued by the Lincoln Highway Association, October 1, 1913.

35. Ibid.; see also Wolfe, "How the Lincoln Highway Snubbed Colorado."

36. Hokanson, *Lincoln Highway,* 14–15.

37. McCarthy, "Lincoln Highway," 37.

38. Jerry Fisher, *Pacesetter,* 114.

39. Hokanson, *Lincoln Highway,* 17–18.

40. Ibid., 19.

41. Ibid.

42. Ibid., 16. See also Wolfe, "How the Lincoln Highway Snubbed Colorado."

43. In 1910, there were about 468,000 vehicle registrations. See Seely, *Building the American Highway System,* 37.

44. Automobile touring was beginning to capture the imagination of Americans, including increasing numbers of working-class families, but most family trips were still confined to relatively small regions. See Belasco, *Americans on the Road.* See also Aron, *Working at Play,* 209–10.

45. Goddard, *Getting There,* 64.

46. Lincoln Highway Association, *Lincoln Highway,* 113–14.

47. For other works analyzing the interaction between automobile promoters and the resort and travel industry, see Berger, *Devil Wagon in God's Country,* and Belasco, *Americans on the Road.* Earl M. Pomeroy's classic *In Search of the Golden West* sheds some light on these issues as well.

48. For an authoritative discussion of these issues, see Seely, *Building the American Highway System.* Jerry Fisher claims that the Lincoln Highway Association retained a vital role in influencing highway development even after 1916: "The Lincoln

Highway Association had become the authority on highways; national education authorities had recommended their highway guides for classroom use. Thousands were used as textbooks, and thousands of students wrote the association for information" (*Pacesetter*, 133).

49. Numerous historians have analyzed the symbiosis between the emergence of progressive ideology, scientific problem solving, and rising professionalism. One of the earliest and most persuasive syntheses of this phenomenon is Wiebe, *Search for Order*.

50. Kennedy, *Over Here*.

51. Chapin to Fisher, December 20, 1917; and Fisher to Chapin, December 26, 1917, box 3, Fisher Papers.

52. *Minutes of the Annual Meeting of Active Members of the Lincoln Highway Association Held at the Detroit Auto Club, December 30, 1918*, 19, 20, mimeographed copy, box 9, Fisher Papers.

53. Hokanson, *Lincoln Highway*, 113.

54. Fisher to A. F. Bement, April 13, May 5, 1920, box 9, Fisher Papers.

55. Fisher to F. A. Seiberling, September 3, 1920, box 8, Fisher Papers, and Henry B. Joy to Fisher, August 30, 1920, box 9, Fisher Papers.

56. Fisher to W. A. Gilbreath, September 17, 1921, box 9, Fisher Papers.

57. Fisher to Thomas W. Milton, January 27, 1938, box 11, Fisher Papers.

Chapter 6. Touring Through Dixieland

1. Two seminal studies tracing the evolution of the nation's interstate highways are Seely, *Building the American Highway System*, and Mark H. Rose, *Interstate*.

2. See Herschell, "Indianapolis-Born Dixie Highway Now Almost 6000 Miles Long," *Indianapolis News*, August 1, 1925, 21.

3. Ibid.

4. Wilson quoted in Hoy, "Governor Samuel M. Ralston," 262.

5. Preston, *Dirt Roads to Dixie*, esp. chap. 1.

6. Quoted in Hoy, "Governor Samuel M. Ralston," 262–63. Hoy cited a letter dated December 4 in the Samuel M. Ralston Papers, Lilly Library, Indiana University. A thorough check of the Ralston collection failed to produce the letter, which has apparently been lost or misplaced.

7. Biographical sketch of Taggart taken from Peckham, *Indiana*, 141.

8. Hoy, "Samuel M. Ralston," 263.

9. Samuel M. Ralston, untitled address in Chattanooga, Tennessee, April 3, 1915, n.p., mimeographed copy in Ralston Papers.

10. Goddard, *Getting There*, 61.

11. Both quotes from Hoy, "Samuel M. Ralston," 260n.49.

12. Preston observed that southerners faced unique issues regarding road building. Although citizens were required by law to spend a certain number of days working on roads, they were unskilled at the task and often "goldbricked" on the job. In addition, many avoided work altogether either by paying small fines or find-

ing friendly local politicians to grant them exemptions from duty. Although many southern states used convict labor gangs for various tasks, many of the gangs were engaged in private projects for well-connected, wealthy elites. As a result, their contributions to the regional road-building projects were, at best, marginal. See *Dirt Roads to Dixie*, 20–23.

13. Ibid., 264.

14. Kleinberg, *Miami Beach*, 47.

15. Hoy, "Samuel M. Ralston," 265.

16. "Eastern Division Inspected," *Dixie Highway: A Monthly Journal* 2 (October 1916): 6.

17. Herschell, "Dixie Highway," 21.

18. Ibid.

19. There is an important and growing body of literature on vacationing and the expansion of leisure in the United States. A good starting point is Aron, *Working at Play*. See also Belasco, *Americans on the Road*. For competition between railroad and highway interests, readers might begin with Goddard, *Getting There*.

20. Fisher to Harold Talbot Jr., October 23, 1919, box 3, Fisher Papers.

21. Fisher to W. T. Anderson, September 11, 1919, ibid. Fisher's main role with Kentucky Rock Asphalt was as an investor, fund-raiser, and occasional adviser. In another letter, a copy of which is in his papers, Fisher described management of the company as "a bunch of coal miners . . . who are hard workers and have all the money they have invested in the company." Fisher thought the company had a bright future, and he promoted both its product and its management to other potential investors for several years. See Fisher to Harold Talbot Jr., October 22, 1919, and Fisher to Frank A. Seiberling, February 23, 1920, box 3, Fisher Papers.

22. Fisher to Haines Egbert, August 23, 1917, box 4, Fisher Papers.

23. For an authoritative account of the development of federal highway policy during the war, see Seely, *Building the American Highway System*, chap. 3. The 1916 Federal-Aid Highway Act specifically required that "the establishment of a state highway department that met with OPR [Office of Public Roads] approval be a condition for obtaining federal funds" (ibid., 42).

24. Fisher to Chapin, May 6, 1918, box 6, Fisher Papers.

25. For wartime cooperation between businessmen and the federal government, see Hawley, *The Great War and the Search for a Modern Order*, 24–27. See also Cuff, *War Industries Board*.

26. Mike M. Allison to Fisher, March 11, 1919, box 4, Fisher Papers.

27. Ibid.

28. Allison to Fisher, April 16, 1919, ibid.

29. A. F. Sanford to Fisher, April 28, 1919, ibid.

30. Fisher to Allison, July 22, 1919, ibid.

31. Fisher to Allison, December 11, 1924, ibid. Jerry M. Fisher observed that disorganization and conflicting interests continued to plague those attempting to develop long-range road-building efforts in the South through the 1920s, long after

federal aid provided much of the funding: "Instead of a coordinated effort to obtain federal aid for the highway after it became available, communities tried to get the money for themselves. The publicity given the Dixie Highway encouraged others to build roads and capture some of the tourist trade for themselves" (Fisher, *Pacesetter*, 221).

32. "To the President and Board of Directors," mimeographed secretary's report, undated (ca. December 1919), n.p., box 4, Fisher Papers.

33. I am indebted to my friend and colleague Mark H. Rose for this insight.

34. Allison to Fisher, June 9, 1921, box 4, Fisher Papers.

35. Fisher to W. S. Gilbreath, September 17, 1921, ibid.

36. Fisher to Mike M. Allison, November 17, 1921, ibid.

Chapter 7. The Accidental Tourist

1. Redford, *Billion-Dollar Sandbar*, 44.

2. For a more detailed account of the early portion of the trip, see chapter 3.

3. Fisher, *Fabulous Hoosier*, 16; Kleinberg, *Miami Beach*, 219n.

4. Fisher, *Fabulous Hoosier*, 16–17.

5. *Miami Herald*, July 16, 1939.

6. Ibid., 17.

7. For Florida's prehistory, see Douglas, *Florida*, chap. 1. For the Spanish conquest, see ibid., chaps. 2–4. See also Jahoda, *Florida*, chap. 2.

8. Kleinberg, *Miami Beach*, 1–3. For more detail, see Nash, *Magic of Miami Beach*, chap. 1.

9. Nash, *Magic of Miami Beach*, 20–21.

10. Akin, *Flagler*, 113.

11. In addition to Akin, *Flagler*, readers interested in further examining his connection with Rockefeller and Standard Oil should also peruse Chernow, *Titan*, 132–36, 209–12, 223–25, 344–46, 537–40.

12. Akin, *Flagler*, 121.

13. Ibid., 145–46.

14. Ibid., 163–65.

15. The 100,000 "patrons" in fact indicates the total number of nights spent by visitors during the season. Obviously, the actual number of tourists was far smaller because some of them stayed for weeks or even months.

16. Nash, *Magic of Miami Beach*, 4.

17. Kleinberg, *Miami Beach*, 5, 7–8.

18. Nash, *Magic of Miami Beach*, 32–33.

19. Redford, *Billion-Dollar Sandbar*, 35–36.

20. Ibid., 39; Nash, *Magic of Miami Beach*, 150–51.

21. Redford, *Billion-Dollar Sandbar*, 36–38.

22. Ibid., 38–39.

23. For informed discussion of the evolution of vacations and the development of tourism, see Aron, *Working at Play*; see also Rothman, *Devil's Bargains*.

24. The literature assessing the cultural impact of the automobile on American society is massive, but readers might begin with Flink, *America Adopts the Automobile*; see also Rae, *American Automobile*. My own work, *From Streetcar to Superhighway*, analyzes the automobile's triumph over mass transit in the early years of the twentieth century.

25. Nash, *Magic of Miami Beach*, 92–93.

26. Kleinberg, *Miami Beach*, 26.

27. Redford, *Billion-Dollar Sandbar*, 42–43.

28. Kleinberg, *Miami Beach*, 37.

29. Elaine Payne to "Dear Fatty," March 31, 1915, L. Payne Manuscript Collection, Lilly Library, Indiana University, Bloomington.

30. Fisher, *Fabulous Hoosier*, 51.

31. The "business on a handshake" image is supported by biographers and local historians alike. Jane Fisher, Polly Redford, and Howard Kleinberg all endorsed it. The Fisher Papers included copies of only a few formal contracts, none involving Collins and Fisher.

32. Ibid., 84.

33. Jane Fisher quoted in Redford, *Billion-Dollar Sandbar*, 44.

34. Jane Fisher interview by Polly Redford, April 4, 1967, Special Collections, Otto Richter Library, University of Miami.

35. Kleinberg, *Miami Beach*, 26–28; McCarthy, "The Man Who Invented America's Playground," 68.

36. Fisher, *Fabulous Hoosier*, 85.

37. Kleinberg, *Miami Beach*, 26.

38. *Miami Herald*, August 18, 1912. Jerry M. Fisher noted that the Lummus brothers platted the first subdivision at Miami Beach on July 9, 1912; John Collins followed on December 11, 1912; and Fisher filed more than a year after Collins, on January 15, 1914. See Fisher, *Pacesetter*, 158.

39. Kleinberg, *Miami Beach*, 46.

Chapter 8. Morning Sun

1. Fisher, *Fabulous Hoosier*, 90.

2. Redford, *Billion-Dollar Sandbar*, 67.

3. Ibid., 45.

4. Nash, *Magic of Miami Beach*, 88.

5. Ibid., 108.

6. Redford, *Billion-Dollar Sandbar*, 71.

7. Ibid., 72.

8. Fisher, *Fabulous Hoosier*, 89.

9. By Jane's calculations, her husband would have been pouring over $18 million per year into the project, a rate of negative cash flow that would have bankrupted him in a few months. Unfortunately, financial records detailing expenses have been lost or destroyed.

10. Mehling, *Most of Everything*, 32.

11. *Miami Herald*, July 16, 1939.

12. Fisher, *Fabulous Hoosier*, 90.

13. Ibid., 114–15. In all likelihood, Jane Fisher significantly romanticized the workers' reaction to her former husband's labor-saving device.

14. Ibid., 115.

15. Ibid., 50, 112.

16. The standard, if dated, treatment of the Red Scare is Murray, Red Scare. For briefer, more recent analysis, see Cooper, *Pivotal Decades*, 324–30.

17. Harry Bastain to Fisher, September 26, 1919, box 10, Fisher Papers.

18. Fisher to Governor John M. Parker, September 16, 1920, box 14, Fisher Papers.

19. Levi to Fisher, October 23, 1924, box 10, Fisher Papers.

20. Fisher, *Fabulous Hoosier*, 25–26.

21. For examples of these types of exchanges, see John LaGorce to Fisher, October 15, 1926, box 9, Fisher Papers; Fisher memo, September 30, 1918, box 14, Fisher Papers; Tom Pancoast to Fisher, September 23, 1920, and Fisher to Pancoast, September 28, 1920, box 3, Fisher Papers.

22. The $2 million figure is taken from Mehling, *Most of Everything*, 32.

23. Later, when Miami Beach reached its heyday in the mid-1920s, the Lummus brothers claimed that they actually sank more money into dredging than had Fisher. For details, see Kleinberg, *Miami Beach*, 41.

24. Redford, *Billion-Dollar Sandbar*, 68.

25. Fisher, *Fabulous Hoosier*, 114–15.

26. Redford, *Billion-Dollar Sandbar*, 127.

27. Fisher, *Fabulous Hoosier*, 110–11.

28. Redford, *Billion-Dollar Sandbar*, 122.

29. Ibid., 98–99; Kleinberg, *Miami Beach*, 63, 104.

30. In his letter to a state senator Fisher considered particularly uncooperative, even intransigent, he pulled no punches: "You . . . overlook the fact that we built and operated a plant and a railway system at Miami Beach and over your lines in the city of Miami at a continuous loss for several years." Fisher to Senator John W. Watson, July 6, 1925, box 10, Fisher Papers.

31. Redford, *Billion-Dollar Sandbar*, 122.

32. *Miami Herald*, December 10, 1913.

33. Quoted in Redford, *Billion-Dollar Sandbar*, 85.

34. McCarthy, "The Man Who Invented America's Playground," 70.

35. Fisher, *Fabulous Hoosier*, 120.

36. Redford, *Billion-Dollar Sandbar*, 97.

37. Fisher, *Fabulous Hoosier*, 124.

38. Ibid., 124–25.

39. Redford, *Billion-Dollar Sandbar*, 104.

40. Kleinberg, *Miami Beach*, 54.

41. W. A. Muller to Fisher, July 28, 1917, box 1, Fisher Papers.

42. Fisher to Major J. G. Vincent, December 31, 1917, ibid.

43. Fisher to Captain Howard Marmon, January 2, 1918, ibid. For further discussion of foul weather conditions in the North and Fisher's ruminations about the government's lack of foresight, see Fisher to Lt. Col. C. G. Edgar, March 6, 1918, ibid.

44. Fisher to H. E. Talbot Jr., August 14, 1918, ibid.

45. Willard Seiberling to Fisher, August 13, 1920, box 2, Fisher Papers.

46. See Fisher to James A. Allison, March 27, 1920, and Fisher to John Levi, June 1, 1920, box 5, Fisher Papers; Fisher to J. J. Cole, June 2, 1920; Fisher to Harold Talbot, November 22, 1921; and Fisher to H. H. Raymond, November 19, 1923, box 16, Fisher Papers. See also Fisher, *Pacesetter,* 266–67.

47. George R. Kline to Fisher, June 30, 1919, box 14, Fisher Papers.

Chapter 9. Dressing Up the Beach

1. Aron, *Working at Play,* 16–17.

2. Ibid., 44.

3. The idea of three "r's" is borrowed from ibid., 23.

4. Rothman develops the concept of scripted scenes in his pathbreaking work *Devil's Bargains,* 3, 12.

5. Ibid., 12.

6. Ibid., 13.

7. Fisher to Frank B. Shutts, April 27, 1921, box 14, Fisher Papers.

8. Fisher to Fred R. Humpage, May 16, 1921, box 5, Fisher Papers.

9. Fisher to Humpage, October 24, 1921, ibid.

10. Rothman offers an intriguing explanation of tensions between "outsider" resort developers and local businessmen: "As places acquire the cachet of desirability, they draw people and money; the redistribution of wealth, power, and status follows, complicating local arrangements. When tourism creates sufficient wealth, it becomes too important to be left to the locals. Power moves away from local decision makers, even those who psychically and socially invest in the new system that tourism creates, and toward outside capital and its local representatives. This redistribution changes internal relations as it eventually consolidates into a dominant template or overlay for the place it develops. The new shape disenfranchises most locals even as it makes some natives and most neonatives . . . economically better off" (*Devil's Bargains,* 11).

11. Fisher to Thomas J. Pancoast, September 19, October 31, 1921, box 14, Fisher Papers.

12. Fisher to John Levi, Irving A. Collins, and Thomas J. Pancoast, June 30, 1919, box 10, Fisher Papers.

13. Redford, *Billion-Dollar Sandbar,* 116–18.

14. *Miami Herald,* July 1, 1925.

15. Fisher to John W. Watson, July 6, 1925, box 10, Fisher Papers.

16. I borrow the term "gasoline aristocracy" from Donald F. Davis, author of *Conspicuous Production*.

17. Fisher to Thomas J. Pancoast, July 28, 1921, box 16, Fisher Papers.

18. Kleinberg, *Miami Beach*, 55.

19. Fisher, *Fabulous Hoosier*, 150.

20. *Miami Herald*, February 21, 1919.

21. Redford, *Billion-Dollar Sandbar*, 113; McCarthy, "The Man Who Invented Miami Beach," 70.

22. Fisher to L. A. Young, September 1, 1920, box 14, Fisher Papers.

23. Fisher to Edsel Ford, September 29, 1924, and Firestone to Fisher, December 29, 1924, ibid. A chukker is one of the periods into which a polo match is divided. It lasts for seven and a half minutes.

24. Fisher to Harold Talbot, Jr., March 20, 1920, ibid.

25. Fisher to Talbot, April 12, 1920, ibid.

26. McCarthy, "The Man Who Invented America's Playground," 70.

27. Ibid., 71, 100.

28. C. W. "Pete" Chase, interview by Polly Redford, September 28, 1966, Oral History Collection, Richter Library, University of Miami.

29. Fisher to James M. Cox, June 29, 1928, box 11, Fisher Papers.

30. Hal Rothman analyzes the frenzied competition among late twentieth-century resort developers, each aiming to provide vacationers with the "perfect experience" (*Devil's Bargains*, 4). Although Fisher would not have described his challenges in academic terms, he clearly recognized how many would-be purveyors of vacationing experiences were ratcheting up the stakes in Miami Beach and elsewhere in the United States during the 1920s.

31. Fisher to S. Bobo Dean, October 9, 1919, box 7, Fisher Papers.

32. Fisher to J. H. Meyer, May 15, 1919, ibid.

33. Redford, *Billion-Dollar Sandbar*, 136–37. Redford got most of the details right except for the date. Fisher initially put up the $5,000 trophy prize in 1919; Allison committed his share of the prize money the same year. See Fisher to J. G. Vincent, January 30, 1919, box 2, Fisher Papers.

34. Fisher, *Fabulous Hoosier*, 154.

35. Ibid., 152.

36. Fisher to Charles F. Kettering, April 3, 1927, box 7, Fisher Papers.

37. Redford, *Billion-Dollar Sandbar*, 89.

38. *Miami Herald*, January 27, 1929. The newspaper was passing along a story that had been making the rounds for years. Several years earlier, Fisher had rejected this account as a fabrication. He reassured Russell, "I am not willing to give Will Rogers or any other human being the original but I will give him a copy. . . . I would like to do it with the understanding that the copy will always be in his possession and never be sold." See Fisher to Charles M. Russell, October 19, 1926, box 16, Fisher Papers.

39. For a description of the club, see "Cocolobo Cay Club," mimeographed manuscript (1919), box 3, Fisher Papers.

40. Fisher, *Fabulous Hoosier*, 157–58.

41. Cindy Aron describes the late nineteenth-century resort ambiance in exquisite detail in *Working at Play*, esp. chap. 3.

42. Several historians have explored the evolution of tanning. In the mid-1980s, Robin Tomlach Lakoff and Raquel L. Scherr observed, "A century ago, white, untanned skin was a necessary part of beauty, and a wise young woman who had to be outdoors in the sun protected her fair complexion with a parasol. A tan was the mark of someone who had to labor under the sun—someone not accustomed to leisure." They concluded that today, the white, or "pasty," skin is a giveaway of someone spending long hours indoors at work, while a tan identifies those with sufficient leisure to vacation in the sun. A tan is a "badge of rank" (*Face Value*, 178). Lois W. Banner pinpoints the emerging status of tanning more specifically, claiming that it emerged in the 1920s: "Tanned skin now also came completely into vogue. Since the 1890s and the beginnings of women's athletic interest, some women had favored a darker skin tone, associating it with sports and new sensual beach behavior and not with lowly peasant women working in the fields. As the vogue of athleticism increased, so did the popularity of tans, particularly when it became apparent that women working in the factories away from the sun had pale, not dark skin. Finally, in the 1920s, Coco Chanel was pictured in the tabloids with tanned skin, and her adoption of it gave the final imprimatur to a style in keeping with class, sensual, and physical-fitness motives" (*American Beauty*, 277). I am indebted to my friend and colleague Pamela W. Laird for directing me to these studies of tanning.

43. Fisher continued this practice even into the 1930s, when his hotels and other investments in Miami Beach were losing money. This is reflected in some of the instructions he gave to his hotel managers. See Fisher to F. L. Abel, November 20, 1931, box 8, Fisher Papers.

44. Ibid., 128–29.

45. Jane Fisher's account implies that she and her husband originated the "bathing beauty" idea. Its originator was most likely Everett Sewell, head of Miami's Chamber of Commerce, who started a bathing beauty contest about 1920. See Fisher, *Pacesetter*, 235. Frederick Lewis Allen, famed historian of the 1920s, dates the first national bathing beauty contest from September 1921, when Atlantic City, New Jersey, hosted a contest that evolved into the Miss America Pageant (*Only Yesterday*, 66–67).

46. Kleinberg, *Miami Beach*, 79–80.

47. Chase interview by Redford, September 28, 1966.

48. Fisher interview by Redford, April 4, 1967.

49. Wood interview by Redford, October 20, 1966.

50. Fisher to Honorable Robert L. Bacon, September 5, 1928, box 14, Fisher Papers.

51. Kleinberg, *Miami Beach*, 57.

52. Fisher to Mrs. Charles F. Kettering, December 18, 1917, box 9, Fisher Papers.

53. Kleinberg, *Miami Beach*, 56.

54. Redford, *Billion-Dollar Sandbar*, 134.

55. Fisher to Charles B. Sommers, October 5, 1920, box 7, Fisher Papers; Kleinberg, *Miami Beach*, 60.

56. Fisher, *Fabulous Hoosier*, 136; Kleinberg, *Miami Beach*, 59–60.

57. See, for example, Fisher to M. Hawley McClanahan, March 24, 1920, box 7, Fisher Papers.

58. Fisher to Lyman B. Kendall, May 11, 1921, ibid.

59. Kleinberg, *Miami Beach*, 59–60.

60. Charles S. Krom to Fisher, July 16, 1920, box 7, Fisher Papers.

61. Fisher to Luke Glennon, June 29, 1921, ibid.

62. Quoted in Fox, *Illustrated History of the Indianapolis 500*, 467.

63. Fisher repeatedly expressed premature optimism that he was turning the corner. See Fisher to James Allison, March 27, 1920, Fisher to A. F. Bement, April 13, 1920, and Fisher to Cecil G. Fowler, May 3, 1920, box 7, Fisher Papers; Fisher to John M. Levi, June 1, 1920, box 5, Fisher Papers.

64. John H. Levi to Fisher, September 23, 1921, box 5, Fisher Papers.

65. Fisher to Emory W. Clark, November 13, 1921, ibid.

66. Fisher to Frank J. McNamara, August 2, 1921, box 9, Fisher Papers; Fisher to Alex Taggart, June 6, 1922, box 7, Fisher Papers.

67. Redford, *Billion-Dollar Sandbar*, 135; Fisher, *Pacesetter*, 265.

68. Curl, *Mizner's Florida*, passim.

69. Kleinberg, *Miami Beach*, 96.

70. Fisher, *Pacesetter*, 250.

Chapter 10. Noonday Sun

1. Fisher to Warren G. Harding, December 6, 1920, box 8, Fisher Papers.

2. LaGorce to Fisher, December 7, 1920, ibid.

3. William M. Miller to Fisher, January 4, 1921, ibid.

4. LaGorce to Fisher, January 11, 1921, ibid. The same day, Senator Miller wrote along the same lines, suggesting that although it was unlikely that Harding would stay with Fisher, he would probably accept his invitation either to fish or to play golf. See Miller to Fisher, January 12, 1921, ibid.

5. Harding to Fisher, January 12, 1921, ibid.

6. Fisher to LaGorce, January 14, 1921, ibid.

7. LaGorce to Fisher, January 21, 1920, ibid.

8. Rossiter to Fisher (n.d., ca. January 1921), ibid. One may infer sexual innuendoes in Rossiter's remarks, and she may well have hinted at her "availability" to the president-elect. Carl S. Anthony's recent biography of Harding's wife, Florence, provides a portrait of Harding as a compulsive adulterer even more damning than those provided in earlier works. See Anthony, *Florence Harding*, passim.

9. Quoted in Kleinberg, *Miami Beach*, 62.

10. Fisher, *Fabulous Hoosier*, 137.

11. Redford, *Billion-Dollar Sandbar*, 112.

12. David Jameson to Batch, January 31, 1921, box 8, Fisher Papers.

13. Kleinberg, *Miami Beach*, 62. In his seminal book on tourism in the late twentieth-century American West, Hal Rothman addresses the inevitable tensions generated between monied "outsiders" and local elites when the former challenge for regional leadership in promoting resorts (*Devil's Bargains*, 11).

14. Fisher to Thomas J. Pancoast, November 7, 1921, box 10, Fisher Papers.

15. Fisher, *Fabulous Hoosier*, 128.

16. The literature on the increasing sophistication of advertising from the late nineteenth to the early twentieth century is both massive and impressive. Interested readers might begin with Laird, *Advertising Progress*. See also Jackson-Lears, "From Salvation to Self-Realization" and *Fables of Abundance*, and Horowitz, *Morality of Spending*.

17. Redford, *Billion-Dollar Sandbar*, 114.

18. McCarthy, "The Man Who Invented America's Playground," 70–71.

19. Donald Curl, author of *Mizner's Florida*, makes such a claim: "Many of the sales techniques originated by Fisher on Miami Beach became standard with later real estate promotions. He built a hotel to house prospective purchasers of his lots. Later developments almost always began with announcements of plans for a large hotel" (135).

20. See numerous acerbic interoffice memos between the two men in the early to mid-1920s in boxes 7 and 8, Fisher Papers.

21. Fisher, *Fabulous Hoosier*, 143.

22. Jane Fisher, interview by Polly Redford, April 4, 1967, Oral History Collection, Richter Library, University of Miami.

23. Mehling, *Most of Everything*, 132.

24. Gar Wood, interview by Polly Redford, October 20, 1966; Fisher to Harry Klein, March 19, 1927, box 7, Fisher Papers. Jerry M. Fisher, a distant relative who wrote a generally admiring book about Carl, essentially affirmed Kleinberg's balanced assessment of Fisher's attitude toward Jews. See *Pacesetter*, 257–63.

25. Fisher to Mrs. E. A. Rickmers, January 14, 1920, box 10, Fisher Papers.

26. Fisher to James H. Snowden, May 5, 1921, box 5, Fisher Papers.

27. Fisher to Oscar Daniels, June 14, 1922, ibid.

28. Kleinberg, *Miami Beach*, 93.

29. Ibid., 95.

30. Curl, *Mizner's Florida*, 136.

31. Kleinberg, *Miami Beach*, 93.

32. Armbrister, *Life and Times of Miami Beach*, 25.

33. Curl, *Mizner's Florida*, 138–40. For an extended discussion of the Boca Raton project, see ibid., chap. 5.

34. Ibid., 142.

35. McCarthy, "The Man Who Invented America's Playground," 100.

36. For good descriptions of the tactics of the "binder boys," see ibid., 100–101, and Redford, *Billion-Dollar Sandbar*, 150–51.

37. Redford, *Billion-Dollar Sandbar*, 152.

38. Mary M. Bethune to Fisher, February 5, 1930, box 3, Fisher Papers; Fisher to Frank D. Stalnaker, October 1, 1920, box 13, Fisher Papers.

39. Fisher, *Fabulous Hoosier*, 160–61; *Indianapolis Star*, July 16, 1939; Riggs, "Carl G. Fisher," 78.

40. Fisher, *Pacesetter*, 209.

41. Fisher to Mother, March 26, April 2, 1919; Ida Fisher to Fisher, March 21, 1922; Albert Fisher to Fisher, December 25, 1917, January 31, 1918; Fisher to Father, April 25, May 20, 1918; Albert Fisher to Son, December 24, 1919; Fisher to Frank B. Shutts, October 21, 1921; all in box 4, Fisher Papers.

42. Fisher, *Fabulous Hoosier*, 28.

43. Fisher, *Pacesetter*, 73.

44. Fisher, *Fabulous Hoosier*, 29–30.

45. Ibid., 95–97.

46. Ibid., 164–65.

47. Riggs, "Carl G. Fisher," 77.

48. Mazie Rothay to Jane Fisher, May 5, 1922, box 4, Fisher Papers.

49. Rothay to Jane Fisher, May 17, 1922, April 13, 1923, ibid.

50. Kleinberg, *Miami Beach*, 94; Redford, *Billion-Dollar Sandbar*, 158; Fox, *Illustrated History of the Indianapolis 500*, 469.

51. Late in 1922, Fisher provided a $500 annual payment to Mrs. Rothay, to be delivered in two separate checks. See Fisher to George L. Denny, December 2, 1922, box 6, Fisher Papers. See also Rothay to Jane Fisher, May 14, 1923, and Rothay to Carl Fisher, August 8, 1923, box 4, Fisher Papers.

52. Fisher to George L. Denny, December 9, 1922, box 6, Fisher Papers.

53. Former lovers occasionally wrote him, recalling their trysts. See, for example, Laura Wilson to Fisher, undated letter (ca. 1930), box 16, Fisher Papers.

54. Riggs, "Carl G. Fisher," 77.

55. Jane Fisher interview by Polly Redford, April 4, 1967, Oral History Collection, Special Collections Department, Richter Library, University of Miami.

56. Fisher, *Fabulous Hoosier*, 166.

57. Separation agreement dated November 24, 1924, box 18, Fisher Papers.

58. Frank B. Shutts to Fisher, February 24, 1926, box 6, Fisher Papers.

59. Redford, *Billion-Dollar Sandbar*, 52–53. In later years, as Jane married time after time, Carl felt a compulsive need to "screen" prospective spouses. It almost seemed that he wanted to protect, or control, her long after their divorce. See Fisher, *Fabulous Hoosier*, 196–97.

60. Fisher, *Pacesetter*, 293, 310.

Chapter 11. Seeds of Doubt

1. *Five Years Afterwards*, 3.
2. Chase to Fisher, October 23, 24, 1924, Fisher to Chase, October 24, 1924, box 10, Fisher Papers.
3. Fisher to James Cox, July 29, 1925, box 2, Fisher Papers.
4. Anderson to Fisher, November 6, 1925, box 10, Fisher Papers.
5. Fisher, *Fabulous Hoosier*, 177.
6. C. W. "Pete" Chase to Fisher, October 1, 1925, box 10, Fisher Papers.
7. Fisher, *Fabulous Hoosier*, 179. Fisher's ethics were constantly tested by the lure of easy profits in a fast-rising real estate market. He repeatedly demonstrated his rock-solid character. For example, a year after the boom collapsed, when he desperately needed funds for other projects, Fisher refused to lease property to a developer interested in laying out an air strip because it would disturb earlier buyers who had assumed their area would always be residential. See Fisher to Richard F. Hoyt, November 11, 1927, box 14, Fisher Papers.
8. According to another historian of Miami Beach, it was N. B. T. Roney who took the lead in driving out the "binder boys." See Kleinberg, *Miami Beach*, 41.
9. Curl, *Mizner's Florida*, 153–54.
10. Redford, *Billion-Dollar Sandbar*, 163.
11. Chase to Fisher, September 30, 1925, box 2, Fisher Papers.
12. Redford, *Billion-Dollar Sandbar*, 163–64.
13. Kleinberg, *Miami Beach*, 105.
14. *Five Years Afterwards*, 3.
15. *Miami Daily News*, September 17, 1927.
16. Anonymous letter from Miami Beach resident to his mother, quoted in Kleinberg, *Miami Beach*, 107.
17. Report quoted ibid., 107–8.
18. Parrish, *Anxious Decades*, 227.
19. Fisher, *Fabulous Hoosier*, 202.
20. Fisher to La Gorce, October 8, 1926, box 8, Fisher Papers.
21. Carl Fisher to Jane Fisher, quoted in Redford, *Billion-Dollar Sandbar*, 175.
22. Fisher to E. W. Preston, October 18, 1926, box 8, Fisher Papers.
23. C. W. "Pete" Chase to Fisher, October 21, 1926, ibid.
24. Fisher to LaGorce, October 8, 1926, ibid.
25. Fisher to C. J. Iven, November 9, 1926, ibid.
26. Charles S. Krom to Fisher, January 14, 1927, box 7, Fisher Papers.
27. Redford, *Billion-Dollar Sandbar*, 179.
28. Roy D. Chapin to Fisher, December 27, 1927, box 5, Fisher Papers.
29. Galbraith, *Great Crash*, 17.
30. Parrish, *Anxious Decades*, 228.
31. Fisher to F. L. Abel, September 28, 1928, box 8, Fisher Papers.
32. Fisher to B. Lundberg, July 28, 1927, box 14, Fisher Papers.
33. Charles S. Krom to Fisher, April 12, 1929, box 7, Fisher Papers.

34. Charles S. Krom to Fisher, April 8, 1930, ibid.

35. *Five Years Afterwards*, 3.

36. John H. Levi to Fisher, July 3, 1928, box 10, Fisher Papers.

37. Fisher to H. S. Talbot, February 17, 1930, box 14, Fisher Papers.

38. Paul Kunschik to Fisher, June 12, 1930, box 5, Fisher Papers.

39. Fisher to Irving A. Collins, December 17, 1931, box 10, Fisher Papers.

40. Fisher to Irving A. Collins, December 17, 1931 (second letter), ibid.

41. Fisher to C. M. Keys, January 4, 1932, box 5, Fisher Papers.

42. Fisher to Parke G. Haynes, February 6, 1932, box 10, Fisher Papers.

43. Fisher to Arthur Brisbane, April 12, 1932, box 8, Fisher Papers.

44. Fisher to Victor H. Ehrhart, June 18, 1932, box 7, Fisher Papers; Fisher to D. A. Crawford, December 20, 1932, box 10, Fisher Papers.

45. For an incisive analysis of the public policy paralysis at the national level, see Schwarz, *Interregnum of Despair*.

46. Fisher to John Hertz, December 7, 1932, box 8, Fisher Papers; Fisher to Clem M. Keys, February 25, 1933, box 12, Fisher Papers.

47. Fisher to William T. Anderson, March 4, 1933, box 10, Fisher Papers.

Chapter 12. A Search for Greener Pastures

1. Fisher, *Fabulous Hoosier*, 24.

2. For a first-rate analysis of the leadership class in Detroit's automobile industry during the early twentieth century, see Davis, *Conspicuous Production*.

3. Olds to Fisher, August 20, 1919, box 13, Fisher Papers.

4. See Fisher to James Couzens, March 25, 1921, box 8, Fisher Papers.

5. Fisher to Oscar Daniels, July 19, 1921, box 5, Fisher Papers.

6. Ibid.

7. Fisher to G. Maurice Heckscher, August 21, 1921, box 8, Fisher Papers.

8. See Fisher to Caleb Bragg, undated letter, box 3, Fisher Papers.

9. Pell and Tibbits to Fisher, June 21, 1922, box 15, Fisher Papers.

10. Henry R. Tibbits to Fisher, August 16, 1922, ibid.

11. See Tract Map of Bayview Colony, dated April 17, 1925, ibid.

12. Fisher to Hugh W. Davis, January 22, 1930, box 16, Fisher Papers.

13. Fisher to W. A. Kohlhepp, April 28, 1924, box 11, Fisher Papers.

14. Ibid.

15. Fisher to Roy Chapin, June 2, 1924, box 12, Fisher Papers.

16. Fisher, *Fabulous Hoosier*, 187.

17. Irving A. Collins to Fisher, May 18, 1925, box 12, Fisher Papers.

18. Redford, *Billion-Dollar Sandbar*, 54. For a very similar reaction, see Fisher, *Fabulous Hoosier*, 20.

19. Fisher to Collins, May 19, 1925, box 12, Fisher Papers.

20. Redford, *Billion-Dollar Sandbar*, 160; McCarthy, "The Man Who Invented America's Playground," 101; Fisher, *Fabulous Hoosier*, 186.

21. Fisher to Henry B. Joy, August 4, 1925, box 12, Fisher Papers.

330 NOTES TO PAGES 252–264

22. Joseph C. Copps to W. A. Kohlhepp, July 29, 1926, ibid.

23. Fisher to Hugh W. Davis, March 15, 1926, box 14, Fisher Papers.

24. Riggs, "Carl G. Fisher," 69.

25. Fisher to Collins, September 10, 1926, box 3, Fisher Papers.

26. Fisher to Firestone, November 5, 1926, box 12, Fisher Papers.

27. Fisher to C. F. Redden, November 9, 1926, box 11, Fisher Papers.

28. Kohlhepp to Fisher, December 13, 1926, ibid.

29. Fisher to E. W. Preston, December 20, 1926, ibid.

30. Fisher to Hugh W. Davis, December 23, 1926, ibid.

31. Stuart Gayness to Fisher, December 23, 1926, box 3, Fisher Papers.

32. Fisher to the Honorable Robert L. Bacon, December 6, 1926, box 11, Fisher Papers.

33. *East Hampton* (N.Y.) *Star*, April 22, 1927.

34. Fisher to C. W. Barron, April 22, 1927, box 3, Fisher Papers.

35. Fisher to W. A. Atterbury, May 3, 1927, box 11, Fisher Papers.

36. Fisher to Bernhard Lundberg, June 13, 1927, ibid.

37. Bernhard Lundberg to Fisher, June 16, 1927, ibid.

38. Fisher telegram to Ed Ballard, July 16, 1927, ibid.

39. J. G. Caffrey to Fisher, August 24, 1927, ibid.

40. James M. Cox to Fisher, June 28, 1928, ibid.

41. Fisher to Cox, June 29, 1928, ibid.

42. Steve Hannagan to Fisher, September 10, 1926, box 8, Fisher Papers.

43. Fisher to Louis E. Buschmann, September 28, 1928, box 1, Fisher Papers.

44. Fisher to John Oliver LaGorce, April 16, 1930, and LaGorce to Fisher, April 23, 1930, box 9, Fisher Papers.

45. That group included Irving Collins, who sounded the strongest warnings. See Collins to Fisher, May 18, 1925, box 12, Fisher Papers.

46. Fisher to Howard Coffin, December 2, 1926, ibid.

47. Richard Hoyt to Fisher, January 10, 29, 1927, box 11, Fisher Papers.

48. Fisher to Irving Collins, January 11, 1927, box 3, Fisher Papers.

49. Roy D. Chapin to Fisher, March 14, 1927, box 5, Fisher Papers; Chapin to Fisher, March 18, 1927, box 3, Fisher Papers.

50. Fisher to Harvey Gibson, April 12, 1927, box 5, Fisher Papers.

51. J. G. Caffrey to Fisher, June 15, 1927, box 12, Fisher Papers.

52. Ibid.

53. Fisher to Caffrey, August 24, 1927, box 11, Fisher Papers.

54. Fisher to Parke G. Haynes, September 27, 1927, ibid. Carl was, by then, frequently giving employees vague and often contradictory orders. He instructed his manager at Montauk to allow bartenders to "furnish" guests with drinks, "but under no circumstances to *sell* it to them. He will give them drinks with his compliments and if they pay him for it, all right, and if they don't it is entirely his loss and up to him" (emphasis added). See Fisher to Haynes, September 27, 1927, ibid. Evidently, he hoped that in the event of raids by Prohibition agents, upper-level managers could plead ignorance about any violations of the law.

55. Riggs, "Carl G. Fisher," 77.

56. Henry B. Joy to O. D. Treiber, October 19, 1927, box 8, Fisher Papers.

57. Fisher to Walter C. Marmon, November 12, 1927, box 5, Fisher Papers.

58. Fisher to W. A. Drumpelmann, December 9, 1927, box 10, Fisher Papers.

59. Fisher, *Fabulous Hoosier*, 207.

60. Roy D. Chapin to Fisher, December 27, 1927, box 5, Fisher Papers.

61. Fisher to Fred A. Britten, February 29, 1928, box 11, Fisher Papers.

62. Fisher to George LeBoutillier, January 11, 1929, box 12, Fisher Papers.

63. Fisher to George LeBoutillier, March 16, 1929, ibid.

64. For details regarding his troubles with the Internal Revenue Service, see George L. Denny to Fisher, April 7, 1917, Fisher to Lee Olwell, November 23, 1927, and Paul Kunschik to Fisher, August 14, 1930, box 5, Fisher Papers.

65. J. L. Bradley and J. N. Hagerty, "Montauk Beach Development Corporation Report of Audit," September 3, 1929 (mimeographed), copy in box 12, Fisher Papers.

66. Fisher to George LeBoutillier, October 18, 1929, ibid.

67. Fisher to A. J. Jones, November 14, 1929, ibid.

68. Ernest L'Ecluse to Fisher, January 9, 1930, Fisher to L'Ecluse, January 13, 1930, ibid. Raskob was equally well known for his famous dictum, uttered just weeks before the collapse of the bull market in October 1929, "Everybody ought to be rich." See Galbraith, *Great Crash*, 57.

69. L'Ecluse to Fisher, January 25, March 3, 1930, and Fisher to Hugh W. Davis, April 3, 1930, box 12, Fisher Papers.

70. Fisher to Hugh W. Davis, March 6, 1930, ibid.

71. Moses had been working on parkway plans for Long Island since the mid-1920s. For a masterful, if highly critical, biography of Moses, see Caro, *Power Broker*.

72. Robert Moses to W. E. Houghton, April 22, 1930, and Parke G. Haynes to Fisher, April 24, 1930, box 12, Fisher Papers.

73. Montauk Beach Development Corporation, "Report to Stockholder and Land Owners," May 23, 1930, ibid.

74. *New York World*, July 14, 1930.

75. Mrs. Albert Stewart, interview by the author, January 17, 1998, Claremont, California.

76. Fisher to F. E. Moskovics, September 8, 1930, Fisher to Arthur Brisbane, August 18, 1930, Fisher to Irving A. Collins, November 14, 1930, box 12, Fisher Papers.

77. Fred A. Britten to Fisher, November 29, December 3, 1930, box 2, Fisher Papers.

78. Long Island historian Ralph Hausrath reported that the navy exercises off Montauk generated some unfavorable publicity for those involved: "Some newspapers . . . saw in it the distinct possibility of political logrolling to advertise the Carl Fisher development" ("Carl G. Fisher and Montauk," 257).

79. Fisher to Harold E. Talbot Jr., March 17, 1932, box 16, Fisher Papers; Fisher to C. M. Keys, April 8, 1932, box 5, Fisher Papers.

80. "To the Stockholders of the Montauk Beach Development Corporation," mimeographed report, June 3, 1932, 2, copy in box 12, Fisher Papers.

81. Tom Milton to Fisher, May 21, 1931, box 11, Fisher Papers.

82. Jane Fisher to Fisher, October 21, 1932, box 3, Fisher Papers.

83. Fisher to Margaret Fisher, n.d. (August 1935); Fisher to Margaret Fisher, Labor Day 1935, box 6, Fisher Papers.

84. *Long Island Daily Press-Jamaica*, November 27, 1935.

85. Alfred Barton, interview by Polly Redford, May 12, 1967.

Chapter 13. Twilight of a Career

1. Redford, *Billion-Dollar Sandbar*, 112.

2. For more about these developments, see Chandler, *Visible Hand*, and Hawley, *The Great War and the Search for a Modern Order*, chap. 6.

3. For the best, most recent treatment of these issues, see Marchand, *Creating the Corporate Soul*, chap. 6.

4. Howard Kleinberg quoted in *Mr. Miami Beach*.

5. Fisher, *Fabulous Hoosier*, 202.

6. C. W. "Pete" Chase, interview by Polly Redford, October 5, 1966.

7. Fisher to James M. Cox, February 18, 1926, box 3, Fisher Papers.

8. Jane Fisher interview by Polly Redford, April 4, 1967. Capone biographer Robert J. Schoenberg essentially reinforces Jane's account, stating that Fisher "orchestrated" and generally masterminded a collective civic effort to force Capone to leave South Florida (*Mr. Capone*, 252).

9. Redford, *Billion-Dollar Sandbar*, 194.

10. Kleinberg, *Miami Beach*, 113–14.

11. From 1931 until his death in 1947, Capone's presence in Miami Beach was intermittent. He was convicted of income tax evasion in October 1931 and served eight years in prison. By the time he was released in November 1939, he had contracted a serious case of syphilis and was a sick man. Although he returned to Miami Beach, he and his family lived quietly. According to Kleinberg, he "just wanted to be left alone" (ibid., 116).

12. Fisher to Ed Ballard, November 27, 1928, box 7, Fisher Papers.

13. Fisher, *Fabulous Hoosier*, 195.

14. Fisher to William T. Anderson, March 4, 1933, box 10, Fisher Papers.

15. I borrow the term from Donald F. Davis, author of *Conspicuous Production*.

16. Leslie, *Boss Kettering*, 232.

17. Ibid., 229.

18. See, for example, Henry B. Joy to Wallace T. Atterbury, December 13, 1926, box 16, Fisher Papers.

19. Kettering to Fisher, March 3, 1927, box 9, Fisher Papers.

20. Fisher to Kettering, March 8, 1927, ibid.

21. See, for example, W. A. Kohlhepp to Mr. Tyndall, September 23, 1927, box 16, Fisher Papers.

22. Fisher to Henry B. Joy, August 17, 1927, box 8, Fisher Papers.

23. Fisher to Henry B. Joy, July 2, 1929, ibid.

24. Fisher did not specifically spell this out, but that certainly is strongly inferred. See Fisher to Kettering, August 9, 1929, box 9, Fisher Papers.

25. Fisher to Dan J. Mahoney, August 15, 1929, box 16, Fisher Papers.

26. Kettering to Fisher, August 21, 1929, box 9, Fisher Papers; Charles E. Wilson to Treiber, October 4, 1929, box 16, Fisher Papers.

27. Leslie, *Boss Kettering*, chap. 10.

28. See, for example, Fisher to W. K. Vanderbilt, December 9, 1929, box 16, Fisher Papers.

29. Fisher to E. V. Rickenbacker, December 18, 1929, box 15, Fisher Papers.

30. Fisher to Thomas W. Milton, August 18, 1930, box 11, Fisher Papers.

31. Irving A. Collins to Fisher, September 12, 1930, box 16, Fisher Papers.

32. Fisher to Levi, May 10, 1929, box 9, Fisher Papers. Fisher's assessment of Levi's future in regional politics was prescient; he was later elected mayor of Miami.

33. Fisher to Fred A. Seiberling, August 19, 1929, box 15, Fisher Papers. For further evidence that his interest in submitting and underwriting patents continued, see Fisher to Lieutenant Alford J. Williams, Jr., August 28, 1929, and Fisher to Albert T. Bremser, March 8, 1933, box 13, Fisher Papers.

34. For a superb account of the impact of automobile touring on American culture, see Belasco, *Americans on the Road*, esp. chaps. 1 and 3. For two recent works on vacations and tourism, see Aron, *Working at Play*, and Rothman, *Devil's Bargains*.

35. Fisher to Roy D. Chapin, April 30, 1928, box 1, Fisher Papers.

36. Fisher to Arthur Brisbane, September 7, 1928, and Fisher to Stockholders of the Aerocar Corporation, September 4, 1928, ibid.

37. Fisher to B. F. Everett, September 28, 1928, ibid.

38. Kettering to Fisher, April 16, 1929, box 9, Fisher Papers.

39. Fisher to H. Sayre Wheeler, May 21, 1929, box 1, Fisher Papers.

40. Fisher to Thomas W. Milton, August 16, 1930, box 11, Fisher Papers.

41. Fisher to Roy D. Chapin, December 31, 1931, box 1, Fisher Papers.

42. Fisher liked Roosevelt and had some unflattering comments about businessmen who were taking potshots at the new president: "The guys that started a whispering campaign that Roosevelt was weak and vacillating, should apologize to themselves in a God's prayer before each meal. Just what [he] is doing now has headed off a real revolution, and it would not have been bloodless, as you can see from what happened in a few isolated spots about the country." See Fisher to John Oliver LaGorce, May 1, 1933, box 9, Fisher Papers.

43. The health hazards associated with asbestos were not known in the 1930s.

44. Fisher to Hugh W. Davis, May 22, 1933, box 11, Fisher Papers; Fisher to Fred A. Britten, May 22, 1933, box 2, Fisher Papers.

45. Fisher to Thomas W. Milton, February 12, 1935, box 11, Fisher Papers.

46. For a general treatment of the Roosevelt administration's response to the housing crisis, see Gelfand, *Nation of Cities*, Arnold, *The New Deal and the Suburbs*, and Patterson, *America's Struggle Against Poverty*, chap. 3.

47. Fisher to Dan Mahoney, June 22, 1935, box 9, Fisher Papers.

48. N. P. Lowrey to A. D. H. Fossey, July 6, 1935, ibid.

49. Milton to Fisher, February 25, 1935, box 11, Fisher Papers.

50. Fisher to Thomas W. Milton, November 19, 1935, box 13, Fisher Papers.

51. Frank J. Horuff to Fisher, December 11, 1935, ibid.

52. See Fisher to Frank J. Horuff, December 16, 1935, February 14, 1936, ibid.

53. Fisher to E. V. Rickenbacker, May 5, 22, 1936, box 15, Fisher Papers.

54. Fisher to Hartley's Patent Sales Agency, Inc., October 29, 1934, box 13, Fisher Papers.

55. See, for example, Charles Beard to Fisher, February 13, 1936, ibid.

56. C. W. "Pete" Chase, interview with Polly Redford, October 5, 1966.

Chapter 14. Taps

1. Fisher to Barney Oldfield, April 25, 1939, box 1, Fisher Papers.

2. John LaGorce to Fisher, September 26, 1930, Fisher to LaGorce, October 2, 1930, box 9, Fisher Papers.

3. Fisher, *Fabulous Hoosier*, 219.

4. Ibid., 13.

5. Fisher to A. W. Howe, July 10, 1930, box 2, Fisher Papers.

6. Fisher to Albert D. Lasker, May 25, 1929, box 9, Fisher Papers.

7. Robert H. Davis to Fisher, January 31, 1930, box 14, Fisher Papers.

8. McCarthy, "The Man Who Invented America's Playground," 66.

9. Charles A. Bookwalter to Fisher, April 16, 1921, box 10, Fisher Papers.

10. Dr. Charles D. Hume to Fisher, October 26, 1921, box 8, Fisher Papers.

11. Fisher to Charles D. Hume, November 1, 1921, ibid.

12. Charles D. Hume to Fisher, November 14, 1921, ibid.

13. Fisher to Maurice Heckscher, August 27, 1921, ibid.

14. Fisher to Henry B. Joy, June 12, 1923, ibid.

15. Fisher to James Cox, December 22, 1923, ibid.

16. Fisher, *Fabulous Hoosier*, 181.

17. Fisher to Albert D. Lasker, March 8, 1929, box 9, Fisher Papers.

18. Fisher to Charles S. Krom, February 27, 1929, box 8, Fisher Papers.

19. In a lengthy letter to her parents shortly after their marriage, Margaret breathlessly recited a lengthy account of several days in their lives which were filled with endless rounds of excursions to casinos, restaurants, horse races, yacht cruises, and other forms of entertainment. See Margaret to Daddy and Mom, March 4 [ca. 1928], box 7, Fisher Papers.

20. LaGorce to Fisher, November 25, 1930, box 6, Fisher Papers.

21. Redford, *Billion-Dollar Sandbar*, 182; Kleinberg, *Miami Beach*, 134.

22. Fisher to LaGorce, April 10, 1933, box 8, Fisher Papers.

23. See Dr. A. R. Johnstone to Fisher, April 4, November 26, 1934, box 12, Fisher Papers.

24. Fisher to A. R. Johnstone, March 8, 1935, box 13, Fisher Papers.

25. Fisher to A. R. Johnstone, February 12, 1936, ibid.

26. Fisher to Margaret C. Fisher, September 23, 1936, box 7, Fisher Papers.

27. Fisher, *Fabulous Hoosier,* 223.

28. See, for example, Humpage to Fisher, August 31, 1936, box 5, Fisher Papers.

29. Rose Weiss, interview by Polly Redford, April 28, 1967.

30. Walter Dennis Myers, "Recollections" (mimeographed manuscript, undated), 222, Myers Papers, Indiana Historical Society, Indianapolis.

31. Ibid.

32. William G. Alexander to Margaret Fisher, April 7, 1938, box 4, Fisher Papers.

33. Fred Humpage to Margaret C. Fisher, August 18, 1938, box 8, Fisher Papers.

34. Fisher to Frank B. Voris, August 11, 1938, ibid.; Fisher to Mrs. Albert Santos, September 19, 1938, box 6, Fisher Papers; Fisher to Barney Oldfield, December 13, 1938, box 1, Fisher Papers.

35. Fisher, *Fabulous Hoosier,* 225.

36. Fisher to Thomas J. Pancoast, July 10, 1939, box 8, Fisher Papers.

37. Letter quoted in Kleinberg, *Miami Beach,* 134.

38. Ibid.

39. Kleinberg quoted in *Mr. Miami Beach,* PBS video.

40. Riggs, "Carl G. Fisher," 81.

Epilogue

1. Fisher, *Fabulous Hoosier.*

2. Between December 1940 and March 1953, Fred Humpage and C. W. "Pete" Chase exchanged numerous communications with Margaret. All of this correspondence is in box 4, Fisher Papers.

3. For an excellent treatment of the retirement community phenomenon in post–World War II United States, see Findlay, *Magic Lands,* chap. 4.

Bibliography

Adams, Henry. *The Education of Henry Adams.* Boston: Houghton Mifflin, 1918.

Address to the Conference of Governors at Colorado Springs, Colorado, August 26, 1913, on the Lincoln Highway. Pamphlet issued by the Lincoln Highway Association, October 1, 1913, Fisher Papers.

Alderson, Frederick. *Bicycling: A History.* New York: Praeger, 1972.

Akin, Edward N. *Flagler: Rockefeller Partner and Florida Baron.* Kent, Ohio: Kent State University Press, 1988.

Anthony, Carl S. *Florence Harding: The First Lady, the Jazz Age, and the Death of America's Most Scandalous President.* New York: William Morrow, 1998.

Armbrister, Ann. *The Life and Times of Miami Beach.* New York: Knopf, 1995.

Aron, Cindy S. *Working at Play: A History of Vacations in the United States.* New York: Oxford University Press, 1999.

Banner, Lois. *American Beauty.* New York: Knopf, 1983.

Barton, Alfred. Interview by Polly Redford, May 12, 1967. Oral History Collection, Special Collections, Richter Library, University of Miami.

Bederman, Gail. *Manliness and Civilization: A Cultural History of Gender and Race in the United States, 1880–1917.* Chicago: University of Chicago Press, 1995.

Belasco, Warren J. *Americans on the Road: From Autocamp to Motel, 1910–1945.* Cambridge, Mass.: MIT Press, 1979.

Bennett, David H. *The Party of Fear: The American Far Right from Nativism to the Militia Movement.* New York: Vintage Books, 1988.

Berger, Michael L. *The Devil Wagon in God's Country: The Automobile and Social Change in Rural America, 1893–1929.* Hamden, Conn.: Archon Books, 1979.

Bloemaker, Al. *500 Miles to Go: The Story of the Indianapolis Speedway.* New York: Coward-McCann, 1961.

Boomhower, Ray. "Carl G. Fisher: The Hoosier Barnum." *Traces of Indiana and Midwestern History,* 6 (Spring 1994): 24–27.

Brown, Allen E., ed. *The History of the American Speedway.* Marne, Mich.: Slideways Publications, 1984.

Bush, Gregory W. *Lord of Attention: Gerald Stanley Lee and the Crowd Metaphor in Industrializing America.* Amherst: University of Massachusetts Press, 1991.

Caro, Robert A. *Power Broker: Robert Moses and the Fall of New York.* New York: Knopf, 1974.

Case #88,446, Superior Court, Marion County, Ind. Mimeographed manuscript, undated, Fisher Papers.

Cashman, Sean D. *America in the Gilded Age.* 3d ed. New York: New York University Press, 1993.

Cavender, Fred D. "He Planned the Track." *Indianapolis Star Magazine,* May 27, 1962.

Chapin, Roy D. Papers. Special Collections, Bentley Historical Library, University of Michigan, Ann Arbor.

Chase, C. W. "Pete." Interview by Polly Redford, October 5, 1966. Oral History Collection, Special Collections, Richter Library, University of Miami.

Chernow, Ron. *Titan: The Life of John D. Rockefeller, Sr.* New York: Random House, 1998.

Collier, Peter, and David Horowitz. *The Fords: An American Epic.* New York: Simon and Schuster, 1987.

Coontz, Stephanie. *The Social Origins of Private Life: A History of American Families.* New York: Verso, 1988.

Cooper, John M., Jr. *Pivotal Decades: The United States, 1900–1920.* New York: Norton, 1992.

Critchlow, Donald T. *Studebaker: The Life and Death of an American Corporation.* Bloomington: Indiana University Press, 1996.

Cuff, Robert D. *The War Industries Board.* Baltimore: Johns Hopkins University Press, 1973.

Curl, Donald W. *Mizner's Florida: American Resort Architecture.* Cambridge, Mass.: MIT Press, 1984.

Davis, Donald F. *Conspicuous Production: Automobiles and Elites in Detroit, 1899–1933.* Philadelphia: Temple University Press, 1988.

Douglas, Marjory Stoneman. *Florida: The Long Frontier.* New York: Harper & Row, 1967.

"Eastern Division Inspected." *Dixie Highway: A Monthly Journal* 2 (October 1916): 4–5.

Eigenman Family Papers. Special Collections Department, Lilly Library, Indiana University, Bloomington.

Encyclopedia Americana: International Edition. Vol. 15. Danbury, Conn.: Grolier, 1989.

Ewen, Stuart. *PR: The History of Spin*. New York: Basic Books, 1996.

Findlay, John M. *Magic Lands: Western Cityscapes and American Culture after 1940*. Berkeley: University of California Press, 1992.

Fisher, Carl G. Papers. Historical Museum of South Florida, Miami, Florida.

Fisher, Jane. *Fabulous Hoosier: A Story of American Achievement*. New York: Robert M. McBride, 1947.

Fisher, Jane. Interview by Polly Redford, April 4, 1967. Oral History Collection, Special Collections, Richter Library, University of Miami.

Fisher, Jerry M. *The Pacesetter: The Untold Story of Carl G. Fisher*. Ft. Bragg, Calif.: Lost Coast Press, 1998.

Five Years Afterwards. Pamphlet issued by First Company of Florida, October 1, 1930.

Flink, James J. *America Adopts the Automobile, 1870–1910*. Cambridge, Mass.: MIT Press, 1970.

Foster, Mark S. *From Streetcar to Superhighway: American City Planners and Urban Transportation, 1900–1940*. Philadelphia: Temple University Press, 1981.

Fox, Jack C. *The Illustrated History of the Indianapolis 500*. 4th ed. Speedway, Ind.: Carl Hungness, 1994.

Galbraith, John K. *The Great Crash*. Boston: Houghton Mifflin, 1961.

Goddard, Stephen B. *Getting There: The Epic Struggle Between Road and Rail in the American Century*. New York: Basic Books, 1994.

Gustin, Lawrence. *Billy Durant: Creator of General Motors*. Grand Rapids, Mich.: Eerdmans, 1973.

Hausrath, Ralph. "Carl G. Fisher and Montauk." *Long Island Forum*, November 1981 and December 1981.

Hawley, Ellis W., Jr. *The Great War and the Search for a Modern Order: A History of the American People and Their Institutions, 1917–1933*. New York: St. Martin's Press, 1979.

Herschell, William. "Indianapolis-Born Dixie Highway Now Almost 6000 Miles Long." *Indianapolis News*, August 1, 1925.

Higham, John. *Strangers in the Land: Patterns of American Nativism, 1860–1925*. 2d ed. New York: Atheneum, 1988.

History Committee of the Speedway Civic Committee. *The Story of Speedway*. Speedway, Ind.: Speedway Civic Committee, 1976.

"History of Speedway." Undated newspaper clipping (ca. 1966). Speedway Public Library, Speedway, Ind.

Hokanson, Drake. *The Lincoln Highway: Main Street across America*. Iowa City: University of Iowa Press, 1988.

Holden, Albert R. *A Pictorial History of Montauk*. Montauk, N.Y.: Holden's Publications, 1983.

Horowitz, Daniel. *The Morality of Spending: Attitudes Toward the Consumer Society in America, 1875–1940*. Chicago: Ivan R. Dee, 1985.

Hoy, Suellen M. "Governor Samuel M. Ralston and Indiana's Centennial Celebration." *Indiana Magazine of History* 71 (September 1975): 245–66.

Hughes, Robert. *American Visions: The Epic History of Art in America*. New York: Knopf, 1997.

Hugill, Peter. "Good Roads and the Automobile in the United States, 1880–1929." *Geographical Review* 72 (July 1982): 332–40.

Jackson-Lears, T. J. *Fables of Abundance: A Cultural History of Advertising in America*. New York: Basic Books, 1996.

Jackson-Lears, T. J., and Richard W. Fox, eds. *The Culture of Consumption: Critical Essays in American History, 1880–1980*. New York: Pantheon Books, 1983.

Johada, Gloria. *Florida: A Bicentennial History*. New York: Norton, 1976.

Joy, Henry B. Papers. Special Collections, Bentley Historical Library, University of Michigan, Ann Arbor.

Kennedy, David M. *Over Here: The First World War and American Society*. New York: Oxford University Press, 1980.

Kimes, Beverly Rae. "The Rise and Fall of the Empire Automobile." *Automobile Quarterly* 12 (First Quarter 1974): 70–81.

Kleinberg, Howard. *Miami Beach: A History*. Miami: Centennial Press, 1994.

Klingaman, William. *1919: The Year Our World Began*. New York: St. Martin's Press, 1987.

Laird, Pamela W. *Advertising Progress: American Business and the Rise of Consumer Marketing*. Baltimore: Johns Hopkins University Press, 1998.

Lakoff, Robin Tomlach, and Raquel L. Scherr. *Face Value: The Politics of Beauty*. Boston: Routledge & Kegan Paul, 1984.

Leslie, Stuart W. *Boss Kettering: Wizard of General Motors*. New York: Columbia University Press, 1983.

Lincoln Highway Association. *The Lincoln Highway*. New York: Dodd, Mead, 1935.

Lummus, J. N. *The Miracle of Miami Beach*. Miami: Miami Post Publishing Company, 1941.

Madison, James H. *The Indiana Way: A State History*. Bloomington: Indiana University Press, 1986.

Marchand, Roland. *Advertising the American Dream: Making Way for Modernity, 1920–1940*. Chicago: University of Chicago Press, 1997.

Mason, Phillip. "The League of American Wheelmen and the Good Roads Movement." Ph.D dissertation, University of Michigan, 1957.

May, George S. *A Most Unique Machine: The Michigan Origins of the American Automobile Industry*. Grand Rapids, Mich.: Eerdmans, 1975.

McCarthy, Joe. "The Man Who Invented America's Playground." *American Heritage* 27 (December 1975): 64–71.

McShane, Clay. *The Automobile: A Chronology of Antecedents, Developments and Impact*. Westport, Conn.: Greenwood Press, 1997.

Mehling, Harold. *The Most of Everything: The Story of Miami Beach*. New York: Harcourt Brace, 1960.

"Minutes of the Annual Meeting of Active Members of the Lincoln Highway Association Held at the Detroit Auto Club, December 30, 1918." Mimeographed copy, Fisher Papers.

Mr. Miami Beach. PBS American Experience Video, Boston, MDTV Productions, first aired February 2, 1998.

Montauk Beach Development Corporation. "Report to Stockholders and Land Owners, May 23, 1930." Fisher Papers.

Murray, Robert K. *Red Scare: A Study in National Hysteria, 1919–1920*. Minneapolis: University of Minnesota Press, 1955.

Myers, Walter Dennis. "Recollections." Undated manuscript, Myers Papers, Indiana Historical Society, Indianapolis.

Nash, Charles E. *The Magic of Miami Beach*. Philadelphia: David Mackay, 1938.

Nevins, Allan. *Ford: The Times, the Man, the Company*. New York: Scribners, 1954.

Palmer, Arthur J. *Riding High: The Story of the Bicycle*. New York: E. P. Dutton, 1975.

Parish, Michael E. *Anxious Decades: America in Prosperity and Depression, 1920–1941*. New York: Norton, 1992.

Paten, Phil. *Open Road: A Celebration of the American Highway*. New York: Simon and Schuster, 1986.

Patterson, James T. *America's Struggle Against Poverty, 1900–1980*. Cambridge, Mass.: Harvard University Press, 1981.

Payne, L. Manuscript Collection. Special Collections, Lilly Library, Indiana University, Bloomington.

Peckham, Howard H. *Indiana: A Bicentennial History*. New York: Norton, 1978.

Phelps, Clifton J. *Indiana in Transition, 1880–1920*. Indianapolis: Indiana Historical Bureau and Indiana Historical Society, 1968.

Pomeroy, Earl M. *In Search of the Golden West: The Tourist in Western America*. New York: Knopf, 1957.

Prest-O-Lite Incorporation Papers, September 6, 1904. Indiana State Archives, Indianapolis.

Preston, Howard L. *Dirt Roads to Dixie*. Knoxville: University of Tennessee Press, 1991.

Rae, John B. *The American Automobile*. Chicago: University of Chicago Press, 1965.

———. *The Road and Car in American Life*. Cambridge, Mass.: MIT Press, 1971.

———. "Why Michigan?" In *The Automobile in American Culture*, edited by David L. Lewis and Laurence Goldstein, 1–9. Ann Arbor: University of Michigan Press, 1980.

Ralston, Samuel M. Papers. Special Collections, Lilly Library, Indiana University, Bloomington.

———. Untitled address in Chattanooga, Tennessee, April 3, 1915. Mimeographed copy in Ralston Papers.

Raskob, John J., with Samuel Crowther. "Everybody Ought to Be Rich." *Ladies' Home Journal*, August 1929, 80, 99–102.

Redford, Polly. *Billion-Dollar Sandbar: A Biography of Miami Beach*. New York: E. P. Dutton, 1970.

Riggs, L. Spencer. "Carl G. Fisher: Indiana's Best Kept Secret." *Automobile Quarterly* 35 (June 1992): 117–26.

Rodgers, Daniel T. *Atlantic Crossings: Social Politics in a Progressive Era*. Cambridge, Mass.: Harvard University Press, 1998.

Rose, Mark H. *Interstate: Express Highway Politics, 1939–1989*. Rev. ed. Knoxville: University of Tennessee Press, 1990.

Rothman, Hal K. *Devil's Bargains: Tourism in the Twentieth Century American West*. Lawrence: Regents Press of Kansas, 1998.

Schoenberg, Robert. *Mr. Capone*. New York: William Morrow, 1992.

Schwarz, Jordan A. *The Interregnum of Despair: Hoover, Congress and the Great Depression*. Urbana: University of Illinois Press, 1970.

Sears, Stephen W. *The American Heritage History of the Automobile in America*. New York: American Heritage Publishing Company, 1977.

Seely, Bruce E. *Building the American Highway System: Engineers as Policy Makers*. Philadelphia: Temple University Press, 1987.

Slauson, Harold W. "Making a Sport of Speed." *Leslie's Weekly*, May 18, 1916.

Smith, Merrit Roe, and Leo F. Marx, eds. *Does Technology Drive Progress?* Cambridge, Mass.: MIT Press, 1994.

Smith, Robert A. A *Social History of the Bicycle: Its Early Life and Times in America*. New York: American Heritage, 1972.

Stewart, Mrs. Albert. Interview by Mark S. Foster, January 17, 1998.

Taylor, Rich. *Indy: 75 Years of Racing's Greatest Spectacle*. New York: St. Martin's Press, 1991.

Tichi, Cecilia. *Shifting Gears: Technology, Literature, Culture in Modernist America*. Chapel Hill: University of North Carolina Press, 1987.

"To the Stockholders of the Montauk Beach Development Corporation." Mimeographed report, June 3, 1932, Fisher Papers.

Tract Map of Bayview Colony, April 17, 1925, Fisher Papers.

Wade, Richard C. *The Urban Frontier: Pioneer Life in Early Pittsburgh, Cincinnati, Lexington, Louisville and St. Louis*. Chicago: University of Chicago Press, 1959.

Weisberger, Bernard. *The Dream Maker: William C. Durant, Founder of General Motors*. Boston: Little, Brown, 1979.

Weisse, Rose. Interview by Polly Redford, April 28, 1967. Oral History Collection, Special Collections, Richter Library, University of Miami.

Wiebe, Robert H. *The Search for Order, 1877–1920*. New York: Hill and Wang, 1967.

Wolfe, Mark. "How Lincoln Highway Snubbed Colorado." *Colorado Heritage* (Autumn 1993): 3–21.

Index

St. Augustine, Henry M. Flagler's development of, 139
Stanford, Leland, 100
stock market, 235–36
Stoltz, J. Perry, 198, 210
Stutz, Harry C., 42, 211
swimming: bathing beauty "invention," 189; Miami Beach, 189–90

Taggart, Tom, role of in Dixie Highway, 122
Tarkington, Booth, 15
technological "fixes," Americans' faith in, 45, 70–71, 169–70
tennis, in Miami Beach, 181–82
Tequesta Indians, 138–39
Tichi, Cecelia, 45
Tilden, Bill, 182, 255
Tippecanoe, Battle of, 10
Trieber, O. D., and diesel engine development, 282–85
Trotter, Lem, 74
Tunney, Gene, 184
Tyndall, Bob, 17

Underground Railroad, 10
Union Carbide Corporation, purchase of Prest-O-Lite by, 58–59

Vanderbilt Cup, 34
Vanderbilt, Harold, 212
Vanderbilt, William K., 212, 251
von Richthofen, Baron Manfred, 169

Waldon, Sydney D., and route for Lincoln Highway, 108
Wanamaker, Rodman, 212
Watts, James Buchanan (Jane Fisher's stepfather), 63
Wayne, General "Mad Anthony," 10
Webb, Al, 157
Weiss, Rose, 299
Wheeler, Frank H., 75
Willys, John N., 105
Wilson, Charles E., 284
Wilson, Elenor (grandmother), 9
Wilson, Woodrow, 102, 121, 122–23, 201
Wood, Gar, 186, 192, 246
Wright brothers, 57, 79, 87
Wrigley, William K., Jr., 269

Zanesville, Ohio: Fisher's serious racing accident in, 34, 72, 77, 95
Zig–Zag Cycle Club, 15–17, 22, 23, 24, 70; and future business contacts, 17
"Zolene" hoax, 56–57

Mark S. Foster is professor of history at the University of Colorado at Denver. He is the author or coauthor of eight previous books, including *From Streetcar to Superhighway: American City Planners and Urban Transportation, 1900–1940* (1981) and *Henry J. Kaiser: Builder in the Modern American West* (1989).

The Florida History and Culture Series

EDITED BY RAYMOND ARSENAULT AND GARY R. MORMINO

Al Burt's Florida: Snowbirds, Sand Castles, and Self-Rising Crackers, by Al Burt (1997)

Black Miami in the Twentieth Century, by Marvin Dunn (1997; first paperback edition, 2016)

Gladesmen: Gator Hunters, Moonshiners, and Skiffers, by Glen Simmons and Laura Ogden (1998)

"Come to My Sunland": Letters of Julia Daniels Moseley from the Florida Frontier, 1882–1886, edited by Julia Winifred Moseley and Betty Powers Crislip (1998; first paperback edition, 2020)

The Enduring Seminoles: From Alligator Wrestling to Ecotourism, by Patsy West (1998)

Government in the Sunshine State: Florida Since Statehood, by David R. Colburn and Lance deHaven-Smith (1999)

The Everglades: An Environmental History, by David McCally (1999; first paperback edition, 2000)

Beechers, Stowes, and Yankee Strangers: The Transformation of Florida, by John T. Foster Jr. and Sarah Whitmer Foster (1999)

The Tropic of Cracker, by Al Burt (1999; first paperback edition, 2009)

Balancing Evils Judiciously: The Proslavery Writings of Zephaniah Kingsley, edited and annotated by Daniel W. Stowell (2000)

Hitler's Soldiers in the Sunshine State: German POWs in Florida, by Robert D. Billinger Jr. (2000; first paperback edition, 2009)

Cassadaga: The South's Oldest Spiritualist Community, edited by John J. Guthrie Jr., Phillip Charles Lucas, and Gary Monroe (2000)

Claude Pepper and Ed Ball: Politics, Purpose, and Power, by Tracy E. Danese (2000)

Pensacola during the Civil War: A Thorn in the Side of the Confederacy, by George F. Pearce (2000; first paperback edition, 2008)

Castles in the Sand: The Life and Times of Carl Graham Fisher, by Mark S. Foster (2000; first paperback edition, 2023)

Miami, U.S.A., by Helen Muir (2000)

Politics and Growth in Twentieth-Century Tampa, by Robert Kerstein (2001)

The Invisible Empire: The Ku Klux Klan in Florida, by Michael Newton (2001)

The Wide Brim: Early Poems and Ponderings of Marjory Stoneman Douglas, edited by Jack E. Davis (2002)

The Architecture of Leisure: The Florida Resort Hotels of Henry Flagler and Henry Plant, by Susan R. Braden (2002)

Florida's Space Coast: The Impact of NASA on the Sunshine State, by William Barnaby Faherty, S.J. (2002)

In the Eye of Hurricane Andrew, by Eugene F. Provenzo Jr. and Asterie Baker Provenzo (2002)

Florida's Farmworkers in the Twenty-first Century, text by Nano Riley and photographs by Davida Johns (2003)

Making Waves: Female Activists in Twentieth-Century Florida, edited by Jack E. Davis and Kari Frederickson (2003; first paperback edition, 2003)

Orange Journalism: Voices from Florida Newspapers, by Julian M. Pleasants (2003)

The Stranahans of Fort Lauderdale: A Pioneer Family of New River, by Harry A. Kersey Jr. (2003; first paperback edition, 2022)

Death in the Everglades: The Murder of Guy Bradley, America's First Martyr to Environmentalism, by Stuart B. McIver (2003; first paperback edition, 2009)

Jacksonville: The Consolidation Story, from Civil Rights to the Jaguars, by James B. Crooks (2004; first paperback edition, 2019)

The Seminole Wars: America's Longest Indian Conflict, by John and Mary Lou Missall (2004; first paperback edition, 2016)

The Mosquito Wars: A History of Mosquito Control in Florida, by Gordon Patterson (2004)

Seasons of Real Florida, by Jeff Klinkenberg (2004; first paperback edition, 2009)